# THE ACCOUNTANT'S HANDBOOK
# OF INFORMATION TECHNOLOGY

## SUBSCRIPTION NOTICE

This Wiley product is updated on a periodic basis with supplements to reflect important changes in the subject matter. If you purchased this product directly from John Wiley & Sons, Inc., we have already recorded your subscription for this update service.

If, however, you purchased this product from a bookstore and wish to receive (1) the current update at no additional charge, and (2) future updates and revised or related volumes billed separately with a 30-day examination review, please send your name, company name (if applicable), address, and the title of the product to:

Supplement Department
John Wiley & Sons, Inc.
One Wiley Drive
Somerset, NJ 08875
1-800-225-5945

# THE ACCOUNTANT'S HANDBOOK OF INFORMATION TECHNOLOGY

G. Jack Bologna, BBA, CFE, JD
Anthony M. Walsh, BComm, CA

John Wiley & Sons, Inc.
New York • Chichester • Weinheim • Brisbane • Singapore • Toronto

Copyright © 1997 by John Wiley & Sons, Inc.

Library of Congress Cataloging in Publication Data:

Bologna, Jack.
    The accountant's handbook of information technology / G. Jack
Bologna, Anthony M. Walsh.
        p.   cm.
    Includes bibliographical references and index.
    ISBN 0-471-30473-5 (cloth : alk. paper)
    1. Information technology—Management.   2. Database management.
3. Information resources management.   4. Accounting—Data
processing.   I. Walsh, Anthony M.   II. Title.
HD30.2.B65   1997
675'.0285—dc20                                         96-31996

10 9 8 7 6 5 4 3 2 1

# ABOUT THE AUTHORS

**G. Jack Bologna,** BBA, CFE, JD, is president of Computer Protection Systems, Inc., of Plymouth, Michigan, and Assistant Professor of Management, Siena Heights College, Adrian, Michigan. He has authored numerous works on the subject of fraud, commercial crime, and computer security, and is editor of the monthly newsletters *Forensic Accounting Review* and *Computer Security Digest*.

**Anthony M. Walsh,** BComm, CA, Toronto, Canada, is a Chartered Accountant and writer whose previous works include *The Handbook of Information Technology*, an earlier version of this book published in Canada only. He has also been instrumental in the development, management, and production of *The Accountant's Handbook of Fraud and Commercial Crime*, another supplement service published by John Wiley & Sons, Inc.

# CONTENTS

# PREFACE

It's been said that an accountant's job is to make order out of chaos. Historically, this has been known to conjure up images of the stereotypical number-cruncher—equipped with green eyeshades and matching audit pen—as he or she sifts through a shoe box of receipts and vouchers, struggling to make the link to something approximating a statement of income.

Of course, the reality for accountants or auditors today is quite different. They're more likely to be found using a laptop to download a transaction data base file for analytical and ratio analysis. The objective in the broadest sense remains the same—making order out of chaos, synthesizing the big picture from a thousand individual pieces of the puzzle, seeing the forest for the trees—but the skills, training, and tools employed have evolved considerably over the years.

Arguably, information technology has been and remains the most dynamic driving force behind the changes taking place in the accounting profession—indeed, in the business community and the world as a whole. Yet ironically, this very tool that we've been using to help us make order out of chaos has itself become subject to chaos. It's become nearly impossible for individual accountants, and in many cases even organizations, to keep up with all of the important changes and, most important, to manage them. There is simply too much happening too quickly, with no end in sight to the rapid pace of change.

This handbook is intended to assist accountants and financial professionals in making order out of information technology chaos. It's targeted primarily at those who use and manage information technology every day and deal with its effects on their business environment. We've tried to tailor the material to this target audience—the nontechnical but reasonably sophisticated user/manager. We know that your time is valuable, and we've attempted to be as clear and concise as possible, including, for example, practical checklists that summarize key points in several of the chapters. Too much detail doesn't make order out of chaos; it only makes chaos worse. On the other hand, we've tried to give credence to all pertinent areas and to identify sources of additional information that you might require. And, recognizing that current information is often the only useful information, we plan to update the handbook at least once and perhaps twice a year.

If you're the kind of person we've identified as our target audience, we believe you'll find this handbook a comprehensive, useful reference for dealing with information technology chaos. And even if you're one of those technical people who already knows much more than what's contained herein, you still need to relate to the rest of the world that doesn't. This handbook can assist you, too.

The handbook seeks to make order out of chaos for the sophisticated but nontechnical user of information technology by providing:

- Concise definitions and explanations.
- Practical examples (e.g., of financial modeling applications).
- Useful data (e.g., on some popular software products).
- Checklists (e.g., of features to look for in a particular type of software).
- Sources of additional, more specialized information.
- Commentary and recommendations, when appropriate.

The handbook is divided into 15 chapters and two appendices. Each chapter deals with a specific area of information technology (IT). These chapters can also be grouped into the four general categories set out below.

1. *Management Issues*—This section covers the management of IT under the following chapter headings: Organizational and Ethical Issues (Chapter 2), Strategic Planning and Policy (Chapter 3), Productivity and Competitiveness (Chapter 4) and Historical Chronology and Future Directions (Chapter 5).

2. *Hardware and Software*—This part of the handbook covers the different "boxes" that make up computer hardware: Microcomputers (Chapter 6) and Peripherals (Chapter 7). It also covers software, including Word Processing and Desktop Publishing (Chapter 8), Spreadsheets and Database Management (Chapter 9), and Other Software Categories (Chapter 10).

3. *Connectivity and Specialized Topics*—This part deals with connectivity: Telecommunications (Chapter 11) and its practical application, Networking (Chapter 12), It also deals with several specialized topics, including Computer Security and System Recovery (Chapter 13), Information Technology and the Law (Chapter 14), and Artificial Intelligence and Expert Systems (Chapter 15).

4. *Appendices*—Finally, the handbook includes two appendices: an ASCII table (Appendix A), and a Directory of Companies (Appendix B). A glossary, a reference section, and an index round out the material.

The approach taken within each chapter is generally as follows:

- A brief introduction sets out the main topics covered in the chapter, in particular the management issues relating to those topics.
- Where applicable, a summary and checklist set out—in practical form—the main points dealt with in the chapter.
- The main body of the chapter deals with the topics in greater detail. While attempts have been made to keep the nature and tone of this section as practical and useful

as possible, for the sake of completeness, this part of the chapter may also contain somewhat dry background and reference material.

- In a few chapters a catalog of major products is provided, setting out information such as the most recent version number and list price.

This handbook is a supplement service, and over time we hope and intend to provide whatever subscribers want. If you have any suggestions, please feel free to direct them to John Wiley & Sons, Inc., attention Sheck Cho. Alternatively, you can E-mail any comments directly to the authors via the following address: AWalshCA@aol.com.

G. Jack Bologna
*Plymouth, Michigan*

Anthony M. Walsh
*Toronto, Canada*

# ACKNOWLEDGMENTS

The authors would like to thank the following organizations and individuals for their contributions and assistance in producing this handbook:

The Canadian Institute of Chartered Accountants, Toronto, and in particular Peter Hoult, CA and Steve Johnston, CA, who are responsible for overseeing the development and publication of the handbook in Canada.

Coopers & Lybrand, and in particular Donald A. Brown, FCA (currently based in London, U.K.) and David A. Griffiths, BSc, C&L Toronto Partner-in-Charge of Computer Security Services, for their contribution during the planning stages of the book, in contributing certain source material used in producing Part I (Management Issues), and in drafting certain source material used in producing Chapter 13 (Computer Security and System Recovery).

John Wiley & Sons, Inc., New York, and in particular Jeffrey Brown, executive publisher, and Sheck Cho, acquisitions editor, who are responsible for overseeing the development and publication of the handbook in the United States.

Several contributors and advisors who were involved in an earlier book published in Canada only and written by Donald A. Brown and Anthony M. Walsh, including J. Efrim Boritz, PhD, CISA, CA; Dennis Hogarth, BA, CISA, CA; David R.D. Macfarlane, CISA; Sid Markowski, BComm, CA; Richard J. Morochove, BComm, FCA; George Nutter, BA; Larry W. Shick, B.Eng., CMC; and Leigh C. Webber, BA, LL.B., MBA. Whatever praise readers may have for this book is due in part to them; whatever criticisms there are (hopefully constructive!) fall on the shoulders of the authors.

# CHAPTER 1

# What Is Information Technology?

## 1.1  IT DEFINED

Information technology is the name given to the tools and methods used to collect, retain, manipulate, or distribute information. It is most often associated with computers and related technologies.

## 1.2  MAKING ORDER OUT OF CHAOS

As we indicated in the Preface, an accountant's job is to make order out of chaos. Information technology (IT) is one of the most important tools accountants use to do this, and yet IT is itself in an ever-changing, almost chaotic state of flux. To use and manage information technology effectively, accountants need to make order out of this IT chaos—in short, to put the pieces of the puzzle together and see the big picture.

    How to get from chaos to the big picture? With books of account, we take source documents reflecting different transactions, record them in journals, post them to general ledgers, and summarize them in a trial balance and ultimately in a set of financial statements. Of course, it's almost all done by computer, but the essential key to making order out of chaos is the same: systematically categorize everything and use it as input into a hicrarchy that ultimately yields some kind of orderly, meaningful information.

Obviously, there's no uniquely correct system of categorization when it comes to information technology. We've developed one that we think makes sense and is useful, and we've used it in organizing this handbook. In the remainder of this chapter, however, we'll present a brief "big picture" view of IT.

## 1.3 THE IMPORTANCE OF IT

From time to time in the course of history, a product or event comes along that changes everything that follows. Fire was one. Gutenberg's movable type, the steam engine, and Henry Ford's assembly line are other examples. Information technology is one of the most recent.

Henry Ford's assembly line brought momentous changes. It made luxury goods affordable by taking advantage of several key principles, including:

- The use of land, labor, and capital in mass production
- Economies of scale
- People augmenting production machines

But information technology leads to some important new principles that replace the old rules of Henry Ford. Today we're faced with a changing economy that sets many of our basic business premises on end:

- There's now more to business than land, labor, and capital. Information has become a commodity, too, one vital to your competitive advantage.
- Economies of scale, "bigger is better," and even mass production are no longer unchallenged principles.
- Machines are increasingly enhancing people's skills; no longer do people merely provide the dexterity that machines lacked (and incidentally, now have).

### (a) IT IS AN ONGOING REVOLUTION

There's an ongoing business revolution underway, and you—the accounting professional or financial manager—can't afford to watch it go by. It's the information technology revolution, part of a mind-numbing growth in discovery and invention that has seen more knowledge accumulate in the last 30 years than in all of human history before that.

Like most before it, the IT revolution began well before we realized it. Such familiar tools as the telephone and photocopiers and service ideas like telemarketing were the vanguard of the revolution. They allowed people in business to become more productive, to use information better as a business tool. Telephones and photocopiers are still important and useful tools, but it was the computer—and particularly the microcomputer—that signaled that the revolution was really underway.

It isn't information technology itself that heralds the new age; it's the impact the technology has had on society. Information technology now figures in almost every walk of life, every industry, and every major business decision. Large companies are using computers by the hundreds of thousands, and even the smallest businesses are now computerized.

## (b) IT IS A COMMODITY

There is no question that information has always been important to business. It's the *raison d'être* of the accounting profession and has a profound effect on many other professions and industries such as law and financial services. But before information technology, using information was like piecing together history from snapshots. What you saw was essentially all you had, and you could manipulate it only in limited, fixed ways.

Today, information is a commodity that can be captured through information technology and then stored and manipulated in unlimited ways. Information finds its way into new products like on-line databases and into established industries like publishing; it is used as a replacement or supplement for some of the land, labor, and capital of the economist. It enables us to do what we do and make what we make more efficiently.

## (c) IT IS COMPETITIVE ADVANTAGE

To business the revolution means that business decisions can no longer ignore the value of information. To keep ahead of the game, you have to ask yourself some new questions:

- *Is there a product in the information you're collecting?*

  Yes. Newspapers around the world have captured the data that they feed their electronic typesetters and have started retailing it online. The sale of magazine mailing lists is probably the oldest example of business information turned to profit.

- *Can information technology make your business more efficient and competitive?*

  Of course, information technology can easily help monitor revenues, expenditures, and trends. But it can also help you in other areas. You can keep track of your customers and analyze your markets. For example—as American Airlines found—computerized ordering from terminals placed on-site with a customer can reinforce that customer's loyalty.

- *Is your competition using IT effectively?*

  Probably the most compelling reason to adopt—and adapt to—information technology is to keep up with the competition. Any time you lose any type of advantage you're playing catch-up. It's a lesson the North American auto industry learned the hard way from the Japanese.

Information technology is a capital enhancer—a productive commodity—and you can't afford to dally for long. The bottom line is that information has value, and information technology lets you trade on that value.

## (d) IT IS CHANGING THE ECONOMIC RULES

Because of information technology the advantages enjoyed by big producers over small are becoming less important in economic terms in many industries.

For example, look at computers themselves. Until the end of the seventies, they were a luxury that only larger businesses could afford. Today, the fastest-growing market in the computer industry is the microcomputer market, and those computers aren't just going into homes and small offices. Many are going to the banks, insurance companies, and other firms that previously relied on large computer installations.

With a microcomputer, a small firm has publishing capabilities once enjoyed only by printing plants. It has analytic capability beyond a roomful of accounting clerks. A small firm with a computer can tap into outside information sources more extensive than those of any corporate library. Even in manufacturing a key buzz phrase today is *flexible manufacturing,* the ability to produce specialized "one-ofs" (specially designed products not intended for mass production) to meet customer needs. Using computerized job scheduling and other information technology tools, a company can mobilize a plant quickly and regularly to produce the goods its market needs at any given time.

Large companies could always do these things. The difference is that now the small business can, too. We've come a long way from mass production, with its economies of scale. Indeed, the economic rules have been changed by the new technology, and some groups even talk of the need for a new economic paradigm. They propose a model that recognizes the role of information and knowledge in enhancing other capital goods.

### (e) IT IS AUGMENTING PEOPLE

The old science fiction movies notwithstanding, the reality of information technology is that people will be far more important to business growth than machines. In an economy in which information, knowledge, and ideas—not brute mechanical size and muscle—will be the key value-addeds, people will be your key business resource. Machines will only be the tools with which people do increasingly creative work. Machines will augment people; on Henry Ford's assembly line, it was the other way around.

In the information society, training people, keeping good people, and knowing how to manage them will be the mark of the successful business. This isn't a new concept—in fact, it's the subject of Tom Peter's book *In Search of Excellence*—but it's an important one to grasp.

Training people is particularly important to businesses that hope to benefit from information technology. A state-of-the-art microcomputer with word processing and database packages can yield terrific benefits in productivity for a business that relies on direct-mail marketing, but only if its people know how to use these tools to maximum advantage. The importance of training is too often forgotten in the mind-numbing search for the right equipment.

### (f) IT IS THE FUTURE

Chapter 5 of this handbook takes a look at developing trends in technology and their possible impact on business's use of IT. Trends like the increased emphasis on worker training, mentioned earlier, will have a significant impact on business practice. Even tax treatment and accounting procedures might be affected, providing greater recognition to the importance of human resources in the balance-sheet equation. And in an environment where equipment has only a five-year life before it's considered obsolete, keeping on top of developments and trends like these will be vital.

Information technology is changing everything around us. The revolution is not going to go away, and one can hope that when historians look back, they'll see that society has become the better for it.

# CHAPTER 2

# Organizational and Ethical Issues

The organization must be properly set up to manage information technology effectively. This chapter focuses on such organizational issues.

A brief checklist in the next section (Section 2.1) precedes a more detailed treatment of these areas. This checklist serves as a practical executive summary of the main points covered in this chapter. It is followed by these sections:

- Organization Structure (Section 2.2), which deals with the need to (a) integrate the IT function within the organization, (b) establish job descriptions and related controls, and (c) periodically reassess this area to meet the organization's needs. A sample partial organization chart is included.
- Organizational Leadership (Section 2.3), in particular the roles of the Senior IT Officer and of senior management.
- Microcomputer Support Facilities (Section 2.4), including their benefits and related planning and management considerations. These facilities are based on the concept of information centers, which never achieved the popularity predicted for them in the mid-1980s and are rarely found in practice. (It's possible they'll become more common in the late 1990s and beyond.) Microcomputer support facilities—a kind of specialized subset of the information center—are more common today. Whether or not one actually exists, the concept of a microcomputer support facility is an instructive one from an organizational viewpoint, because the related issues must somehow be addressed.

Finally, Section 2.5 deals with some of the ethical issues raised by information technology, its use and potential for misuse.

## 2.1  THE IT MANAGEMENT ORGANIZATIONAL CHECKLIST

The following two-page checklist, summarizing many of the points in this chapter, is designed to assist accountants in dealing with information technology organizational issues in their organizations and those of their clients. Generally, all "No" answers require investigation and follow-up, the results of which should be documented. Where there is such additional documentation, the purpose of the "Ref" column is to cross-reference the checklist to the appropriate working paper (or to the notes on the reverse).

The checklist is intended for general use only. Use of the checklist does not guarantee that information technology organizational issues have been adequately addressed, and the checklist is not intended as a substitute for audit or similar procedures. If information technology organizational issues are an especially vital concern, the advice of an information technology management specialist should be sought.

**IT Management Organizational Checklist**

| | Yes | No | N/A | Ref |
|---|---|---|---|---|

**1. Organization Structure**

a. Is information technology controlled and coordinated through an integrated IT function so that:

| | Yes | No | N/A | Ref |
|---|---|---|---|---|
| • Incompatibility is avoided or minimized? | ☐ | ☐ | ☐ | ___ |
| • Redundancy is avoided or minimized? | ☐ | ☐ | ☐ | ___ |
| • Maximum cost savings are achieved in IT purchases? | ☐ | ☐ | ☐ | ___ |

b. Has a senior executive steering committee been established to monitor and approve:

| | Yes | No | N/A | Ref |
|---|---|---|---|---|
| • IT plans, budgets, and resource allocation? | ☐ | ☐ | ☐ | ___ |
| • Organizationwide IT policies and guidelines? | ☐ | ☐ | ☐ | ___ |

| | Yes | No | N/A | Ref |
|---|---|---|---|---|
| c. Have the scope and mission of the IT function been formally defined? | ☐ | ☐ | ☐ | ___ |
| d. Has the organization structure been documented, perhaps in an organization chart? | ☐ | ☐ | ☐ | ___ |
| e. Do detailed job descriptions exist for all of the IT-related functions? | ☐ | ☐ | ☐ | ___ |
| f. Do the job descriptions reflect adequate segregation of duties, separating record keeping (i.e., information input), asset handling, and expenditure approval? | ☐ | ☐ | ☐ | ___ |
| g. Are job descriptions adhered to, both in practice and as a matter of organizationwide policy? | ☐ | ☐ | ☐ | ___ |
| h. Does the organization structure, taken as a whole, allow for flexibility and diversity in the use of information technology? | ☐ | ☐ | ☐ | ___ |
| i. Are the organization structure and its components periodically reassessed and amended as appropriate? | ☐ | ☐ | ☐ | ___ |

**2. Organizational Leadership**

a. Does the senior information technology officer:

| | Yes | No | N/A | Ref |
|---|---|---|---|---|
| • Understand the business as a whole? | ☐ | ☐ | ☐ | ___ |
| • Have executive-level skills in managing personnel? | ☐ | ☐ | ☐ | ___ |
| • Have executive-level skills in financial management? | ☐ | ☐ | ☐ | ___ |
| • Have good oral and written communication skills? | ☐ | ☐ | ☐ | ___ |
| • Have excellent technical IT skills? | ☐ | ☐ | ☐ | ___ |

|  | Yes | No | N/A | Ref |
|---|---|---|---|---|
| b. Does the senior information technology officer participate in high-level decision making? | ☐ | ☐ | ☐ | ___ |
| c. Does senior management provide regular, appropriate direction to the senior information technology officer? | ☐ | ☐ | ☐ | ___ |
| d. Have performance standards been set for the senior information technology officer and his or her department? | ☐ | ☐ | ☐ | ___ |
| e. Does senior management provide regular performance feedback to the senior information technology officer? | ☐ | ☐ | ☐ | ___ |
| f. Is the IT function given equal status with others (accounting, marketing, production, and so on) through opportunities for advancement of the senior information technology officer to higher management positions? | ☐ | ☐ | ☐ | ___ |

**3. Microcomputer Support Facilities**

| | Yes | No | N/A | Ref |
|---|---|---|---|---|
| a. Has consideration been given to centralizing the microcomputer resource and related user support within a microcomputer support facility, first on a pilot basis? | ☐ | ☐ | ☐ | ___ |

b. If a microcomputer support facility is planned, or if one already exists:

| | Yes | No | N/A | Ref |
|---|---|---|---|---|
| • Are its services defined? | ☐ | ☐ | ☐ | ___ |
| • Are its users identified? | ☐ | ☐ | ☐ | ___ |
| • Are its sources identified? | ☐ | ☐ | ☐ | ___ |
| • Has its budgeting process been established? | ☐ | ☐ | ☐ | ___ |

**4. Ethical Issues in Information Technology**

| | Yes | No | N/A | Ref |
|---|---|---|---|---|
| a. Does the organization have a written, enforced Code of Ethics? | ☐ | ☐ | ☐ | ___ |

b. Does the organization's code of ethics cover the following IT-related issues?

| | Yes | No | N/A | Ref |
|---|---|---|---|---|
| • Maintaining the privacy/confidentiality of information | ☐ | ☐ | ☐ | ___ |
| • Information technology and data security | ☐ | ☐ | ☐ | ___ |
| • Prohibition of software piracy | ☐ | ☐ | ☐ | ___ |
| • Prohibition of personal use of IT assets | ☐ | ☐ | ☐ | ___ |
| • Employee safety and ergonomic issues | ☐ | ☐ | ☐ | ___ |
| • Loyalty and fairness in dealings with employees | ☐ | ☐ | ☐ | ___ |
| • Competence, honesty, and due care in the use of IT | ☐ | ☐ | ☐ | ___ |
| • Where applicable, fairness in IT transactions | ☐ | ☐ | ☐ | ___ |

## 2.2 ORGANIZATION STRUCTURE

Today information technologies have assumed larger and more diverse roles in most organizations than the most farsighted observer could have predicted 20 years ago. Yet in many companies the organizational structure for managing technology has not evolved at the same rate. Clearly, the old maxim applies: if it's not broken, don't fix it. In too many cases, though, the organization for technology is a legacy of early convenience and subsequent inertia. Where this works against a company's ability to use and control its information resources, it should be a subject for management concern.

### (a) INTEGRATING IT WITHIN THE ORGANIZATION

One aspect of organizational concern should be the way in which all of the technology-related components are integrated. For obvious evolutionary reasons, many pieces of the overall information technology complex (central data processing, telecommunications, word processing, engineering/scientific systems, plant automation, microcomputers, and others) may have emerged and remained in different parts of the organization. The overlap and interdependence among these technologies, however, have increased dramatically. If left completely independent, redundancy and incompatibility may result, raising costs, constraining growth, and limiting flexibility and responsiveness.

*(i) Centralizing IT Control and Coordination*

The objective of integration suggests a need for a senior, central point of control and coordination for all information technologies. Some organizations have assigned responsibility for all of the component pieces to a single executive (a chief information officer). This works especially well where technology integration is viewed as critically important and where matrix management processes are well established. Alternatively, coordination of technologies may be accomplished through a senior executive steering committee, chartered and constituted so that it can allocate resources, set guidelines, and direct planning from an organizationwide perspective.

*(ii) Establishing the Scope and Mission of the IT Function*

Another area for attention may be the scope and mission of the central IT function, particularly if it functions in lieu of a chief information officer. Although compatibility and integration are important, they can and should be accomplished in an environment of flexibility and diversity that presents a range of solutions rather than forcing every problem into a single mold. To yield its maximum benefits, technology must be nurtured and exploited across the organization, through end-user computing and departmental-level systems, with appropriate guidance and support. The data-processing function should be directed to grow (or, more often, to continue to grow) beyond its traditional role as author and owner of centralized systems and data so that it can provide more consultation, direction, standard setting, training, problem solving, creativity stimulation, and strategic planning for the rest of the organization. If this cannot be readily or cost-effectively accomplished within the IT function, some or all of these functions may be structured separately at a departmental or corporate level.

*(iii)  Placement of the IT Function Within the Organization*

A third organizational issue to be reconsidered periodically is the placement within the organization's reporting hierarchy of the information technology function (or functions). It is traditional and still statistically typical for this function to report to the chief financial officer, a policy that often reflects sound historical reasons (the first few applications were almost always financial ones) but little recent thought. The appropriateness of this or any other reporting relationship should be revisited periodically.

Where the size and strategic importance of the information technology function warrant it—as often symbolized by the presence of a chief information officer—the reporting level of the function may be elevated (for example, to the chief executive officer or chief operating officer) to good effect. This may broaden the business perspective of the technologists, improve the evenness of technology support across business units, and emphasize the importance of technology to people within and outside the organization.

In other cases it may be more appropriate to shift the information technology function laterally on the organization chart to provide closer support to a business area of greater need or strategic importance (for example, manufacturing or operations). For other environments and corporate cultures, an alternative approach would be to decentralize some (or even all) of the traditional IT function into multiple business units; this may be highly effective for application development in a larger organization.

## (b)  JOB DESCRIPTIONS AND RELATED CONTROL CONSIDERATIONS

Another key aspect of the organization structure is ensuring that formal, detailed job descriptions exist for all of the IT-related functions and that these job descriptions are fulfilled. This is an especially important control and fraud-prevention tool, especially in information technology functions that can be a kind of "black box" to those who aren't involved. Job descriptions should spell out exactly what each employee is expected to do. As a general rule, employees should not perform duties outside their job description.

Job descriptions should reflect the important principle of division of duties. For example, employees with physical control over an asset should not also keep the records relating to that asset. (This makes undetected error more likely and makes it easier to cover up fraud.) Likewise, asset-handlers should not have access to the computerized accounting system, except on a limited basis (for example, to confirm inventory availability). Other especially sensitive duties—for example purchasing and check signing—should also be segregated.

The need for job descriptions goes beyond the widely recognized concept of segregation of duties, although that is certainly one of the important consequences of job descriptions. In some cases a duplication of duties may result—entirely appropriate, for example, in the case of the double-signing of checks. The job description should also specify that annual vacations must be taken (another well-known fraud-prevention tool, because the perpetrators of an ongoing fraud scheme are more likely to be found out when they're removed from the scene).

The foregoing should make it apparent that the process of formulating job descriptions for IT-related functions—indeed, for all employees—must be approached in an integrated fashion. From an internal control and fraud prevention point of view, different tasks performed by different individuals may be interrelated; therefore, an appropriate job description for one employee will often depend on the job descriptions of others.

The need for formal job descriptions is very often ignored or underestimated—written off as more useless paper. At other times existing job descriptions might be ignored. This attitude invites trouble. As one leading fraud investigator put it, "When people begin to do things outside their job description, you have reason to be concerned. It could be a red flag that something is going on. Even if it isn't, some employees can develop a justification to steal if the additional workload goes unrewarded. It's very important that job descriptions be clear, agreed upon, and adhered to."

### (c) THE NEED FOR ONGOING REASSESSMENT

Because the structures and management styles of organizations are so different, it is very difficult to generalize about strategies for structuring information technology resources. In the long run the organizational structure for technology management that will work best is the one most closely attuned to the structure, style, and personalities of the business as a whole. The organizational approach for technology should be periodically reconsidered and adjusted as the importance of technology within the business evolves and as the sophistication and structure of the rest of the organization changes.

The organizational structure for managing the various information technologies in a typical business can easily become a serious obstacle to coordination, compatibility, creativity, flexibility, and responsiveness. Unless the scope, role, and placement of the technology function are revised to grow with the technologies themselves and the business as a whole, the effectiveness and competitive value of the firm's investment in information systems may be drastically reduced.

### (d) SAMPLE PARTIAL ORGANIZATION CHART

A sample partial organization chart, reflecting many of the concepts dealt with in this chapter, appears in Figure 2.1.

## 2.3 ORGANIZATIONAL LEADERSHIP

To a very large extent, the organization's ability to manage and use technology to best effect has always been dependent on the leadership provided by the senior IT officer and by his or her capability to address difficult business technology issues. However, senior management also has an important leadership role to play. Each of these areas is dealt with below.

### (a) THE SENIOR IT OFFICER

As information technology has assumed a greater role in business strategy and competition, two things have become clear: first, the importance of the senior IT officer's skills has increased dramatically; and second, the skills required of the senior IT officer have changed at least as dramatically. Rapid growth in the size, scope, and importance of the information technology function has been (at best) a mixed blessing for the senior IT officer. The pressures and challenges described herein translate into more than

**Figure 2.1**   Sample Partial Organization Chart

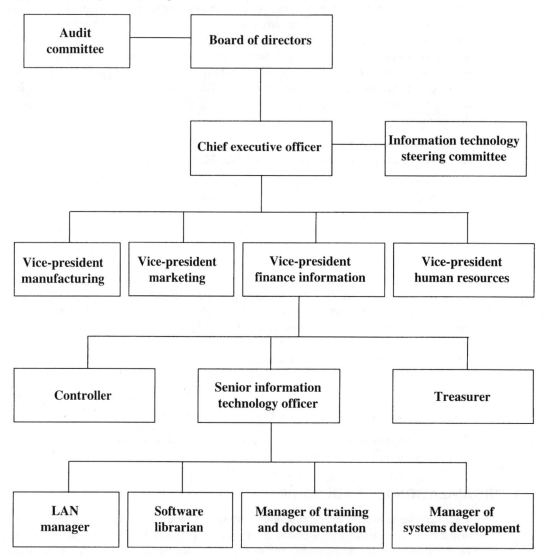

just day-to-day headaches; they are forcing a difficult transformation in the job itself (and, of course, in those who fill it).

*(i)  Meeting Senior Management's Expectations*

A measure of the senior IT officer's changing role in many businesses can be taken from a survey commissioned by C&L of senior executives in the financial services industry. The survey found that 74 percent of the organizations in the sample expected their senior IT officer to participate in high-level decision making and strategic planning beyond the technology function. The same study, however, found that fewer than half of that number were fully satisfied with their senior IT officers appreciation of the overall needs of the organization or their ability to recommend strategic uses of technology—a discrepancy that underscores the problems senior IT officers face in meeting senior management's escalating expectations.

*(ii) Critical Success Factors*

The critical success factors for management of the information systems function have clearly changed as the technology environment and the typical organization using technology have changed. Less than two decades ago, the senior IT officer's role was focused inside the central data processing department, managing the creation and operation of transaction processing systems. Although that function may remain part of the job in some organizations, a greater part is now directed outward, in supporting and guiding other business units, and upward, in advising and responding to senior management.

Today's key requirements for the lead technology officer reflect this transition. An informal survey of successful senior IT officers identified the following critical skills, listed in descending order of importance:

- *Understanding of the business*—active familiarity with industry, products, markets, regulatory environment, and other external factors; a broad-based view of the structure, style, and needs of the organization.
- *General management skills*—executive-level abilities to hire, develop, motivate, delegate to key lieutenants, and to plan, allocate, and control resources.
- *Interpersonal communications skills*—particularly skills in communicating with the rest of the management team to develop and maintain progress toward shared objectives.
- *Technical skills*—management-level competence to direct the technology function, coupled with awareness of directions and new developments in technology for application to the needs of the business.

## (b) SENIOR MANAGEMENT'S ROLE AND RESPONSIBILITY

Although the burden of growing with the job falls primarily on the information technology officer, senior management retains the critical responsibility of providing meaningful direction and feedback to the senior IT officer and, when necessary, for making a leadership change. Unfortunately, senior management has often had some difficulty in appraising the performance of the senior IT officer. Frequently, senior management has had little familiarity or significant contact with the information systems function in its historic role as a "back office" support activity. In the past—especially because senior IT officers have not often been in line for higher positions in the organization—this unfamiliarity has deprived the senior IT officer of motivation and feedback and has resulted in some inevitable stagnation in leadership.

In the evolving technology environment, senior management must set somewhat different standards for its technologists and communicate standards more effectively than in the past through selection and measurement. Key expectations for the senior IT officer are increasingly executive in nature. They require little technical insight on the part of senior management. The cost of not performing an honest assessment or taking appropriate action may be an IT function that fails to provide the leadership and guidance needed by the entire organization.

As the role of information technology increases in importance to the business as a whole, more leadership and new skills are required from the leader of the technology function. If senior management fails to assess accurately the quality of leadership, provide corrective feedback, and make changes when necessary, the effectiveness and usefulness of the organization's IT function will suffer along with long-term competitive posture and even profitability.

## 2.4  MICROCOMPUTER SUPPORT FACILITIES

### (a)  THE CONCEPT

Microcomputer support facilities are akin to the broader concept of the information center. The term "information center" became popular in the first half of the 1980s. At first it referred to the department responsible for computer user support, particularly in an IBM mainframe environment in which there are hundreds, sometimes thousands, of users. The traditional computer or management information systems (MIS) department is often ill-equipped to deal with and support users in this kind of environment. It's too busy running the system.

Today, there is no widespread agreement on what an information center is or ought to be. Very few organizations have formally implemented one, and there are some who believe that the whole concept will never take hold. On the other hand, we're in the middle of an information revolution with new developments in connectivity (more powerful hardware capabilities and groupware such as Lotus Notes) that are changing the way business operates. And to business, information means not just competitive advantage but competitive survival. In this environment, and also considering the high cost of information, it makes more and more sense to integrate the information management function within one area for the benefit of the whole organization. Information centers are one way of achieving this integration.

Defined somewhat broadly, an information center is the department within an organization responsible for managing information resources and responding to the information needs of users. A microcomputer support facility, a specialized subset of the information center, is the department within an organization responsible for managing microcomputer resources and responding to the needs of microcomputer users.

### (b)  THE BENEFITS OF MICROCOMPUTER SUPPORT FACILITIES

The benefits of establishing a microcomputer support facility include:

- Better identification of the microcomputer needs of the organization and of the individuals within it.
- Reduced microcomputer hardware and software costs resulting from microcomputer compatibility throughout the organization and avoidance of duplication among departments.

- Improved microcomputer control and security, which is especially important in the case of sensitive programs and data.

- Better corporate strategy, policy, and decision making, because the quantity and quality of microcomputer-generated information increases when it is managed by a department dedicated to that function.

- Greater efficiency throughout the organization, because other departments know where to obtain the microcomputer support they need and are relieved of the burden of driving and/or coordinating the microcomputer function themselves.

The following sections set out some of the more important considerations in planning and managing microcomputer support facilities.

## (c) PLANNING MICROCOMPUTER SUPPORT FACILITIES

Planning a microcomputer support facility involves four main steps: defining the service to be provided, identifying the users of the service, identifying the sources of supply to be used in providing the service, and setting the necessary budget. These steps are more interdependent than sequential.

### (i) Defining the Service

A microcomputer support facility manages the microcomputer resource and responds to the microcomputer needs of users. However, this doesn't mean that every microcomputer is controlled by the microcomputer support facility. Microcomputers still pervade the organization and are a vital part of everyone's day-to-day activities; they are simply coordinated through the microcomputer support facility.

When you make the initial commitment to implement a microcomputer support facility, you may decide to do so in stages or as a pilot project. In fact, especially in large organizations, it is advisable to do so. For example, a manufacturing company might decide that it needs a new inventory-control and job-costing system. This might be the new microcomputer support facility's pilot project, and it would include coordinating the development of a system that ensures that:

- Materials are obtained in the most timely and cost-efficient manner when needed.

- Inventory records are accurate and kept up to date.

- Understocking and overstocking problems are minimized.

- Alternative sources of supply are identified during a main supplier's strike or other interruption.

- Users are properly trained in the operation of the new system.

Subsequently, if the pilot project is successful, the microcomputer support facility's scope might be expanded to include other functions.

### (ii) Identifying the Users

This will normally be done in conjunction with defining the service. In the preceding example on inventory control and job costing, the purchasing department would be a major user (e.g., to determine what, when, and how much to buy), as would the accounting department (e.g., to determine values for inventory, cost of goods sold, etc.).

This and the previous step are highly interdependent, since it is the users who must to a large extent determine the service or services they want from the microcomputer support facility.

### (iii) Identifying Sources

Once the services have been defined and the users identified (or vice versa), the source of microcomputer hardware and software must be determined. Hardware will generally be purchased outside. Depending on the circumstances, the possible sources of software generally fall into one of the following three broad categories:

- Information-generating systems developed in-house (for example, a custom-designed Lotus 1-2-3 model to handle budgeting, or an in-house database accessed by the entire organization through Lotus Notes).
- Information-generating systems purchased from outside (for example, an accounting package).
- Information obtained directly from outside sources (for example, a legal database subscribed to by a law firm to research cases).

Even after the choice has been narrowed down to one of the broad categories set out above, or some combination thereof, there will likely still be a secondary process to go through. For example, which of the available accounting packages should you buy, or which external database should you subscribe to? These decisions should, of course, be based on a cost-benefit analysis of the features of a particular source.

### (iv) Budgeting

Although prices have declined considerably over the past ten years, the investment in microcomputer hardware and software can still be expensive. In large organizations the cost can be measured in hundreds, thousands, or even millions of dollars. In some cases, microcomputer needs may determine the budget required; in others, the available budget may influence how microcomputer needs are defined. Once again, the budgeting process is linked to the other steps previously set out.

The important point is that there must be a budgeting process. To implement a new microcomputer support facility—indeed, to embark on any information system-building—without such a process is a prescription for disaster. Information is certainly critical to the success of business, but not at any cost.

## (d) MANAGING MICROCOMPUTER SUPPORT FACILITIES

For those who do set up a microcomputer support facility—as part of a pilot project or otherwise—the ongoing management of the department must be considered, as set out in the following sections.

*(i)  Organization Structure*

The nature and scope of a Microcomputer Support Facility's functions are such that one person—or even one type of person—is unlikely to have the skills necessary to address all tasks. For example, there may be a need for several specialties: microcomputer LANs; maintenance of database management systems (DBMSs); and user training. One would therefore expect a microcomputer support facility to be staffed by people from a number of different backgrounds.

The microcomputer support facility must deal with and serve all departments and may often have to balance the needs of one department against those of another, or against the interests of the organization as a whole. To be effective, it must therefore be an independent department with a relatively senior executive in charge of it.

*(ii)  Control and Maintenance*

In addition to responding to the needs of users as they arise—a process that involves the steps set out in the earlier section on planning—microcomputer support facilities have a control and maintenance function, which includes:

- Ensuring microcomputer compatibility across the organization, to the extent appropriate (including making sure that the same version of software is being used).

- Ensuring that the organization's microcomputer resource is secure by being responsible for the issuance of network user IDs and passwords, and making sure that sensitive materials (e.g., diskettes) are properly disposed of when no longer required.

- Monitoring the effectiveness of existing systems, primarily through feedback from users and updating those systems as required.

## 2.5  ETHICS IN THE INFORMATION AGE

### (a)  ETHICAL ISSUES

Every organization should have a written code of ethics covering all aspects of the organization's activities. While the need for such a code extends well beyond information technology, the ethical issues surrounding information technology should not be ignored. Makers, distributors, owners, managers, and users of information resources have ethical responsibilities for the products and services that they own, sell, manage, and use. They should be especially aware of the following ethical issues: privacy, piracy, safety, data security, data integrity, competence, honesty, loyalty, and fairness. Each of these is dealt with in the following sections.

*(i)  Privacy*

Data are collected today by a myriad of private- and public-sector organizations for a wide variety of purposes. The U.S. government alone has gathered and stored several billion records on individuals. The development of database management software for personal computers has extended these capabilities to anyone with a few hundred dollars. Although databases have grown explosively, controls over access and disclosure of confidential data have not kept pace. Unauthorized access to databases and disclosure of confidential information contained therein are commonplace.

There are legal constraints on the improper collection and dissemination of personal data in the United States and Canada, embodied in their respective constitutions, court decisions, tort law, and in federal and state/provincial privacy and consumer rights regulations. However, these laws and rulings are not clear enough to reach consensus. For example, on the question of ethical concern over access to personal history databases versus an individual's right of privacy, an ethicist might ask:

- Who is collecting the data?
- Why is it being collected?
- How, to whom, and for what purpose will it be disseminated?
- How well protected are those data against unauthorized access and disclosure?
- How accurate, complete, and timely are the data?
- What degrees of confidentiality should be accorded to such disparate data as medical, psychiatric, credit, employment, school, and criminal records?

If medical records are considered the most confidential of the lot, the ethical standard for the care accorded such data would be higher; that is, medical records should be gathered, stored, and disseminated with great care and caution.

*(ii) Piracy*

Using the creative software work of another or duplicating it without permission and/or payment of royalty is software piracy. The definition assumes that the creator of the software has complied adequately with the legal requirements of the federal copyright law. The software pirate therefore commits an act of infringement and may be sued civilly for damages, criminally prosecuted, or both.

Software piracy is probably the most common breach of ethics in the field of information technology. For each software program sold, developers claim that another two to five copies are bootlegged. The lost royalties of developers are staggering.

*(iii) Safety*

Computers and peripheral devices, such as terminals and on-line PCs, are driven by power sources that may expose humans to radiation. High levels of such radiation may cause miscarriages and cancer. The intensive use of terminals and PCs may also bring about muscular or skeletal damage to the neck and shoulders, eye strain, and repetitive action injuries like carpal tunnel syndrome.

Proper shielding of terminals and PCs can minimize radiation exposure. Manufacturers should, therefore, see to it that their products are designed and constructed to minimize risks to users. Users should be made aware of the risks and be accorded special considerations to ensure against physical harm.

*(iv) Data Security*

The protection of personal information from unauthorized access, disclosure, and duplication obligates a database owner to:

- Formulate and enforce standards for the proper use of the data
- Communicate, educate, and train users with respect to their responsibility for protecting such information
- Plan for likely contingencies
- Establish adequate security controls
- Monitor control exceptions

### (v)  Data Integrity

An incorrectly entered arrest report, credit report, insurance rejection, debt default, or lab test can cause great emotional and financial damage. Yet the error rates of databases with such sensitive information are often higher than the standards of quality set by the original designers of these systems. Accuracy, timeliness, completeness, and relevance are what give information its value. Creators of personal history databases have, in particular, a special obligation to compile and process such data accurately and protect it from the prying eyes of snoops, browsers, and hackers.

Information can be collected, processed, and disseminated at a high speed today. If information is irrelevant to the needs of users or flawed in logic, assumptions, or conclusions, relying on such specious data can cause catastrophic damage. Quality therefore begins with clear objectives, exacting designs, flawless development, and proper training of users. The obligations of people and organizations involved in software development and database design are to make products that are fit for their intended use and have no fundamental defects.

### (vi)  Competence

The field of information technology is notable for its fast growth, complexity, and the sweeping social, economic, and political changes it has wrought. At times, change seems overwhelming. Skills and products become obsolete overnight. Large sums must be invested in research and product development.

Compromises in quality, safety, and security often result from the race to get new products out of the labs and into the market. New products sometimes contain design flaws, software errors, bugs, glitches, and other impediments to proper functioning that can be costly, especially to uninformed and unsophisticated users. Makers and providers of information technology products—both hardware and software—must take great care and caution in their work to avoid damage or interruption of service to their users. Providers of information technology should seek the most competent people available for sensitive design and product development projects. They should also create an ethical climate in their firms and foster responsible behavior among all employees.

### (vii)  Honesty

Makers, sellers, dealers, distributors, and installers of information technology products, like all other businesspeople, must be honest in their dealings with one another. Representations must be truthful, advertising should be honest, labeling should be accurate, and contract requirements should be fulfilled.

*(viii)  Loyalty*

The information technology industry is large, complex, fast-changing, and highly competitive. Indeed, some information products—such as chips and PCs—have become commodities. The atmosphere surrounding buyers and sellers is changing from trust, confidence, and faith into caution and *caveat emptor* (let the buyer beware). Sellers attract buyers on the basis of price alone. The service-after-sale element is too often forgotten.

These same industry dynamics have also changed the relationship of employers and employees. Loyalty is supposed to be a two-way street. In today's competitive environment, some high-tech, high-talent employees are loyal only to their paycheck. Obligations, therefore, have become blurred between employers and employees, sellers and buyers, and manufacturers and suppliers.

*(ix)  Fairness*

Business is normally conducted on the basis of faith and trust. One cannot provide for all contingencies in a formal contract. The writing and execution of such a contract would take so long that the objectives of both parties would be frustrated.

If business ethics is a matter of the common rights and obligations of the transacting parties, the implication is that fairness is the rule by which we measure whether a transaction is right or wrong. In theory, the bargaining power of both sides in a commercial transaction is equal; therefore, it is ethical to leave the parties to their own negotiations. But all too often in the information industry, both parties are not of equal size, competence, skill, knowledge, or experience. In such circumstances fairness may mean that the more powerful side has an added measure of obligation. The English common law treated buyers and sellers as equally competent to transact business. Yet in the modern era, the notion of *caveat emptor* has been diluted. Sellers with superior knowledge, skills, and resources ought to be more forthcoming in providing information to buyers. Fairness may no longer be a fifty-fifty proposition; it may depend on the relationship between the parties, their relative power positions, and on the context of the business transaction.

## (b)  A FRAMEWORK FOR THE ANALYSIS OF ETHICAL ISSUES IN INFORMATION TECHNOLOGIES

*(i)  Utilitarianism*

Applying a moral yardstick to a particular act is no simple task. The first obstacle is the multiplicity of moral yardsticks. The utilitarian school would suggest, for example, that an act be judged by its results—does it result in the greatest good for the greatest number? A comparison of social cost and benefits could then be made to determine whether that result was or could be achieved. If so, the act is good.

*(ii)  Contractarianism*

The contractarian school of thought questions whether a given act is fair, just, and equitable to the parties. Although the utilitarian theory discounts the interests of a minority in its concern for the "greatest good for the greatest number," the contractarian theory avoids that argument and speaks to a universal or categorical imperative as proposed by Immanuel Kant: "Act only according to that maxim by which you can, at the same time, will that it should become a universal law." In other words, if everyone should act that way, it is ethical.

*(iii) Pluralism*

The third major school of ethics, pluralism, focuses on the priority of our duties and obligations, evaluating acts from the perspective of whether they are right or wrong, bad/bad, not-so-bad, not bad at all. More pragmatic than the other two schools, pluralism emphasizes that there is often no "right answer," and that any decision must balance a variety of considerations, many of which may conflict.

*(iv) Commonality Among the Three Schools of Thought*

Each of the three major schools tends to agree on some basic, fundamental, or common-sense rules. Mathews et al. (1985)[1] suggest the following:

- Avoid harming others.
- Respect the rights of others.
- Do not lie or cheat.
- Keep promises and contracts.
- Obey the law.
- Prevent harm to others.
- Help those in need.
- Be fair.

Authorities in ethics generally use the following criteria in making their critical assessments:

- The intentions of the parties.
- The circumstances under which the transaction occurred: that is, time, place, and the physical and mental capacities—age, education, and experience—of the parties.
- The act itself: that is, its inherent or relative goodness or badness.
- The foreseeable consequences of the act: that is, the likely adverse impacts on the parties themselves, on others, and on future generations.
- The relationship of the parties: for example, any special duties or obligations owed by one party to the other.

---

[1] John B. Mathews, Kenneth E. Goodpaster, and Laura L. Nash, *Policies and Persons: A Case Book in Business Ethics*, Second Edition, published by McGraw-Hill, 1985.

*(v) Summary and Suggested Approach*

We can now summarize the three approaches to ethical decision making as follows:

- Utilitarianism is goal-based and asks what action or policy maximizes social benefits against costs.
- Contractarianism is rights-based and asks what action or policy most fairly respects the rights of the parties.
- Pluralism is duty-based and asks what action or policy reflects the stronger duty or obligation.

For ease or breadth of analysis, you might merge the three approaches. Ask yourself these questions:

1. Does it violate
   A criminal law?
   A civil law?
   A company policy?
   A professional code?
   An industry code?
   My personal values?
2. Is it fair, just, and equitable to all parties?
3. Does it serve the common good and the public's interest?
4. Does it provide the greatest good for the greatest number?
5. Does it cost more than its social benefits?
6. Would you like it if it were done to you? (The "golden rule")
7. Does it do the least harm to the greatest number?
8. Would your mother approve of the act?

## (c) THE ETHICS OF COMPUTER OWNERSHIP AND USE

To some extent, owning a computer is not unlike owning anything that can do harm to yourself or others—like a gun or automobile, for example. Car or gun ownership entails a fair measure of responsibility for the way the car or gun is used and operated. Failure in that responsibility may result in charges of unethical, tortuous, or criminal conduct.

When the object is a gun or car, we can understand the ethical requirement that we should responsibly use a potentially dangerous object. When the object is a computer, such thoughts do not usually cross our minds. Computers are not dangerous, we rationalize. Computers are just toys.

Indeed, like cars and guns, computers can be viewed as playthings in some respects. Yet most people concede that responsible use and operation of cars and guns are critical to our safety, security, and survival. So it is with computers. Computers can do many things to enhance our work lives, our social lives, our economic lives, and even our political lives. Computers, improperly used or operated, can also cause physical and psychological damage and can dilute our individual rights of privacy. What, then, are the obligations of computer owners and computer users?

*(i) Obligations of Owners*

Computer owners are responsible for the following:

1. Providing standards and controls for data security, accuracy, integrity, and completeness
2. Monitoring for exceptions to standards and controls
3. Providing plans for contingencies
4. Providing a safe and healthy work environment for users
5. Educating users to treat and use computer resources responsibly
6. Protecting confidential information from unauthorized access and disclosure
7. Formulation, communication, and enforcement of standards that ensure no unauthorized access nor disclosures are made.

*(ii) Obligations of Users*

Computer users are responsible for the following:

1. Complying with all safety, security, and internal control standards
2. Using computer resources safely, securely, and for company purposes only
3. Sharing computer resources equitably
4. Accessing only those data, files, and programs over which one has authority
5. Disclosing only information that one is authorized to disclose and only to those authorized to receive it
6. Protection, preservation, and proper maintenance of computer resources at one's disposal
7. Refraining from conflicts of interest
8. Refraining from theft or personal use of computer time, computer supplies, or other corporate assets.

# CHAPTER 3

# Strategic Planning and Policy

The last chapter dealt with organizational issues—i.e., ensuring that the organization is properly set up to manage information technology. The next logical area to deal with is the top-level process of IT management, strategic planning, and policy-setting. Specifically, this chapter covers:

- Strategic approaches to IT (Section 3.2), including approaches to IT change (e.g., downsizing and outsourcing), human resources, connectivity, and control, security and disaster recovery (the strategic implications of two other issues—(i) end user computing, and (ii) mergers, acquisitions, and divestitures—are also briefly covered).

- Strategic planning to control IT costs (Section 3.3), a process that involves several elements such as establishing a control mechanism, assessing the level of IT investment, and controlling the costs of hardware, development, application creation, maintenance, and communications.

- Setting IT policies (Section 3.4), the necessary link between IT strategy and the topic covered in the next chapter: the successful use of IT to maximize productivity and competitiveness.

Section 3.5 concludes the chapter by setting out some challenges in the strategic management of IT. But first, a checklist—serving as a practical summary of the main points covered in this chapter—is provided in Section 3.1.

## 3.1 THE IT STRATEGIC PLANNING AND POLICY CHECKLIST

The following five-page checklist, summarizing many of the points in this chapter, is designed to assist accountants in dealing with IT strategic planning and policy issues, in their organizations and those of their clients. Generally, all "No" answers require investigation and follow-up, the results of which should be documented. Where there is such additional documentation, the purpose of the "Ref" column is to cross-reference the checklist to the appropriate working paper (or to the notes on the reverse).

The checklist is intended for general use only. Use of the checklist does not guarantee that IT strategic planning and policy issues have been adequately addressed, and the checklist is not intended as a substitute for audit or similar procedures. If IT strategic planning and policy issues are an especially vital concern, the advice of an IT management specialist should be sought.

## IT Strategic Planning and Policy Checklist

|  | Yes | No | N/A | Ref |
|---|:---:|:---:|:---:|:---:|

**1. Strategic Approach to IT Change**

a. Does a formal program of IT monitoring exist (i.e., the assessment of important IT trends and new directions and their implications— evolutionary or revolutionary—for the business)?   ☐ ☐ ☐ ___

b. Where appropriate, does the organization subscribe to IT forecasting services, participate in IT seminars and conferences, and subscribe to IT publications?   ☐ ☐ ☐ ___

c. In implementing IT change, are strategies and policies in place to ensure that there is:

- Thorough advance preparation?   ☐ ☐ ☐ ___
- Adequate testing and beta-testing?   ☐ ☐ ☐ ___
- No operational disruptions?   ☐ ☐ ☐ ___
- No interruption in the functioning of internal controls?   ☐ ☐ ☐ ___
- Monitoring, feedback, and adjustment as appropriate?   ☐ ☐ ☐ ___

d. Are priorities in place, measured against the objectives of the organization as a whole, and involving senior management?   ☐ ☐ ☐ ___

e. Are executive- or decision-support systems in place to ensure that senior management has all the relevant, timely, reliable, and secure information necessary to make IT-related decisions?   ☐ ☐ ☐ ___

**2. Strategic Approach to Human Resources**

a. Especially for scarce and/or critical IT functions, is a wide range of IT recruitment alternatives pursued in the following ways?

- In-house, including relocation if necessary   ☐ ☐ ☐ ___
- Specialized search firms   ☐ ☐ ☐ ___
- Advertising, including advertising out-of-area   ☐ ☐ ☐ ___
- Campus-level, by trained recruitment specialists   ☐ ☐ ☐ ___

b. Where conventional recruitment is unsuccessful, have alternatives such as outsourcing been considered?   ☐ ☐ ☐ ___

|  | *Yes* | *No* | *N/A* | *Ref* |
|---|---|---|---|---|

c. Especially for scarce and/or critical IT functions, are strategies and policies in place to retain personnel, including such elements as:

|  | *Yes* | *No* | *N/A* | *Ref* |
|---|---|---|---|---|
| • Good physical work environments? | ☐ | ☐ | ☐ | ___ |
| • Fair performance measurement systems? | ☐ | ☐ | ☐ | ___ |
| • Recognition, rewards, and incentives? | ☐ | ☐ | ☐ | ___ |
| • Fair compensation? | ☐ | ☐ | ☐ | ___ |
| • Promotion opportunities? | ☐ | ☐ | ☐ | ___ |
| • Training and education? | ☐ | ☐ | ☐ | ___ |
| • Management styles that promote creativity and productivity? | ☐ | ☐ | ☐ | ___ |
| • Job satisfaction surveys? | ☐ | ☐ | ☐ | ___ |
| • Exit interviews? | ☐ | ☐ | ☐ | ___ |

## 3. Strategic Approach to Connectivity

a. Does an overall strategy formally:

| | *Yes* | *No* | *N/A* | *Ref* |
|---|---|---|---|---|
| • Define communications requirements? | ☐ | ☐ | ☐ | ___ |
| • Identify alternative solutions, including costs? | ☐ | ☐ | ☐ | ___ |
| • Select the best (most cost-effective, flexible) solution? | ☐ | ☐ | ☐ | ___ |
| • Provide support to users? | ☐ | ☐ | ☐ | ___ |

b. Are strategies and policies in place to take advantage of the following opportunities for cost savings and productivity gains?

| | *Yes* | *No* | *N/A* | *Ref* |
|---|---|---|---|---|
| • Networking of microcomputers | ☐ | ☐ | ☐ | ___ |
| • Relocation of IT operations to less expensive areas | ☐ | ☐ | ☐ | ___ |
| • Telecommuting | ☐ | ☐ | ☐ | ___ |
| • Outsourcing of communications needs | ☐ | ☐ | ☐ | ___ |
| • Resale of PBX, leased lines, private networks, etc. | ☐ | ☐ | ☐ | ___ |

c. If not already in place, does the organization have a plan to integrate its voice, data, and image communications (e.g., through ISDN)?     ☐  ☐  ☐  ___

## 4. Strategic Approach to IT Control, Security, and Recovery

a. Has the organization, and senior management in particular, actively conveyed to all employees— not just those directly involved in IT—the critical importance of IT security issues?     ☐  ☐  ☐  ___

|  | *Yes* | *No* | *N/A* | *Ref* |
|---|---|---|---|---|
| b. For particularly sensitive IT positions, is there an adequate program of screening prior to hiring and an awareness of potentially important changes in individual behavior that may pose a danger to the organization's IT resources? | ☐ | ☐ | ☐ | ___ |
| c. Is there a comprehensive disaster recovery plan in place, covering all conceivable threats to the organization's IT resources? | ☐ | ☐ | ☐ | ___ |
| d. Has or will the checklist on computer security and system recovery (Chapter 13) been filled out? | ☐ | ☐ | ☐ | ___ |

## 5. Strategic Approach to End User Computing

|  | Yes | No | N/A | Ref |
|---|---|---|---|---|
| a. Does the organization have end-user computing strategies and policies in place (who, when, how, etc.)? | ☐ | ☐ | ☐ | ___ |
| b. Is a cost-benefit analysis performed before each major application of end user computing is approved? | ☐ | ☐ | ☐ | ___ |
| c. Have the security and integrity issues surrounding end user computing been adequately addressed? | ☐ | ☐ | ☐ | ___ |

## 6. Strategic Approach to Acquisitions, Mergers, and Divestitures

|  | Yes | No | N/A | Ref |
|---|---|---|---|---|
| a. In considering the merits of any acquisition, merger, or divestiture decision, have compatibility, integration, and synergy in the following IT-related areas been thoroughly considered? | | | | |
| • Hardware and software | ☐ | ☐ | ☐ | ___ |
| • Data | ☐ | ☐ | ☐ | ___ |
| • Networks | ☐ | ☐ | ☐ | ___ |
| • IT human resources | ☐ | ☐ | ☐ | ___ |
| b. For all entities that are to be acquired, merged with or divested, has the value of all IT-related products, services, and capabilities been fully assessed and considered? | ☐ | ☐ | ☐ | ___ |

## 7. Strategic Planning to Control IT Costs

|  | Yes | No | N/A | Ref |
|---|---|---|---|---|
| a. Are there effective planning and control mechanisms in place (e.g., a senior management steering committee) to ensure that IT priorities are consistent with the goals and priorities of the organization as a whole? | ☐ | ☐ | ☐ | ___ |

| | Yes | No | N/A | Ref |
|---|---|---|---|---|
| b. Is there an effective cost-accounting mechanism for IT-related expenditures across the organization? | ☐ | ☐ | ☐ | ___ |
| c. Is there an appropriate mechanism for charging IT cost to departmental units, taking account of the overall objectives of the organization? | ☐ | ☐ | ☐ | ___ |
| d. Are there mechanisms in place to ensure that costly and unnecessary duplication in IT systems is avoided between different departments or divisions? | ☐ | ☐ | ☐ | ___ |
| e. Has the overall level of investment in IT been assessed against a wide range of benchmarks (e.g., industry averages, and even more importantly, the organization's strategic IT plan)? | ☐ | ☐ | ☐ | ___ |
| f. Are hardware acquisition costs controlled by: | | | | |
| • Assessing user needs to avoid unneeded options? | ☐ | ☐ | ☐ | ___ |
| • Centralizing buying, for large volume purchases? | ☐ | ☐ | ☐ | ___ |
| • Buying from discount retailers, for smaller volumes? | ☐ | ☐ | ☐ | ___ |
| g. Is there a process in place for analyzing and choosing from available alternatives for acquiring IT applications (e.g., in-house development by systems personnel, prototyping, end-user development, acquisition of packaged systems, etc.)? | ☐ | ☐ | ☐ | ___ |
| h. Are controls in place to ensure that IT systems (e.g., software packages on microcomputers) are compatible with one another and with the objectives and policies of the organization? | ☐ | ☐ | ☐ | ___ |
| i. Are existing IT systems appropriately monitored and maintained to ensure continued and efficient service? | ☐ | ☐ | ☐ | ___ |
| j. Are maintenance costs controlled by considering all of the following options and choosing the most cost-effective? | | | | |
| • Retrofitting old applications | ☐ | ☐ | ☐ | ___ |
| • Porting applications to new, more efficient platforms | ☐ | ☐ | ☐ | ___ |
| • Outsourcing | ☐ | ☐ | ☐ | ___ |

|  | *Yes* | *No* | *N/A* | *Ref* |
|---|---|---|---|---|
| k. Are maintainability and maintenance costs considered in the acquisition and development of new systems? | ☐ | ☐ | ☐ | ___ |
| l. Has specific responsibility been assigned for the management of communication costs? | ☐ | ☐ | ☐ | ___ |

## 8. IT Policies

| | | | | |
|---|---|---|---|---|
| a. Do specific, written policies with respect to IT exist, and have the policies been conveyed to all employees? | ☐ | ☐ | ☐ | ___ |
| b. Do the IT policies cover the following? | | | | |
| • Overall approach and commitment to IT | ☐ | ☐ | ☐ | ___ |
| • Organization charts | ☐ | ☐ | ☐ | ___ |
| • Job descriptions | ☐ | ☐ | ☐ | ___ |
| • Human resources (training, awards, ergonomics, etc.) | ☐ | ☐ | ☐ | ___ |
| • Hardware and hardware use | ☐ | ☐ | ☐ | ___ |
| • Software and software use (e.g., no copying software) | ☐ | ☐ | ☐ | ___ |
| • Security and backup procedures | ☐ | ☐ | ☐ | ___ |
| • System and file documentation procedures | ☐ | ☐ | ☐ | ___ |
| • Other relevant IT areas (e.g., charging of costs) | ☐ | ☐ | ☐ | ___ |

## 9. Summary

| | | | | |
|---|---|---|---|---|
| a. Is IT viewed as a critical success factor throughout the organization and given commensurate weight in strategic planning at the highest levels? | ☐ | ☐ | ☐ | ___ |
| b. Overall, do the organization's IT strategies and policies seem to strike the right balance between structure (rules, centralized control) and flexibility (innovation, creativity)? | ☐ | ☐ | ☐ | ___ |
| c. Do IT strategies and policies adequately take into account the organization's employees (e.g., early employee involvement in changes, adequate direction and training, etc.)? | ☐ | ☐ | ☐ | ___ |

## 3.2  STRATEGIC APPROACHES TO IT

### (a)  STRATEGIC APPROACH TO IT CHANGE

Major advances in information technology continue to occur with great frequency. These include not only advances that are clearly evolutionary in nature, representing straightforward and logical extensions of technology already in place, but also more revolutionary changes that have the potential to alter significantly either the uses or management of information systems. The ability of the organization to recognize and act on both kinds of changes has important financial and strategic implications.

### (i)  Evolutionary Change

Evolutionary changes are more frequent now than at any time in the history of information technology. Technology product life cycles—for both hardware and software—are significantly shorter than ever before. The steady stream of such changes may have major consequences for many technology decisions: vendor and product selection, timing of hardware growth or software migration, method of acquisition for new systems, and so on. Poor or poorly timed choices may result in overspending for technology, large financial adjustments (e.g., writedowns or lease-termination charges), or avoidable product conversions or migrations.

### (ii)  Revolutionary Change

Revolutionary changes may have even more serious organizational consequences, including new products or applications of technology that may shift the way a business operates or the competitive posture of organizations in an industry. In the past such changes have ranged from the personal computer to the automated teller machine. The penalty for failing to react may be steep, including operational cost disadvantages, loss of market share, or even deterioration of public image. Conversely, organizations that anticipate and take full advantage of such changes may be well positioned to improve their competitiveness.

### (iii)  Formal Programs to Deal with IT Change

Coping with technological change poses special problems. Many changes involve long lead times—sometimes measured in years—especially when significant software development is required. Today's integrated and interdependent system environments add geometrically to the complexity of seemingly straightforward changes. Often the magnitude of the long-term investment entailed or affected by a technology decision may be larger than it appears.

The consequences of technological change and the problems surrounding it are large enough that most organizations must work actively to minimize them. For many companies this should begin with a formal program to anticipate change through technology monitoring; for example, assessing important trends and new directions and their implications for the business. Although comparatively few organizations seek to be on the cutting edge of technology (a C&L sponsored study found that a scant 23 percent of senior commercial bank executives felt their companies were "trailblazers in the use of technology"), all need to consider future directions in their planning.

The form of the program will vary from one enterprise to the next, depending on company size, nature of the industry, and many other factors. In some organizations it may be necessary to create a separate unit (within the IT function or elsewhere) to evaluate future technologies, with the objectivity to assess them and the funding to experiment with and "seed" further use of those that appear promising. In others it may be adequate to subscribe to technology forecasting services and participate in seminars and conferences focused on relevant trends and directions. In every case, however, management should assign specific responsibility for forecasting and evaluating changes in technology and its impact on the organization and for planning of appropriate measures to take advantage of them.

### (iv) Implementing IT Change

The complexity and importance of change require close attention to ways in which major changes are implemented. Migrations or conversions—from one application to another, from one vendor's hardware to another, or from one operating system to another—are as difficult and involved as the word "migration" implies. The potential for costly delays and operational disruptions during major changes is very high, demanding thorough advance preparation and testing and rigorous, well-monitored procedures to manage and control the process.

Less obvious—and often overlooked in the urgency of change schedules—is the potential for interruption of the operation of normal controls during a major system change. Controls that were adequate for the old environment are often inadequate for the new environment and even less so for the transition between them. Thoughtful attention to internal control risks must be part of change control procedures and migration/conversion planning. Depending on the change, the exposure may be high enough to demand attention not just by the control community (both internal and external auditors) but by senior management as well.

Rapid changes in technology will continue to affect every system decision as well as the operational stability of existing systems. Without a formal program to monitor and evaluate future technology directions, the organization will risk excessive costs and strategic disadvantage in its marketplaces. Without a well-disciplined and well-controlled process for managing the implementation of changes, the organization may face serious and costly operational disruptions.

### (v) Assigning Priorities

Industry studies have consistently found that average application backlogs range from two to three years. This means that once an application project has been identified, formally requested, and approved, it faces a long delay before actual development is even begun. Most organizations have a hidden or invisible backlog of additional projects that are known and wanted by users but that have not been requested or approved—one study found that the hidden backlog averaged 168 percent of the average known backlog!

The backlog reflects the surplus of demand for new information technology services over the supply of development resources to deliver them. Many factors contribute to the problem, including high maintenance burdens, slow growth in development productivity, rising application complexity, high staff turnover, and budget constraints.

Because information technology has grown increasingly important to corporate profitability and competitive product differentiation, the backlog has grown from an irritant to a major business problem. There are many steps that can and should be taken to reduce the backlog (e.g., increasing development productivity, making greater use of software packages, outsourcing the development of systems or maintenance activities), but a critical responsibility of management is to ensure that scarce IT development resources are used for maximum corporate benefit. In many cases this cannot be accomplished by the existing prioritization mechanism for application projects.

Within many organizations priorities among pending projects are assigned by the information systems department itself or by a middle management user committee on the basis of internal plans, cursory cost-benefit analysis, organizational priority, "first in, first out," or even corporate politics. None of these approaches—regardless of professional competence or good intentions—is likely to capture the true strategic view of senior management. And yet, given the importance of information systems and the long lead times associated with their development, that is the critical element in effective prioritization.

Senior management, with its long-range strategic view of the business, must be directly involved in prioritization. A common mechanism for achieving this, as noted in the last chapter, is a senior management steering committee. To be effective, such a committee must be supported by adequate staff resources and techniques to evaluate projects thoroughly against multiple factors, including:

- Return on investment, developed in accordance with the company's financial standards and subjected both to management scrutiny and postaudit.
- Contribution to other (nonfinancial) corporate goals and objectives, such as market share or public image, that represent strategic intangible benefits.
- Responsiveness to external regulatory, technological, or industry imperatives.

If scarce application development resources are not focused squarely on the long-range strategic targets of senior management, the most important information and systems requirements of the business will not be met in a timely or cost-effective manner.

*(vi) Executive Support Systems*

To make decisions about IT change, management needs relevant, timely, reliable, and secure information. Indeed, this is true for any decision, not just one related to IT, but IT change is the focus of this section.

Among the promised features of recent developments in computer technology are executive support systems or decision support systems, combinations of hardware and software capabilities that provide an easy-to-use, "English-like" interface to powerful query and analysis facilities. The concept is to allow a decision-maker direct access to corporate data and the tools to manipulate it without extensive technical training. Although executive (often graphic reporting systems) and decision (generally analytical modeling systems) support functions are different in principle, they overlap heavily in actual practice.

Traditional information technology systems are at their best in dealing with large numbers of predictable, structured transactions. In contrast, many key management activities are strategic in nature—unstructured and unpredictable—and not readily supported by conventional applications of technology. Decision support systems represent a positive attempt to use technology to support some of the most critical and financially significant activities of the business. Where better informed and/or faster decision-making results, the company may gain a major financial or competitive edge.

Good facilities exist for the front-end portion of a system for decision/executive support: natural language interfaces; easy-to-use packages for analysis, forecasting, graphics, reporting, and so on; and even high-level languages for more complex problems. These may be delivered on an executive desk through a microcomputer, a terminal attached to a mainframe system, or a client/server configuration.

Arguably the most important and certainly the most difficult element of a decision support system is providing an executive easy and flexible access to the required data resources, which are typically fragmented among many application files on a central computer system or even across multiple computer locations. Providing this access requires consideration of the following issues:

- Data management, to ensure that data are planned for, organized, properly defined, and readily retrievable (some organizations attempt to substitute IT technicians for sound data management practices, so that each executive request triggers a flurry of staff work, a short-term solution at best).
- Privacy and security standards and controls, to ensure confidentiality of key data in an environment of widespread ad hoc inquiry.
- Support organization and staff to minimize the waste of valuable executive time in locating the correct, timely version of any desired data or in dealing with residual user unfriendliness in hardware and software.

Clearly, executive/decision support systems can improve corporate decision making, and eventually change the way managers conduct their daily activities. The implementation of such systems, however, requires more than just the installation of some hardware and software. It requires creation of an appropriate technical environment (especially data management) as well as organizational support to ensure secure and cost-effective use.

Without a sound foundation of planning, data management, and technical support, it will be difficult for the organization to make its information resources available for executive decision making. Organizations that fail to plan for and work toward integrated executive support capabilities will find it increasingly difficult to make strategic decisions on IT change as well and as quickly as their competitors.

*(vii)  Change Examples: Downsizing and Outsourcing*

An example of IT change—one that has become prevalent in mid- to large-size organizations—has been the downsizing from mainframe to client/server configurations. (In smaller organizations upsizing has been the trend as standalone microcomputer workstations become wired into a network.)

Downsizing is driven by:

- The lower cost combination of (1) standard microcomputer and network hardware, and (2) client/server software solutions, as compared with related costs in the mainframe environment.
- The greater speed, flexibility, and user appeal of the client/server environment (e.g., graphical user interfaces as opposed to the "green screen uglies" common to the mainframe environment).

A formal program to deal with IT change would have recognized the downsizing trend and its implications for the organization. Whether or not it represents an evolutionary or a revolutionary change would depend on the organization and its approach to implementation. For example, a phased approach is one recommended way of making it an evolutionary change. One mainframe application at a time would be ported and introduced to the client/server configuration, with both run in parallel until the bugs are worked out.

Outsourcing is another, often overlooked, example of change. There is no natural law that says the best and most cost-effective IT solution resides within the organization. If internal solutions have become too expensive, unwieldy, or ineffective, outsourcing becomes a legitimate option for change. It can be applied to any number of IT-related areas: microcomputer support and training, hardware maintenance, payroll, almost any software application, and even to management issues such as IT security.

Once again, a strategic approach to IT change would include a formal program to identify change and change options, including outsourcing. Such change can then be managed and implemented on an evolutionary basis.

## (b) STRATEGIC APPROACH TO HUMAN RESOURCES

### (i) Supply and Demand

Staff costs for information systems have grown into the largest single part of the information technology budget—averaging roughly 40 percent by some estimates. Even more important are local shortages of certain technical and managerial skills, which have focused attention on the fact that the development, support, and operation of information systems have remained highly people-intensive processes; accordingly, the inability to locate, attract, or retain needed skills is critical.

Computer programming and systems analysis will likely be among the fastest-growing occupations during the next decade. This demand for growing numbers of programmers and analysts has not yet created a national crisis—in fact, in some areas entry-level programmers are having difficulty finding jobs. However, significant shortages have been observed in many specialties, including:

- Operating systems programmers (especially for very large systems)
- Database technicians and administrators
- Telecommunications and networking technicians

- Experienced application programmers (with industry expertise or for selected development environments)
- Artificial intelligence "knowledge engineers"
- Client/server application developers
- Executive-level information technology and communications management

Moreover, competition for these and other skills has resulted in relatively high turnover among IT professionals, with frequently disastrous effects on project costs and schedules and significant operational disruption. As the use and competitive importance of information technology continue to rise, the impact of staff shortages and turnover will become even more damaging.

*(ii)  Recruitment and Retention*

The problems of recruitment and retention are complicated by the often-observed fact that computer specialists are not necessarily motivated by traditional rewards. Several years ago, a *Business Week* article on the subject summed up the problem in its title: " 'Computer People': Yes, They Really Are Different." Studies have generally confirmed that technologists, as a group, are less motivated than their non-IT peers by money, job title, responsibility, and autonomy; conversely, they are relatively more motivated by the opportunity to learn new skills and grow within their specialty.

Retention measures within the IT department deserve greater attention than they typically receive from either corporate personnel functions or IT management. Work environments, measurement systems, recognition and incentive systems, management styles, training and educational programs, and career paths within the technology organization should be adjusted to support the desired personnel objectives and reflect the competitive realities of the local job market. Exit interviews with departing employees and periodic job satisfaction surveys will help focus attention on potential issues before they become disastrous for morale and head counts.

Recruitment programs benefit directly from retention measures, since the same factors that work to motivate and retain good people will attract others. Aggressive recruitment—including campus-level activity by specialized recruiters, out-of-area advertising, attractive relocation packages, and use of specialized search firms—will be increasingly common in many areas. These measures should be used in combination with in-house recruitment and development wherever possible; in-house recruitment may help build more loyalty to the company.

Many sought-after IT skills (especially in scarce technical disciplines) are the product of long experience rather than university curricula. Thus, although shortages will vary somewhat with changes in what technologies are "hot," competition to attract the best people will grow more serious.

Without recruitment and retention programs to maintain an adequate supply of skilled, experienced, and motivated IT technical and managerial talent, an organization will find it hard to create and support new information systems. As the competitive importance of technology increases, the potential impact of key staff deficiencies can become a significant and costly handicap.

## (c) STRATEGIC APPROACH TO CONNECTIVITY

### (i) Taking Advantage of Opportunities

Rapid changes in the telecommunications industry and marketplace have made many aspects of communications management more difficult: for example, the proliferation of competing services and sources, the growth in technological alternatives, and the newly volatile pricing environment. The changes have forced many companies to assume new responsibilities for their communications service, to add technical and managerial support staff, and, in many cases, to absorb higher total costs.

At the same time, however, the dynamic technological environment has opened new opportunities for many organizations. Repricing of services, repackaging of services, and new services and capabilities have combined to open many new avenues for a communications user to increase profitability and even revenues. The most obvious strategies involve lowering costs for the organization's communications use by improved planning and management and enhancing the productivity of computer systems by networking them.

There are many other, less obvious, opportunities that the organization should assess and be prepared to take advantage of, including the following:

- *Resale of communications services*—by selling unused communications capacity on a corporate PBX (private branch exchange), leased communications links, or private networks, the company can generate additional revenue and/or help justify more cost-effective, higher-capacity solutions to its own communications needs. Pursued on a large scale, this may become a line of business in its own right; or it may merely help defray expenses. Attractively priced, such resale can help add value to other products or services, as in a "smart building" or shared tenant service.

- *Relocation of operations*—by using economical bulk communications facilities, a company may find it cost-effective to relocate some parts of its administrative operations to less expensive or otherwise attractive locations away from major metropolitan areas. This is often particularly applicable to data entry or data processing activities, where significant savings in staff and occupancy costs can be realized without much operational impact.

- *Telecommuting*—using computers (e.g., laptops) and communications links, many white-collar functions can be performed from home—common examples include telephone order entry, reservation processing, and computer programming. Telecommuting does have limitations and risks (ranging from insurance liability to management and motivation), but it affords opportunities for cost reduction (reduced office space), increased staff productivity, and recruitment of scarce or otherwise unemployable staff.

- *Product or service differentiation*—creative use of communications may provide significant competitive advantage through enhanced marketing or delivery capabilities. Simple examples include telemarketing, direct telephone follow-up on product registration or service performance, and toll-free numbers for product suggestions or support.

- *Outsourcing*—companies may choose to outsource the implementation and management of their communications facilities.

Many other capabilities and opportunities either exist now or will exist as the communications environment changes. The organization should be prepared to identify and evaluate those that can contribute to profitability or help advance other corporate strategies. This requires that the technical support organization be properly staffed, trained, and oriented toward business requirements. It also requires that the functional management of the business be knowledgeable about communications capabilities and motivated to use the technology to full advantage.

If the organization fails to equip and motivate its technical staff and business management to identify and pursue new communications opportunities, it will miss expanding opportunities to improve overall profitability, increase revenues, and/or enhance and differentiate its products and services.

### (ii)  Integrating Voice, Data, and Image

Communications technologies make it possible for voice, data, image, and text traffic to share a single physical communications network. In many organizations this may open the way to large potential savings in telecommunications line costs and facilities wiring costs through consolidation of multiple networks. Opportunities exist for reductions in in-building wiring costs, equipment costs (e.g., modems), and interlocation carrier charges.

Because many businesses have not placed the responsibility for data communication and voice communication in a common reporting and/or planning structure, they face significant problems in evaluating the feasibility of network integration and in determining current and expected requirements, capabilities, and costs.

Significant capital outlays (for rewiring and equipment) may be required for network integration, and, in many cases, cost-effective products and services are only now becoming available. Moreover, normal financial analysis of these costs against network operating savings is complicated by several other factors:

- Difficulty of anticipating future network traffic volumes and functional requirements.

- Difficulty of projecting future network operating costs in the wake of deregulation and the evolving competitive environment.

- Difficulty of selecting from among competing, incompatible vendor technologies and strategies for building integrated environments.

The long-term direction of major communications and systems vendors is toward fully integrated network services through common facilities. Major users of communications will benefit from this direction in both financial savings and enhanced capabilities—provided their equipment, communications service, and organizational strategies have been farsighted enough to work towards network integration. Without a long-range commitment to planning for network integration, the organization will find it costly and difficult to take full advantage of communications technology.

If the organization does not orient its long-range communications strategies and organizational structure toward the eventual integration of voice, data, and image networks, it will pay an increasingly large penalty in communications service costs and functional limitations.

*(iii)  Integrating Information Systems*

Most organizations have experienced tremendous growth over the past decade in their use of information technology. Much of the growth has come in the form of additional systems—personal computers, word processors, and departmental computers as well as new applications on existing computers. Only rarely have all of the additional pieces of hardware and software been acquired with a long-range view of how all would work together.

Unfortunately, there are major differences between vendors and even between product families from a single vendor in the architecture, design, and implementation of computer hardware and system software. These incompatibilities can often make the transfer of application software or even effective exchange of information between systems difficult, time-consuming, and expensive. Moreover, "compatibility" is a complex and widely misused term in the information industry. In the 1980s, for instance, personal computer vendors describing their product as "IBM-compatible" may in reality have offered a machine that variously ran all or some of the same applications or only the same operating system as the IBM Personal Computer. Meaningful assessment of compatibility among different systems may in fact require sophisticated technical analysis of a specific set of requirements.

Although not a new problem in the information systems industry, compatibility has become a more serious issue with the proliferation of diverse devices and increased acquisition outside the traditional IT or data-processing department. Systems acquired for a single local purpose almost always evolve toward more sharing of data and application programs with other systems, a potentially costly and complex afterthought. Less obviously, incompatible systems complicate training and support activities and may result in lost volume purchase economies.

Greater use of packaged application software and unconventional development strategies (like end-user development and prototyping) may complicate the task of information interchange in other ways, working against the consolidation of data in an integrated data architecture. More subtly than in the case of hardware, incompatible software adds complexity and cost when greater future integration is required.

Where the long-range needs and growth of the business require diverse systems to cooperate actively, thorough planning for compatibility and integration of both hardware and software may be very important. Although technical differences between systems can be and often are bridged, the cost of post hoc integration may well exceed the initial acquisition investment.

The problem may become acute without a broad-based strategic plan for information resources, or with a plan that is poorly understood by all units of the business. Planning and managing hardware and software acquisitions does not require subordination of the needs of end users and operating departments to those of the IT or data processing department (as in the bad old days before microcomputers). The trade-off between individual flexibility and corporate control must be managed carefully to avoid dampening the creativity and initiative of users and generating organizational friction. Guidelines and policies, however, can be established that provide a good framework for long-range integration without foreclosing user interests.

Unplanned and uncoordinated growth of information systems hardware and software will add significant cost and complexity to any future efforts to increase integration or to share data. The organization can reduce risks through an information system plan that applies appropriate guidelines and policies for system procurements.

*(iv)   Networking of Microcomputers*

Rapidly increasing microcomputer use in business is a function of the revolutionary increase in functional capabilities, data storage capacity, and availability of powerful software. Nevertheless, some office microcomputers are still used as standalone devices. The drawbacks are obvious: most data must be entered manually through the keyboard (with adverse implications for productivity, accuracy, etc.); expensive peripheral devices (e.g., color laser printers) cannot be shared; and messages, documents, and data cannot be communicated electronically and shared with others.

Networking is the establishment of direct communications among computer systems. It is an area that has significant potential for improvement of staff productivity and resource utilization. Networks range in scope and complexity from comparatively low-speed connections between microcomputers in the same work area to high-capacity networks linking many microcomputers to one another and to larger systems (e.g., departmental or corporatewide mainframes). Conceptually, functions include:

- *Resource sharing*—common access to and use of expensive input/output devices (high-capacity data storage or archival units, communications "gateways" to other networks, etc.).

- *Information sharing*—joint use of shared data files or software programs (where permitted by license) or electronic mail for messages and sending documents between systems.

- *Micro-to-mainframe link*—a generic term for connections between personal computers and larger systems for a range of capabilities from simple terminal emulation for accessing host (mainframe) applications to sophisticated data extraction, download (to the micro) and upload (back to the host) capabilities (with the increasing power and capabilities of micros, this function is being supplanted by client/server technology in all but the largest applications).

Any of these functions require both physical and logical connections among the systems involved. The physical connections are complex enough, consisting of an appropriate communications channel (chosen from among a wide and very dynamic assortment of competing and often incompatible technologies and vendors) and corresponding hardware to attach devices to the communications channel. The logical connections may be even more complex, encompassing network management software, operating system and application software extensions, protocol and data format conversion software, and so on.

Defining networking solutions that will integrate efficiently and cost-effectively with current systems and future requirements is a complex task that is complicated by the flux in technologies for local area networking and the lack of a single recognized standard. Moreover, any network solution will require technical and operational support, from planning and selection through implementation and maintenance. Micro-to-mainframe or client/server connections raise issues of central data management, security and privacy, performance, training and staff support.

It is not surprising that the "fully loaded" costs of a connection between a microcomputer and other systems may exceed the cost of the microcomputer. On the other hand, it is also not surprising that networking is already in place in most organizations, and it is likely to grow rapidly as the cost per connection declines (physical connection costs have declined steadily in recent years, and some software barriers have been reduced).

Costs are often outweighed by the potential productivity and operational benefits resulting from faster and more accurate movement of information. The critical component is a well-defined strategy to identify real requirements, select appropriate and compatible solutions, implement them in an orderly, cost-effective manner, and provide necessary organizational support.

Without a farsighted and comprehensive strategy and program for computer systems networking, a company will pay a significant long-term penalty in implementation costs and time, in the cost and effectiveness of eventual network solutions, in missed productivity and operational benefits, or in all of these.

## (d) STRATEGIC APPROACH TO IT CONTROL, SECURITY, AND RECOVERY

Chapter 13 covers this topic in greater detail, but it has very important IT management significance and merits some additional coverage here.

### (i) Recognizing the Risks

The dramatic growth in the use and importance of information technology has led to increased security risks that result from these developments:

- Much more information is stored electronically than was the case in the past, including much information of inherent value (e.g., product designs) or of strategic and competitive importance (e.g., marketing plans or business forecasts).
- Data are far more dispersed than before: in departmental processors, at plant sites, remote offices, stores, in personal computers, and elsewhere.
- Access to systems has become far more widespread, both within the organization and among its customers and suppliers. Data move faster, and reliance on public networks is greater.
- With the spread of computer literacy, the number and capabilities of potential external threats have increased apace.

Not surprisingly, the incidence of security violations has grown as well. A study of senior executives in the financial services industry commissioned by C&L found that 14 percent of the organizations surveyed had sustained unauthorized access to their computer systems over the previous five years (including 20 percent of top tier commercial banks and brokerage firms). Allowing for both executive unawareness of some intrusions and an understandable reluctance to admit to security problems, it is likely that the actual percentage is even higher. The impact of such intrusions ranges from nuisance to disaster and may include lost time and resources to correct electronic vandalism, lost data, operational disruption, and damage to public image and credibility.

Fortunately, hardware and software protective measures have also improved. Techniques include comprehensive access control software packages, data encryption tools, call-back systems to control network access, and improved security features in many database and network management packages. Any of these impose some cost, both direct (initial acquisition, support, and maintenance) and indirect (system performance impact, operational restrictions, and organizational overhead). It is also unrealistic to consider any of these techniques completely foolproof. But a reasonable investment in appropriate countermeasures (keyed to the level of risk and operational environment) can provide an acceptable technical base for security.

A workable security program must encompass more than just hardware, software, network tools, and the physical security of corporate processing facilities. Other critical elements are:

- Sound security policies and procedures, tied to the overall corporate security program (for all assets) and focused especially on establishing a security awareness and good practices among users and management.

- Appropriate organizational support, to create an effective security function not just in the central IT shop but in each department or unit, to monitor and support security across all of the computer resources of the business.

- Staff security programs, to reduce internal security exposures by better screening at time of hire (especially for technical staff), and by programs to heighten management awareness of potentially important changes in individual behavior.

Unless the organization assesses its growing security risk and improves its overall security program accordingly, it will likely face financial loss, operational disruption, and public embarrassment.

*(ii)  Control and the Auditor's Role*

The increasing use and capabilities of information systems present special challenges for both internal and external auditors. Today's systems differ from those of the recent past in these ways:

- Short-lived or computer-embedded transaction trails (less evidence)
- Wider access to stored data
- Less division of duties
- More dependence on computer controls
- Significant links to external computer systems (e.g., suppliers and customers)
- More integration among processes (automatically generated transactions)

Although information technology does not change the objectives of control procedures in today's environment, they must keep pace with the systems themselves. As more conventional techniques of testing and ensuring control become less efficient and less effective, more reliance becomes necessary on (a) audit trails and controls integrated into automated application systems, and (b) the general controls (often referred to as integrity controls or information technology controls) surrounding the overall systems environment (including controls over application development, application maintenance, program security, data security, system software, and computer operations).

Internal auditors in particular must ensure proper safeguarding and efficient operation of the corporation's increased investment in information technology. Training and hiring programs will often require regular revision to keep the technological capabilities of auditors current with the systems they must audit.

In addition, earlier and more active participation by auditors in the development of new systems (to review the effectiveness of controls design, operational efficiency, and compliance with other management objectives) will be required to avoid serious control weaknesses or expensive remedial modifications late in the development life cycle. Special attention must be paid to control weaknesses that can arise from the conversion or migration from one system (hardware or software) to another or from major changes to existing systems.

External auditors face comparable challenges in executing their responsibilities thoroughly and cost-effectively. The changing competitive environment, and changing regulatory and legal conditions dictate that external auditors focus to a far greater extent on computer systems and controls over them. The corporation should regularly reevaluate for the effectiveness and value of the tools and skills employed by its external auditors against its current and projected information technologies.

Overauditing—often referred to as the "belt-and-suspenders" approach—can occur as readily as underauditing in a computer environment. Although technology creates new exposures, it mitigates others: for example, the risk of unintentional (random) error. And evaluation of and reliance on information technology controls may significantly reduce costly and time-consuming testing.

Although information technology poses special challenges for auditors, it offers new capabilities as well. These range from the fairly basic (e.g., automation tools for maintenance of documentation and interlocation communications, and microbased spreadsheets for analysis), to those that are becoming more common (e.g., specialized audit software packages for testing and planning, data inquiry and manipulation tools to probe data files, and micro-mainframe links to extract and manipulate mainframe-based data on a microcomputer), and to those that are only now becoming practical (e.g., audit-related "expert systems" for planning, risk assessment, and testing support, and programmer "workbench" tools for graphic analysis of applications). Internal auditors should evaluate available and potential technologies for their environments and work toward installing those that can improve the quality and/or productivity of the control process.

Increasingly, the successful performance of both internal and external audit functions demands greater understanding of and emphasis on technology-related controls. Unless auditors are equipped with the training, experience, and tools appropriate to the organization's current and planned environment, it will be more costly and difficult for them to ensure effective management controls.

*(iii) Preparing for Disasters and Other Contingencies*

The automation of any business process creates some degree of dependence on the means of automation—computer hardware, programs, data, communications networks, support staff, and so on. Any of these resources are subject to failure or interruption. With increasing computerization of critical business processes, the company's vulnerability to such failures or interruptions rises dramatically. A major system failure can be catastrophic. A study by the University of Minnesota estimated how long various companies could survive in the face of a data processing system failure: on average, banks could survive for approximately 2 days, manufacturing companies for 4.8 days, and insurance companies for 5.6 days.

Good systems design and operational procedures can mitigate the effects of short or partial outages, including those encountered in normal operations. Other vulnerabilities are less common but more devastating, including:

- Natural disasters (e.g., fire, flood, earthquake)
- Criminal or even terrorist acts external to the organization, especially acts of electronic vandalism by hackers
- Fraud or sabotage by disgruntled employees
- Loss of staff because of strike or mass resignations

Such disruptions are more common than many realize. In the aforementioned C&L study, 10 percent of the study sample had sustained physical damage to their data processing or data storage facilities as a result of fire, vandalism, or natural disaster during the previous five years. Once again, the level rose to 20 percent among top tier commercial banks.

There are no completely foolproof precautions against all contingencies, even without considerations of cost-effectiveness. However, there is a broad range of preventive measures that can reduce risk by varying degrees.

A prudent contingency strategy begins with senior management awareness of business risks and a commitment to reducing them. Technical management and user management share the responsibility for identifying critical exposures and appropriate, cost-effective, realistic responses on a continuing basis. Contingency plans may include many elements, such as:

- Manual procedures
- Reciprocal agreements with other companies
- Contractual arrangements with a subscription recovery facility
- Alternative company processing sites

Effective countermeasures require careful planning, proper documentation, regular updating, training, testing, and rehearsal. Such contingency preparation is an increasingly essential investment in corporate survival today; without it, management is accepting a significant and unnecessary risk to the survival of the organization in the event of a disaster.

## (e) STRATEGIC APPROACH TO END-USER COMPUTING

End-user computing is the array of techniques that an information technology nonprofessional may use to attack a business problem with a computer. The term includes many different hardware and software strategies, ranging from simple spreadsheet programs on a microcomputer to fourth generation programming languages on a corporate mainframe system. Although the mix of products will differ in various organizations, the great majority have seen and will continue to see rapid growth in end-user computing.

*(i)  Costs vs. Benefits*

Strategically, end-user computing offers the opportunity for significant productivity improvements, both for the individual and for the organization as a whole. Properly trained and supported, end-users can solve many of their own computing problems, releasing IT professionals to work on more complex problems and drastically reducing the opportunity costs and frustrations of waiting through the typical application backlog for an IT solution.

On the other hand, the rapid growth in end-user computing can be a mixed blessing. Neither the tools of end-user computing nor end users themselves are well suited to the development of all applications; some guidance and control will prevent lost productivity, wasted resources, and unsatisfactory applications. The staff resources to train, guide, and support end users represent a significant (and often hidden) cost. Incremental computer resources at the departmental and central processor level to drive user-friendly but inefficient end-user software can drive up costs.

*(ii)  Security Issues*

Some of the most critical implications of end-user computing growth revolve around the security and integrity of the corporate data asset. Many organizations have taken steps to improve the planning for and management of centralized data—often developing an overall data architecture implemented by a specialized staff through a database management system and/or other tools. Only very rarely do the planning and policies for data extend to the rapidly growing percentage of electronically stored data created outside the immediate scope of the central IT shop in end-user and departmental systems. Data security, consistency, accuracy, timeliness, efficiency of data capture, backup, and recoverability become increasingly problematic with the growth in noncentralized systems. Without going overboard in the direction of restrictive control and bureaucracy, organizations should broaden the scope of data planning and management activities to focus on the support of and control over nontraditional data processing systems.

*(iii)  Staying Focused*

IT strategy and policy should foster efficient and productive links between end users and centralized data resources. Technology—in the form of data network hardware and connection-conversion-interface software—increasingly facilitates such links. Staying focused is critical, however, and difficult questions must be addressed:

- Are the data organized and managed well enough for users to locate what they need?
- Can acceptable levels of performance be sustained for the potential numbers of users and volumes of data?
- Are procedures and controls adequate to maintain data security and privacy, as well as cost-effectiveness of data use?
- How will data integrity be preserved when data is modified or created under end user control?

If the technology of end-user data access is allowed to grow without commensurate growth in the scope and sophistication of data planning, management, and support, the impact on the corporate data asset may be serious. Overall security, integrity, cost-effectiveness, and performance of corporate data and systems may be adversely affected. In addition, the very substantial benefits of end-user computing may not be fully realized.

### (f)  STRATEGIC APPROACH TO ACQUISITIONS, MERGERS, AND DIVESTITURES

Finally, as automated information systems have become more pervasive, essential, and complex, their potential importance in business combinations has increased dramatically. Obviously, the degree of integration in business operations will largely dictate the extent to which information systems must also be integrated. For a holding company or con-glomerate with autonomous or functionally unrelated operating units, integration of infor-mation systems may be undesirable, serving more as a barrier to subsequent divestiture than as an aid to operations. But where the degree of central control or interunit cooper-ation is significant, the integration of systems merits careful consideration. In industries where information systems are strategic, integration of systems may be vital.

An acquisition or merger situation involving some integration of systems might entail great time and expense. During the period of conversion—which may easily be two to three years in a complex system environment—additional costs can result from business disruption, productivity loss, manual integration of data, and "opportunity loss" on other IT projects awaiting resources. Where systems are compatible, comple-mentary, or wholly dispensable, financial implications may be relatively minor. On the other hand, it is common for the real and opportunity costs of systems integration to range into many millions of dollars. Divestiture of a business unit can produce com-parable costs if shared information systems must be separated. Massive revision may be required; the time and resources required to accomplish this and the resulting oper-ational disruption caused are often underestimated.

Less obviously, a business combination may also provide significant benefits from newly acquired information resources or technological capabilities. Application soft-ware, data resources, IT technical and managerial resources, and/or other technology-oriented products, services, and capabilities may be extremely valuable acquisitions. Major combinations intended specifically to advance a technologically driven market strategy are becoming far more frequent. The technology value (as well as cost) in any acquisition or merger may be significant and should be evaluated.

Even though constrained by time or circumstance, a reasonable assessment of the information systems implications may be pivotal in accurately determining the financial desirability or even viability of acquisitions, mergers, and divestitures.

## 3.3  STRATEGIC PLANNING TO CONTROL IT COSTS

### (a) ESTABLISHING AN EFFECTIVE CONTROL MECHANISM

Although the costs associated with information systems can grow rapidly, the tools and reporting mechanisms needed to manage those costs effectively often do not keep pace. Unless costs can be collected, broken down, and associated with specific activities and services, IT management and users alike will find it difficult to make efficient use of IT resources and to plan for future needs.

### (i) Cost-Accounting Objectives and Elements

Cost-accounting principles can be readily adapted to the financial control of information systems resources. A properly designed and implemented financial control architecture should:

- Encourage effective utilization and management of information systems resources.
- Establish standards for performance and fiscal measurement.
- Improve communications between users and providers of information systems resources.
- Provide senior management with timely information for investment analysis and performance monitoring.
- Improve efficiency and accuracy of planning and budgeting.

The essential elements are the collection, analysis, and assignment of costs to specific services and the integration of cost allocation with budgeting and planning activities. Software facilities for medium-size and larger computer systems can help the mechanics of the process, but the overall design of the financial controls and the way they are used must be carefully developed to fit organizational structure and style and to support specific corporate objectives.

### (ii) Achieving the Desired Effect

Consideration should be given to whether costs should be charged out to users fully, partially, or not at all; to which kinds or categories of costs will be subject to allocation; to the method of cost allocation; to the method of internal pricing; and, most important, to the impact on IT and user behavior. Costing and pricing strategies for IT resources will produce changes in organizational behavior and can support corporate strategies. Care must be taken to avoid building in unintended incentives that run contrary to long-range corporate plans.

For example, as the organization evolves toward multilevel processing and application development (with increased use of departmental and end-user computing), fully loaded charges may force users away from use of some central services that may be strategically, technically, or financially desirable from an overall corporate perspective. Data processing services (especially new application development) may be more heavily utilized by prosperous divisions or mature operating units with the ability to pay, as opposed to areas of the business where the benefit to the corporation might be higher or the need greater. Innovative use of new software or hardware—where the first user must bear the incremental cost—may be discouraged unnecessarily. And the revenue loss implications of purging old, unneeded applications may encourage the IT department to keep running them.

On the other hand, the market mechanism introduced by a cost-allocation system may engender some healthy scrutiny of IT productivity and costs and introduce some constructive reexamination of alternative approaches to providing cost-competitive information services. Cost allocation, however, is clearly not a substitute for either long-range planning or senior management involvement. If anything, a financial control system may increase the need for strategic guidelines and management involvement to ensure that overall corporate interests are not diluted by unintended side effects of the cost-allocation mechanism.

*(iii)  Benefits and Caveats*

The information developed by a sound financial control system should enable users of IT services to make better, more efficient use of information resources and to provide more meaningful projections of future requirements. It should enable providers of IT services to manage resources more effectively, improve overall service, and forecast future growth more accurately. It should also provide senior management with an understandable set of standards and measurements for evaluating the fiscal performance of the IT function.

Without an effective system to allocate and manage costs, the IT function and its users will be seriously handicapped in making cost-effective use of resources and planning for future growth. In general, costs for information resources will be higher, budgeting and planning less accurate, and user satisfaction lower than if a properly implemented system for financial control were in place.

## (b)  ASSESSING THE LEVEL OF INVESTMENT IN IT

*(i)  Cost Benchmarks*

Spending for information technology has increased both in total and as a percentage of corporate expense. Spending under the control of the information systems department rose an average of about 15 percent per year from 1980 until the onset of the recession in the late 1980s. Additional spending for information technology outside of central control (often including much of the investment in office automation, personal computing, engineering/scientific computing, telecommunications, and other areas) added significantly to both the growth rate and total.

Management often finds it difficult to evaluate the level of spending for information technology. Is it so high that financial resources are being wasted on unnecessary bells and whistles or technology for technology's sake? Or is it too low, with the grave risk that competitors may be building up strategic advantages and productive efficiencies that will be difficult to overcome?

The use of gross comparisons—spending as a percentage of gross revenues versus an industry average, for example—is common but very misleading. Aggregate measures ignore differences in past investment levels, what costs are included, how they are compiled, and, most important, the needs of the business. Such comparisons also obscure fundamental issues of whether or not the spending is efficient (relative "bang for the buck") or effective (targeted at key business objectives). It is certainly possible to spend more and get less; it is even possible to accomplish the opposite.

As noted earlier, it is not possible to perform any serious evaluation without accurate and comprehensive information on technology spending across the organization. The rapid decentralization in many organizations has caused the central IT budget to include only a minority of total information technology expenditures. The remaining pieces—

micros, communications, office systems, departmental systems, plant floor systems, and so on—must be assembled if management is to have any idea of total spending, year-to-year increases, or allocation among functions.

*(ii)  Assessment Issues*

A good financial management control mechanism for information systems (as also described earlier) is one key element in assessing the level of investment. Where costs are charged back to users and budgeted for by users, the budget process and level of investment in systems can become (at least partially) a function of user demand for services. Although a financial control system may not produce an ideal allocation of resources (for example, the least profitable operating units may be the best areas for technology investment but will be less able to afford service), it can provide a valid market mechanism to test IT costs. It also provides a reliable source of information for management's assessment of its information technology investments.

   Meaningful analysis of the level of investment demands attention to other issues: human resources, planning, leadership, prioritization, system development, maintenance strategies, and so on. Even when information technology resources are productive and well managed, it may prove very difficult to fix a specific "best" level of investment. Incremental investments in new systems should be evaluated against one another, against investment in other areas of the business, and against corporate financial criteria. But often the full benefits of proposed information systems are not captured in financial analyses, and strict financial analysis may produce serious underinvestment in technology.

*(iii)  IT Investment vs. the IT Strategic Plan*

In the long run, the most successful strategy is to assess overall investment level against a comprehensive strategic plan for information resources, which encompasses the systems activities necessary to support future business objectives. A sound information systems plan, combined with active management measures to ensure that spending is as productive and well-controlled as possible, should provide a good target for evaluating investment in systems. It should include an explicit link to business strategies and corresponding time-phased systems activities. Level and allocation of investment can then be calibrated against plan objectives and time frames.

   There are no easy guidelines to follow in setting an optimal level of investment in information technology, and the problem is complicated by difficult questions of how efficiently investments in technology are being managed. As the competitive importance of system capabilities rises, however, management must learn to evaluate the level of funding—on one hand to avoid serious long-term competitive disadvantage and on the other to avoid wasting scarce financial resources on unneeded technology.

## (c)  HARDWARE ACQUISITION

Although the cost of IT hardware—in particular microcomputers—has fallen steadily over the past 15 years, the total investment in hardware remains high for many organizations, partially because of the proliferation of microcomputers and partially because of the tendency to buy state-of-the-art machines found near the top end of manufacturers' price ranges.

IT hardware has essentially become a commodity item. The market during the past five to ten years has been characterized by fierce competition, including the entry of discount chains into the fray. Prices on last-generation machines (e.g., 486-based microcomputers after Pentium-based units were released; Pentiums as P6 machines come on the market) are routinely driven down to bargain-basement levels within six months to a year. It's possible to pick up a complete last-generation system, including CD-ROM and laser printer, for under $2,500. State-of-the-art systems with all the bells and whistles run more than double that. In large organizations that purchase hundreds or even thousands of machines per year, the potential costs are obviously significant.

Of course, there are often good reasons for the cost differences. The higher speeds of newer machines are quite noticeable when running today's graphic user interface (GUI) versions of popular software (e.g., Lotus or Excel for Windows, Word, or Word-Perfect for Windows). Last-generation machines may also come up short on memory (4Mb just won't do anymore, and 8Mb is barely enough), and on hard-disk capacity (240Mb is rapidly used up, 420-540Mb will usually suffice, but more is preferable). Nevertheless, the key questions concern user needs. For example, if the machine is to be used primarily for word processing, then it's possible to get by quite well with less.

Some key steps in controlling hardware costs include the following:

- Assess user needs and ensure that expensive, unneeded options and features are not included in the hardware.
- For small volume purchases of basic microcomputers, shop around for the best price. This usually means discount retailers. Although vendor support is limited, these retailers sell a wide range of reputable brand names, and manufacturer support is available.
- For large volume purchases, centralize buying to get the best volume discount, and/or tender the contract to at least three reputable, independent suppliers.

## (d) CONSIDERING ALL APPLICATION DEVELOPMENT OPTIONS

*(i) Option 1: Custom Development*

Conventional methodologies for application development have been blamed for many of the current problems in today's systems environment: large backlogs, long lead times, high costs, "unfriendly" designs, significant project failures, and so on. Although some of the blame belongs elsewhere, one aspect of conventional development methodologies clearly contributes to many of these headaches—the prescription of a full-blown, custom development solution for every application problem.

Major advances have been made in improving the productivity of custom development. The rapid changes in the information technology environment have also added a long list of significant new alternatives for creation of an application. Important examples include purchased application packages, prototyping, and end-user development.

None of these is an ideal solution for every kind of problem. If used in appropriate situations, however, one or more of them may prove faster and more cost-effective than traditional methods. Since application projects vary widely in complexity, expected longevity, transaction volume, number of users and locations, and other factors, it makes sense to have a range of solution strategies available.

*(ii)  Option 2: Purchased Packages*

Purchased application packages represent an excellent solution for many common business problems. They are available in growing numbers for general applications, industry-specific variations, and more technical environments than ever before. Where a suitable software package can be found, it will generally be less expensive than custom development and should also result in faster implementation and lower risk of project overrun or failure. Software package selection requires a good understanding of requirements, risks associated with the vendor and package itself, skills necessary to install and modify the package, and the legal protection necessary in any software contract. Recent trends in the software market—including integrated design (e.g., of multiple financial applications) and flexible user-customization options for data capture and formatting—increase the attractiveness of the packaged software option.

*(iii)  Option 3: Prototyping*

Prototyping is a strategy for application creation that replaces the highly structured and detailed processes of requirements definition, design, and analysis with a quick and dirty iterative process. Using high-level tools, a team of users and developers creates a simple working prototype system, places it in use, and refines it progressively.

Prototyped systems produce much better communications between IT and users, generally resulting in higher levels of user satisfaction with the end product as well as a shorter development cycle. Most experience with prototyping has focused on small-to-intermediate projects of moderate complexity where team size can be kept to a minimum and where some inefficiency of operation or structure is not a major concern.

*(iv)  Option 4: End-User Development*

As described earlier, end user development encompasses many different varieties of programming by non-IT professionals, e.g., micros using report generators and other "user friendly" software tools, or mainframes using high level languages. End-user development, of course, lacks the structure and controls that surround traditional development and may lack documentation, audit trails, security features, and other desirable characteristics of standard development.

*(v)  Choosing the Best Option*

For most intermediate and larger businesses, alternative development strategies (like packaged software, prototyping, and end-user development) complement rather than replace conventional IT development. Each strategy has efficiencies and limitations that best suit it to certain development problems. More complex applications with more users and higher transaction volumes will be better addressed by conventional development; less complex, smaller-scale problems may be most effectively addressed by prototyping; and the least complex, lowest-volume applications may be best handled by end users. Packages may substitute for any of these if a good solution can be found.

In practice, the problem of selecting the best strategy is more complex. Detailed criteria are needed to reflect the specific concerns and environment of the organization. Diverse, somewhat incompatible tools and packages can necessitate a very costly and time-consuming retrofitting of applications into an integrated structure for information management. Short-term gains in application development efficiency should not come at the expense of long-range system planning.

Unless the organization broadens its methodology for systems development to incorporate alternative strategies, it will experience significant unnecessary costs, delays, and user dissatisfaction in the creation of new systems. Conversely, new strategies used without consideration of their limitations and inefficiencies may result in unnecessary costs, user frustration, and less control over the information asset.

## (e) CONTROLLING APPLICATION COSTS

*(i) New System Development Strategies and Techniques*

Traditional methods of application development combine a structured system development life cycle and methodology with a procedural programming language (e.g., C, COBOL). This conventional approach typically optimizes the efficiency of system design, hardware utilization, and adherence to corporate standards; it does not optimize either the use of development staff resources or the total time needed to complete a system. As a result, IT development productivity has scarcely improved over the last two decades, and project costs have grown steadily with staff costs. Over the same period, computer hardware costs have fallen dramatically, and user demand for new applications has increased. The result has been long application lead times, significant opportunity costs, and soaring user frustration.

Until recently, few information systems organizations have made significant use of alternative development approaches or programming tools that promised productivity improvements. The reasons—product functional limitations, machine inefficiency, IT staff reluctance, and so on—often have much to do with the cultural heritage of information technology. In today's environment, such objections are less appropriate and more costly to the organization.

New system development techniques and technologies are available that can materially reduce the time to define, design, and develop computer applications. Nonprocedural fourth-generation languages can greatly reduce programming time for many applications; other software facilities, such as automated design tools, data modeling aids, screen generators, application generators, report writers, and query products have improved steadily over the past decade and can also contribute significantly to development productivity. The integration of powerful software facilities in system development workbenches (combining design aids, data dictionary, high-level languages, and documentation tools) is increasingly practical and potent. The advent of graphic user interfaces (GUIs), sophisticated database management systems, and system query languages is revolutionizing systems development. Although such tools are not inexpensive (either in initial acquisition cost or hardware overhead), productivity gains can be dramatic.

New development strategies and methodologies that deviate from the traditional system development approach can also improve productivity and user satisfaction. One good example is the previously mentioned prototyping, in which small teams of users and development professionals create, use, and refine a quick and dirty solution through multiple iterations (in lieu of drawn-out specification, analysis, and design). And again, greater use of application packages and development by end users themselves should also be part of the overall corporate development strategy.

*(ii)  The Importance of Management Control and Coordination*

Unfortunately, none of the tools or techniques described in the last section is a complete panacea for the application development "problem." Product limitations, operational inefficiencies, integration considerations, learning curves, and so on, all necessitate good business judgment. For example:

- Proper analysis, evaluation, and testing of all development tools under consideration (most effectively by an independent, objective, and technically qualified staff).
- Comprehensive training.
- Adequate support, at an appropriate level of technical expertise.
- Incorporation of appropriate standards and quality controls.
- Establishment of guidelines to ensure that different tools and techniques are matched to appropriate kinds of problems.

Moreover, such analysis, guidelines, and support should be coordinated across all of the organization's development groups—including the department-level and other dispersed development activities that are increasingly common in many larger organizations. Management should consider possible adverse effects of the new development tools on application system integration and compatibility or on overall data management. A profusion of new programming languages and their associated data handling facilities can fragment an organization's systems and information resources as thoroughly as a proliferation of incompatible hardware.

Used inappropriately, without necessary training, technical expertise, guidance, and support, advanced development tools may prove worse than just costly and counterproductive—in some cases results have been disastrous. One executive victimized by a textbook case of fourth-generation language misuse said of such tools, "They are the only way information technology will be able to deliver the services users are demanding at a reasonable cost. But as with any powerful tools, if you put them in the hands of amateurs, someone is going to get hurt."

If the organization is not evaluating and exploiting tools and techniques in an appropriate manner to improve its development productivity, then application development will inevitably be costing more, taking longer, producing less, and impairing the company's profitability and competitive posture.

## (f)  MAINTENANCE—A KEY COST FACTOR

Many organizations have a significant portfolio of application systems that were originally developed in the 1980s, 1970s, or conceivably even the 1960s. Maintenance of these older systems has become a major activity of the typical information technology department, often consuming 65 to 100 percent of the total application development staff time in a large organization.

As generally defined, maintenance comprises the following activities:

- Repairs to correct errors or failures in the application.

- Changes to the application to reflect changes in the underlying business process or environment (e.g., new product line, new organizational structure, new computer hardware or software).

- Enhancements to the application to add new functions or capabilities requested by users.

As application programs age, maintenance activities become more difficult and time-consuming because of cumulative program "patches," inadequacy of application documentation, and turnover of knowledgeable staff. In IT shops with large portfolios of old applications, maintenance may consume all the development resources.

The cost of application maintenance is reflected not just in staff time and other resources (hardware and software) that sustain old systems, but also in the opportunity cost of delays to new development projects—delayed benefits, inadequate management information, lost competitive opportunities, and so on. Major unplanned changes to old applications (e.g., due to a significant regulatory change) pose an additional risk of unplanned costs, serious operational disruption, and even effective obsolescence of basic systems.

Maintenance is what keeps applications relevant and functional beyond their useful lives, and it cannot be eliminated. It can and must be managed, however, to avoid crippling of new application development activities. At a minimum, management must track and assess the level of maintenance activity and the age and condition of major application systems. Other appropriate measures may include:

- Evaluation and prioritization of all major changes and enhancements through a management steering committee to restrict unnecessary maintenance.

- Identification and replacement of troublesome, maintenance-prone modules.

- Use of "retrofit" software packages to structure and improve maintainability of older applications.

- Revision of development standards to improve maintainability of future systems.

- Use of new tools, techniques, or organizational approaches to improve the productivity of development staff resources.

- Outsourcing of maintenance activity.

- Porting of older systems to a new technology base to take advantage of new tools available to maintain programs.

Unless the resource drain imposed by maintenance of old application systems is understood, measured, and managed effectively, the organization will be seriously handicapped in controlling IT operational costs, responding to changes in the technical or business environment, and addressing new application opportunities. In the long run, inadequate maintenance management will directly reduce IT effectiveness and corporate profitability.

## (g) MANAGING COMMUNICATION COSTS

Some businesses spend almost as much on telecommunications as they do on all other information technology activities combined. Moreover, although communications costs are rising faster than data processing costs, many organizations lack either a consolidated budget or a responsible manager to control costs. Surprisingly often, companies do not even have a complete picture of how much they are spending on communications products, services, and support.

At the same time, the telecommunications industry is undergoing rapid change. Under the impetus of both regulatory and technological changes, fresh (or, in some cases, newly cost-effective) alternatives to plain old telephone service are available in every category of telecommunications. A sampling of service alternatives in different range categories would include:

- Computerized voice-and-data private branch exchanges, local-area and wide-area networks, and shared tenant services for in-building service.
- Private microwave, fiber optic, or wire networks; two-way cable TV (leased bandwidth); or cellular for metropolitan area service.
- Wireless LAN technology.

As these and other options become available, the choice of a corporate telecommunications strategy becomes more important and more difficult. As with hardware and software selection for computer systems, selection of communications vehicles must be based on comprehensive cost/benefit analysis and long-term, business-driven planning combined with thorough technical analysis.

Issues of business planning are increasingly important because many communications decisions represent long-term, capital-intensive commitments (as basic as what kind of wire to place in the walls of a new building, for example) which may be affected dramatically by strategic moves—new products, new markets, new locations, and so on. The implications for performance, capacity, compatibility, growth, control, security, support, and training are obviously important and must be considered. Particular emphasis in planning should be placed on flexibility because of the continuing state of flux in communications costs, products, and service capabilities.

In addition, management should ensure that communications planning is conducted either as part of or in close conjunction with planning for other information technology systems. Nearly all of the capabilities of planned computer-based systems will be delivered through or as a part of the corporate communications network, and integrated planning is the only way to provide required levels of performance and functionality. Integrated planning is also essential to minimize costly incompatibilities and redundancies of hardware, services, and staff.

An important development in recent years has been the "unbundling" of support services previously provided by telephone companies. In addition to the planning, selection, and procurement responsibilities discussed above, each organization must now assume overall responsibility for the implementation, operation, and maintenance of its communications facilities. Although some vendors and other sources may provide many—or at least some—of these functions, the key evaluations and some support requirements will fall on the using organization.

Without a qualified manager and technical support organization appropriate to the size and complexity of the communications environment, businesses will find it difficult to control communications service costs, integrate diverse products and services, maintain acceptable service levels, and support needed planning and support activities. Experienced managerial and technical communications specialists are in comparatively short supply, but many organizations will find it far more costly and difficult to do without such skills than to hire or develop them.

Without a comprehensive strategy for communications—based on business requirements and closely integrated with information systems planning—the organization will spend more than necessary on telecommunication services and often get less than required. Without appropriate management and technical support staff and a responsible communications organization, many companies will find it difficult to develop or implement the viable communications strategy they need.

## (h)  PITFALLS TO AVOID

Many of the other issues raised in this chapter introduce the logical consequences of not doing an adequate job of long-range information technology planning. Strategic planning for information technology offers the organization an opportunity to define the role of its IT functions, set objectives, assign priorities, and forecast capital requirements based on a realistic assessment of future needs. In today's environment of IT resource scarcity, long lead times, and critical competitive significance, long-range planning is the only consistently effective approach to building a reliable information and technology foundation for the business. As the use of information technology spreads throughout the organization and the rate of technological change accelerates, strategic planning for information resources becomes more difficult and critical.

Good intentions and an awareness of the importance of planning are not enough to guide strategic planning in any area of the business—least of all in information technology. Planning projects fail for many reasons (usually casting a pall on future planning efforts):

- Too little structure or too much structure in the planning approach.
- Too narrow a scope or too little participation from users.
- Too broad a scope (for available time or resources) or too much participation.
- Not enough senior management sponsorship and participation.
- Ineffective links to strategic business planning and future business directions.
- No provision for reaching a common understanding of how the business does work and how it should work.
- Inadequate assessment of current systems and technology. (How well are they performing? What problems need to be addressed? What problems may exist in the future?)
- Ineffective link to systems implementation (plan too theoretical).
- Failure to use appropriate automated tools to improve the discipline, cost-effectiveness, and maintainability of the plan.
- Too little objectivity or inadequate planning skills on the part of the planning team.
- Insufficient attention to how the plan will be used and kept alive—adapting to changes in the business and environment, monitoring progress, and functioning as a working tool of management.

Effective long-range information resource planning must provide the means to address all of these pitfalls directly and in a manner appropriate to the style, structure, and sophistication of the organization. Ineffective planning may actually do more harm than no planning at all, not just because of wasted time and resources in the planning process but because of ill-chosen long-term commitments and a false sense of preparedness.

## 3.4  SETTING IT POLICIES

Senior management should oversee strategic planning for information technology. Ultimately, the strategies that are developed have to be implemented throughout the organization by ensuring that specific, written policies are set out and conveyed to all employees.

The strategic sources of IT policy have already been dealt with in this chapter. For greater certainty, some of the key elements to be covered in the organization's information technology policies are briefly described in the following sections.

### (a)  APPROACH AND COMMITMENT TO IT

IT policy should begin with a general statement on the organization's approach and commitment to IT. Does it want to be at the leading edge of IT innovation? Is increased productivity the key objective of its IT strategy, or is it minimizing costs, maximizing competitiveness, and finding new opportunities? If it's a combination of all these and other goals, how do they rank? And how do the organization's employees fit into the picture?

### (b)  ORGANIZATION CHARTS

It's been said that a picture is worth a thousand words. If so, a chart ought to be worth at least several hundred, especially in the case of information technology, which pervades the organization. By illustrating how IT fits into the big picture (who's in charge, etc.), organization charts can reinforce the general policy statement referred to in the last section.

### (c)  JOB DESCRIPTIONS

The last chapter referred to the critical importance of job descriptions, especially for IT-related functions. Job descriptions represent another element of the organization's policies. Even functions that are not directly related to IT should refer to the employee's relationship and involvement with IT, including his or her responsibilities.

### (d)  HUMAN RESOURCES

Information technology can be intimidating, especially for employees not directly involved. Setting out policies in this area can help reduce anxiety and provide focus. What is expected of employees in IT? What is the organization's policy on training? Will the organization acquire its IT human resources by promoting from within wherever possible? Are there incentive or award programs for valuable employee suggestions on how to use IT more effectively and efficiently?

Another germaine issue is ergonomics, as further described in the next chapter. For example, employees who spend most of their day in front of a terminal or microcomputer should be guaranteed ergonomically sound furniture and directed to take breaks once an hour.

Finally, if the organization has arranged special pricing with an outside supplier for employee purchases of new IT products or for used products being put out of service by the organization, those policies could be included in this section.

## (e) HARDWARE AND HARDWARE USE

Hardware policy includes what makes and models are approved, what suppliers the hardware can be purchased from, what the approval and purchase process is, and so on. It also includes policy on the use of hardware; for example, whether or not employees can take laptops home with them. Other prohibitive policies (for example, no personal long distance calls) could also be included here.

## (f) SOFTWARE AND SOFTWARE USE

Similarly, software policy would include all issues related to the purchase and use of software, including any packages that have been standardized. To protect the organization from severe civil and even criminal penalties, it is also extremely important that policy specifically and strongly prohibit the copying or movement of software from machine to machine. (This is also a good computer virus-protection policy.)

Other useful prohibitions are no computer games allowed on microcomputers and no end-user development of important applications (e.g., spreadsheet models) without appropriate authorization and control.

## (g) SECURITY AND BACKUP

Security policy should cover a wide range of issues: physical security of the premises and microcomputers, password and other access restrictions, backup procedures and the off-site storage of backup media, shredding and other disposal procedures, and so on. Security issues were briefly covered in this chapter and are more fully covered in Chapter 13 of this handbook.

## (h) SYSTEM AND FILE DOCUMENTATION

The organization's policies should include the complete documentation of all systems by IT staff, as well as the procedures to be followed by users in documenting important word processing, spreadsheet, and similar files.

## (i) OTHER POLICIES

Depending on the circumstances and the type of organization, there may be other IT issues that need to be addressed. For example, there may be policies and procedures for the release of hard copy and electronic information (to clients, etc.). There may also be instructions with respect to the charging of IT-related costs and time.

## 3.5 CHALLENGES IN THE STRATEGIC MANAGEMENT OF IT

Many of the issues presented here have a familiar ring, reminding us that few of the underlying problems are new. For example, questions of compatibility, development productivity, and the need for planning are as old as the technology.

Although much is familiar, even more has changed. As we have seen and will see, the scope and impact of information technology issues are far broader than ever before, directly affecting more businesses, more processes, more products, more employees, more of the competitive posture, more of the business plan, more of the public image, and more of the profitability.

There has been a tremendous reversal of the conventional wisdom about technology and its management. Fundamental principles—like the economies of scale in computer hardware—have been turned upside down. Many other conventions have been called into question, including:

- Where and how applications should be developed.
- How the technology function should be organized.
- The principal role and uses of technology in the business.
- How projects should be justified and prioritized.

These changes have a common, overriding implication: They demand a different level of involvement and a new attitude toward technology on the part of senior management.

In the preceding material we have highlighted a very broad range of complex problems and their implications for the organization. Each of them is potentially important enough to warrant serious attention by management. But it is also possible to draw out of these diverse issues some common general themes that represent the challenges that senior management must face directly.

### (a) BUILD A DIFFERENT FRAMEWORK TO MANAGE TECHNOLOGY

Technology has evolved in numerous ways that should alter both the organization of technology and the organization for technology. The traditional view of the function—focused on the central data-processing shop—is far too narrow for the realities of most organizations' information technology activities.

Technology management must be broadened to provide consolidated planning and policy control for all of today's overlapping and interdependent information technologies—including telecommunications, office computing, plant floor automation, engineering and scientific systems, and so on. The technology function and its leadership must assume new responsibilities for guiding, counseling, and supporting the diverse and dispersed information systems activities of other organizational units—departmental systems and end-user computing, for example.

Numerous other organizational issues have to be addressed: How do we institutionalize the systems planning process and link it to business planning? How will we provide for ongoing and objective evaluation of new system development tools and other key technological directions? What mechanism will we put in place to formalize project prioritization and force line management involvement?

These and many other organizational questions require the attention of senior management. Every organizational unit is affected, and all of their needs must be balanced as objectively as possible against the strategic needs of the business as a whole. Only senior management can find and implement the best solutions for the organization. Management's success in making the technology organization work well is a prerequisite resolving many of the issues raised.

### (b) VIEW TECHNOLOGY AS A CRITICAL SUCCESS FACTOR

The first challenge overlaps with the second, which is to view technology in its broad sense as a critical success factor—something that the business must do well in order to be successful. Success in managing and using information technology affects the success of all of the units of virtually every organization: operations, administration, finance, marketing, personnel, and on across the entire organization chart.

Success in using technology has come to affect far more than a company's productivity and operational efficiency. It has enormous implications for just about every aspect of the business, including competitive posture, public image, relations with buyers and suppliers, internal control and security, and even the selection of the product set. The conventional distinction between information-intensive industries (that know they need to worry about technology) and everybody else is fast disappearing.

Viewing technology as critical to success requires more than lip service. It means providing an appropriate level of investment, ensuring strong leadership for the technology function, actively integrating planning for the business and technology, funding technology monitoring and experimentation with promising technologies, motivating the management team to seek out creative applications for potential competitive advantage, and taking a serious interest in contingency and disaster preparedness.

### (c) GET INVOLVED AND STAY INVOLVED

Most of all, it means recognizing that information technology has become far too important to be directed by proxy. Although technology specialists, corporate planners, and middle management all have essential roles, they cannot bring to bear the broad, strategic view of the business that has become absolutely essential in guiding technology. General management must get personally involved in directing the use of technology—and must find the time to stay involved.

No one who has tried it will minimize the difficulty of this task. It is important to institutionalize the involvement—through a senior management steering committee, for example, with a well-defined charter and appropriate staff support. The critical ingredient in sustaining effective involvement (especially in the face of other priorities and "progressive delegation syndrome") is active, visible commitment from the top of the business. Many companies have assigned the responsibilities for technology management to a senior executive called a chief information officer (CIO). As described in the last chapter on organizational issues, this person's role reflects a business perspective rather than a purely technical one.

Executives must assume responsibility for educating themselves in information technology. It is not particularly important to understand how a computer adds and subtracts, but it has become vitally important to know what information technology can and cannot do in your industry and environment; what are the competitive, organizational, operational, personnel, and other implications surrounding your present and planned uses of technology; and what questions you should be asking and how you can test the answers.

### (d) QUESTION EVERY SIGN OF "BUSINESS AS USUAL"

Questioning is the single most important function that senior management can perform. Consider how much and how quickly information technology has changed in the past fifteen years. Consider the "reversal of truths" described earlier in this section. Consider the present and future importance of technology and the impact on your business of its changes.

Next, ask whether or not your organization has overcome natural inertia and kept pace. In many cases, the "cultural heritage" of traditional information technology is compounding the issues raised here rather than working toward their resolution. Old organizational, technological, and managerial solutions are being forced on new and changing problems. Often this continues to happen despite the best intentions of everyone involved.

Senior management is ideally positioned and inevitably responsible for providing the voice of constructive suspicion, challenging old assumptions and questioning every sign of business as usual in the area of information technology. If senior management sets as its only technology-related goal for the next three years to test and reexamine every information technology strategy, standard, convention, and policy, most of the issues raised herein will be addressed. The potential improvements in technology effectiveness and productivity could be enormous.

# CHAPTER 4

# Productivity and Competitiveness

Ensuring that the organization is properly set up to manage information technology (Chapter 2) and that a process is in place for strategic IT planning and policy-setting (Chapter 3) are both important steps. However, the ultimate objective of these steps is the use of IT to maximize the productivity and competitiveness of the organization.

There is some degree of overlap and interrelationship between the management issues of organization structure, strategic planning, and productivity and competitiveness.

For example, in the last chapter we referred to productivity as it relates to application development. In this chapter, however, we refer to the productivity of the end user of IT and to the effect of IT on the overall competitiveness of the organization.

As in Chapters 2 and 3, a brief checklist is provided in the next section (Section 4.1) to serve as a practical executive summary of the main points covered in this chapter.

Next, Section 4.2 deals with a number of issues from a productivity and competitiveness viewpoint: balancing centralization and decentralization, integrating IT and human resources, making full and effective use of data resources, and using information technology to full competitive advantage.

Finally, Section 4.3 sets out a practical scenario for information technology in the workplace. Since this section demonstrates how the various pieces fit together, there are several cross-references to subsequent chapters in the handbook.

## 4.1  THE IT PRODUCTIVITY AND COMPETITIVENESS CHECKLIST

The following two-page checklist, summarizing many of the points in this chapter, is designed to assist accountants in dealing with IT productivity and competitiveness in their organizations and those of their clients. Generally, all "No" answers require investigation and follow-up, the results of which should be documented. Where there is such additional documentation, the purpose of the "Ref" column is to cross-reference the checklist to the appropriate working paper (or to the notes on the reverse).

The checklist is intended for general use only. Use of the checklist does not guarantee that IT productivity and competitiveness issues have been adequately addressed, and the checklist is not intended as a substitute for audit or similar procedures. If productivity and competitiveness issues are an especially vital concern, the advice of an IT management specialist should be sought.

**IT Productivity and Competitiveness Checklist**

|  | Yes | No | N/A | Ref |
|---|---|---|---|---|

**1. Maximizing Productivity and Competitiveness**

a. Is there an effective balance between centralization and decentralization (i.e., one that does not stifle productivity, creativity and innovation)? ☐ ☐ ☐ ___

b. Is there an incentive and reward program to promote creative and innovative employee suggestions on the use of information technology? ☐ ☐ ☐ ___

c. Does the organization actively attempt to identify and remove productivity obstacles—e.g., telephone tag—through more effective use of information technology? ☐ ☐ ☐ ___

d. Does the organization identify and experiment with innovative attempts to enhance productivity and cost-effectiveness (e.g., telecommuting), with a view to wider implementation of successful programs? ☐ ☐ ☐ ___

e. Are the productivity and work force effects (morale, job satisfaction, etc.) of IT-related decisions carefully considered through early employee involvement? ☐ ☐ ☐ ___

f. So far as is known, is the organization's use of and investment in IT comparable with that of its major competitors? ☐ ☐ ☐ ___

g. Have opportunities to develop a competitive advantage through IT been explored, using IT to:
  - Enhance the marketing of existing products/services? ☐ ☐ ☐ ___
  - Speed up market analysis/decisions on new products? ☐ ☐ ☐ ___
  - Create new information-based products? ☐ ☐ ☐ ___
  - Create closer links with customers and suppliers? ☐ ☐ ☐ ___
  - Increase the allegiance of customers and suppliers? ☐ ☐ ☐ ___

h. Does the organization recognize the importance of being first in the taking of IT initiatives that yield competitive advantage, and does it act accordingly? ☐ ☐ ☐ ___

i. Are there guidelines for the creation, architecture, storage, and use of data throughout the organization to ensure data are compatible? ☐ ☐ ☐ ___

| | Yes | No | N/A | Ref |
|---|---|---|---|---|
| j. Is data centrally accessible through electronic "card catalogs" or through bulletin boards and databases created with Lotus Notes or other groupware? | ☐ | ☐ | ☐ | ___ |
| k. Has the organization considered opportunities for the use of IT resources in revenue-generating activities (e.g., the sale of database information that is not strategically or competitively sensitive)? | ☐ | ☐ | ☐ | ___ |

## 2. IT in the Workplace

| | Yes | No | N/A | Ref |
|---|---|---|---|---|
| a. Does the organization have a common standard on hardware, software, and networking? | ☐ | ☐ | ☐ | ___ |
| b. Are the following aspects of maximum productivity and cost-effectiveness being gained from IT? | | | | |
| • Sharing of expensive peripherals in LANs | ☐ | ☐ | ☐ | ___ |
| • Voice and electronic mail systems | ☐ | ☐ | ☐ | ___ |
| • Use of OCR scanners for large input jobs | ☐ | ☐ | ☐ | ___ |
| • Manager and executive use of word processing, and so on. | ☐ | ☐ | ☐ | ___ |
| c. Is teleconferencing considered as an option before physical travel is approved? | ☐ | ☐ | ☐ | ___ |
| d. Are employees adequately trained in the use of IT as a productivity tool? | ☐ | ☐ | ☐ | ___ |
| e. Are ergonomically sound policies followed, including: | | | | |
| • Adjustable chairs and workstations? | ☐ | ☐ | ☐ | ___ |
| • Good quality monitors and surrounding lighting? | ☐ | ☐ | ☐ | ___ |
| • Regular 5–10 minute breaks every hour? | ☐ | ☐ | ☐ | ___ |
| f. Is management wary of IT productivity pitfalls ("analysis paralysis," draft 19 of reports and memos, etc.)? | ☐ | ☐ | ☐ | ___ |

## 4.2 MAXIMIZING PRODUCTIVITY AND COMPETITIVENESS

### (a) BALANCING CENTRALIZATION AND DECENTRALIZATION

Because it's integral to the organization's structure and strategic planning approach, the issue of centralizing control of IT is one that was touched on in each of the last two chapters. Striking the right balance between centralization and decentralization is also a key productivity issue. If the organization's employees are overly concerned and intimidated by policy, procedures, and other top-down edicts, it will be a struggle just to maintain productivity at a low level. To achieve high and increasing productivity levels, sufficient breathing room must be left for creativity and innovation.

With the steady increase in the price/performance, ease of use, and availability of computer hardware and software, the traditional economies of scale in centralizing all corporate computing have become much less compelling. On the other hand, in many organizations the emergence of cost-effective decentralized options has been more a source of confusion and debate than an opportunity for better use of technology. User dissatisfaction, large application backlogs, and internal politics often obscure more critical issues.

In most organizations significant decentralization has occurred almost by default, in particular with the proliferation of microcomputers and other standalone systems. At the same time the centralized component in many of those same organizations is growing faster than ever.

So the either/or issue of centralization vs. decentralization, (or distributed processing in all of its myriad forms) a major debate in the 1970s and 1980s, has almost become moot. Today, the issue has become one of finding a good balance between centralized and decentralized resources. The best balance is the one that is most effective and efficient in supporting the information needs of the company and maximizing productivity. This balance will vary, of course, depending on a wide range of factors including:

- Industry structure and nature of the business
- Company organizational structure
- Corporate (and IT) culture and management style
- Current and planned technical environments
- Long-range business strategy

Certainly, there are some important technical considerations that complicate the issue, especially those surrounding the nature and use of data. In most cases and with proper planning, a wide range of approaches between centralization and decentralization can be implemented without significant functional limitations. Moreover, the difference in costs (if developed objectively) between more centralized and more decentralized solutions is rarely large enough to override all of the other issues surrounding the decision.

Given the increasing importance of information systems to business success, a broader view of the issue is essential. The most satisfactory systems architecture will be the one that best integrates the control and use of information technology with the corporate style and structure.

Unfortunately, that kind of balance almost never happens by coincidence. The centralized and decentralized components often acquire enormous momentum of their own—

and neither frustrated user executives nor protective IT managers are wholly objective in their view of the matter. Active intervention is required by senior management to find and force a workable balance through planning, standards, and financial controls. If management fails to exercise that responsibility, every unit in the organization (IT included) will eventually chart its own course. And the long-term results will be far more costly and less satisfactory to the organization.

Another tool that can help in striking the right balance, while at the same time boosting employee morale and sense of involvement in the process, is an incentive and reward program for employee suggestions on the use of information technology. Employees who actually use the technology have a unique perspective, especially with respect to productivity. Why not exploit this perspective for the organization's benefit?

In any case, if the distribution and control of information technologies and resources are not adapted to support the management style, organizational structure, human resources, business processes, and strategic purposes of the organization (within reasonable constraints of cost-effectiveness and technical efficiency), internal friction, user frustration, and operational inefficiency must be expected.

## (b) INTEGRATING IT AND HUMAN RESOURCES

Along with centralization, integration was an important theme of the last two chapters—integrating IT into the organization structure, integrating information systems with one another and with communication systems, and so on. Often overlooked is the fact that people, too, must be integrated with IT (or vice versa). Clearly, how well people and information technology work together will have a critical effect on productivity.

We might have used the term "office automation" in the title of this section, since it has often been used to describe the merging of information technology and human resources in the typical business environment. Office automation is the technique of making any office apparatus, process, or system operate automatically or in such a way as to reduce the expenditure of human time and effort. It is most often associated with the use of computers in the office environment.

The term has several drawbacks, however, including the fact that it's become so overused—to the point that it's become almost useless. (This is a common phenomenon in the hype-prone world of IT—anyone tired of the "information superhighway" yet?) The term "office automation" was highly misleading for years, since office workers were not replaced by robotic equivalents; it suffers from a decade of abuse by technology vendors, who have defined it in terms of their existing product lines; and for a time it became a code word for word processing in the minds of many. Finally, if automation means the movement from manual to computerized systems, then it's a process that took place many years ago in almost all business environments.

We've therefore chosen a different phrase—"IT in the workplace"—that we think better defines the issue: the use of computer and communications technology to improve both the productivity and the quality of tasks performed by workers—managers, professionals, administrators, support staff, and others. Why is the issue so critical? Not only do wages and salaries for office workers represent a very large expense for most companies, and consequently a large potential for savings; but also the tasks performed in the workplace are critical to business success, and any improvement in productivity can enhance long-term profitability.

From a technology standpoint, the building blocks of IT in the workplace consist of familiar tools applied to office bottlenecks: personal computing functions like spreadsheets, modeling, graphics, reporting, project management, and data retrieval; word processing functions like test preparation, document filing and retrieval, document printing, and reproduction; and communication functions like telephone and message handling, document, data and message interchange (electronic mail), and schedule matching.

IT in the workplace can certainly develop—and is developing in many organizations—without benefit of plan or direction. The proliferation of microcomputers, software packages, and local area networks is testimony to that. It is clear, though, that the greatest benefits and cost-effectiveness result when all of the necessary building blocks combine into an integrated and functionally compatible whole. Any workstation should be able to get to any authorized resource, and comprehensive planning is the most effective means to that end.

IT in the workplace can be viewed as a complex set of applications, and these applications should be approached conceptually in a conventional way, from broad requirements definition through design to phased testing and implementation. Nevertheless, it does present some special issues that should be considered carefully, including the following:

- *Assignment of responsibility*—IT in the workplace affects multiple organizational units and draws on technologies (e.g., data processing, voice communications, electronic mail, word processing) that are often controlled in different parts of the organization. In order to provide direction and continuity to IT in the workplace, a single point of control may prove necessary. How responsibility is assigned will influence the content and success of the result. Unless care is taken to place responsibility at a high enough level, parochial or partial solutions will result.

- *Justification*—because their jobs lack clear-cut products and processes, the productivity of many office workers is hard to measure and improvements hard to quantify. This nonquantifiable character makes it hard to justify projects, a difficulty that can be partially offset by piecemeal assessment of specific tasks and measurement of peripheral effects (e.g., impact on recruitment, employee morale, or subjective views of productivity) defined through well-constructed experiments with the technology. It may also prove helpful for the organization to focus on obstacles to white collar productivity (e.g., telephone tag or time spent scheduling meetings) and assigning value to relieving those obstacles.

- *Work force impact*—because of the size and importance of the organization's white collar work force, the impact of technology on their morale, job satisfaction, job content, and career pathing, should be carefully considered. Consequences ranging from alienation to job enrichment, from flattening the organizational pyramid to multiplying the bureaucracy, have already been noted. How the technology is designed and implemented and how the work force is prepared for it are critical to its success. Without experimentation (e.g., identifying candidates and soliciting volunteers for a pilot program on telecommuting), careful planning, preparation, and monitoring after implementation, the results may impair rather than help productivity.

Although the costs, complexity, and organizational issues surrounding IT in the workplace may be somewhat daunting, the potential benefits are enormous. And although many of the benefits are difficult to identify as direct cost savings, they are real nonetheless. The results of better decision making, faster intraoffice communications, and improved professional staff retention, for example, are not only significant; for many organizations they may be critical to competitive success.

Without a comprehensive strategy for IT in the workplace, the inherent problems of technology and organizational fragmentation will make white collar productivity a difficult, time-consuming, and costly goal. Responsibilities and objectives must be assigned at an appropriate level in the company to ensure that the overall IT in the workplace program effectively addresses the diverse functional requirements, multiple technical components, and special problems of the office workplace.

## (c) MAKING FULL AND EFFECTIVE USE OF DATA RESOURCES

Computer technology has allowed organizations to collect and produce unprecedented amounts of raw data. In the mid-1980s, one estimate stated that it would take five trillion human clerks to manage the volume of data processed by the world's computers! To be useful for operation and management of the business, however, data must be organized and accessible—and the task of extracting needles of accurate, timely, and relevant information becomes increasingly difficult with the exponential growth in the haystacks of raw data. It is often very frustrating to managers and senior executives that the information needed to improve decision-making is somewhere out of reach in the computer.

It is generally accepted that information has become an important asset of nearly every business. Like any other asset, it must be planned for, managed, and safeguarded by skilled managers and professionals armed with appropriate tools and techniques. In many companies the management of data has not received adequate attention. With the increasing use of information as a competitive weapon and the increasing tendency to fragment data resources among distributed, departmental, and personal processors, data asset management has become both more important and more difficult than ever.

Appropriate techniques for data management vary with size, complexity, technical environment, and sophistication. In almost every case, however, it will be increasingly difficult for the organization to manage and use its data effectively without an overall data architecture: a master plan for the creation, storage, and use of data across the organization, driven by the underlying business processes and strategies. In addition, to deal with the complexity and broad scope of the corporate data resource, it is usually essential to create a data administration function with responsibility and commensurate authority for organizationwide data management.

Other tools may prove to be indispensable in implementing effective data management. These include:

- Database management systems to collect and organize corporate data within a consolidated, integrated file structure (databases offer clear advantages over traditional file structures in developing and maintaining productivity, flexibility of use, control, and security; relational database systems add ease of use and powerful ad hoc retrieval capabilities).
- Data dictionaries, to serve as an integrated "card catalog" and central control point for corporate data.

- Data modeling and planning tools to assist in structuring and maintaining data relationships.

Groupware such as Lotus Notes can also be very effective in making the organization's information resources available to all through bulletin boards or databases. This is especially important in large knowledge- and expertise-driven service businesses such as management consulting firms. There is nothing more unproductive for professionals and their clients than time spent solving a problem that may already have been solved by someone else in the firm. Electronic access to the experience of others within the organization dramatically reduces the chance of that happening.

Implementation of data management measures may prove complex, time-consuming, and costly, but an appropriate investment in improved data management will be necessary for an enterprise, both to control its data asset effectively and to leverage it across the organization.

Without an overall plan for the data asset and the necessary organization, staff, and tools to implement it, the organization will find it increasingly difficult to manage and use its data resources effectively. This will result in excessive costs for information processing and an increasingly serious barrier to using information for competitive and operational advantage.

## (d) USING INFORMATION TECHNOLOGY TO FULL COMPETITIVE ADVANTAGE

Since its very early days, information technology has contributed to corporate success, primarily by lowering costs of manual activities (especially transaction processing). Cost reduction is still a fertile area for further technology application—through techniques as diverse as microcomputer-based office productivity tools, plant floor robotics, and computer-aided design.

Increasingly, though, attention is being given to the other ways in which technology can contribute to the success of business strategies, such as:

- Enhancing the content or marketing of products and services to create significant product differentiation.
- Speeding up market analysis, decision-making, and product development to improve responsiveness to market shifts and niche opportunities.
- Creating closer ties to customers and suppliers through cost-effective, information-enhanced links.
- Allowing the creation of new and distinctive information-based products and services.
- Raising new barriers to competition by increasing the allegiance of customers and suppliers and by increasing the technological ante.

Numerous examples of the competitive impact of these techniques exist—classic cases include American Hospital Supply's customer-sited order entry system, American and United Airlines' industry-dominant on-line reservation systems (enhanced with automated frequent flier capabilities and sophisticated market tracking/analytical facilities), and the ground-breaking integrated Cash Management Account from Merrill Lynch.

Strategic systems are not limited to large companies and traditional "information-intensive" industries. They are become increasingly common in virtually every industry segment and business size range. In the mid-1980s a C&L-commissioned study of top executives in the financial services industry found that 34 percent had invested in technology primarily to gain a strategic advantage up to the time of the study; the level of those planning to invest primarily for strategic advantage in subsequent years rose to 46 percent.

In addition to their often potent competitive implications, strategic uses of information technology warrant management attention for other reasons. Frequently, the actual technology used is not particularly sophisticated. Rather, creativity in application is the critical ingredient. This creativity as applied to business opportunities is most often found outside the IT department, among marketers, product designers, line managers, and so on, where the business need or niche is most visible. Timing is very important—the advantage often accrues to the first company to create the new product or establish unique links to customers or suppliers, for example. A "me too" strategy of response to competitive initiative may be important for market share damage control, but it will not yield competitive advantage.

With these considerations in mind, the following questions become significant:

- Do we have a sound technical base for competitive innovation? This question goes to the heart of many other complex issues, but clearly any organization will find competitive use of technology more difficult if the underpinnings are in disarray.
- Is there a working partnership between the IT function and users? Organizational barriers and friction will discourage many creative ideas and delay the discussion and implementation of others.
- Are we motivating line management and others to find creative opportunities for technology? This is a primary responsibility of senior management; techniques may range from a high-level "Creativity Council" to cash awards and internal recognition.

If the organization does not prepare itself and motivate its staff to identify and exploit creative strategic uses of technology, it will find itself at a growing competitive disadvantage in a wide range of product areas and markets. Direct effects like lost market share may be compounded by the indirect effects of lost marketing initiative, damage to public image, and lost shareholder confidence.

## 4.3  IT IN THE WORKPLACE—A PRACTICAL SCENARIO

Information technology is pervasive; it affects virtually all areas of society. No area, however, is more greatly affected than the typical workplace environment—the office. This section deals with the impact of information technology on that environment.

This is by no means a new subject, but the technology and its impact are changing so rapidly—and continually—that it remains a perennial hot topic. The office of the future always seems to be offering us some new product, system, challenge, or opportunity that promises to change the way we work.

Depending on your point of view, the term IT in the workplace can have a benevolent or a sinister connotation: benevolent if you view it as the freeing up of human resources and creativity to take on less mundane tasks; sinister if you view it strictly as the replacement of humans by machines. This handbook takes the former view. But whatever your outlook, one thing is certain—IT in the workplace is here to stay.

## (a) OVERVIEW

Hardware and software are the primary tools used to automate the office, but they cannot be considered in isolation. The way in which they are linked together—and their effect on people—are vital concerns that also need to be addressed. Each of these areas is dealt with in the following sections. First, it may be useful to envisage a workplace IT scenario that brings all of these elements together. Specifically, a fully automated office might include:

- A series of microcomputer workstations used for various purposes such as word processing, daily input of accounting transactions, and on-line customer account enquiries. A small mainframe might control the accounting system in this environment.

- A local area network or LAN connecting together all of the workstations, thereby enabling them to share files and a high-quality laser printer. An electronic mail system might also be a part of the LAN; alternatively, it might reside on a mainframe. Groupware such as Lotus Notes might also be used as a connectivity tool.

- A PBX telephone system that includes features such as call forwarding and call conferencing. In some offices the PBX system might also provide the infrastructure for the local area network described above.

- A photocopy and fax center (the latter is increasingly controlled and executed via microcomputers). For example, fax technology might be used to send sales representatives in remote regions copies of each week's sales summary for their territory.

## (b) HARDWARE TOOLS

*(i) Workstations*

A workstation consists of a terminal or microcomputer and related equipment at which individuals carry out their job functions and communicate with other workers. Some authorities give the term a more specific definition—for example, restricting it to networked environments where the terminal or microcomputer is linked to a larger computer that acts as a file server (i.e., one that is storing all of the data and programs for use by other workstations in the network).

Because of falling hardware costs, the microcomputer has almost eliminated the terminal-based workstation. Microcomputers obviously afford much greater power and flexibility. They are also necessary if the workstation is to include its own peripherals such as disk drives, printers, or other devices designed to generate output.

*(ii)  Shared Peripherals*

Except in very high-volume applications, many peripheral devices—printers in particular—are often left unutilized much of the time if they are based at a single workstation. This can be wasteful of the organization's resources, especially in the case of expensive devices such as high-end and color laser printers.

Whenever possible, it makes sense to treat peripherals as shared devices that can be called upon by any number of workstations, often as part of a local area network. The sharing of peripherals affords the added benefit of greater control—an especially important concern in the case of the storage devices that hold the organization's programs and data.

*(iii)  Photocopiers and Fax Machines*

Photocopiers were one of the vanguards of the information revolution in general and office automation in particular. (We use the term "office automation" on purpose here, because in those days that was the term used.) Over the years they have become increasingly sophisticated—as anyone who has tried to make full use of the features of the latest models knows—and have spawned related technologies and devices such as laser printers and scanners.

Faxes, or facsimile machines, receive or send digitized information over a communications line. In a sense, they are a printer, scanner, and modem in one package.

The trend in audio and video technology has been toward modular components. The same is true for photocopier and fax technology. Photocopiers and laser printers use the same basic mechanism to produce images, as do scanners and fax machines to read them. The trend is toward a general-purpose machine or "generic iron," perhaps composed of different add-on modules, that can be used to perform many of these functions. Another example of this trend is that fax capability is now routinely built into microcomputers.

*(iv)  Storage Devices*

The so-called paperless office is actually a myth; as long as people work in offices, they'll want hard copy output. Nevertheless, there are a number of hardware tools that assist in the storage of documents and help reduce the sheer volume of paper. These include:

- Electronic storage in the form of disks or tape.
- Microfiche, a high-resolution photographic material on which documents can be captured in miniature form (microfiche is a common form of storage that has been available for many years and that is still widely used).
- Compact disk, an increasingly popular form of storage discussed in "Peripherals," Chapter 7 of this handbook.

*(v)  Other Devices*

There are numerous other devices that have given impetus to the development of IT in the workplace, including simple ones like the telephone. In recent years the generic iron or multipurpose phenomenon has taken hold here as well—telephones have become increasingly integrated with other devices. For example, they are often linked in to their own computer system and/or make use of their own computer software.

Other devices typically found in the automated office include:

- The aforementioned scanner, also referred to as an image digitizer—in particular, optical character recognition (OCR) scanners—which can read text and can therefore cut down considerably on typing time and effort—are an increasingly popular device (related document imaging systems are also being used more frequently to electronically store large volumes of data).
- Communications equipment such as modems and multiplexers, which are used to link various devices to one another within the office and to the outside world.

### (vi) Standardizing Hardware

Given all of this hardware and the fact that there are so many manufacturers and models to choose from, questions naturally arise about what to buy and whether to standardize on one kind of machine officewide.

Answers to these questions will depend on the circumstances in each case. Generally, however, it's important to ensure as much compatibility between devices as possible. In some instances this is obviously a necessity—for example, your microcomputer has to be able to work with your laser printer. In other cases—for example, regarding the ability to exchange information between workstations in two different departments—the need may not be as obvious until it is too late.

Fortunately, hardware manufacturers have become increasingly aware of the user's need for compatibility and are responding. For example, Apple's latest product line offers IBM compatibility. In fact, manufacturers that ignore the compatibility question can scarcely expect to penetrate the market.

In practice, despite the fact that compatibility is the wave of the future, most offices will adopt one manufacturer's equipment unless there is some persuasive reason to do otherwise.

## (c) SOFTWARE TOOLS

Some of the more important software tools used in the automated office are set out below. Many of these are dealt with in greater detail in other chapters of this handbook.

### (i) Decision Support

Decision support software (for example, Lotus 1-2-3) has become an indispensable part of the office environment. Such software is used by the finance department to handle budgets, by the marketing department to analyze sales performance, by the production department for job costing, and so on.

Most business decisions ultimately hinge on an assessment of cost vs. benefits over time. For example, deciding whether or not to acquire a piece of capital equipment will depend on its cost and on the anticipated revenues (or cost savings) that would result from its acquisition. Similarly, the decision whether to increase prices by 10 percent will depend on the increased profit per unit (benefit) vs. the potential loss in market share or number of units sold (cost). Decision support software is ideal for handling these types of cost/benefit analyses, because different parameters can easily be studied across a wide range of values, and any number of "what if" scenarios can be considered. This provides managers with more complete information. In theory, better decisions should result.

### (ii)  Information Storage and Retrieval

If information is the key to an organization's competitive advantage—indeed, survival—then the ability to manage that information is equally important. Information storage and retrieval software—in particular, database software—is one of the primary tools available to manage information.

Some information storage and retrieval applications that are particularly significant to the workplace include:

- Inventory
- Customer and mailing lists
- On-line inquiry (e.g., of account data)
- The accessing of commercial data bases outside the office

In addition, accounting software packages—which are essentially a specialized form of data base—are used to satisfy the basic information needs of virtually all businesses.

### (iii)  Word Processing

One of the earliest applications of information technology to automate the modern office was the dedicated word processor, which in the mid-1970s actually preceded the microcomputer to the marketplace. More than any other device or application, word processing has become an indispensable part of day-to-day business operations.

During the early years of the microcomputer revolution (the 1980s), dedicated word processors and word processing pools were the norm in many offices. Early word processing packages for microcomputers did not offer the power and flexibility of dedicated machines. By the late 1980s the balance had shifted, however, and the 1990s have seen the introduction of extremely powerful packages that include spell and grammar checkers, automatic indexing, database and mail merge, graphics, and templates for a variety of formats.

Another trend has been the increasing use of microcomputers by executives and other end users, so that the role of the dedicated word processing operator has changed. Original input through longhand or dictation is all but extinct. The role of the dedicated operator, if any, is limited to polishing the format of the final document or executing the more sophisticated, high-volume features such as mail merge.

### (iv)  Other Applications

A variety of other software is also having an impact on IT in the workplace. For example:

- Desktop publishing
- Graphics (including graphics built into other applications such as spreadsheets)
- Computer-aided design and computer-aided manufacturing (CAD/CAM)
- Project management and scheduling

While these applications may not be as widely used as those previously described, they nevertheless yield significant benefits in environments where they are relevant. Desktop publishing can be important wherever printed reports are critical to the business. (However, it may not be necessary to have a top-of-the-line desktop publishing program—e.g., PageMaker—in order to achieve the desired effect. Graphics built into spreadsheet programs, a word processor, and a high-quality laser printer can combine with creative expertise to yield publishable output.)

CAD/CAM has become an indispensable part of the auto industry, and project management and scheduling are critical to the resource sector. For these sectors the impact of IT in the workplace obviously extends far beyond the office itself.

*(v) Standardizing Software or Software Suites*

The need to standardize software is sometimes overlooked. A lot of attention is devoted to the hardware purchase decision; less attention is given to what that hardware will be used to accomplish.

Finding a suitable software package is a topic dealt with in the various software chapters of this handbook, Chapters 8 through 10. (Software "suites" containing several applications are also becoming commonplace: e.g., Lotus SmartSuite, Microsoft Office.) Once a suitable package or suite is identified, standardization of that package or suite is highly desirable. Consider the following:

- Training costs, in the form of direct out-of-pocket expenses and hours spent on training, are a significant but often overlooked element of total software cost. (Training costs will be kept to a minimum if the organization standardizes one package.)

- File sharing between departments or workstations will be facilitated (the ability to transfer files between packages has increased significantly in recent years; however, certain attributes of the data, such as font and format, may not survive the transfer).

- Personnel from one area of the organization will be more readily available to assist in another area when required.

- When temporary or part-time help is brought in, a specialist in the particular software package can be requested, rather than a generalist who may not be as efficient.

## (d) LINKING IT ALL TOGETHER

Hardware and software are well-established tools of the information revolution, having been around in their microcomputer variety for over fifteen years. A relatively new development, however, is the way in which these and other tools have become integrated in the modern office. Some of the ways in which this integration has been accomplished are set out below.

### (i) PBX

A PBX—or private branch exchange—is essentially a sophisticated telephone system that gives an organization many of the switching capabilities of a telephone company central office (hence the term "exchange"). PBX systems have been used for years to handle voice communications; more recently they have also been used to transmit and receive data signals.

PBX capabilities have expanded considerably over the years. Today it is not unusual in large offices to find PBX systems linked in to their own computers and costing tens of thousands of dollars. These systems often have sophisticated features such as voice messaging, call forwarding, call conferencing, and automatic charging of long-distance calls to the originator's budget.

PBX systems are described in greater detail in Chapter 11 of this handbook, "Telecommunications."

### (ii) LANs

LANs, or local area networks, involve the linking together of several workstations for the purpose of sharing data files, programs, and peripherals. LANs can even be interconnected with other LANs and can take a number of different forms, including PBX.

Although LANs were successfully implemented in many offices during the 1980s, they were at that time "leading edge" technology, and their benefits were often overlooked by many microcomputer users. The perception was that they were somehow too complicated or technical to set up and operate. Only Apple, with a built-in LAN called AppleTalk, seemed to escape this perception. In the 1990s this is no longer true. LAN technology has become much more widely accepted and implemented.

The benefits of LANs in the office environment include:

- Hardware cost savings that, as noted earlier, flow from the sharing of expensive devices such as high-end and color laser printers.
- Assured compatibility and standardization across the organization (for example, everyone will be using the same version—and the most current version—of the company's word processing software).
- Enhanced security, because control over programs and data files is centralized in one location.
- Better and more efficient communication between those on the LAN, enhancing productivity.

These and related topics are dealt with in greater detail in Chapter 12 of this handbook, "Networking."

### (iii) Electronic Mail

LANs also make it possible for users on the network to send and receive messages via "electronic mail." Each user has a specific ID or "mailbox" address where mail is instantly delivered and stored by the system until read. Sophisticated electronic mail systems offer user-friendly interfaces and advanced features such as the sending of messages at a specific time, tracing (the ability to confirm whether a message has been delivered and read), and mail forwarding (passing on a message to another user for action or comments).

Electronic mail systems can also be found in non-LAN environments. For example, terminals or microcomputers can be connected to a mainframe that has an electronic mail system, and many commercial data bases and "gateways" also offer electronic messaging.

Electronic mail continues to grow in popularity. It is interesting to note that in environments where both voice and electronic messaging are available, many users show a preference for electronic messaging. In addition to providing a more formal record of the communication, electronic mail puts an end to "telephone tag" in cases when one or the other party can be difficult to reach.

*(iv)  Notice Boards*

Another tool related to electronic mail is the notice board. Most organizations will have a LAN administrator responsible for setting users up on the system, handling security and training, and so on. The administrator can also set up a form of global electronic mail—the notice board—which can be used to inform all users in the LAN of important company developments and news.

The popularity of groupware such as Lotus Notes is fueled partly by electronic notice and bulletin boards. The groupware concept is not restricted to the LAN environment, however. Neither are notice boards, which are also found on larger networks such as the commercial data bases and gateways.

## (e)  MAKING IT ALL WORK

IT in the workplace isn't simply a matter of plugging in a lot of hardware and linking it together. Too often, the importance of people in the process is overlooked.

*(i)  The Effect on People*

For many employees, especially those who have no control over the process, change can create psychological stress. Will they be able to cope with the new technology? If not, will they be passed up for promotion in favor of those who can? Worse still, will they become obsolete and lose their jobs? All these questions weigh on the minds of employees faced with the ominous prospect of IT in the workplace.

If the effect on people is not addressed, the entire process can actually be counterproductive. To ensure successful implementation, those affected by the changes should be:

- Consulted early on in the process, both to obtain their cooperation and also to provide valuable feedback to management on how improvements can be made.

- Well trained in any new procedures and the operation of any new systems.

- Given an appropriate forum to express any concerns over health, safety, job security, and so on, and to have these addressed by management.

Training and health are discussed in the following sections.

### (ii) The Importance of Training

The best hardware and software will be of no use if people don't know how to operate it. The cost of proper training can be high, in terms of both direct expenses and hours devoted to the process. But the cost of improper training can be much higher.

Some of the key principles that should be followed in designing or choosing a training approach include the following:

- Training should take place during regular office hours to reinforce the fact that learning the new technology is considered a part of the employee's job responsibilities. Key personnel can be trained on a rotational basis to avoid any disruption in regular business operations.

- To the extent possible, training should take place in a location designated for that purpose, preferably off-site. Training employees in their normal work environment is much more difficult, mainly because the employees' regular duties inevitably encroach on training time and act as a distraction.

- When the employee is expected to learn some computer-related task—for example, using a new piece of software—hands-on training is vital. If many employees are being trained at once, there should be one terminal or workstation for every student, and an instructor should be available to supervise and answer questions.

Often, especially in the case of widely used hardware and software, training seminars are offered by the manufacturer and/or by independent consultants. These seminars are usually a better value than courses developed in-house.

### (iii) Health Concerns

The information revolution has radically changed the office environment and has raised a number of health-related questions that have been given varying degrees of media attention in recent years. The study of these and related questions is part of the increasingly important discipline of ergonomics, which deals with the interaction of people and their work environment.

Some of the more important health questions are briefly dealt with below.

1. *Posture*—The advent of the workstation has meant that more and more people—for example, word processing operators—are spending their time fixed at one position for most of their work shift. As a result, poor posture—or a poorly designed workstation—can result in discomfort, back and neck problems, and headaches.

   The best solution is adjustable furniture—for example, chairs that can be raised and lowered to suit individual needs and desks that allow keyboards and monitors to be similarly moved or tilted. Adjustable furniture allows different users to work in their optimum position, which is usually back straight and eyes level with the top of the display screen. A good chair that supports the small of the back is also important.

2. *Eye Strain*—A poor display screen and/or poor surrounding lighting can lead to eye problems and headaches. A number of things can be done to alleviate this problem. First, the area surrounding a workstation should not be too brightly lit, because display screens themselves do not emit much light. A large difference in light levels will make the screen more difficult to read.

   Second, glare can be minimized by proper positioning of the workstation away from sunlight or other direct light sources. Any reflective surfaces in the work environment that may cause indirect glare—for example, mirrors or chrome—should also be properly positioned to avoid problems.

   Finally, the display screen itself should provide good resolution and allow adjustments to be made to brightness and contrast to suit the individual user's preferences. Display screens are discussed in greater detail in Chapter 7 of this handbook, "Peripherals."

3. *Fatigue*—Spending long uninterrupted periods at a workstation, especially if the work is repetitive and boring, typically results in fatigue, a greater error rate, and less efficiency in the long run. A five- to ten-minute break away from the workstation, every hour, is an advisable policy.

4. *Radiation*—The radiation emitted by video display terminals (VDTs) and other office equipment has been the subject of considerable research and controversy for several years. Government standards exist for the emission of radiation. Despite considerable scrutiny, there is still no direct or conclusive evidence that these devices pose any health hazard. In fact, the known hazard is far greater from other problems such as those set out above.

## (f)  SUMMARY

IT in the workplace, as the phrase implies, is the tying together of a number of different information technology areas in the typical workplace environment. In that context, the process is often more important than any specific decision on what hardware or software to buy.

The most important point to note about IT in the workplace is its inevitability. As technology advances, offices can expect to see a steady stream of new equipment and new systems to replace the old way of doing things. Accepting this environment of constant change—learning to live with it—is an important and necessary first step in getting through the process.

Remember also the importance of people in the equation. People make IT in the workplace a success or failure, and many of the problems that sometimes occur arise from a failure to recognize that fact.

Finally, IT in the workplace can sometimes be a simple matter of injecting a little common sense into the process. We're living and working in an age when technology is outpacing the ability of most organizations to effectively harness it. Productivity pitfalls, such as going through countless drafts of memos, and analysis paralysis—the overuse of technological tools like the spreadsheet without ever arriving at a decision—are rampant. In this environment, it's important not to let IT in the workplace get out of hand, not losing sight of the forest for the trees, or the office for the microchips.

# CHAPTER 5

# Historical Chronology and Future Directions

The issues covered in the first four chapters—seeing the big picture, setting up an appropriate organization structure, strategic planning and policy, and maximizing productivity and competitiveness—substantially cover the important management concerns about information technology. However, there's at least one other element that can be an important management advantage, and that's perspective. Understanding the history and future direction of information technology provides such perspective.

## 5.1  THE RAPID GROWTH IN IT

Even from the few chapters in this handbook thus far, one truism should have definitely become clear—information technology is a moving target. New developments occur daily. And thanks to the high-powered marketing that drives the computer industry, every development seems critical to your business's future. You almost wonder how your business survived before.

In this chapter we look at the history of information technology, some of the developments on the horizon, and at what the new developments might mean to your business's use of information technology. Picture a computer smorgasbord where it's up to you to pick and choose from the menu. But choose carefully—there's no free lunch.

The computer industry has to this point been largely experimental. You have been the guinea pig, adopting new ideas that sometimes went somewhere, sometimes didn't. It's been worthwhile because so many developments have worked out well. Early adopters were well rewarded for their efforts by greater business efficiency, a little extra edge.

The rapid growth of information technology won't slow. One rule of thumb in the industry holds that every two years computers will store twice the information and take half the physical space—a good thing, too. Today you process the same information in less than a day that your grandparents processed in a year at your age. And that trend won't slow either.

What is changing now, and what is one of the most important considerations for the future, is that technological development is outstripping our ability to use it. A bigger, faster computer is only important if your applications, needs, and expectations can take advantage of it. An analogy can be drawn to the automobile industry. Indy racers can top 200 miles per hour. They're at the forefront of automotive technology. Would you really recommend one as a fleet car?

Early computers, like early cars, represented great innovation but left a lot of room for improvement. The industry, in both cases, moved rapidly to fill the gaps. Cars can now go faster than is practical or even safe. Today's computers are perfectly adequate for many business applications well into the future. Computer buying tomorrow will require careful analysis of whether the purchase of new features and capabilities is justifiable. It's no longer true that newer, bigger, and faster is necessarily better.

That said, intelligent computer users will have to be even better acquainted with the developing technology and how it relates to their needs.

## 5.2  LOOKING FORWARD BY LOOKING BACK

Before we look at current and projected future developments in information technology (Sections 5.5 through 5.8), a little history is in order. Computers have been with us as useful business tools for such a short time that it's hard to believe they have a history. But they do indeed—a surprisingly long and rich history. It's a story befitting a revolution—like any history of revolution, the story of the computer offers important insights into the future.

That's why we've devoted the first half of this chapter to history. Understanding something of the computer's past may better prepare you to make decisions about the computer's future as it affects you and your organization. Some questions you may want to keep in mind as you read on are these:

- How do I tell what's leading edge?
- Do I want to be at, ahead, or behind the leading edge?
- Where will future computer breakthroughs come from?

Of course, looking at the past is an imperfect way of predicting the future. But it's an interesting tool and, for computers, an interesting story.

In looking at any history of the computer, we're really looking at trends and developments in three interconnected but different areas, each of which will be dealt with in turn. First, and with the longest history, is computer hardware (Section 5.3). Second, with a far shorter history, is the development of software (for our purposes, business software, Section 5.4). Third—and through it all, we need to consider the changes in the use of computers—the users, the marketing channels and the expectations (Section 5.5).

## 5.3  A HISTORY OF COMPUTER HARDWARE

The first computer—in the modern sense of the word—is widely recognized as being ENIAC (an acronym for electronic numerical integrator and calculator). This section has therefore been divided into "Pre-ENIAC" and "ENIAC and Beyond."

### (a)  PRE-ENIAC

Since humans first matched ten fingers to ten objects, they've been using devices to help order the things around them. In fact, the French word for computer, *ordinateur*—the loose translation means "order keeper"—is perhaps a better word than the English computer. The earliest computers were simple improvements on the finger counting that is still the basis of our number system. Looking again at the language, consider the words *digital* and *digit*.

The sand table of the early Egyptians was perhaps one of the earliest efforts at a manufactured computing device. Three columns scratched in the sand, ten pebbles in each, were used to keep track and make calculations. The Arabian abacus, still used in that and other parts of the world, made the sand table portable—the first "laptop" digital computer. Digital, because it helped answer the question how many; in other words, it tallied numbers of like things. It's this tallying that is still the basis of most modern computers.

A second type of computer measures flows rather than tallies. These are called analog computers and they measure things like speed and time. They were also used by the Egyptians—for example, the sundial. Analog computers today are a technology just coming into their own in the world beyond gauges. For example, some microcomputers use analog technology to exercise more control over their display screens.

For the most part, though, the history of computers is the history of the digital computer, and the first modern attempts in the field are usually credited to Blaise Pascal.

### (i)  Blaise Pascal—1642

Although various mathematical aids—like slide rules and Napier's rods, which assisted in multiplication—were developed earlier, the first mechanical calculator was developed in the seventeenth century. The first commercial attempt was Blaise Pascal's arithmetic machine, the Pascaline, which was capable only of addition. It worked using a series of interconnected cogs, like a car odometer.

Pascal, a French mathematician and philosopher, gets credit for the mechanical calculator because he made it a marketable device. In actual fact, a German professor, Wilhelm Schickard, created the calculating clock in 1623, but the device fell into obscurity as a result of the Thirty Years' War. Pascal's machine—similar in principle to Schickard's—was developed independently and was designed to assist in the collection of taxes.

### (ii)  Gottfried Wilhelm von Leibniz—1673

Pascal's machine suffered from quality control problems, and, as mentioned, was capable only of addition (and in a roundabout way, subtraction). Leibniz, a German, improved on the device with his "Stepped Reckoner," which could perform all four of the basic mathematical operations.

Leibniz's device pioneered the movable carriage of later calculators and typewriters, but it suffered from severe mechanical-quality problems of its own and never reached market. Nevertheless, imitators of the Leibniz machine dominated the calculator market through the eighteenth century.

Even more lasting was Leibniz's fascination with binary mathematics, which uses only ones and zeroes to create numbers. The binary system is easily simulated by electronic on/off switches and has since become the basic building block of modern-day electronic calculators and computers.

*(iii) Charles Babbage—1822*

By the nineteenth century, calculators improving on the Leibniz model had become commonplace but were still limited to the four basic operations. The Babbage machine, named after Charles Babbage, took advantage of the precision machine tool industry and was able to calculate navigation and other similar tables. In fact, it was financially supported by the British government for its contribution to navigation.

Babbage's first machine, called the difference engine, was limited to calculating tables that were based on constant differences between numbers, but it did pave the way for a more general machine. Actually, Babbage never completed a full working model of the later machine—only partial models and documentation.

In any case, Babbage's proposed analytical engine had many of the features of modern computers. It was a general machine, not restricted to any one kind of calculation. It used programs, and data was input by punchcards. While the earlier machines of Pascal and Leibniz could be quite properly called calculators, the proposed Babbage machine of the late 1860s, had it been built, would have been the first real mechanical computer.

*(iv) Herman Hollerith—1890*

While Babbage's musings would have produced the first real computer, credit for the first tangible device goes to the American Herman Hollerith. He designed his tabulator and related equipment to speed the U.S. census of 1890. The tabulator used punched cards and was electrically powered (the Babbage machine was purely mechanical). It also used equipment—typewriterlike keyboards, for example—that we associate today with computer equipment.

The 1890 census published its tally in a mere six weeks, but the cost was nearly double that for the 1880 census. Full compilation of the numbers took seven years, compared with nii e for the manual 1880 census. Why the high cost and still lengthy compilation time? The answer would become familiar to our generation of computer users—there was a tendency to use available equipment to the fullest, to tackle new tasks, and to tackle the old more thoroughly. Statistics never before possible were prepared. The data was checked and double-checked.

In any event, Hollerith's machines impressed the world. They were used not only by many U.S. companies, but also by Austria, Canada, France, and Russia for their census work.

Hollerith's company—the Tabulating Machine Company—became a part of International Business Machines.

*(v) Konrad Zuse—1938*

Hollerith had given the world its first real taste of computers in a business application, and he was the first to make computing a business. Others, however, actually developed the basics of computer technology though they did not always enjoy Hollerith's commercial success.

Konrad Zuse, a German student at the outbreak of the Second World War, proposed a general-purpose computing machine that had many of the important elements of today's computers. His work focused on the binary system of numbers championed by Leibniz and borrowed a logical structure from Boolean algebra. Boolean's operators—and, or, and not—are familiar to most modern database users. They take full advantage of the binary number system.

The Zuse machines also replaced mechanical parts with electrical telephone relays. Zuse built several special-purpose machines for the German war effort—for example, to calculate such things as aircraft wing flutter.

## (b)  ENIAC AND BEYOND

### (i)  John Mauchly—1943

The American war effort also spurred computer development in a series of projects that led to ENIAC, the first popularly recognized mainframe computer.

John Mauchly, an American physicist, and Lt. Herman Goldstine developed an electronic calculator with a purpose somewhat akin to Babbage's differential engine—the calculation of tables. This time, though, it was firing tables for gunners.

The new machine went a step beyond Zuse's, replacing telephone relays with electronic vacuum tubes. But surprisingly, despite its high tech (for the day) design, ENIAC used decimal rather than binary notation and did not use Boolean algebra. Nevertheless, it was thousands of times faster than any previous calculating machine. Once finished in 1946, it touched off the electronic computer revolution.

ENIAC's first task was to complete the complex calculations that led to the hydrogen bomb.

### (ii)  John von Neumann—1946

Mauchly and the core of scientists who developed ENIAC recognized its shortcomings. Though powerful, the computer had no way of storing information or programs. Both had to be entered each time the unit was used. For complex calculations—the kind whose expectations ENIAC fueled—storage was a necessity.

John von Neumann, one of America's most respected scientists, lent the new effort his mind and credibility. Given the skepticism that still surrounded the development of purely electronic computers—there being a strong constituency in favor of the slower but more reliable relay—it's hard to say which was more important. In any case, the result was EDVAC.

EDVAC borrowed on ENIAC's vacuum tube technology but paired it with the more powerful logic system of binary and Boolean operators. It was finished in 1952, but as is often the case in the computer industry, was beaten to the marketplace by an imitator. The imitator, the British Colossus computer series developed by Alan Turing, sported many technical enhancements and, for a time, set the new standard.

### (iii)  Remington Rand—1950

Remington Rand was a company, not an individual. Listing it here as a subtitle is indicative of a change that the computer industry was undergoing at the time. Previously, from Pascal to Babbage to ENIAC, computers were developed largely as a government exercise. Of course, government was always a key computer customer and remains so to this day. However, when Remington Rand invested in the UNIVAC project, it marked a change in focus; in the manner pioneered by Hollerith at the turn of the century, computers had gone commercial.

UNIVAC was the brainchild of Mauchly and his partner Eckert. Unlike other computers, which had a specific target market or function in mind at the time of their design, UNIVAC was intended from the start to be a truly flexible business computer system. UNIVAC in fact stands for universal automatic computer.

Also unlike earlier machines, UNIVAC could process both numeric and alphabetic data, although it still utilized decimal as opposed to binary math. It was nevertheless the state of the art, with 12K RAM and a magnetic tape drive storage system. Subsequent UNIVAC models would go as high as 120K RAM.

It was UNIVAC that awoke the world to the power of electronic computing when, in 1952, it accurately predicted the results of the U.S. presidential election.

### *(iv)   International Business Machines—1952*

Both Remington Rand and International Business Machines were in business long before the 1950s (Hollerith's tabulating company had merged with others to form IBM). In fact, both companies—and other major computer firms like Burroughs and NCR—had started by marketing traditional business equipment lines. Remington Rand entered the computer market with UNIVAC. IBM, after toying with several near-computers based on its calculating machine technology, entered the fray in 1952.

The first IBM product was designed in response to the Korean War, but it aimed beyond the defense industry. IBM wanted its share of the fledgling commercial computer market as well. That share rapidly grew when the company was picked to commercialize Lincoln Lab's innovative magnetic core memory, developed for the U.S. military's air defense computer system, SAGE. The SAGE system also pioneered the television-like monitor, computer networks, and real-time processing, all of which are commonplace in today's systems.

SAGE technology helped ensure IBM's dominance of the computer industry. By 1961—the zenith of the vacuum-tube computer era—IBM had garnered 71 percent of the then $1.8-billion-dollar market, with Remington Rand a distant second at only 10 percent. By 1964, when $5.8 billion worth of computers had been installed, 76 percent were IBM.

### *(v)   The Integrated Circuit—1953*

The first commercial use of the transistor was in 1953. The device did much the same job as a vacuum tube but was much smaller and more durable. The first use of transistors in computers occurred in 1957. The result, by UNIVAC and Philco, was a computer far more powerful than its predecessors or competitors as well as smaller, faster, more reliable, and more economical.

An English engineer, G.W.A. Dummer, later took the technology a step further, integrating several transistors, resistors, and similar components into a single circuit; hence the term "integrated circuit" (IC). Dummer's idea was sound, but the day's technology wasn't. It was not until 1959 that an engineer for Texas Instruments, Jack Kilby, pioneered a miniature integrated circuit, the forerunner of today's chips.

The Texas Instruments chip was soon surpassed by a technically superior chip from Fairchild Semiconductor. However, it wasn't until the mid-to-late sixties that integrated circuits were used in IBM computers, eventually replacing the ceramic core memory developed in the 1950s. It was in 1971, when a computer's central processor was installed on a chip, that the modern computer era—that of the microprocessor—began.

### (vi)  The Minicomputer—1963

Nestled between the mainframe and micro in the history of computers is the minicomputer. Although it has fallen out of use in the era of the supermicro, the minicomputer remains an important development.

Ken Olsen, founder of Digital Equipment Corporation, can perhaps be considered the father of business computing. He recognized that most business computing needs didn't require the size or justify the expense of a mainframe computer. His initial PDP-1, priced at $120,000, and the later PDP-8, priced at $18,000, were simple machines but filled a real business need.

Finding its market niche, Digital became one of the world's largest computer companies.

### (vii)  The Personal Computer—1974

Although DEC had looked into the potential home computer market, it and all the other computer companies ultimately decided that this market didn't have any real potential. The development of the home computer, at least in its early stages, remained in the hands of individual visionaries. Instead of being driven by government grants or academic pursuits, the home computer—which led to the business personal computer—was driven by hobbyists.

The first home computer appeared as a cover story in *Radio-Electronics* magazine; it was designed by Jonathan Titus, a hobbyist with no real business interest in computers. Although the machine did very little, it sparked a lot of interest. Riding on that interest, a small one-man company called MITS launched a machine called the Altair 8800 in *Popular Electronics'* January 1975 issue. By April MITS had 4,000 orders for a computer that could do little more than play simple games. But what it did offer was potential—now anyone could own a computer.

The Altair lacked software and most of the add-ons necessary to make it really useful. Nevertheless, over 50 firms were soon manufacturing peripherals and competitive equipment. In fact, Microsoft—later to become the leading software house—was formed to develop an Altair BASIC language. Other companies took the Altair concept further. For example, ISMAI bundled an Altair clone with a working operating language, disk drives, and marketing persistence to create a personal computer for business use.

But of course it was Apple Computer, begun out of a garage by two friends, Stephen Wozniak and Steve Jobs, that ultimately took the microcomputer out of the hobbyist's workshop and into the family room. In 1977 the Apple II, the first home computer manufactured on a large scale, hit the market. Apple's production began doubling every three or four months.

### (viii)  The Business Microcomputer—1981

Although the Apple II brought the personal computer respectability, it wasn't a business machine. Business interest was raised by the introduction of VisiCalc and other Apple software (the history of software will be looked at later), but the computer itself wasn't aimed at the business market.

Adam Osborne took the first hardware steps toward a business computer with his launch of the Osborne portables. To make the machine more attractive to buyers, he included a bundle of business software—BASIC, a word processor, and a spreadsheet—all for $1,795. At its peak, the Osborne was selling 10,000 units a month, sparking such imitators as Kaypro.

Other companies, including Xerox and Hewlett-Packard, also tested the business micro market. Then, in 1981, IBM launched its personal computer. The PC, backed by the IBM name, blessed the microcomputer for business and changed forever the way businesses operated. The IBM machine sold 13,000 units in its first five months, 40 times that over the next two years. It quickly set the industry standard, as did its operating system, Microsoft's MS-DOS.

*(ix)  The Revolution Drives On—the 1990s*

Though IBM remains a powerful industry force, it faces equally powerful competition from Compaq and, to some extent, other companies. No company today can claim to be the technology leader. It's almost as if the technology is driving itself. Significant developments come out of firms most people haven't heard of and, unlike in the early days, many of these firms remain nonentities while still enjoying great success.

For example, who other than computer industry insiders or stock market watchers thought much about Intel, at least before those "Intel Inside" ads started appearing on television several years ago? Yet it's Intel's product line—integrated circuits—that has really changed the face of computing. The integrated circuit allowed computers to move beyond the limits of vacuum tubes. Integrated circuits—yesterday's transistors, today's chips, and tomorrow's variants using surface mount technology—have changed computers as much as Babbage, von Neumann, or IBM.

Although there have been incremental improvements in hardware since the introduction of the IBM machine—hard disk drives, better printers, graphics boards, and bigger and faster processors (e.g., based on Intel's 286, 386, 486, Pentium, and now P6 microprocessors)—it was with the IBM PC that the technology really reached a plateau. Later, with the introduction of inexpensive IBM clones in the mid-1980s, microcomputers and related equipment became a basic commodity. Competition became fierce, and prices fell. Even Intel now faces competition from clone chip makers and new chip technologies.

Indeed, by the late 1980s, it was clear that the hardware industry was no longer driving the revolution. Software had become the hot new market.

## 5.4  A BRIEF HISTORY OF COMPUTER SOFTWARE

In the first 35-year history of the modern computer, the focus was almost exclusively on the mechanical or electronic components of the system. Software, programming, instructions—however called—were an afterthought. In computers like ENIAC, programming meant virtually rewiring the machine. And the first personal computers, like Altair, had to be programmed each time the machines were turned on.

That all changed when software finally arrived, increasing the power of hardware tenfold.

## (a) LANGUAGES AND OPERATING SYSTEMS

Languages and operating systems are the software "interface" between the central processing unit of the computer, and what is external to it: disk drives, programmers, users. These are the programs which enable everything in the system to communicate.

### (i) Machine Language and Assemblers

With machines that offered stored program capability, like the British Colossus or Mark 1 machines, programming initially meant using the keyboard to enter the exact string of ones and zeroes that made up the binary code or "machine language." Obviously this was inconvenient and error-prone; an alternative was badly needed.

For the Mark 1, Turing created a simple assembler that let him substitute a single letter code for longer strings like "01001100011." A similar coding system was developed for UNIVAC, but like Turing's, it still required a complex command set. A higher-level language was necessary.

### (ii) FORTRAN—1957

The first higher-level language for computers was released in 1957 for the IBM 704. FORTRAN, short for FORmula TRANslation, was developed by a team headed by John Backus. Its breakthrough concept was the use of logical words, like PRINT and STOP, to control the computer.

FORTRAN was designed as a scientific and engineering language; it wasn't well suited to business applications. Other languages, like COBOL (COmmon Business Oriented Language) were soon developed to better meet the needs of business.

### (iii) UNIX—1969

This historical list wouldn't be complete without UNIX, a cryptic but powerful language loved by many "techies" and hated by many others because of the difficulty in remembering commands. (Want to delete a file? How about "rm" for remove?)

UNIX was originally designed by AT&T's Bell Labs around 1969. One of its main selling points was its portability from machine to machine, which eventually made it the language of choice in network operating systems, particularly in the academic world. (Because AT&T gave free licenses to academic institutions, it quickly became a staple in that environment.)

As academia moved from large time-sharing machines to individual workstations around 1980, UNIX migrated to the networked workstation environment. Since the Internet started as a network of academic (and government) networks, UNIX is prevalent on network servers throughout the Internet. It is also found extensively in client/server environments within industry.

It should be noted that UNIX comes in several different flavors nowadays. Over the years, AT&T has licensed the product, and third parties have tailored it to suit their needs. Some manufacturers offer proprietary versions that run only on their machines—a somewhat ironic development considering the portability feature that spurred UNIX's early success.

*(iv)  CP/M—1973*

BASIC eventually became the standard language for microcomputers. A greater challenge was to develop an operating system that would allow computers to use disk drives for data storage. CP/M was the first such operating system for micros.

Gary Kildall, a computer science professor at the U.S. Navy's Postgraduate School, developed CP/M to connect a disk drive to a small microcomputer. Kildall marketed the program through his own small company, Digital Research, and it remained the standard operating system until IBM chose Microsoft's MS-DOS as the operating system for the IBM PC.

*(v)  BASIC—1974*

Easily the most popular language of all, BASIC (beginners' all-purpose symbolic instruction code) is the mainstay of the hobbyist and business do-it-yourself programmer. The language was initially developed in the early 1960s for minicomputers, but its most noteworthy use has been in personal computers.

Bill Gates and Paul Allen developed BASIC for the Altair in 1974, which made the home computer usable by hobbyists. At the same time they also launched Microsoft, which became the leading microcomputer software house a decade or so later. But developing BASIC languages was not difficult, and Microsoft faced competition from a number of other firms, for example, Compiler Systems, which developed CBASIC.

*(vi)  MS-DOS—1981*

The adoption of MS-DOS as the operating system for the IBM PC radically changed the microcomputer industry. It also represented a major departure for IBM, which had never before looked outside for a component as critical as MS-DOS would be to the PC. Microsoft was in fact a very small company. It did have an impressive track record, having provided most of the early BASICs and having developed hardware to allow its products to run on Apple computers. Still, the IBM invitation was unprecedented.

MS-DOS was designed as an open software product—that is, other software developers would have access to it to develop software for IBM's new machine. That and the open nature of the IBM PC itself—which allowed easy add-ons and, ultimately, easy cloning—established MS-DOS and the PC as industry standards very shortly after their introduction in 1981.

*(vii)  Windows 3.0—1990*

Although MS-DOS did establish itself as the dominant microcomputer operating system during the 1980s, it was not without its detractors, who viewed it as cumbersome and decidedly unfriendly to users. To this group MS-DOS was simply piggybacking on the success of the IBM standard and was the market leader by default in spite of its own limitations.

The dogged market popularity of the Apple Macintosh throughout the 1980s tended to support this damning judgment of MS-DOS. If there was one clearly superior feature of the Macintosh, it was its user-friendly graphic interface. In the late 1980s IBM finally threw in the towel with the announcement of its own graphic-based operating system—the OS/2—for its Personal System/2 line.

Nevertheless, the large installed base of MS-DOS applications software remained an impediment to the final victory of the graphic-based interfaces. This impediment was all but removed in May 1990, however, with the introduction of Microsoft's own Windows Version 3.0. Windows was originally conceived as a "shell" system that would envelop MS-DOS and make it visually intuitive in the same way as the Macintosh. However, earlier versions of the software suffered from memory and performance restrictions.

Windows 3.0, which at the time required a system based on Intel's 386 or 486 microprocessor, overcame earlier limitations by offering access to up to 16Mb of memory, as well as multitasking of both MS-DOS and Windows applications. Its introduction signaled the end of the transition to the era of the graphic-based microcomputer operating system.

Subsequent versions of Microsoft Windows have included Windows NT (for networks) and Windows 95. The latter went through a series of name changes internally at Microsoft, as its release date was repeatedly pushed back. Beta copies of the software finally did start shipping to willing guinea pigs in 1995, but not before the constant delays had enhanced Microsoft's reputation (among some critics) as a purveyor of "vaporware."

## (b) APPLICATIONS SOFTWARE

Applications software, sometimes referred to as productivity tools, are programs that enable users to perform specific tasks more effectively and efficiently than the manual method.

### (i)  Word Processing Software—1976

Word processing, one of the key business applications on the personal computer, began as has much software—as a hobbyist's recreation. Electric Pencil was written for the Altair by Michael Shrayer in California. Numerous versions were written for other computers, including the Radio Shack TRS-80.

Electric Pencil started things rolling, but it did not become the industry's standard word processor. WordStar, released by MicroPro in 1979, did become the standard for a time.

Today, there are numerous word processing packages competing for market share. However, WordPerfect and Microsoft Word have emerged as the clear market leaders during the 1990s.

### (ii)  Spreadsheet Software—1979

If any one program was the catalyst for business's interest in personal computers, it was VisiCalc. Spreadsheets which allow complicated financial modeling and the easy manipulation of "what if" situations, are today an indispensable business tool.

VisiCalc was the first spreadsheet widely marketed for personal computers. It was developed by Software Arts, a partnership of Daniel Fylstra and Dan Bricklin. The first release shipped 500 copies per month. By 1981, the company was shipping 12,000 per month.

Initially released only for the Apple, VisiCalc was rewritten for several other machines. IBM ensured that an MS-DOS version was available when its PC was released in 1981. But competition rapidly ensued, to the point that virtually every major software house began offering a spreadsheet program.

Today, the leading spreadsheets are Microsoft's Excel and, of course, the venerable Lotus 1-2-3. The latter, originally introduced in 1983, was designed with the MS-DOS operating system in mind and had features well beyond what the "translated" VisiCalc could offer.

### (iii)  Database Software—1981

The database management software market for the PC began with Ashton-Tate's dBase II (now dbase V), released in 1981. Business had already grown familiar with database programs from the mainframe and minicomputer environments.

Really useful database programs required the development of hard disk drives and faster processors. That is why few programs were developed for the CP/M and Apple markets in earlier years.

### (iv)  Other Software

Software is a fast-moving industry, and today's star is likely to be outdated tomorrow. Areas that have shown rapid growth over the years include desktop publishing, graphics programs, presentation software, and some home-based applications such as financial planning packages (particularly Quicken).

## (c) GROUPWARE—LOTUS NOTES, 1990

Arguably, the most recent milestone in the history of software was the introduction of Lotus Notes in 1990. Although few realized it at the time, Lotus Notes would go on to become spectacularly successful, and would in fact launch a whole new category of software called groupware. IBM's takeover of Lotus in 1995 was motivated in very large part by the success of Lotus Notes and IBM's desire to build on that success.

What does groupware allow you to do? In a sense, groupware is a very user-friendly network manager containing, controlling, and/or coordinating a number of elements: E-Mail, electronic bulletin boards, remote database searches, on-line connections allowing people to work on the same document at the same time, and even "platforms" on which to build user-specific applications (e.g., to manage a sales force).

Why groupware, and why did it take so long into the IT revolution to catch on? The answer has to do with telecommunication technology and its related connectivity and networking applications, which really only began to mature early in the 1990s. Certainly most organizations of any size already had local-area networks (LANs) before then, and larger organizations had long been familiar with micro-to-mainframe links, and more recently client/server configurations. But it wasn't until the early 1990s that the entire world became "wired"—right down to the last micro with its high-speed modem, Internet connection, and so on. The spectacular growth in the 1990s of many commercial on-line services (CompuServe, America Online, Prodigy), after a decade of relative stagnation, is part of the same trend.

## 5.5  CHANGING PATTERNS OF COMPUTER USE

After looking at computer hardware, and then the development of software, there's one further series of trends worth examining. Patterns of computer use have changed dramatically over the years.

### (a)  WHO'S USING COMPUTERS?

In the brief history of computers, their use has undergone a radical change. In the beginning, as experimental tools, they were of course the preserve of a few academics. To others, even in the business world, access to computers was limited. This was as much a function of cost as of any grand plan: large mainframe computers were obviously beyond the reach of small businesses and individuals. Time sharing, when the technology allowed it in the 1960s, permitted some use by smaller organizations, but even this service was expensive, and the applications available quite limited.

The development of the personal computer, first as a hobbyist's toy, later as a viable business machine, democratized the computer. It is now available to virtually every business and to most nonprofit organizations and is appearing in an increasing number of homes.

### (b)  WHAT ARE COMPUTERS USED FOR?

This too has changed over the years. Remember that the early machines of Pascal and Babbage were single-purpose machines. Even ENIAC was designed with one purpose in mind—the construction of firing tables. It wasn't until UNIVAC that a commercial multipurpose computer was available; and although it was multipurpose, it was far from flexible.

As computer costs came down and the number in use increased, the range of applications expanded. Computers today are used in offices, factories, and schools. Almost all of their applications—virtually anything beyond the batch processing of information—had to await development of the mini and microcomputer in the sixties and seventies.

### (c)  HOW ARE COMPUTERS MARKETED?

The early modern computers were room-size and were not sold in a traditional sense. As with supercomputers today, purchasing time was the common means of use.

With UNIVAC and subsequent computers by IBM and its competitors, there was finally an opportunity for the marketing skills of the business equipment industry to be brought back into play. Mainframe computers were sold through fairly sophisticated networks of company salespeople. Minicomputers were sold in much the same way, and often a single vendor provided the software, hardware, and service.

The microcomputer changed the marketing structure even further. The first personal computers were generally sold by direct mail, with virtually no formal follow-up support. As the technology grew more sophisticated, so did the marketing, but manufacturers have never had the same kind of hold on customers that was common with larger systems.

Today with hardware increasingly becoming a commodity differentiated largely by price there is more consumer choice—and confusion. In a somewhat circular turn of events, value-added retailers are picking up an increasing share of the market, bringing together hardware, software, and service in one package.

## 5.6 DEVELOPMENTS IN COMPUTER HARDWARE

Developments in computer hardware will continue in all areas, from the speed and size of machines to the quality of displays and printing. Many changes will be incremental and, aside from helping manufacturers compete on criteria other than price, will have little real impact on the user. A sharper monitor, for example, may be very important to some people but of little relevance to others.

Such changes may be important when applications are developed that take advantage of hardware developments. Today's spreadsheets, for example, are worlds apart from the state of the art when machine memory was only 64K.

So long as the old applications suit your purposes, so too should the old machines. On the other hand, if you're feeling constrained by memory size or processing speed, improvements are never very far away.

### (a) MEMORY SIZE

Until the latter half of the 1980s, MS-DOS–based machines were limited in full-use operating memory to 640K. A variety of add-ons on the market allowed limited use of greater memory, but 640K still marked a real limit. At that time it was thought to be a generous limit—but no more.

Newer operating systems, like OS/2 Warp and Windows 95, and more powerful microprocessors like Intel's Pentium, offer far greater capacity and are allowing the development of more memory-hungry, sophisticated applications. Machines based on the 80386 microprocessor, for example, routinely came with a standard 4 megabytes (4Mb, i.e. 4,000K) of random access memory (RAM), expandable to 16Mb. IBM's first 80486-based machines, released in October 1990, were expandable to 32Mb. Later, faster versions of the 80486 chips could access 64Mb and even 128Mb of RAM. Pentium processors and their equivalents are continuing the upward trend, although you rarely see them equipped with more than 8Mb to 16Mb unless they're being used as servers in a network configuration.

A P6 or 80686 microprocessor is already coming on the market, and there seems little reason to stop there. Over the course of the industry, memory has increased tenfold every five years.

### (b) PROCESSING SPEED

In the mid-to-late 1980s, a standard IBM PC or XT ran at a speed of 4.77 megahertz (MHz), considered blazingly fast in its day. The newest Pentium- or equivalent-based machines now on the market offer speeds of up to 166 MHz or more. Once again, the upward trend will continue.

At present, the biggest barriers to making use of increased processing speed are not found in the microprocessing technology itself; rather, they involve the graphics and other cards that run at slower speeds, and the various application software packages that were originally designed for slower machines.

Nevertheless, unlike memory capacities that are in a state of overkill for most applications, the higher speeds are welcome and often much-needed in order to effectively run (a) huge, otherwise very slow operating systems such as Windows 95, and (b) server machines in network environments.

## (c) STORAGE

Just as system memory and speed have increased substantially over earlier machines, so too has the capacity to store information for later use.

### (i) Diskette Drives

Technology has moved from cassette tape to 8-inch diskettes to $5\frac{1}{4}$-inch diskettes to the current $3\frac{1}{2}$-inch diskette standard. The new, smaller diskette packs two to four times more information than its larger predecessor.

The $3\frac{1}{2}$-inch diskette has eclipsed the standard $5\frac{1}{4}$-inch floppy because of its capacity and because it is more durable, its casing being a protective rigid plastic. Another factor was that, as the physical size of the computer itself decreased, an even smaller disk became desirable.

IBM adopted the $3\frac{1}{2}$-inch diskette with its PS/2 (business) and PS/1 (home) microcomputer lines in the early 1990s. It was already the standard for the Apple Macintosh line, and is really the only solution for laptop computers. Virtually all major software manufacturers have moved to the $3\frac{1}{2}$-inch standard.

Smaller diskettes, under 3 inches in size, have been developed, but the $3\frac{1}{2}$-inch size seems a good compromise between compact size and easy handling. The format will likely endure for some time.

### (ii) Hard Disk Drives

Hard disk drives, which store information on a disk permanently mounted inside the computer, have progressed from an expensive and unreliable option to an essential component of any serious business system. In fact, it was the widespread acceptance of the hard disk that led software developers to abandon copy protection on their programs.

Now that hard disks have become commonplace, the same mad rush for capacity that took place with active memory is under way. Hard disks are now available with capacities of one gigabit (Gb)—that's one billion bytes or 1,000 Mb—and even higher. As technology improves and prices fall, there's no reason to expect the capacity to stop increasing.

### (iii) CD-ROM

Compact disks, which during the 1980s enjoyed increasing popularity with audiophiles, have been a growing presence in the computer industry of the 1990s. On a single disk that is indistinguishable from its stereophonic cousin, over 550 megabytes of data can be stored. That's the equivalent of over 1,500 standard floppy disks. Put another way, it stores enough data to replace every phone book in Canada, a country with about 30 million people. In fact, some companies have been doing just that kind of thing—a good example of an application for which CD-ROM is well suited.

CD-ROM stands for "compact disk—read only memory." You can read the disk but can't alter what's on it. Other existing applications for the technology include electronic encyclopedias, newspaper databases, technical manuals, and computer programs.

At first CD-ROM's popularity was limited by the relatively high cost of CD-ROM as well as the dearth of applications for it. A number of developments in the 1990s have changed that. One is the familiar downward trend in price as more and more units are installed. Another is called "hypertext," which establishes a complex series of linkages between words in a database to allow easier searching for what you want. This capability is important when you're facing a sea of 550 Mb of data. (Hypertext is also one of the key reasons for the popularity of the World Wide Web, a major component of the Internet.)

Finally, important developments have taken place and will continue to take place in "CD-I," or interactive compact disks. While hypertext assists in using CD-ROM in its bibliographic role, CD-I holds promise as an educational and entertainment media. In its simplest forms, it takes advantage of the large data capacity of the disk to allow the viewer to make choices, for example, about how a movie is going to end.

*(iv) WORM*

CD-ROM only allows you to read what's already been written. Writing to a CD-ROM is an expensive, specialized process. In the most general terms, WORM, or "write once, read many," is a do-it-yourself CD-ROM system. WORM has a comparable storage capacity but allows you to write or record your own information on a disk. The technology is at least three to four times as expensive as CD-ROM and is not yet widely in use. However, it is a reliable technology and should come down in price.

Another related technology is the erasable optical disk. These disks combine the mass storage of the other laser-based systems with the easy alteration common to traditional magnetic disks.

## (d) INPUT DEVICES

Enough of how we might store data in the near future—what options will we have for getting it there in the first place? Today, data is manually input in one of two main ways: the keyboard and pointing devices like the mouse. Each has advantages and disadvantages. Mouse supporters claim the device is a more natural way to handle drawing and pointing applications. The keyboard is a traditional way of entering data. Although there will be variants and improvements, these two devices will dominate manual data input for some time to come.

*(i) Alternative Keyboards*

The keyboard arrangement currently in use, the familiar QWERTY typewriter keyboard, was designed to slow typists down to the speed of their machines. Several alternative keyboards, like the Dvorak, arrange the more frequently used keys under the most dexterous fingers. They've failed to catch on, however, and as straight copy typing and typing speed become less important, they are unlikely to.

Similarly, another device that has the capability to generate characters A to Z using only six keys and that emulates a mouse, is unlikely to catch on for other than limited text entry on engineering drawings.

### (ii) Pointers

The mouse is definitely here to stay. As the graphic interface (dealt with later in this chapter) continues to grow in utility, pointing devices will become as prominent. The current mouse, which glides over your desktop, will face increasing pressure from stationary "track balls" built into the keyboard, and from penlike attachments that use light as a comfortable drawing tool.

### (iii) Voice

Speech recognition and its corollary, voice activation, are still at least a few years away from being commercially viable and efficient. Given the many homonyms in language, effective voice input mechanisms have awaited advances in artificial intelligence that can tell similar words apart by context.

Voice input mechanisms are being tested and are already used by some disabled computer users. For speed and reliability, they cannot yet compare to keyboarding.

### (iv) Scanners

Given that a WORM holds the equivalent of several hundred books—something like 10,000 pages—mass storage would be a daunting prospect for any typist. Concurrent with the increase in storage capacity has been an increase in the popularity of another technology, the scanner, which ends the need to directly input previously typed material.

A scanner reads text from paper and translates the characters to standard ASCII code, which is the character set your computer understands. Some scanners are equally adept with graphics. In the future nearly all will be.

Scanners are already going through the familiar cycle in which function improves rapidly while price declines. They will likely soon become as indispensable as a hard disk drive.

## (e) PRINTERS

So the future holds great promise in processing more, storing more, and inputting more. How about getting the information out?

### (i) Impact Printers

Until the early to mid-1980s, printers for business computer use were generally one of two types of impact printer: daisy wheel or dot matrix. The daisy wheel, which borrows from typewriter technology, has essentially suffered the same fate as its parent—relegation to a very limited number of low-speed applications.

Dot matrix, which, as the name implies, uses dots to construct images, benefited from rapid increases in print quality and speed. It took over for a time as the low-cost workhorse but was eventually replaced by the rapidly expanding range of non-impact printers, of which the laser represents the commercial vanguard. Non-impact printers generally offer higher speed—up to 18,000 lines per minute, compared with the impact printer's peak of 3,600—and high-quality images.

*(ii) Laser Printers*

Borrowing from office copier technology, the laser printer uses a photoconductive drum to attract toner and form an image. They have grown in reliability and fallen sharply in cost over the past decade. Some laser printers are now cheaper than many top-of-the-line dot matrix printers. They offer virtual-typeset quality (600 dpi is replacing 300 dpi as the standard; 1,200 dpi machines are available) and are ideal for mixing text and graphics on a page. Lasers have set the new industry standard and will likely remain the printer of choice.

Color lasers are becoming more readily available, although they are still rather expensive ($5,000 to $20,000 or more). As with any technology, they will become much more common over the next few years as prices fall.

*(iii) Magnetographic Printers*

With speeds up to 90 pages per minute—about nine times that of most office lasers—and with similar quality, this technology is still in the developmental stage. It uses a dot matrix-style printhead to magnetically charge a drum and attract toner.

*(iv) Ion Deposition Printers*

Whereas lasers use light and electricity and magnetographic printers use magnetic charge, ion deposition printers use ions from the air to attract toner and form images. They offer speeds approaching 120 pages a minute and unparalleled reliability. They may one day supplant lasers for low-resolution applications.

*(v) Other Printers*

Both ink-jet and electrostatic printers have been around for some time—the latter for two decades. Both have been given new life through technological improvement.

Ink-jet printers allow high-quality printing on virtually any texture of paper, "spraying" ink onto the page. New solid inks have further enhanced print quality, and the technology easily supports color printing.

Electrostatic printers use electric charges to make special papers absorb ink. The technology is expensive and requires special paper but offers printing speeds up to 18,000 lines per minute.

## (f) FAX AND FAX-MODEMS

Combine a printer, a scanner, and a telephone modem (for communications), and you have a fax, or facsimile machine. These devices allow the transmission of documents over telephone lines for no more than the cost of a phone call. Faxes have been around for decades but never took off until improved data transmission speeds and scanners made them practical. They are now one of the fastest-growing products in office technology.

The fax machine is a bit of an anomaly in that it is a single-purpose, standalone device. For several years now, there has been software that allows a microcomputer, equipped with a fax-modem and a scanner, to act as a fax machine. As this option becomes more and more widely used, the market for standalone fax machines will continue to decrease.

### (g) "GENERIC IRON"

In wrapping up any look at computer hardware development, there's a final trend that can't be ignored. At one time computers were developed for specific purposes. Today, the trend is toward hardware whose function comes totally from software. This is known as the "generic iron" phenomenon. An example is the combined fax-scanner-printer being offered by some manufacturers.

The merger of television and computers is also on the horizon—in fact, it's already begun, with real-time video capability being built in or offered as an add-on to many high-end microcomputers. The next generation of set-top TV converters will include a microprocessor that can run software to help users navigate the 500-channel universe, do home banking and teleshopping, and so on. Cable companies will also be offering very high speed modems that can be used to navigate the Internet and make the downloading of video—video on demand—more practical than it is now.

The move toward generic iron also means that understanding developments in computer software will be critical for businesses that want to maximize the advantage of computers.

## 5.7 DEVELOPMENTS IN COMPUTER SOFTWARE

Most of the common business applications of microcomputers—word processing, simple spreadsheets, databases—automate clerical functions. The newer applications are aimed more at executives and professionals. Complex modeling spreadsheets and business graphics are probably the two most common, but there are others. Project tracking can be assisted by computers. Spell checkers have been a common enough part of word processors for years; more recently, grammar and style checkers have become standard on the top-of-the-line packages.

Desktop publishing has become an accepted part of business and a basic tool for getting a message across. Presentation software, which does with the computer screen what desktop publishing software does for paper, is changing the way business and sales presentations are made.

Software is also being customized to meet the needs of specific occupations and industries; this is the opposite of generic iron. Keeping track of the software that is available and suitable for your work means a little reading and intelligence gathering. In particular, you should watch for the trends set out below.

### (a) INTEGRATION

As computers themselves become integrated more fully into business operations, the data must be more easily moved from person to person and application to application. At one time, microcomputer users had a choice between full-function applications that could not easily (or not at all) share data and limited function programs that could share data "within the family."

Integration of data between powerful applications has become easier as standards for data become more commonly accepted and as the capacity of computers allows for the concurrent running of several applications. There are currently several formats that allow various spreadsheet programs to share data, and the same is true for word processors. Apple Macintosh machines have been able to read and convert data from MS-DOS-formatted disks for years, and, more recently, even run MS-DOS software.

The trend towards integration will continue because the market will demand it. Customers will shun new, standalone platforms or applications that may quickly become obsolete (or never even get a foothold in the market). Groupware such as Lotus Notes fuels the integration trend, which at its core reflects the increasing need for connectivity in IT applications.

### (b) GROUPWARE

Speaking of groupware, we indicated earlier in the chapter that Lotus Notes is by far the leader in the marketplace. Others are scrambling to get a foothold; Microsoft is developing a program called Exchange. However, Lotus isn't sitting on its laurels. Its Network Notes will tap into AT&T's long-distance network and allow databases to be converted into the Internet's World Wide Web format known as HTML. With such capabilities organizations will be able to create their own private Internet (intranet) without the lack of control (some would say chaos) in the Internet environment. Taking it a step further, groupware may eventually act as a secure "gateway" from the Internet or other private networks anywhere in the world into an organization's own network (e.g., for purposes of electronic commerce, advertising, and customer support).

Nevertheless, the main benefit of groupware is and will probably continue to be the productivity gains and opportunities it creates within the organization. It remains to be seen whether it's a cost-effective alternative to the Internet for the corporate world. The Internet is free, and one centralized Web Page for it can be developed fairly cheaply. Groupware, on the other hand, costs $200 to $300 per installation.

### (c) GRAPHIC USER INTERFACES (GUIs)

Controlling a computer via on-screen graphical "icons" has become the accepted standard since Microsoft's Windows first replaced MS-DOS's "A-prompt." Most new applications will use Windows or some similar graphic system of control such as OS/2 Warp or the Macintosh Operating System (which Apple began to license out in 1995).

Although easier to use and understand, the downside of GUIs is that they make the computer do more work. They have therefore had to await faster and more powerful computers.

### (d) SOFTWARE MARKETING

As mentioned earlier, copy protection devices in software have gone out of fashion, largely as a result of the hard disk. To an extent, tougher copyright laws in many jurisdictions will reduce outright piracy. However, software developers face a new danger—cloning.

As computers themselves become more generic and pricing and marketing practices approach those for commodities, the real competition will be in the software market.

When industry standards in software appeared, we saw copycat programs enter the marketplace. This trend will continue, with the same results as in computer hardware—an overall lowering of prices and margins.

### (e)  SOFTWARE DISTRIBUTION

Software is currently distributed on diskettes, CD-ROM, or even on tape (e.g., with some large computer systems). Remote distribution via modem—i.e., downloading from bulletin boards, the Internet, etc.—has also become very popular. There are other alternatives as well. As far back as the late 1970s, one company tried to distribute computer programs and data via cable television. They proved that while the technology was there, the market wasn't. Today's more ubiquitous personal computer, and the merger of TV and computers, will very likely change that.

Similarly, it is possible to transmit computer software and data via FM radio waves. Suggestions for using this technology have already been made, particularly as a low-cost way for small businesses to transmit data.

## 5.8  DEVELOPMENTS IN CONNECTIVITY

Continuing the trend of the past several years, connectivity will play an increasingly critical role, even in small business's application of information technology. Indeed, the integration of computers and telecommunications facilities has sparked the second phase of the microcomputer revolution: the end of the micro as a standalone tool and its evolution towards supporting communicating and exchanging information, the basis of most business life.

### (a)  THE TECHNOLOGIES THAT MAKE IT POSSIBLE

Digitization—treating information sent by telecommunications as pulses rather than the waves of analog—allows much more information to be sent over current facilities. This means that telephone lines can handle both voice and data in increasing volumes.

At the same time facilities that use electricity to create pulses are being replaced by fiber optics, which use light. The capacity of fiber optics is enormous compared with other technologies.

Finally, as we've already seen, there are tremendous increases underway in computer capacity; at the same time, prices are falling dramatically. Taken together, all these technological changes are making it possible to finally achieve totally integrated computer communications.

### (b)  INTEGRATED SERVICES DIGITAL NETWORK

Known as ISDN, the integrated services digital network (also dealt with in Chapter 11 of this handbook, "Telecommunications") is likely to be a major factor in the integration of computers and telecommunications technology. In effect, ISDN permits the transmission of data as easily as you plug a telephone into its jack. By effectively standardizing the way data are handled and providing data-handling capability through the telecommunications network, a computer at one location can easily have access and virtual compatibility with a computer across the country.

ISDN has moved out of the concept stage and through the stages of implementation. The first incarnations have been adjuncts to the phone system, with phone companies offering ISDN lines to business (and even residential customers in larger markets). The installation and setup fees, including needed equipment, can run as high as a few thousand dollars for a single installation. Monthly costs can run in the hundreds of dollars, although some base prices have come down below $100 per month.

ISDN may help sustain the strong growth of commercial database and on-line services which, Internet access notwithstanding, still suffer from the limitations of existing data transfer systems. Computer service bureaus, which suffered as the price of computer systems plummeted in dollar-per-byte terms, may also be resurrected. Indeed, ISDN will benefit any application that involves computers exchanging data.

### (c) THE INTERNET

We'll try not to dwell too long on this topic and its potential because it's already been hyped beyond all reason. Suffice it to say that there are two rather extreme views on the subject:

1. The Internet is or will become a panacea for the world's problems, the greatest equalizer in the history of humanity, and so on. Think the 500-channel TV universe is mind-boggling? How about every individual on the face of the planet (with a computer and Internet hookup) having his or her own TV channel? Information will flow freely, anywhere and everywhere, to anyone. The democratic process will become instantaneous. Governments and big multinationals will worship at the altar of You, the Individual Citizen/User.

2. The Internet is or is becoming a cesspool, filled with (a) the computer-equivalent of infomercials; (b) pornography; and (c) gigabytes of sundry, useless, unedited noise masquerading as information. The promise for the future is that there will be more and more waste flowing into the cesspool, making Internet cyberspace the worst environmental disaster of the twenty-first century.

We'll go out on a limb and suggest that the truth probably lies somewhere in between.

### (d) BANDWIDTH—THE NEXT HOLY GRAIL

The quest for connectivity is fueling the rush towards increased bandwidth—essentially, the widening of the information pipeline to get as much information through as quickly as possible. A decade ago 2,400 bps modems were commonplace. A few are still around today, although 9,600 bps (most fax machines), 14,400 bps (most fax-modems), and 28,800 bps (some fax-modems and commercial on-line services) are now the norms.

Fiber optics, ISDN, and cable companies offering modems all have one thing in common: bandwidth. Anyone who has used a 2,400 bps modem knows how excruciatingly slow it can be. Anyone who has surfed the World Wide Web on the Internet with a 14,400 bps modem knows that it just doesn't cut it. If we're going to be downloading real-time video and other massive quantities of information, we need bigger pipelines and faster speeds. We need more bandwidth. Rest assured that just about everyone—especially the telephone and cable companies—are falling over themselves trying to deliver it to us.

## 5.9 SOCIETAL IMPACT

No look at the future direction of information technology would be complete without some examination of the impact the technology will have on people. As information technology changes the economy and offers us new tools and opportunities, society will change.

### (a) ECONOMIC DISLOCATION

First, the bad news. It's undeniable that technology has, at the very least, caused economic dislocation and job loss. Some argue that technology hasn't caused a net loss of jobs in the economy as a whole and that the types of jobs have simply changed. Such arguments fly in the face of considerable anecdotal evidence and even of common sense. (Can it really take as many technicians and programmers to run a newly automated shop as the employees who were replaced, and if there was no net savings in employment costs, then what economic sense did the conversion make?) In any case, even if the "no net job loss" arguments were true, not everyone whose job has been replaced by technology can retrain to become a computer programmer.

In fact, several developments—many technology-related in one way or another—have been fueling economic dislocation and job loss since the early 1980s. In no particular order, these include:

- The general advance of technology, as noted above.
- Globalization—for example, the almost instantaneous movement of capital across borders, made possible by information technology—which has led to competition among jurisdictions for higher interest rates and lower labor costs, with attendant job losses, especially in industrialized countries.
- The increasing concentration of capital in large pools such as mutual and pension funds, which, combined with globalization and technological advances such as computer trading programs, means that nearly all of the available capital is less likely to flow to job-producing investments and more likely to seek short-term gain (some put the argument another way: Back in the 1950s, 60s, and even 70s, capital would be used to dig a hole in the ground, build a plant, hire workers, produce a product, and compete in a free market where success would lead to profit; today capital moves at the touch of a button into whichever government bond is offering the highest interest rate, regardless of the effect on employment and sometimes to its detriment).
- The collapsing public sector and the inability of deficit- and debt-wracked governments to prop up employment using old strategies based on Keynesian economics. Competition for lower tax rates—another effect of globalization, which is

in turn made possible by technology—puts additional stress on the revenue side, further aggravating the already serious deficit and debt problems.

Other factors also come into play, such as the widespread industry shakeouts, rationalizations, downsizing, mergers, and acquisitions of recent years, especially among larger employers. The decision to downsize and slash jobs is almost always a competitive necessity for the executives that make it, and few suggest that the executives are to blame. Still, many lose faith in a system that yields such results. Debacles such as the junk bond and U.S. savings and loan frauds of the 1980s also destroy confidence and seem to suggest a fundamental deterioration in our economic model. Is the system running amok?

Indeed, some argue that technology and the other developments previously described have caused a permanent shift in the balance that is at the heart of the capitalist system—i.e., in the capital-labor-government equation. Through technology and globalization, capital has been set free to roam anywhere, subject to ever-decreasing government regulation and taxation. Governments have been left fiscally impotent, unable to deal with economic stagnation. Often they are even being forced to abdicate their historical role as rulemaker and referee for fear that capital may instantly seek less regulated and less heavily taxed jurisdictions. In the middle of all this upheaval, has labor been left to whither on the vine? Is the economic dislocation and job loss of the last 15 years irreversible and uncorrectible? And if so, has an endless and vicious circle been entered, with lower incomes further eroding the tax and economic base, putting greater stress on what's left of the social safety net and causing even more decay in our social fabric?

There are at least two reasons to hope not. First, if a majority comes to the conclusion that the system is broke, democracy will presumably lead to government action that fixes it. Theoretically at least, it's possible that coordinated government action could mitigate the effects of many of the ills previously described. Measures sometimes suggested include:

- Labor-related reforms, such as a legislated reduction in the work week and heavy tax surcharges on overtime expenditures, to spread the available work better.
- Overhauling the entire tax system to discourage undesirable phenomena (high debt, speculation, widespread job slashing, etc.), while encouraging job-producing investments and employment spending, through such measures as:

    Higher income taxes on interest income;

    Higher capital taxes on debt;

    A flat corporate income tax with all loopholes and special deductions eliminated except for employment-related expenditures;

    The elimination of payroll taxes and similar taxes that discourage hiring; and

    Much higher taxes on speculative, short-term, non job producing investments and transactions.

Practically speaking, however, there seems to be no appetite anywhere—let alone worldwide unanimity—for such government intervention. And so what's the second reason to hope that the sky isn't really falling?

The human ability to adapt to difficult and changing conditions is enormous. Nature abhors a vacuum, and even if all of the existing jobs were eliminated through technology, people would, of necessity, invent new ones. We are already starting to see this trend. Ever-increasing numbers of people have been forced into self-employment and telecommuting, whether they like it or not (and often, they do like it). All of which brings us to the next topic.

## (b) TELECOMMUTING

Early pundits of the information age predicted that computers would free us from the office. Office workers were to become part of an electronic cottage industry, working from their homes, but the reality has been different. Telecommuting offered a short-term solution for some businesses and workers. But it also eliminated person-to-person contact.

Nevertheless, in addition to the factors described in the last section, there are several trends that suggest telecommuting is finally becoming as widespread as was earlier predicted:

- Microcomputer and telecommunication technology are close to providing practical and affordable video teleconferencing, so it isn't necessary to actually be in the office in order to "meet" with the people there. (In fact, this capability already exists, but it's still a bit sluggish.)
- The economic costs of physical commuting—fuel and transportation costs, lost time and productivity, and so on—are almost certainly greater than the incremental hardware, software, and telecommunication costs involved in telecommuting. (If they aren't now in any given situation, they will be soon because the former costs are constant or rising, while the latter are falling.)
- The environmental costs of physical commuting—pollution, burning of limited fossil fuels, global warming—remain a major concern.
- Company savings in office space costs can be substantial.
- Personal costs also come into play. The "cocooning" trend noted and predicted by some social scientists—the attractiveness of staying home as much as possible to spend more time with family, avoid traffic jams, crime, and pollution, and so on—clearly plays into the telecommuting trend.

## (c) TRAINING

The rapid pace of technological change will mean employers and employees will face a constant struggle to keep up. Adult education will be a burgeoning field, taking up the slack in the education system left by the baby boom generation. The importance of training will be further magnified because workers in the information age can reasonably expect to go through two or three careers in the course of their working life.

For companies the emphasis on keeping abreast of technology and on maximizing the creativity and skills of its employees will mean an increased training budget. A company that doesn't train its staff might just as well not maintain its equipment. Both are resources that will have to be kept in top working order if the company is going to stay competitive.

### (d) THE GLOBAL VILLAGE

In the information age staying competitive means being the best in the world. Information as a commodity is cheap to ship. Information age goods—or goods in which information is a component, and that means anything—will increasingly be produced wherever it is cheapest to do so. Protectionist measures will simply result in an economy that falls behind.

At the same time, for companies that have mastered a production process—including its information component—the world will be an enticing market.

### (e) WORK AND LEISURE

As mentioned earlier, there has been some concern about the impact of information technology on employment. Just as early machinery freed human beings from physical drudgery, information technology has freed society from much intellectual drudgery. Optimists have been hoping that jobs will not be lost but only changed, and changed for the better. While many believe otherwise, let's look at the bright side:

- We have the benefit of having seen the impact on society of an unplanned industrial revolution. Society can plan now to adjust to—not try to stop, or retard, but adjust to—the information revolution.
- Technology undeniably provides an opportunity for greater leisure pursuits. Such pursuits—of which video games are perhaps a regrettable example—will continue to benefit from information technology. Whole libraries can be made available on CD-ROM or via networks. We touched earlier on interactive video. And how about virtual travel—the ability to visit major attractions, exhibits, and sights anywhere in the world, anytime, through permanently stationed cameras accessible by your computer?

## 5.10  SOME FINAL REFLECTIONS

The computer industry has changed a great deal over the years, but some things have remained constant. Ever since Babbage, new technology often has surpassed budgets and timetables, and in doing so has disappointed customer expectations. Leading-edge technology gives its users an advantage, and there is a seemingly instinctive attraction to it. At the same time, the leading edge—like any frontier—has its risks.

If the history of the computer has any lesson for business today, it must simply be to balance any perceived gains with the risk that expectations may not be met. As in all other business deals, success in balancing the risks leads to profit.

The course of the future will always remain uncharted, but a forward-looking executive or a forward-looking society should always try to anticipate what lies around the next corner. With information technology—and the dizzying pace at which it is changing and changing us—keeping one eye a little ahead of today is sound advice.

# CHAPTER 6

# Microcomputers

The second part of this handbook deals with hardware and software. The central hardware component in most environments is the microcomputer, the subject of this chapter. The following material consists of:

- A checklist (Section 6.1), summarizing many of the main points in this chapter.

- A brief treatment of the management, user, and market issues surrounding microcomputers (Section 6.2).

- A section on the features and applications of microcomputers (Section 6.3) (some of this is fairly basic background or training material that experienced users may wish to skip).

- A discussion of user needs assessment and hardware evaluation (Section 6.4).

## 6.1 MICROCOMPUTER CHECKLIST

The following checklist is designed to assist accountants in decision-making and management relating to microcomputers, in their organizations and those of their clients. Generally, all "No" answers require investigation and follow-up, the results of which should be documented. Where there is such additional documentation, the purpose of the "Ref" column is to cross-reference the checklist to the appropriate working paper (or to the notes on the reverse).

The checklist is intended for general use only. If microcomputers are of especially vital concern to an organization, the advice of a specialist should be sought.

## Microcomputer Checklist

| | Yes | No | N/A | Ref |
|---|---|---|---|---|

### 1. Management Issues—Acquisition

a. Have an appropriate process, timetable, and budget been established for the assessment of user needs, the evaluation of available microcomputers, and purchase, training, and implementation?   ☐ ☐ ☐ ____

b. Has the participation of the ultimate users of the microcomputer(s) been ensured throughout the process?   ☐ ☐ ☐ ____

c. Have the major user needs been identified—such as required capacity, speed, availability of support, and so on—and has a preliminary identification been made of those microcomputers that might meet these criteria?   ☐ ☐ ☐ ____

d. For each microcomputer that might be purchased, have the following issues been addressed:

- Compatibility with preferred operating systems?   ☐ ☐ ☐ ____
- Compatibility with preferred applications software?   ☐ ☐ ☐ ____
- Compatibility with all printers in use?   ☐ ☐ ☐ ____
- Compatibility with existing or preferred networks?   ☐ ☐ ☐ ____
- Compatibility with possible future upgrades of above?   ☐ ☐ ☐ ____
- Adequacy of RAM and hard disk capacity?   ☐ ☐ ☐ ____
- Manufacturer and/or vendor warranties?   ☐ ☐ ☐ ____
- Availability of manufacturer and/or vendor support?   ☐ ☐ ☐ ____
- Adequacy of documentation and manuals?   ☐ ☐ ☐ ____
- Availability of skilled operating personnel?   ☐ ☐ ☐ ____
- Availability of training (self-study, seminars, etc.)?   ☐ ☐ ☐ ____

e. Has the microcomputer been user-tested for appropriateness and ease of use?   ☐ ☐ ☐ ____

f. Are security features adequate?   ☐ ☐ ☐ ____

g. Is the microcomputer price (taking into account the required number of machines, training costs, etc.):

- Competitive with other comparable hardware?   ☐ ☐ ☐ ____
- Within budget?   ☐ ☐ ☐ ____

|  | Yes | No | N/A | Ref |
|---|---|---|---|---|
| h. Once a microcomputer is decided upon, have the related purchase documents (sales agreements, etc.) been reviewed, by legal counsel if appropriate? | ☐ | ☐ | ☐ | ___ |

## 2. Management Issues—Implementation and Use

|  | Yes | No | N/A | Ref |
|---|---|---|---|---|
| a. Have all appropriate applications for the microcomputer been identified to ensure that maximum use and value are obtained from the microcomputer investment? | ☐ | ☐ | ☐ | ___ |
| b. Have appropriate policies, procedures, standards, and controls been put in place with respect to: |  |  |  |  |
| • Microcomputer documentation? | ☐ | ☐ | ☐ | ___ |
| • Microcomputer security? | ☐ | ☐ | ☐ | ___ |
| • Data backups, including off-site backups? | ☐ | ☐ | ☐ | ___ |
| • Are appropriate mechanisms in place to ensure that the microcomputer(s) are properly maintained and that repair service is available when needed (e.g., through signing of a maintenance contract)? | ☐ | ☐ | ☐ | ___ |
| • Has the reasonableness of maintenance costs been established, e.g., through competitive bids? | ☐ | ☐ | ☐ | ___ |

## 3. User Issues

|  | Yes | No | N/A | Ref |
|---|---|---|---|---|
| a. Are users adequately trained in the basic use of the microcomputer, including refresher or update courses when required? | ☐ | ☐ | ☐ | ___ |
| b. Where appropriate, are users adequately trained in the advanced features of the microcomputer? | ☐ | ☐ | ☐ | ___ |
| c. Both in theory and in practice, are users aware of the importance and necessity of: |  |  |  |  |
| • Microcomputer security? | ☐ | ☐ | ☐ | ___ |
| • Frequently backing up documents? | ☐ | ☐ | ☐ | ___ |

## 6.2 MANAGEMENT, USER, AND MARKET ISSUES

### (a) MANAGEMENT AND USER ISSUES

Most managers have become users of microcomputers themselves, and to that extent manager and user concerns have overlapped. However, from a purely management perspective, the main issues are:

- Making purchase, upgrade, and standardization decisions (this will be based on an analysis of user needs, the available microcomputers and features, available budgets, etc.).
- Ensuring that policies and procedures are in place to optimize the use of microcomputers throughout the organization, including:

  Identifying appropriate applications for the microcomputers

  Hiring and training of staff

  Standardization

  Integration with networks

  Controlling related costs
- Establishing good security, backup, and record destruction controls.

Your buying decision should be based on a proper assessment of your needs as described later in this chapter. It is impossible to make specific recommendations that cover all users, but the following points should be considered:

- If price is an important factor, new product introductions should be avoided. Last year's state-of-the-art technology can often be purchased at significantly lower prices and may well be enough to meet your needs. Also, there may be more software available for established machines.
- For accounting, database, conventional word processing and other high-volume applications, the large base of installed IBM and compatible equipment has resulted in a wealth of software on the market. An IBM or compatible may be the best choice in these areas.
- For graphics and desktop publishing applications, and in environments requiring low-cost networking and sharing of peripherals, the Apple Macintosh is a viable alternative. However, if you already have a large installed base of IBM-compatible equipment, IBM-compatible may be a more cost-effective choice.
- The major compatibles have for the most part proved themselves to be acceptable alternatives to IBM, so long as the equipment is purchased from a reputable vendor. Buyers should not hesitate to go this route if compatibles suit their needs.

### (b) MARKET ISSUES

*(i) Historical Background*

In the 1960s, before the arrival of the micro, only the largest organizations could justify the purchase of a computer. Indeed, the mainframe, the cost of which was prohibitive for small- and medium-size businesses, was the only type of computer available.

In the mid-1970s, Apple introduced the microcomputer to the marketplace with its Apple II line. Apple continued to lead the way until IBM entered the fray in 1981 with its IBM PC, which established a new standard in the industry. However, Apple still retains a significant market share with its Macintosh series, and IBM has lost market share in recent years to the makers of IBM-compatibles such as Compaq.

When IBM entered the microcomputer market in 1981, it made little attempt to conceal the technical specifications of its products. The primary rationale was that such exposure would attract a host of disciples and boost its own prestige in the data processing field. Other factors may have included:

- The fact that most IBM-PC components were purchased from outside suppliers (and could therefore not be protected).
- The possibility that IBM did not expect the machine to be as successful as it turned out to be.
- The threat of potential antitrust action arising from IBM's market domination.

In any case, the strategy backfired, as it opened the door for the compatibles. By the mid-1980s, many of these were arguably better and often less expensive than the IBM-PC. The rapid growth and acceptance of compatibles came at the expense of IBM's market share.

IBM's Personal System/2 posed a new threat to compatibles for several reasons:

- Its design eliminated one of the major competitive disadvantages of its predecessors—slow response time.
- It had many more standard features.
- Most importantly, it had a new operating system (OS/2), new proprietary hardware, and new processors. As a result, the advantage of existing compatibles was reduced and the new system became more difficult to emulate.

During the early 1990s the business microcomputer market was essentially split into three parts:

- IBM's old standard and the compatibles, which, because of their huge installed base of hardware and software, continued to thrive.
- The Apple Macintosh line, which remained popular especially for graphics, desktop publishing, and in environments requiring low-cost networking.
- IBM's new standard based on the Personal System/2, the long-term success of which was still in question.

Another development in the industry in the early 1990s was the trend toward graphics-based operating systems and shells, such as Microsoft's Windows and IBM's own OS/2. (The Apple Macintosh's operating system has always been graphics based.) A special advantage of OS/2 is that it complies with IBM's Systems Application Architecture (SAA), a common standard that facilitates the linking of varying levels of IBM machines from the user's point of view.

In the mid-1990s, a new element was added to the market mix with the joint development of the PowerPC chip by Apple, IBM, and Motorola. Machines based on the PowerPC can run software from earlier IBM and Apple machines, and new software is being developed to take advantage of its greater capabilities. Apple was the first to introduce a machine based on this technology in early 1994; several introductions were expected from both Apple and IBM in subsequent years.

*(ii)  Market Analysis and Trends*

Microcomputers have made computing power drastically more accessible and have revolutionized the computer industry to the extent that, as far back as 1983, the total number of all microcomputers sold had surpassed that of all other computers combined.

By the beginning of the 1990s, there were over 100 million microcomputer systems in operation worldwide. As a result of this tremendous market, the microcomputer marketplace has been extremely dynamic, characterized by a steady stream of new entrants into the market and exits by those who cannot compete. More and more makes and models are being offered by manufacturers in an attempt to keep pace with advances in technology.

Although there are well over 100 microcomputer manufacturers, the marketplace is dominated by a smaller number of players. IBM and Apple have been the market leaders throughout the 1980s and into the 1990s, accounting for over one third of the market between them. Other significant players have included Compaq, Dell, Hewlett-Packard, and NEC.

Despite its eroding market share during the 1980s, IBM clearly set the industry standard to the extent that over 100 companies are now manufacturing IBM-compatible microcomputers or clones. In fact, the very word *compatible,* within the context of the microcomputer industry, implies compatibility with IBM products. To say that a microcomputer is IBM-compatible essentially means that it will run compatible software, which in turn means that it uses the same processor (Intel 8088, 8086, 80286, 80386, 80486, 586, Pentium, or Intel's P6) and operating system (MS-DOS, OS/2, Windows) as the IBM line of microcomputers.

The compatibles often offer more standard features than IBM at somewhat lower prices. In fact, some models sold by smaller, one-product vendors who access parts manufacturers in the Far East have in the past been priced as much as 70 percent lower. Although these products are often lacking in vendor support, the combination of lower prices and superior standard features has helped to make compatibles a viable alternative to IBM products. IBM had, however, become much more price-competitive by the mid-1990s, as with its *Ambra* line.

In 1987 and 1988 IBM addressed the threat to its dominance by introducing the Personal System/2, which consisted of four models (30, 50, 60, and 80) that offered more speed, power, primary memory, and storage capacity than any personal computer then on the market. These machines were more difficult to design compatibles for, as described in the Historical Background section of this chapter. Nevertheless, the old IBM MS-DOS-based machines and compatibles remained a force to be reckoned with in the market. In a tacit admission of this fact, IBM introduced a lower-end model of its Personal System/2 line in 1988. Unlike other PS/2 models, it was compatible with the old MS-DOS machines.

Meanwhile, as IBM and the compatibles fight for market share based on the Intel/MS-DOS standard, Apple manages to maintain a significant market share with its Macintosh line. Recently, it has introduced newer models based on the PowerPC chip—jointly developed with IBM and Motorola—which can run Apple, DOS, and Windows applications.

Finally, two other emerging trends have contributed to the proliferation of microcomputers in recent years, even in environments that previously relied on mainframes:

- *Client/server architecture*—this is an expansion of the LAN concept, whereby a powerful microcomputer holds the primary processing and file server capability at the center of a network. Many large organizations are backing down from their mainframes and using this type of configuration.

- *Graphic workstations*—these are very powerful machines offering enhanced graphic capabilities. Based on RISC (reduced instruction set computer) technology such as that found in IBM's own RISC 6000, these workstations represent one of the fastest growth areas of the market. Sun Microsystems and Silicon Graphics are among the market leaders.

## 6.3 MICROCOMPUTER FEATURES AND APPLICATIONS

Because of rapid changes in technology and the proliferation of so many different makes and models of computers, it is difficult to define the term *microcomputer* with any precision. Lacking a better definition, we can say that a microcomputer is a relatively small and inexpensive computer capable of satisfying most of the computing needs of a single user or, in some cases, a small group of users.

In reality, the prefix *micro* can be misleading because these computers have very powerful capabilities. Indeed, many of today's microcomputers approach or surpass the raw processing power of their much larger predecessors.

The term *personal computer* or *PC* is often used synonymously with the word *microcomputer,* since micros were originally designed to be used by one person at a time. However, this has begun to change, since multiuser microcomputers are now available that make it possible for more than one user to access microcomputer files.

### (a) CAPABILITIES AND LIMITATIONS

Today, the breadth of capabilities of microcomputers is truly impressive; and the current rate of technological advancement suggests that the range of microcomputer applications is likely to continue expanding.

Some of the more common capabilities of microcomputers include the following:

- *Sorting information*—arranging data in a specific order of interest;
- *Summarizing information*—compiling desegregated data into a more manageable form;
- *Calculating*—performing a series of computations or operations on input data, and generating output documents that show the results;
- *Updating*—changing stored data to reflect more current information;

- *Query processing*—extracting information from a database to answer a series of questions of interest.

Other capabilities of micros that are in widespread use include:

- Word processing and desktop publishing, which are described in Chapter 8 of this handbook.
- Graphics, including computer-aided design, and computer-aided manufacturing (CAD/CAM).

Most of your microcomputer applications will probably fall into one or more of these categories. Once you decide that a given function should be computerized, the benefits that you can expect if an appropriate system is acquired are formidable. Reduction of time, effort, errors, more up-to-date information, and improved decision-making are among the benefits that will accrue.

Microcomputers do, however, have limitations:

- In relative terms, the speed of a micro's input/output devices is slower than that of the processor itself, which can often limit the overall processing speed of the system.
- Both the internal memory and secondary storage capacity sometimes fall short of the needs of the user, although this is less true since the arrival of advanced micros such as those based on Intel's Pentium and P6 microprocessors.
- Except for powerful micros with advanced operating systems, most microcomputers now in use can still only process one application at a time.
- Malfunctions or "bugs" can be a problem, in particular with micro software.
- Nevertheless, a judicious matching of user needs with appropriate hardware and software can circumvent many of these limitations.

### (b) COMPARISON TO MAINFRAMES AND MINIS

Mainframes are the largest kind of computer; they have very few limitations in their capabilities and processing capacity. They are intended to be used by many people simultaneously and often run programs that are custom-designed by the user.

Minicomputers also have very significant capabilities; however, both the processing capacity and number of simultaneous users are subject to more constraints than is the case with mainframes.

The processing capacity of microcomputers is somewhat limited compared with both mainframes and minis. In addition, micros are largely intended to be used by one person at a time. However, the emergence of the multiuser micro has resulted in a blurring of the mini/micro distinction to the point that the minicomputer category has or will disappear.

### (c) TYPES OF MICROCOMPUTERS

Microcomputers can be classified into four broad categories: pocket or hand-held micros, portable or laptop micros, desktop micros, and super or multiuser micros.

*(i)  Pocket (Hand-Held) Micros*

As is obvious from the name, this category consists primarily of those computers that look and behave like pocket calculators. Pocket micros are in fact sophisticated programmable calculators and often have features such as multiline character displays, printers, input/output ports for peripheral devices, and even handwriting recognition capability.

Electronic diaries or business organizers have enjoyed increasing popularity in recent years. Such machines, a major submarket of this category, are essentially pocket micros with one or more built-in software applications—for example, an appointment calendar and business card file.

*(ii)  Portable (Laptop) Micros*

Portable (laptop) micros, like pocket micros, are small enough to be easily transported but have considerably more processing capability than the hand-held variety. Laptop micros are ideal for users who need to use a computer while they are traveling—for example, sales representatives.

Laptop micros have been the fastest-growing segment of the market during the late 1980s and early 1990s. Toshiba was quick of the mark in this area, but by the mid-1990s all the other major manufacturers had begun offering laptop models, and the market has become very competitive.

*(iii)  Desktop Micros*

Desktop micros are still the most popular variety of microcomputer, primarily because they do not have to forgo the user conveniences of a spacious keyboard and a large display screen in order to achieve portability.

*(iv)  Super (Multiuser) Micros*

Super or multiuser micros, which can be accessed by more than one user simultaneously, emerged as a major force in the market during the late 1980s. The multiuser feature of these micros allows them to approximate the attributes of a minicomputer but at substantially lower cost.

## (d) COMPONENTS OF A MICROCOMPUTER SYSTEM

Microcomputers, like mainframes and minicomputers, operate as part of a system that typically consists of several devices designed to handle input, processing, output, and storage. A very typical microcomputer system or configuration would include the following hardware devices:

- Central processing unit (CPU)
- Keyboard
- Display screen
- Secondary storage devices
- Printer

In addition, a microcomputer system will of course include the software applications that the user intends to run.

Depending on the kind of microcomputer system selected, the various components listed above can be purchased either separately or as part of a single unit. Each of the components is dealt with in the following sections.

*(i)  The Central Processing Unit*

The central processor, as the name implies, is where the actual processing occurs. It is the most important component in a microcomputer configuration, primarily because the particular unit chosen largely determines the makeup of the rest of the system.

The CPU contains one or more microcomputer chips that enable the unit to execute programs and control the operations of the other system components. Thus, when you select a processor, you are really selecting a particular microcomputer chip. This choice is critical, since the type of chip selected greatly affects the processing speed as well as the range of applications software programs that can be used with it.

The CPU consists of three primary components:

- The control unit
- The arithmetic/logic unit
- Primary storage

The control unit is responsible for retrieving an instruction from primary storage, translating it into electrical signals, and routing these signals to other electronic components. The arithmetic/logic unit is responsible for performing the required mathematical or logic operations. Primary storage is the memory used during active processing.

The CPU performs three basic operations: input, processing, and output. Each of these operations is controlled by software, which can be either applications software or specialized system software known as the operating system (explained later in this chapter); therefore, you must take care to ensure that the CPU is compatible with the particular software that you own or intend to acquire.

The base cost of a CPU generally ranges from $500 to $5,000. Microcomputers are often described in terms of the type of processor they use. Intel (IBM and compatibles) and Motorola (Apple, plus the Apple/IBM PowerPC chip) are two of the major manufacturers of microprocessors.

*(ii)  The Keyboard*

The keyboard provides users with a means of inputting data and/or programs into the computer system. Keyboards typically consist of:

- Alphanumeric keys, similar to what you would find on a typewriter
- A 10-key numeric keypad to facilitate entering numeric data
- Special function keys that can initiate a particular command or even an entire computer program

The most popular type of keyboard is the "QWERTY." This is the typical typewriter design and derives its name from the first six keys on the top row. The Dvorak keyboard design, which is far less popular, places the most frequently used characters in the center so that 4,000 different words can be entered from the home row, as opposed to 100 with the QWERTY layout.

### (iii)  The Display Screen

The display screen is a temporary output device that visually displays data or the eventual hard copy output. It also makes it possible for the user to benefit from the directions and prompts issued by the software in order to simplify the use of the microcomputer.
Display screens are discussed in greater detail in the next chapter.

### (iv)  Secondary Storage Devices

Secondary storage devices hold data and programs in electronic form for use or processing by the CPU at a later time. The most common forms of secondary storage are floppy and hard disks, which are discussed in greater detail in the next chapter.

### (v)  Printers

A printer is an output device that produces hard copy or typed representations of information processed by the computer. It is a relatively independent hardware component in the sense that one printer can typically be exchanged easily for another in a given microcomputer system. Printers are also dealt with in the next chapter.

### (vi)  Software

Software is to the computer what records are to the phonograph. The utility of a microcomputer depends on the software you can run on it.

## The Operating System

The operating system is a specialized piece of software consisting of a set of programs and instructions that make it possible to:

- Run applications software
- Control the movement of data
- Make use of disk drives, printers, and other peripheral devices

The operating system also serves as the communication link between the user and the computer in that it initiates prompts and error messages on the display screen. In short, the operating system frees the user from concern about the internal operations of the computer.
The operating system is usually supplied by the computer system vendor at a cost of between $200 and $800.

## Applications Software

Typical software applications in a microcomputer system include spreadsheets and financial modeling, database management, word processing, desktop publishing and graphics, and accounting. These applications are dealt with more fully in separate chapters of this handbook.

The type of applications software to be used often determines which operating system is appropriate.

*(vii) Expansion Cards*

At the time of purchase, users often underestimate or overlook their future needs. Fortunately, expansion cards make it possible to upgrade the capabilities of a system—for example, to add primary memory, increase the speed of processing, enhance the system's graphics and color capabilities, and even add more expansion slots to the system.

The procedure by which expansion cards increase a system's capabilities is simple. The card is inserted into one of the microcomputer's expansion slots, and the microcomputer immediately acquires the additional capabilities offered by the card.

The market is dominated by IBM and compatible expansion cards. Some of the more popular ones include:

- Graphics adapters
- Memory expansion cards
- Speedup boards
- Multifunction cards that contain clock/calendars, additional ports, and in some cases software

Having identified the type of performance enhancement you need, the most important considerations when choosing an expansion card are quality and reliability. You should seek established products that have been debugged by feedback from past users. If possible, test the cards before purchasing them to ensure that they perform as intended.

## (e) ASSESSING MICROCOMPUTER SYSTEMS

In order to make rational comparisons between the many microcomputer systems available to you, it is useful to identify the attributes that distinguish one micro from another. You can then use these attributes as your evaluation criteria, in order to arrive at the decision that best meets your needs.

Generally speaking, microcomputer system components can be evaluated for quality and reliability, speed, capacity, expandability, compatibility, and ease of use.

*(i) Quality and Reliability*

The most important considerations here are the brand of microcomputer you select and the vendor you purchase it from.

Buying quality brands—and virtually all the major vendors produce quality brands—reduces the frequency of breakdowns and also helps to ensure that good software will be available.

Selecting a reliable vendor ensures that efficient, timely repair and maintenance services are available should breakdowns occur. A good vendor that carries the products of several manufacturers can also assist you in making your purchase decision—a decision discussed in greater detail later in this chapter.

It should also be noted here that hard disks are generally considered more reliable than floppy disks or diskettes, since the latter are more easily damaged and, with repeated use, can wear out. (Hard and floppy disk or diskette drives are discussed in greater detail in the next chapter). Since most hard disks are not removable, they therefore are not handled, so the risk of losing data is much reduced. Nevertheless, accidents can happen and hard disks should be regularly backed up, to either diskettes or tape.

### (ii) Speed

The processing speed of a microcomputer system depends primarily on the specifications of the CPU. The specs of the secondary storage devices and the printer, dealt with in the next chapter, are also important.

The speed of the CPU is affected by the number of processing chips in use, the speed of the chip(s) and the word length of the processor.

- *Number of chips*—a CPU normally resides on one miniature circuit board made of silicon and referred to as a microchip or chip; however, in some cases a CPU may consist of more than one chip, each of which may be responsible for different functions. For example, one chip might handle processing operations while another chip handles input and output. Generally speaking, if the CPU contains more than one chip, the processing speed will be greater.

- *The speed of the chip*—the processing speed of the chip refers to the "machine cycle" of the CPU, which is essentially the length of time it takes to retrieve, interpret, and execute a single program instruction. Machine cycles are measured in milliseconds (thousands), microseconds (millionths) and nanoseconds (billionths). Generally speaking, the shorter the machine cycle, the faster the processor. Speed is often expressed in terms of the number of machine cycles per second, or Hertz (Hz). Chip speeds of the more recent machines range start at 100 to 166 million Hertz (100 MHz to 166 MHz).

- *Word length of the processor*—word length refers to the number of bits of information that can be moved or operated on in a single machine cycle. In effect, it represents the number of bits that can be handled as a single unit. The most common word length for microcomputers nowadays is 32-bit, although some 16-bit and even 8-bit machines are still in use. Generally speaking, the greater the word length, the faster the processor.

### (iii) Capacity

The capacity of a microcomputer depends primarily on the CPU, although the capacity of secondary storage devices, dealt with in the next chapter, is also important.

In the case of the CPU, primary storage or main memory is used to store data or programs as they are executed. This primary storage is subdivided into random access memory (RAM) and read only memory (ROM). A distinguishing feature of RAM is that it can be read from or written to; new information can be recorded in it. Conversely, ROM contains permanent prerecorded information that can only be read. ROM is responsible primarily for readying the computer system for use ("booting") and displaying the initial prompt on a display screen.

The amount of RAM contained in a CPU is the key capacity consideration because its size, measured in kilobytes (1,024 bytes) or megabytes (1,048,576 bytes), directly affects the size of the application programs that you can run on your system.

The amount of RAM that the CPU can access depends primarily on the word length of the CPU (e.g., 16-bit or 32-bit). Most micros offer several sizes of memory. The most commonly found capacities were 512K or 640K for the now-outdated 16-bit machines. The latest machines have much higher addressable memories (most now have a minimum of 8 megabytes, and more are coming equipped with 16 megabytes).

### (iv)  Expandability

Typically, at least during the 1980s, first-time microcomputer purchasers tended to under-estimate the power and capacity they required. It is therefore important that you be aware of your system's expansion capabilities in advance. Expandability depends primarily on the number of expansion slots on your processor and on the operating system used.

Expansion slots allow you to enhance the power and capacity of your system by adding on various peripherals or boards—for example, to improve graphics resolution. Users should ensure that their system has enough expansion slots to meet future needs.

The operating system affects expandability because it determines what other software the system can run and whether one or several users are permitted by the system. Specifically:

- If the operating system is an obscure one (or indeed a very new one), the choice of applications software will be limited.
- Some operating systems, such as XENIX and the higher-end versions of MS-DOS and Windows, can accommodate more than one user.

### (v)  Compatibility

The CPU you choose must be compatible with the applications software that you will use with it. Some applications software simply cannot be run on certain processors. As previously noted, the compatibility of the CPU with the operating system is especially important.

If you intend to write specific application programs to meet your needs, then you must also consider whether the programming language(s) you will use are compatible with the CPU. The basic choice here is between an assembly language, which is essentially a more readily understandable version of a machine language, and a higher-level language such as BASIC, FORTRAN, Pascal, or C.

Assembly languages are generally unique to a particular computer and thus cannot easily be used with another type of processor. Conversely, higher-level languages can be moved from one processor to another with fewer changes and translated to the individual machine language with the help of systems software called compilers and interpreters. Thus, higher-level languages are more flexible than assembly languages.

### (vi)  Ease of Use

A microcomputer that is easy to use will be more productive in the long run. It will have a positive impact on employee morale, increase the speed with which tasks can be completed, and decrease the number of errors that are made. The major ease-of-use considerations involve the operating system, the keyboard, and the display screen.

- *Operating system*—a well-designed operating system, through its use of prompts that guide the user, makes it easier to perform functions such as loading programs, creating files and sorting data. It also anticipates many of the errors that a user is likely to make and provides error messages and relatively simple means of making corrections.

   Graphics-based operating systems, which involve the use of a mouse and pictorial representations on the display screen, are replacing keyboard-only command systems as the new standard.

- *Keyboard*—easier to use if they have a numeric keypad, are detachable from the CPU, and have an extensive number of function keys. Placement of the various keys (especially the return and cursor keys) is also important, as is an adjustable-angle keyboard.

- *Display screen*—the ease of use of a display screen depends on the resolution of the screen and the choice of foreground and background colors.

High-resolution monitors project very clear images that can approximate the detail typical of photographs and are especially desirable in graphics applications.

Black lettering on a white background, such as was available on the Apple Macintosh SE and Classic, is gaining in popularity because it more closely approximates the typical black-on-white lettering of the printed page. However, some prefer white on black, which was available on the IBM monochrome monitor, or amber on black, which is available from Zenith and other manufacturers. Green on black has generally lost popularity.

Using other colors tend to be harder on the eyes, especially at lower resolutions. Certain high-resolution RGB (red-green-blue) color monitors overcome this problem by offering a much crisper image.

## 6.4 USER NEEDS AND HARDWARE EVALUATION

### (a) NEEDS ANALYSIS

You should make sure that the benefits you expect to accrue from a microcomputer system justify the time, effort, and cost associated with acquiring and implementing it. The starting point in making such a determination is to analyze your needs as a user.

You should evaluate each potential application in terms of the types of functions involved, the volume of those functions, and the steps involved in performing each function. Such an evaluation will enable you to identify what can be done more quickly and accurately with the aid of a computer, the amount of work that your computer must be able to accomplish within specified time periods, and the storage capability that your computer must have.

*(i) Software Needs*

Suitable applications software is the most important component in your computer system purchase decision and should therefore be one of the first needs you identify. If you do not have the applications software to perform the desired functions, having the ideal microcomputer system in every other respect will be of little consolation.

Keep in mind, however, that your hardware and systems software needs are inter-related with your applications software needs. Most applications software explicitly states its operating requirements.

The major types of applications software are dealt with in separate chapters of this handbook. However, you should be aware that unless you resort to developing custom-made applications software to meet your particular needs—a far more expensive and time-consuming alternative requiring programming tools and system design expertise—no software package will meet all of your needs exactly. Your goal should be to select software that provides you with whatever combination of cost, needs satisfaction, and timeliness of implementation you find most agreeable.

### (ii) Hardware Needs

Your hardware needs should be assessed relative to the various attributes set out earlier in this chapter: quality, reliability, speed, capacity, expandability, compatibility, and ease of use. Software needs, as previously discussed, are a related concern. As part of your needs analysis, you should prioritize each of these attributes or categorize them along the lines of "musts" vs. "wants." This will help you to match your needs with the available hardware and to make a wise purchase within your price range.

It is important that you be as specific as possible when identifying your hardware requirements. The more specific your requirements, the fewer alternatives there will be that can suit those requirements and the easier it will be to arrive at appropriate hardware choices. Even so, it is still very probable that you will not be able to meet your optimum hardware requirements at the price that you are willing to pay, and you may well have to compromise to some extent: for example, you may decide that you can accept another processor with 8 instead of 16 megabytes of primary memory, or a 90 MHz clock speed instead of 133 MHz.

### (iii) Other Needs

When attempting to pinpoint your computer needs, you should involve the ultimate users of your microcomputer system. After all, the system is going to have to be implemented, and it is those users who will be implementing it.

Specifically, involving users at an early stage will have two benefits:

- It is likely that they will be able to assist you in specifying exactly what your soft-ware and hardware needs are.
- Users are much less likely to resist change in their working environment—which is what the presence of a computer system will represent—if they are consulted dur-ing the planning stages.

## (b) WHERE TO BUY

Once you've identified your needs and decided more or less what to buy, you will need to decide where to buy it. Computer vendors vary widely in terms of reliability, service, and knowledge. These factors should not be underestimated, since you will likely need some help when it comes to maintaining and/or expanding your system. You should therefore ensure that your vendor:

- Is financially stable (this is most often evidenced by the vendor having been in business for a number of years).
- Has a good service and repair department and is able to provide replacement equipment should your system break down.
- Has training facilities and/or the ability to offer training at your site.
- Has a reputation for standing behind its products.

Good recommendations from other customers are one of the best indications of a vendor's suitability.

## (c)  A BUYING PROCESS SUMMARY

To summarize, your overriding objectives should be to choose the right combination of hardware and software, to avoid buying too much or too little computer, and to buy within your price range. The following summarizes the steps you should take to achieve those objectives:

- Identify your needs in general terms, including the price you can afford.
- Choose appropriate applications software packages (or candidates) to satisfy those needs.
- Specify hardware configuration requirements based on the above needs.
- Evaluate the various hardware attributes identified earlier (quality and reliability, speed, etc.), distinguishing between "musts" and "wants."
- Select an appropriate vendor and make the purchase.

## (d)  OTHER SOURCES OF INFORMATION

The two major additional sources of information are:

- Computer books and magazines (a list of the major ones appears in Appendix A of this handbook).
- The microcomputer manufacturers and vendors (a directory of information technology companies also appears in Appendix B).

Other possible sources include computer or management consultants and public accountants.

# CHAPTER 7

# Peripherals

A peripheral is any hardware device, other than the central processing unit or CPU, that is used with a computer. Peripherals include display screens, secondary storage devices, printers, plotters, scanners, and modems. This chapter describes each type of peripheral, as well as some factors to consider when assessing each device. Two factors that are not discussed are quality and cost, since these apply equally to all equipment. Obviously, any purchase decision entails trade-offs among needs, features, cost, and risk. The purchase of quality brands from reputable dealers generally yields the lowest risk, although the cost may be higher.

The following material consists of:

- A checklist (Section 7.1), summarizing many of the main points in this chapter.
- A brief treatment of the management, user, and market issues surrounding peripherals (Section 7.2).
- Several sections on the features and applications of each category of peripherals (Sections 7.3 to 7.6). Some of this is fairly basic background or training material that experienced users may wish to skip.
- A discussion of the user needs assessment and hardware selection process (Section 7.7).

## 7.1 PERIPHERALS CHECKLIST

The following checklist is designed to assist accountants in decision-making and management relating to peripherals, in their organizations and those of their clients. Generally, all "No" answers require investigation and follow-up, the results of which should be documented. Where there is such additional documentation, the purpose of the "Ref" column is to cross-reference the checklist to the appropriate working paper (or to the notes on the reverse).

The checklist is intended for general use only. If peripherals are of especially vital concern to an organization, the advice of a specialist should be sought.

**Peripherals Checklist**

|  | Yes | No | N/A | Ref |
|---|---|---|---|---|

**1. Management Issues—Acquisition**

a. Have an appropriate process, timetable, and budget been established for the assessment of user needs, the evaluation of available peripherals, purchase, training, and implementation?

b. Has the participation of the ultimate users of the peripheral(s) been ensured throughout the process?

c. Have the major user needs been identified—such as required quality, speed, availability of support, and so on—and has a preliminary identification been made of those peripherals that may meet this criteria?

d. For each peripheral that might be purchased, have the following issues been addressed?
   - Compatibility with microcomputers
   - Compatibility with other hardware
   - Compatibility with applications software
   - Compatibility with existing or preferred networks
   - Compatibility with possible future upgrades of above
   - Adequacy of peripheral capacity
   - Manufacturer and/or vendor warranties
   - Availability of manufacturer and/or vendor support
   - Adequacy of documentation and manuals
   - Availability of skilled operating personnel

e. Has the peripheral been user-tested for overall ease and appropriateness of use?

f. Are peripheral security features adequate?

g. Is the peripheral price (taking into account the required number of machines, training costs, etc.):
   - Competitive with other comparable hardware?
   - Within budget?

h. Once a peripheral is decided upon, have the related purchase documents (sales agreements, etc.) been reviewed, by legal counsel if appropriate?

| | Yes | No | N/A | Ref |
|---|---|---|---|---|

**2. Management Issues—Implementation and Use**

a. Have all appropriate applications for the peripheral been identified to ensure that maximum use and value are obtained from the peripheral investment? ☐ ☐ ☐ ___

b. Have appropriate policies, procedures, standards, and controls been put in place with respect to:

- Peripheral documentation? ☐ ☐ ☐ ___
- Peripheral security? ☐ ☐ ☐ ___
- Data backups, including off-site backups? ☐ ☐ ☐ ___
- Are appropriate mechanisms in place to ensure that the peripheral(s) are properly maintained and that repair service is available when needed (e.g., through signing of a maintenance contract)? ☐ ☐ ☐ ___
- Has the reasonableness of maintenance costs been established (e.g., through competitive bids)? ☐ ☐ ☐ ___

**3. User Issues**

a. Are users adequately trained in the basic use of the peripheral(s), including refresher or update courses when required? ☐ ☐ ☐ ___

b. Where appropriate, are users adequately trained in the advanced features of the peripheral(s)? ☐ ☐ ☐ ___

c. Both in theory and in practice, are users aware of the importance and necessity of peripheral security? ☐ ☐ ☐ ___

## 7.2  MANAGEMENT, USER, AND MARKET ISSUES

### (a)  MANAGEMENT AND USER ISSUES

Most managers have become users of peripherals themselves, and to that extent manager and user concerns have overlapped. However, from a purely management perspective, the main issues are:

- Making purchase, upgrade, and standardization decisions (these will be based on an analysis of user needs, the available peripherals and features, available budgets, etc.).
- Ensuring policies and procedures are in place to optimize the use of peripherals throughout the organization, including:

    Identifying appropriate applications for the peripherals

    Hiring and training of staff

    Standardization

    Integration with networks

    Controlling related costs
- Establishing good security.

Your purchase should be based on a proper assessment of your needs. It is impossible to make specific recommendations that cover all users, but the following points should be considered:

- Categorize each feature or attribute as a "must" or "want" or "don't need." This will do much to make sense of the choices available in your price range. Identify your requirements as specifically as possible.
- If price is an important factor, new product introductions should be avoided. Last year's state-of-the-art technology can often be purchased at significantly lower prices and may well be enough to meet your needs.
- Take a balanced approach to buying peripherals. Consider the capabilities of the entire system rather than the features of one particular peripheral device.
- Always consider whether peripherals are compatible with your CPU and with one another.

### (b)  MARKET ISSUES

Because of increasing competition, prices for monitors of all types are on the decline. CRTs are expected to continue to dominate the microcomputer market; the alternatives still must undergo substantial technological improvement before they can present a credible challenge. Monochrome monitors suffice for most applications; however, the cost of color has come down substantially in recent years, making it more of a standard.

Hard disk drives are much more affordable than they used to be. They are also much faster and have much greater storage capacity (1 gigabyte and up is becoming commonplace). CD-ROM also continues to grow in popularity.

By the late 1980s more than $7 billion per year was being spent on printers in the United States alone. Although impact printers outsold nonimpact printers throughout the

1980s, the emergence of the laser printer reversed this situation during the 1990s. Laser printers are now the norm, except in the color market, where ink jet technology is less expensive.

Hayes became a standard in modems in the 1980s, dominating to a greater extent than any other manufacturer did for any other type of peripheral (although Epson also had a very significant share of the dot matrix printer market). However, the trend today (as with the Compaq Presario) is for an internal modem/fax capability to be included with the microcomputer package. External modems from third-party manufacturers will therefore become less common.

Plotters, scanners, and expansion cards are still rather specialized peripherals, appealing generally to the more sophisticated users of micros. Plotters are being supplanted by color ink jet and laser printers. Scanning technology is becoming a subset of fax technology—for example, combine a fax machine with a micro that includes a built-in capability to receive faxes, and you have a scanner.

## 7.3 SECONDARY STORAGE DEVICES

Secondary storage devices enable information to be filed away electronically for later retrieval and use. They are an essential part of a computer system, and some form of secondary storage is included with the purchase of almost all systems.

### (a) TYPES OF SECONDARY STORAGE DEVICES

The two most popular types of storage devices are floppy disk drives and hard disk drives.

#### (i) Floppy Disk and Diskette Drives

Floppy disks, so named because they are made of flexible plastic, are a common storage media for peripherals. Programs and data are magnetically recorded on them along concentric tracks. Floppy disk drives are used to rotate the disks at high speed while a read/write head directly accesses data or programs that are stored thereon. Such disks generally store between 360 kilobytes and 1.25 megabytes of information—more if data is compressed.

Floppy disks come in three sizes: $3\frac{1}{2}$-inch, $5\frac{1}{4}$-inch and 8-inch. For microcomputer use, the $5\frac{1}{4}$-inch disks were originally the most popular and were often referred to as floppy diskettes. By the late 1980s, however, the $3\frac{1}{2}$-inch format began to emerge as the new standard. These are normally referred to as simply diskettes or micro diskettes, since they are encased in a rigid plastic and do not really look floppy.

Floppy disk drives usually come with the computer system and are rarely purchased separately.

#### (ii) Hard Disk Drives

Hard disks—sometimes referred to as Winchester disks or fixed disks—fulfill the same function as floppy disks but have much greater storage capacity, much faster access time, and a correspondingly higher price. They are made of rigid rather than flexible plastic, and several platters are typically stacked together one on top of the other. In the 1980s these disks typically stored 20, 40, or 80 megabytes of information at the lower end of the market, and over 100 megabytes at the higher end. By the mid-1990s, several hundred megabytes had become standard, and 1 to 2 gigabytes (billions of bytes) had become increasingly common.

Currently there are several dozen companies manufacturing disk drives, including Quantum, Seagate, and Western Digital. Prices generally range from $500 to $2,000.

Because the volume of data stored on them is great, hard disk drive crashes are a particular danger that should be guarded against. Crashes can occur for a number of reasons: for example, a power failure during use or a hard physical jolt. It is advisable to back up the hard disk data, which can be done in several ways. For hard disk drives with limited stored data, using diskettes as backup is feasible but still cumbersome. For hard disks with a large amount of stored data, removable disk drives are sometimes used that allow users to store a backup in another location. Using a cartridge tape backup system is another possibility.

As higher-capacity hard disk systems become available, the implications of a crash will become more serious. In this environment the practice of backing up a hard disk drive will have to become much more than an afterthought.

*(iii)  Other Secondary Storage Devices*

Disk is still the dominant storage media. The two other available media are:

- Tape, which is most often used as a backup system for disk.
- CD-ROM, a relatively more recent technology that has become increasingly popular, especially as a storage medium for large databases and/or multimedia files (CD-ROM is dealt with very briefly in Chapter 5, "Historical Chronology and Future Directions").

## (b)  ASSESSING SECONDARY STORAGE DEVICES

The important factors to consider when assessing secondary storage devices (and in particular disk storage devices) are set out below.

*(i)  Capacity*

The capacity of a disk is determined by disk or platter size, data density, whether one or both sides are used, and the number of tracks on each side of the disk.

**Platter Size**

As previously noted, disks come in diameters of $3\frac{1}{2}$, $5\frac{1}{4}$ and 8 inches. Generally speaking, larger disk diameters allow for greater capacity.

**Data Density**

Data density refers to how tightly data is packed on the disk tracks. Disks are typically referred to as being single density, double density, or quad density.

### Number of Sides

Some disks are manufactured and processed for use on only one side, others for both sides. Obviously, a double-sided disk has twice the capacity of a single-sided one.

### Number of Tracks

The number of tracks on each side of the disk also influences its capacity. Typically, the number of tracks ranges from 40 to 80 on each side.

Finally, the capacity of hard disks is affected by the number of platters contained in the disk pack. The greater the number of platters, the greater the capacity.

### (ii) Speed

Regardless of the type of storage media used, the key measure of the speed of a secondary storage device is its access time, the time interval between a request by the CPU for a transfer of data to or from a secondary storage device, and the completion of the operation. In the case of a disk drive, this involves the time it takes the access arm to move to the appropriate track (seek time); the time it takes for the appropriate record to be positioned under the read/write head (rotational delay time); and the time it takes to transmit the data to primary storage (transfer time).

Access time is influenced by the number of read/write heads used by the drive, the number of drives that are on-line, and whether the disk is "soft" or "hard" sectored, as described below.

### Number of Read/Write Heads

The number of read/write heads attached to the access arm(s) of the disk drive directly affects access time. If, for instance, the drive has separate heads for reading/writing to the inside and outside disk tracks, the seek time can drop significantly since the access arms have less distance to move.

Access arms are either fixed access or movable access. A fixed-access arm has a read/write head for each track on every disk surface. Information on the disk is always close to one of the heads, which reduces seek time.

### Number of Drives On-Line

The number of drives that are on-line—or available to the computer while processing— can influence the speed with which data or programs can be brought into primary memory. If two drives are being accessed simultaneously, data and programs can be absorbed by primary memory more quickly than if only one drive were being used (assuming data are properly stored and formatted).

### Soft- and Hard-Sectored Disks

Sectoring divides the disk into manageable pie-shaped pieces. A soft-sectored disk can be sectored by the operating system; a hard-sectored disk is presectored. In general, hard-sectored disks are faster.

Hard-disk access time is generally much faster than that of floppy disks—typically 5 to 20 times faster.

*(iii)  Compatibility*

There are several concerns here. If a disk is hard sectored, you may not be able to use it with certain processors and operating systems. Soft-sectored disks, which can be used with virtually any processor, are becoming more popular because they offer more flexibility.

Another consideration is the number of tracks on each side of the disk. For instance, drives designed to read 40-track disks would not be able to read 80-track disks.

Finally, the other hardware and software, in particular the operating system, must be able to address the total storage capacity of the disk.

# 7.4  DISPLAY SCREENS

A display screen, also referred to as a video display or monitor (although the latter is actually a specialized form of display screen), allows the user to interact with the computer system and to visualize what his/her printed output will look like. It also makes it possible to benefit from the directions and prompts provided by computer software.

Display screens are either detachable or attached to the processor. Most often they are purchased as part of a complete system. When bought separately, their cost typically ranges from $200 to $2,000; some top-of-the-line models can run even higher.

Choosing a display screen is usually simpler than choosing other peripherals, since there are fewer factors to consider and relatively fewer choices available. Nevertheless, it is important to choose a display screen carefully.

## (a)  TYPES OF DISPLAY SCREENS

The most common types of display screens are monochrome and color, also known as CRTs (cathode ray tubes). Each of these types is described below.

*(i)  Monochrome Monitors*

Monochrome monitors display images in one color—usually amber, green, or white—and were the most common type of display screen through the mid-1980s. They generally provide very good resolution for text and adequate resolution for graphics (other hardware permitting).

Nevertheless, both monochrome and color monitors have some disadvantages: high electrical requirements, small amounts of radiation emission, cumbersome size and weight, and, possibly, a distracting glare.

*(ii)  Color Monitors*

Color monitors operate much like monochrome units except that, as their name implies, they produce more than a single color. They are typically classified as either composite or RGB (red-green-blue, the three primary colors).

Composite color monitors use one video signal to generate an image that combines the three primary colors. This tends to dilute the image and make it less crisp, although high-quality composite monitors are available.

RGB color monitors use three separate video signals—one for each primary color—to generate a picture. They therefore generally produce crisper images.

*(iii)  Other Display Screens*

Other types of display screens include liquid crystal displays (LCDs), electroluminescent displays, and plasma displays. These types of displays are most often attached to the central processor (typically a portable microcomputer or laptop) and are rarely purchased separately.

LCDs use liquid crystal molecules and positive and negative electrical charges to form characters on the screen. They overcome some of the disadvantages of CRTs in that they do not emit radiation, do not have high electrical requirements and are more portable. However, LCDs typically suffer from poor resolution and a small screen size. They are also angle-dependent, meaning that the user must generally look at them straight-on to be seen.

Electroluminescent displays operate much like LCDs except that they have a higher resolution and are back-lit so that they can be easily seen in the dark. The popularity of these screens has in the past been inhibited by their price. However, those prices, particularly for screens used with laptop portable peripherals, have been declining steadily of late.

Plasma display screens use an ionized gas—typically neon gas—to form characters. The use of gas instead of liquid speeds up response time and improves resolution. Plasma screens are also less angle-dependent.

## (b)  DEPENDENCE ON OTHER HARDWARE AND SOFTWARE

It should be noted that the capabilities of a display screen cannot be considered in isolation from the software and other hardware components in a computer system.

*(i)  Hardware*

The maximum resolution of a display screen can only be taken advantage of if the computer itself is capable of addressing it. For example, some high-resolution monitors can produce one million or more pixels. Some machines may be unable to generate resolutions this high, or may require the addition of special graphic adapter cards. (In fact, some older computers required cards just to produce any kind of nontext images on a video display, even if the display itself was designed for graphics.)

*(ii)  Software*

Video displays, like printers and other peripherals, require specific kinds of instructions from the computer in order to function. The software that provides these instructions is referred to as a device driver.

It is important to ensure that the applications software (e.g., the desktop publishing or graphics package) has the appropriate device driver to take advantage of a display screen's capabilities and/or those of any graphic adapter cards added to enhance the system.

## (c)  ASSESSING DISPLAY SCREENS

The more important factors to consider when assessing display screens are set out below.

*(i)  Resolution*

Resolution refers to the number of dots or pixels (picture elements) that the display screen can generate to form images. The more pixels within a given area, the higher the resolution. Resolution varies widely from monitor to monitor, and is expressed as *a x b*. The first figure *a* refers to the number of pixels horizontally across the screen, the second figure *b* to the number of pixels vertically down the screen. For the higher end monitors, both *a* and *b* can be greater than 1,000, providing very fine resolutions for both text and graphics.

*(ii)  Readability*

The overall readability of a display screen is a function of its resolution, as enhanced by:

- The display controls, which allow the user to adjust the color hue and brightness.
- The tilt and/or swivel features of the screen, which allow the user to position the screen according to preference.

(Before the emergence of color as a standard, another comfort factor—largely a personal preference—was the color chosen for a monochrome monitor. Amber, green, and white were the most common colors, although green generally lost popularity in later years.)

*(iii)  Other Factors*

Two other factors to consider when assessing a display screen are its size and capacity.

The size of a display screen refers to the physical area of the screen's surface. It is often measured diagonally in inches (e.g., a 15-inch or 17-inch monitor). The size of a screen is less important than its resolution, but the two are related. The same resolution on a smaller screen actually appears sharper because the pixels are condensed into a smaller area. Obviously, however, the image is larger on a bigger screen.

The capacity of a display screen is measured by the number of characters and lines that can appear on it. In the early years of microcomputers, this factor was especially important if you were using a large spreadsheet application package and wanted to view as much of it as possible. The most common screen size displayed up to 25 lines of 80 characters each. Other common sizes were 32 by 80 and 25 by 132. Nowadays, software and hardware combine to enable users to manipulate these sizes much more easily.

## 7.5  PRINTERS, PLOTTERS, AND SCANNERS

Printers enable users to obtain hard copy output of their work and are a vital part of any computer system. Often purchased separately, they are also the peripheral that offers the widest range of choice to the buyer.

### (a)  TYPES OF PRINTERS

Printers can be classified in several ways. First, a distinction can be made between impact and nonimpact printers. With impact printers, type elements apply an inked ribbon against the paper to generate printed output. With nonimpact printers, printing takes place without any mechanical contact with the paper. Nonimpact laser printers dominate the market.

Printers can also be categorized as serial, line, or page printers. Serial printers print one character at a time. Line printers, as their name implies, print a whole line at a time, while a page printer can print a complete page at a time.

The main printer classifications used for purposes of this chapter are daisy wheel, dot matrix, ink jet, and laser. The first two are actually subcategories of impact printers, which are falling out of use (daisy-wheel printers are all but obsolete); the latter two are nonimpact. A fifth category of printer is the thermal printer, which "burns" characters onto specially treated paper. However, these printers are relatively uncommon.

### (i) Daisy Wheel Printers

Daisy wheel printers and mechanically similar "golf ball" printers use a print element to produce letter quality output. Daisy wheel printers, by far the most popular letter-quality printer in the late 1970s and early 1980s, contain a flat, spoked wheel that has characters positioned around the outer edge of the spokes. The wheel rotates to the appropriate character, which is then struck against the paper, through an inked ribbon, by a metal hammer.

Golf ball printers, which use a spherical print element that rotates to the appropriate position, similarly strike an inked ribbon against a paper.

With both daisy wheel and golf ball printers you can utilize different fonts (Courier, Prestige Elite, italics, etc.), simply by changing the wheel or the golf ball element.

### (ii) Dot Matrix Printers

Dot matrix printers form each character with a pattern of dots. The dots are arranged in a matrix of rows and columns and are applied to the paper by a printhead that contains a needle for each dot in the matrix. The needles strike the ribbon against the paper in a pattern that corresponds to the particular letter or character.

One early standard dot matrix printhead size contained nine needles or pins. While such a matrix of print needles is capable of producing legible print, it does not represent letter quality since the blank spaces between the dots that form the characters tend to diminish the clarity of the print. However, dot matrix printers with a greater number of dots per matrix later became standard (e.g., 24-pin machines), providing greatly enhanced print quality.

In other respects, dot matrix printers are superior to daisy-wheel printers. Their graphics capabilities are far better; they are also faster and can print in various type sizes and fonts.

### (iii) Ink Jet Printers

Until the advent of laser printers, ink-jet printers were the most common type of nonimpact printer. They are similar to dot matrix printers in that they produce hard copy with dots of ink; they are different in that they "squirt" the ink from a nozzle onto the paper.

A distinctive feature of ink jet printers is that they can produce multicolor output.

### (iv)  Laser Printers

Laser printers produce hard copy in much the same way as a photocopier, except that a laser beam is used to expose the text or graphics image. These printers are extremely fast and produce excellent print and graphics.

In 1985 Apple helped pioneer the field of desktop publishing (for which laser printers were especially well suited) by introducing the LaserWriter, which had outstanding text and graphics capabilities.

Nowadays, laser printers dominate the market, and many are available for well under $1,000.

## (b)  ASSESSING PRINTERS

The main factors to consider when choosing a printer are set out below.

### (i)  Quality of Print

Although daisy wheel printers are relatively slow and noisy, their ability to produce letter-quality output made them the preferred choice of many users for years. However, with advances in dot matrix technology and the arrival of high-resolution laser printers, the print quality of daisy wheel printers was no longer superior.

Ultimately, the decision comes down to a simple inspection of a printer's sample output.

### (ii)  Speed

While printer speed varies widely, the following observations can be made:

- Nonimpact printers are typically faster than impact printers by a wide margin. For example, nonimpact laser printers can usually print up to eight pages per minute as opposed to less than a page per minute for fast daisy-wheel printers.
- Dot matrix printers are generally faster (60-220 characters per second) than letter quality printers (20-60 characters per second), but not as fast as lasers.

### (iii)  Compatibility

Although printers are normally an interchangeable hardware component, the applications software must have a device driver that can issue instructions to the specific printer model being used. Be sure that the software has the correct driver; otherwise you will not be able to use it with your printer.

### (iv)  Other Factors

Other factors to consider when assessing a printer include the following:

**Capacity**

Capacity refers to carriage width. The carriage width you choose almost certainly must be nine or more inches in order to accommodate the standard 8 1/2-inch paper. In practice, wider carriages of 14 to 15 inches are far more common.

**Noise**

The sometimes considerable noise of a printer is often a problem if it is close to other people or if the user is working at the computer while printing is taking place.

Without exception, the much quieter nonimpact printers are preferable if noise is a consideration.

## (c) PLOTTERS

Plotters are specialized printing devices, but whereas the emphasis with most printers is on text output, the emphasis with plotters is on high-resolution graphics. Most printers can print graphics; however, at least until recently plotters provided superior resolution at a comparable or lower price. Plotters therefore tended to be the device of choice for users who required sophisticated, high-quality graphics.

Essentially, a plotter produces its output using pens that are attached to a horizontal carriage. There are three types of plotters:

- Flatbed plotters, which produce graphics on a stationary sheet of paper by moving the pens in various directions.
- Drum plotters, on which the pens move horizontally only (vertical points are plotted by moving the paper vertically).
- Hybrid plotters—by far the most popular—which combine the features of both flatbed and drum plotters.

Be sure that the plotter will run with your microcomputer. Plotters are significantly less flexible than printers in terms of the micro matching. You should also ensure that your graphics software can be used with the plotter.

## (d) SCANNERS

There are scanners that can eliminate the need to keystroke text into a computer or to cut and paste pictures or photographs for inclusion in a document or report. Historically, there were two types of scanners—optical character recognition (OCR) scanners and image scanners (also referred to as graphics digitizers), although nowadays the trend is towards one type of scanner, with separate software handling the OCR function.

### (i) OCR Scanners

OCR scanners make it possible to enter a wide variety of typed material directly into a computer system. The scanner identifies characters through light-sensitive devices and then converts the input into computer format.

*(ii) Image Scanners*

Image scanners, as their name implies, scan an image or object and translate it into computer-readable digital codes. This enables the user to manipulate and reproduce the image later.

The benefits of scanners are obvious. An OCR scanner can accomplish in minutes what might take a typist hours. It also makes fewer mistakes than most typists; and, as previously noted, pictures and graphs appearing in other source documents can easily be reproduced.

Many companies produce scanners, including Canon and Hewlett-Packard. Despite their substantial benefits, OCR and image scanners have yet to enjoy mass appeal, probably because of their high cost. However, the price of these devices is coming down (many are now available for less than $1,000), so they will very likely gain in popularity.

## 7.6 MODEMS

Computer modems make it possible to transmit data from one computer to another over a telephone line. With the aid of specialized communications software, modems enable you to transfer files, send and receive messages, and access on-line information databases.

As further described in Chapter 11, "Telecommunications," the need for modems arises from the fact that telephone lines (at least historically) have been designed to transmit analog signals, whereas data is transmitted by digital signals. A modem translates digital signals into analog signals at the sending end, and analog signals into digital signals at the receiving end. Because of this, a modem is required at both ends of the communication link.

There are various types of modems, generally priced between $100 to $1,000, although very sophisticated models can cost more.

### (a) TYPES OF MODEMS

Modems can be external (standalone) or internal (board unit).

*(i) External Modems*

External or standalone modems are detached from the computers or computer terminals they serve. They are of two major types: acoustic couplers and direct-connect modems.

**Acoustic Couplers**

Acoustic couplers, seen very rarely these days, make use of the familiar telephone headset. To establish a connection, the user simply dials a specified telephone number, listens for a high-pitched sound, and places the headset into a cradle. The coupler then converts the digital signals of the sender into analog form, which allows the data to be transmitted to the receiving end, where the analog signals are reconverted to digital form for further processing.

**Direct-Connect Modems**

Direct-connect modems do not require a telephone headset; rather, they are plugged directly into a telephone wall outlet and the computer itself. Mainly because of their faster data transmission time and comparable price, direct-connect modems have replaced acoustic couplers.

*(ii) Internal Modems*

Internal or board-unit modems are built onto plug-in boards, which are then inserted into an expansion slot inside the computer itself. Board unit modems typically cost less than standalone modems and take up less space; however, they have two disadvantages that have limited their popularity:

- They are computer-specific, meaning they can only be used with a specific type of microcomputer.
- They use up one of a limited number of expansion slots, thereby reducing the number of other peripherals that can be added to the system later.

## (b)  DEPENDENCE ON COMMUNICATIONS SOFTWARE

Like other hardware devices, modems require software—in this case, communications software. The nature and variety of the features associated with a modem depend largely upon the communications software that it uses. Communications software is typically bought when the modem is purchased. In some cases it is included in the price.

Among other things, communications software allows the user to:

- Access a microcomputer from a remote location.
- Access electronic mail services and computer bulletin boards.
- Access information databases such as America Online or  CompuServe.
- Communicate with a mainframe or minicomputer.

## (c)  DATA TRANSMISSION CHARACTERISTICS

Some important data transmission characteristics are described below. These will affect the type of modem required and/or the modem settings to be used.

*(i) Parallel/Serial Bit Transmission*

In parallel transmission all bits of information are transmitted at once using a separate channel for each bit. Conversely, if the bits are transmitted serially, they are sent one at time through a single channel.

Parallel transmission is much faster than serial. But because the communications lines for parallel are much more expensive than those for serial, serial transmission modems are used for long-distance data communication, whereas parallel transmission modems are often used over short distances when there is a need to communicate at high speeds, such as with secondary storage devices.

*(ii) Synchronous/Asynchronous Transmission*

The term *synchronization* relates to the serial transmission of data. With asynchronous transmission, data are transmitted unevenly or in spurts, like the manual keying in of data from a keyboard. Conversely, synchronous transmission of data takes place at a continuous pace, such as when data is read into a CPU from a storage device.

The method of synchronization used is important because it determines the efficiency and, ultimately, the cost of data transmission. Synchronous transmission is more efficient but also more expensive.

*(iii) Transmission Modes*

There are three transmission modes available with modems: simplex, half duplex, and full duplex. Simplex transmission allows communication in one direction only; half duplex transmission allows for two-way communication, but only in one direction at a time; and full duplex transmission permits communication in both directions simultaneously.

*(iv) Error-Checking Protocols*

When data are transmitted within a communications network, transmission errors are inevitable because of interference from weather or other sources. In fact, the higher the transmission speed of a modem, the greater the chance of transmission error.

In order to ensure the reliability of data transmission, various controls are built into communications software that can identify errors and retransmit data if required. These controls essentially add bits to each character or character-block at the originating end, which are then checked and verified at the receiving end.

## (d) ASSESSING MODEMS

The more important factors to consider when choosing a modem are set out below.

*(i) Speed*

The speed of a modem is expressed in "bps," a measure of the number of bits that are transmitted per second. For a communications link to work, the bps rates of the modems at both ends of the link must be the same. Most modems permit data transmission at speeds of at least 9,600 bps to 14,400 bps; 28,800 bps is becoming increasingly common.

*(ii) Compatibility*

Nowadays, compatibility is usually transparent from the user's point of view. Historically, however, there were three compatibility issues to be considered, as set out below.

- *Are the originating and receiving modems compatible with each other?*
  Modems must be technically compatible in terms of their frequency, phase, and amplitude; they must also be capable of transmitting data at the same speed.
- *Are the modems compatible with the computer?*
  Modems must be compatible with your computer. Normally, the modem indicates which system or systems it is designed to work with. In addition, any modem that must be plugged into a computer requires a compatible serial port.

- *Is the communications software compatible with the modem being used and the operating system of the computer?*

This must be the case for the software to work.

*(iii) Special Features*

Modems have a wide range of features that have become standard on nearly all models nowadays. Among these are:

- Auto dial (the ability to dial a telephone number without a telephone)
- Auto answer (the ability to respond to an incoming call without a telephone)
- Call progress reporting
- Variable transmission speeds (discussed earlier)

## 7.7  USER NEEDS AND HARDWARE EVALUATION

### (a)  NEEDS ANALYSIS

You should make sure that the benefits you expect to accrue from a peripheral justify the time, effort, and cost associated with acquiring and bringing it on-line. The starting point in making such a determination is to analyze your needs as a user.

When evaluating your peripheral needs, each potential application should be analyzed in terms of the types of functions involved, the volume of those functions, and the steps involved in performing each function. Such an evaluation will enable you to identify what can be done more quickly and efficiently with the aid of the peripheral.

Your hardware needs should be assessed relative to the various attributes set out earlier in this chapter: quality and reliability, speed, capacity, expandability, compatibility, and ease of use. Software needs, as previously discussed, are a related concern. As part of your needs analysis, you should evaluate each of these attributes or categorize them along the lines of "musts" versus "wants." This will help you to match your needs with the available hardware and to make the best purchase within your price range.

It is important that you be as specific as possible when identifying your hardware requirements. The more specific your requirements, the easier it will be to arrive at appropriate hardware choices. Even so, it is still very probable that you will not be able to meet your optimum hardware requirements at the price that you are willing to pay, and you may well have to compromise.

When attempting to ascertain specifically what your peripheral needs are, it is important to involve the ultimate users of the peripheral. After all, those are the users who will be implementing it.

Specifically, involving users at an early stage will have two benefits:

- It is likely that they will be able to assist you in specifying exactly what your needs are.
- If they are consulted during the planning stages, users are much less likely to resist change in their working environment, which is what the presence of new equipment will represent.

## (b)  WHERE TO BUY

Once you've identified your needs and decided more or less what to buy, you will need to decide where to buy it. Note that peripheral vendors vary widely in reliability, service, and knowledge, since you will likely need some help when it comes to maintaining and/or expanding your system. You should therefore ensure that your vendor:

- Is stable from a business and financial standpoint (this is most often evidenced by the vendor having been in business for a number of years).
- Has a good service and repair department and is able to provide replacement equipment should your peripheral break down.
- Has training facilities and/or the ability to offer training at your site.
- Has a reputation for standing behind its products.

Good recommendations from other customers are one of the best indications of a vendor's suitability.

## (c)  SUMMARY AND OTHER SOURCES OF INFORMATION

To summarize:

- Identify your needs in general terms, including the price you can afford.
- Prioritize the various hardware attributes identified earlier (quality and reliability, speed, etc.), distinguishing between "musts" and "wants."
- Select an appropriate vendor and make the purchase.

The two major additional sources of information are:

- Computer books and magazines (a list of the major ones appears in Appendix A of this handbook).
- The microcomputer manufacturers and vendors (a directory of information technology companies also appears in Appendix B).

Other possible sources include computer or management consultants and public accountants.

# CHAPTER 8

# Word Processing and Desktop Publishing

Two of the most common and useful office applications of information technology are word processing and desktop publishing. Although the line between the two has become somewhat blurred in recent years—as more powerful hardware capacity has allowed many of the popular word processing packages to incorporate desktop publishing features—the distinction still exists, at least from the point of desktop publishing users.

The following material consists of:

- A checklist (Section 8.1), summarizing many of the main points in this chapter.
- A brief treatment of the management, user, and market issues surrounding word processing and desktop publishing (Section 8.2).
- Sections on the features and applications of word processing (Section 8.3) and desktop publishing (Section 8.4) (this is fairly basic background or training material that experienced users may wish to skip).
- A discussion of the user needs assessment and software selection process (Section 8.5).
- A catalog of selected word processing and desktop publishing software, including current version numbers and list prices (Section 8.6).

## 8.1 WORD PROCESSING AND DESKTOP PUBLISHING CHECKLIST

The following two-page checklist is designed to assist accountants in decision-making and management relating to word processing and desktop publishing software, in their organizations and those of their clients. Generally, all "No" answers require investigation and follow-up, the results of which should be documented. Where there is such additional documentation, the purpose of the "Ref" column is to cross-reference the checklist to the appropriate working paper (or to the notes on the reverse).

The checklist is intended for general use only. If word processing and desktop publishing are of especially vital concern to an organization, the advice of a specialist should be sought.

## Word Processing and Desktop Publishing Checklist

|  | Yes | No | N/A | Ref |
|---|---|---|---|---|
| **1. Management Issues—Acquisition** | | | | |

a. Have an appropriate process, timetable, and budget been established for the assessment of user needs, the evaluation of available packages, purchase, training, and implementation?

| | ☐ | ☐ | ☐ | ___ |

b. Has the participation of the users of the word processing or desktop publishing software been ensured throughout the process?

| | ☐ | ☐ | ☐ | ___ |

c. Have the major user needs been identified—such as the system environment (Mac, OS/2, Windows), size of documents that must be handled, availability of support, and so on—and has a preliminary identification been made of those packages that may meet these criteria?

| | ☐ | ☐ | ☐ | ___ |

d. For each package that might be purchased, have the following issues been addressed?

| | Yes | No | N/A | Ref |
|---|---|---|---|---|
| • Compatibility with hardware and operating systems | ☐ | ☐ | ☐ | ___ |
| • Compatibility with all printers in use | ☐ | ☐ | ☐ | ___ |
| • Compatibility with other software in use | ☐ | ☐ | ☐ | ___ |
| • Compatibility with all networks in use | ☐ | ☐ | ☐ | ___ |
| • Compatibility with possible future upgrades of above | ☐ | ☐ | ☐ | ___ |
| • Adequacy of RAM and hard disk capacity | ☐ | ☐ | ☐ | ___ |
| • Availability of manufacturer and/or vendor support | ☐ | ☐ | ☐ | ___ |
| • Adequacy of documentation and manuals | ☐ | ☐ | ☐ | ___ |
| • Availability of skilled operating personnel | ☐ | ☐ | ☐ | ___ |
| • Availability of training (self-study, seminars, etc.) | ☐ | ☐ | ☐ | ___ |
| • Ability to handle required size of documents | ☐ | ☐ | ☐ | ___ |

e. Has the software been user-tested for appropriateness and ease of use?

| | ☐ | ☐ | ☐ | ___ |

f. Is the software price (taking into account the required number of copies and/or site licenses, training costs, etc.):

| | Yes | No | N/A | Ref |
|---|---|---|---|---|
| • Competitive with other comparable packages? | ☐ | ☐ | ☐ | ___ |
| • Within budget? | ☐ | ☐ | ☐ | ___ |

g. Once a package is decided upon, have the related purchase documents (sales agreements, site licenses, etc.) been reviewed, by legal counsel if appropriate?

| | ☐ | ☐ | ☐ | ___ |

|  | Yes | No | N/A | Ref |
|---|:---:|:---:|:---:|:---:|
| **2. Management Issues—Implementation and Use** | | | | |
| a. Have all appropriate applications for the software been identified to ensure that maximum use and value are obtained from the software investment? | ☐ | ☐ | ☐ | __ |
| b. Are appropriate mechanisms in place to ensure that: | | | | |
| • The organization is aware of future software upgrades? | ☐ | ☐ | ☐ | __ |
| • All users have the most current software version? | ☐ | ☐ | ☐ | __ |
| c. Have appropriate policies, procedures, standards, and controls been put in place with respect to: | | | | |
| • The hiring of operators (permanent and temporary)? | ☐ | ☐ | ☐ | __ |
| • Ongoing training of operators, as needed? | ☐ | ☐ | ☐ | __ |
| • Scheduling of operators (overnight turnaround, etc.)? | ☐ | ☐ | ☐ | __ |
| • Requisitioning and prioritization of operator time? | ☐ | ☐ | ☐ | __ |
| • Document formats and/or templates? | ☐ | ☐ | ☐ | __ |
| • Quality reviews (for grammar, spelling, style, etc.)? | ☐ | ☐ | ☐ | __ |
| • Costing of specific jobs, for budget or billing purposes? | ☐ | ☐ | ☐ | __ |
| • Follow-up review of high-cost jobs ("Draft 15," etc.)? | ☐ | ☐ | ☐ | __ |
| • Document/file backups, including off-site backups? | ☐ | ☐ | ☐ | __ |
| • Document security, both electronic and physical? | ☐ | ☐ | ☐ | __ |
| • Document destruction, both electronic and physical? | ☐ | ☐ | ☐ | __ |
| **3. User Issues** | | | | |
| a. Are users adequately trained in the basic use of the word processing or desktop publishing software, including refresher or update courses when required? | ☐ | ☐ | ☐ | __ |
| b. Where appropriate, are users adequately trained in the advanced features of the word processing or desktop publishing software (e.g., mail merge)? | ☐ | ☐ | ☐ | __ |
| c. Both in theory and in practice, are users aware of the importance and necessity of: | | | | |
| • Frequently saving documents? | ☐ | ☐ | ☐ | __ |
| • Frequently backing up documents? | ☐ | ☐ | ☐ | __ |
| d. Are users aware of, and in practice do they follow, procedures with respect to: | | | | |
| • Document formats? | ☐ | ☐ | ☐ | __ |
| • Diskette labeling and storage? | ☐ | ☐ | ☐ | __ |
| • Physical security? | ☐ | ☐ | ☐ | __ |
| • Physical destruction (hard copy, diskettes, etc.)? | ☐ | ☐ | ☐ | __ |

## 8.2 MANAGEMENT, USER, AND MARKET ISSUES

### (a) MANAGEMENT ISSUES

Most managers have become users of word processing software themselves, and to that extent manager and user concerns have overlapped. However, from a purely management perspective, the main issues are as follows:

- Making purchase, upgrade, and standardization decisions—this will be based on an analysis of user needs, the available software packages and features, available budgets, etc.
- Ensuring policies and procedures are in place to optimize the use of word processing and desktop publishing software throughout the organization—this includes

  Identifying appropriate applications for the software

  Hiring and training of staff

  Standardization (e.g., on document formats, diskette labeling, and storage procedures, etc.)

  Integration with networks

  Ensuring the smooth operation of word processing departments or pools

  Controlling related costs
- Establishing good security, backup, and record destruction controls—this applies to both hard copy and electronic media.

For many businesses, the availability of skilled temporary help is important. Most of the major packages are supported in this regard, but you may want to check with your employment agency before adopting a piece of software as your office's standard.

Finally, it is worth remembering that the primary benefit of word processing ought to be improved efficiency—that is, the elimination of the need to retype entire documents in order to correct errors. Too often, however, these benefits are lost when the technology is used as a recurring excuse to go through "one more draft" of a document. Just as some people argue that the photocopier was one of the worst inventions of the century (more and more paper!), a word processor may have become a destructive tool by the time you reach the fifteenth draft of a simple memo.

### (b) USER ISSUES

Users should balance their needs—current as well as future—with their ability to master a word processor. Full-featured programs can end up being no different from simple ones if the user does not learn to exploit the software's power. On the other hand, if a user is experienced or willing to invest some time, he or she can master a full-featured package. Remember that the limitations imposed by a simpler program may prove frustrating.

The simpler and less costly programs are often sufficient for correspondence such as letters and memos, or for shorter reports that have no sophisticated business presentation requirements. For a novice user with little inclination to become involved with a computer beyond word processing, a simpler program should be sufficient.

Full-featured programs are intended for more serious applications, such as preparing manuscripts and legal documents or presenting material requiring differing fonts, styles, layouts, or graphics. Longer documents are easier to manipulate with the additional features offered by the more expensive packages.

The best way to learn word processing is through practice on actual documents. The tutorials provided with many of the popular packages can also assist. Here are some especially important points to note:

- Save your documents to a disk file frequently, say every five to ten minutes or after each page of typing. Writing is a creative process, and lost work can be very difficult to re-create.

- Maintain a current backup of files on a second storage media. Also make sure you have a hard copy printout.

- For longer documents, break down and plan the work by topics, headings, or subject areas. Try to plan the idea or thought that each paragraph will develop. An outline processor, although it takes some getting used to, can be a very useful tool in the planning stages.

For most users, desktop publishing is an extension of word processing, not a replacement for it. Most desktop publishing software packages have relatively limited word processing features; it is more typical that they accept files from popular word processing packages and use them as inputs to the page composition process. At the same time, many of the recent enhancements to popular word processing software have been in desktop-related areas. One example is improved graphics capability (e.g., the drawing of boxes and lines).

## (c) MARKET ISSUES

### (i) Historical Background

The dedicated word processor—an electronic machine that performed only word processing—preceded the microcomputer in acceptance by the business community. From the mid-1970s until the mid-1980s, these machines offered the widest and most sophisticated variety of features. For example, they had customized keyboards with special keys not found on the microcomputer keyboards of the day. In addition, they sometimes offered multistation systems with several input terminals connected to a central processing unit. Most dedicated word processors required specially trained operators. Among the leading manufacturers were AES, IBM, Wang, and Micom.

The proliferation of microcomputers, along with better word processing software, resulted in a shift away from the dedicated machines. The trend started with the introduction of the IBM PC in 1981. WordStar was one of the first successful packages brought to market; it was quickly followed by a number of other packages such as DisplayWrite, WordPerfect, Microsoft Word, and MultiMate.

By the last half of the 1980s, WordPerfect had emerged as the clear market leader in the IBM and compatibles environment, mainly because a number of large corporations standardized on it. Microsoft Word has always been the leading program for the Apple Macintosh, and in the last few years has surpassed WordPerfect in the IBM environment. (As many have noted, the latter environment is today more aptly referred to as the Windows or "Wintel" environment, since it is characterized more by the dominance of Microsoft's Windows and Intel's microprocessors than it is by IBM.)

The emergence of desktop publishing as one of the major applications of microcomputer systems did not occur until the mid-1980s, several years after the arrival of the word processor. Most of the earlier microcomputer systems, including the original IBM PC, had a number of drawbacks that prevented serious desktop publishing work. The limitations of earlier systems included:

- A lack of adequate memory to store desktop publishing programs and files, which are typically very memory-intensive.

- Inadequate hardware—in particular, display screens that did not meet desktop publishing needs (i.e., for high resolution) and printers that were not of sufficient quality (dot matrix printers) or were at the time too expensive (laser printers).

- Earlier operating systems were generally not well suited to desktop publishing, which virtually demands a graphic user interface (GUI) such as that provided by Microsoft Windows, IBM's OS/2 Warp, or the Apple Macintosh.

Indeed, it was the Apple Macintosh and LaserWriter printer that first overcame the limitations described above. The appeal of the Macintosh system was based primarily on its GUI operating system and on the LaserWriter's built-in Postscript page description language, which together produced very high-quality, professional-looking output.

Subsequently, workable desktop publishing systems were introduced for IBM and compatible microcomputers. One of the leading page layout software packages, in both the Macintosh and Wintel environments, is PageMaker from Aldus. (Aldus was acquired by Adobe Systems in 1994.) Another popular package, especially for the Macintosh, is Quark XPress.

*(ii)  Market Analysis and Trends*

Unlike spreadsheets (Lotus 1-2-3) and databases (dBase), a single word processing package did not emerge as the clear market leader right out of the starting gate, at least not in the IBM-and-compatibles environment. Instead, numerous programs, each offering different combinations and compromises that appealed to the personal tastes of different users, competed for market share during the 1980s. Among the reasons are the following:

- WordStar, which was the first major package to establish a presence, suffered in its earlier versions from a lack of user friendliness because, although very powerful, it was considered difficult to learn. This enabled other packages to encroach on WordStar's dominance.

- The usefulness of spreadsheet software—and other types of software—depended to a degree on the availability of related products or "add-ons" (such as prepackaged spreadsheet models). As a result, market leaders tended to be self-perpetuating because they became better supported, which made them more attractive to buyers, and so on. With word processing, there was no "add-on" market per se to support the market leader.

The era of successful standalone packages may be waning. Software suites such as Microsoft Office (including Microsoft Word), Corel Suite (including WordPerfect) and Lotus SmartSuite (including Word Pro) are becoming increasingly common and popular. The primary advantages are the ease of sharing data between the different program functions, the common user interface, the cost savings in the initial purchase, and the productivity benefits of standardizing on one suite.

The trend towards software suites is mimicked industrywide by various acquisitions and mergers that have taken place during the 1990s as companies try to enhance their competitive position and/or create synergy with another company's product line. An example from the turn of the decade was Borland's acquisition of Ashton-Tate. The trend accelerated through the mid-1990s, with the Novell/WordPerfect combination (subsequently, Novell sold off WordPerfect to Corel), Adobe's acquisition of Aldus, Microsoft's failed attempt to acquire Intuit, IBM's mega-buyout of Lotus, and Symantec's purchase of Delrina. Competitive pressures and the market demand for integrated and networked software solutions seem to be creating a feeding frenzy among the industry's leading players.

The sale of many computer systems has been driven by desktop publishing since the mid-1980s. In fact, probably more than any other single application, it was responsible for the success of the Apple Macintosh and LaserWriter combination. Desktop publishing capabilities are now widely available, however, and the hype has long since dissipated. The power of word processing software has reached the stage where it is now possible to envisage the disappearance of desktop publishing as a distinct application. We're not quite there yet for users with the most sophisticated desktop publishing requirements, but even for them the merger (figuratively speaking) will probably be complete within the next five years.

## 8.3  WORD PROCESSING FEATURES AND APPLICATIONS

Word processing is the creation, manipulation, and printing of written material through a computer system, which allows the user to refine, insert, delete, copy, and move blocks of text; change the margins and justification; and otherwise manipulate documents. Computers, because they can perform all these tasks, have all but replaced typewriters.

With a word processor, a user can restructure and display a document on the screen, at any stage and after any required changes, and print it exactly as it appears, eliminating the labor of retyping a document several times because of typos and changes. This frees up the creative talents of the user, allowing him/her to quickly and easily experiment with alternative presentations.

Gradual improvements in word processing software have led to features that do more than imitate manual tasks. These include new computerized dictionaries, grammar checkers, and outliners or "thought processors" that enable users to organize their ideas better.

### (a)  GENERAL FEATURES

Once the software is loaded, the document is presented in an on-screen window, that displays only a portion of it at any one time. Many programs paint a solid line around the edges of the input area, reserving several lines at the top or bottom of the screen for messages, indicators, and a menu system. Optional screen display items include a ruler at the top or bottom to illustrate the margins and tab settings, markings to indicate page breaks, and messages indicating the amount of memory used by the document.

A cursor indicates the position at which typed characters from the keyboard will be placed in the document. The cursor is typically a solid (highlighted) box or a flashing (blinking) underscore. Some programs show the page number and/or line number of the current cursor location. A set of directional keys (up, down, left, and right), or more typically a pointing device such as a mouse, is used alone or in combination with other keys or function keys to position the cursor within the document. Most of the software's features are activated by invoking commands that are often selected from a menu, again using a mouse or other pointing device.

### (i)  Entering Text

Text is keyed continuously for each paragraph. The user need not enter carriage returns at the end of each typed line—only at the end of a paragraph. The program automatically establishes where each line should end within a paragraph and places the next word at the start of a new line. The program breaks lines only at whole words or hyphens. This feature is called word wraparound and allows the user to change the line margins easily for any portion of the document that has already been input.

Many programs display a paragraph mark on the screen to show where the paragraph ends. Some programs also display a mark for a line break. For the major packages the display of these marks can be activated or deactivated.

Line margin controls are usually for both the left and right margins. The program calculates the line width from the specified page width and the font size or pitch. Most programs allow line widths that exceed the typical display. The screen window can then be scrolled horizontally in order to view the entire document.

### (ii)  Editing and Formatting Text

The editing and formatting features offered by the software allow the user to shape the appearance of a document. Once again, these features are generally invoked by selecting menu commands with a mouse or pointing device, or by using special function keys, or both.

Many word processing commands, such as those for moving or copying text, operate on a portion of the document, often called a block. The block can be any number of characters or words, from one up to the entire document. The user selects a block of text, using the mouse or cursor keys, and then executes a command on that block.

Typically, the program displays the block selected in reverse video (e.g., with the characters dark on a bright background if the normal text display is bright characters on a dark background). The user then instructs the program to execute the command on the selected block of text.

The commands that can typically be executed to edit and format text include the following:

- *Moving and copying text*—a block of text can be moved or copied to any place within the document. Typically, the process is to cut or copy the block to a temporary storage area (called the clipboard) and then to paste or copy the block from the clipboard to the desired spot in the document.

- *Formatting text*—changing formats alters the physical appearance of the printed document. Options vary greatly, and the breadth of options offered is one measure of a program's power. Some of the typical formatting features include type of justification (such as centered, left justified, right justified, or proportional spacing); page margins (top, bottom, left, and right); indentation for the first line of each paragraph or for subsequent lines ("hanging indents"); line spacing; capitalization and decapitalization, character format (bold, italics, capitals, small capitals, or underlined); character pitch; and typestyle or font.

  Many programs are able to alter the text on the screen to reflect the format options selected, to the extent that the video monitor is capable of displaying the changes. This is known as WYSIWYG ("What You See Is What You Get").

- *Search and replace*—most programs can search for a word or phrase and move to its location in a document. The search object can be any string of characters specified by the user. Special options include ignoring upper and lower case letters, searching forward or backward through the document from the current cursor location, and searching only for whole words as opposed to a string of characters appearing within a word.

  The replace command enhances the search function by exchanging the search object with a specified string of text. For example, the name Smith could be replaced with the name Jones. Additional options include replacing all occurrences of the search term in the entire document automatically or requesting confirmation from the user at each occurrence.

- *Windows*—as noted earlier, the display screen represents a window onto a portion of the document. The better programs allow the user to create more than one window simultaneously, dividing the screen for each of the windows selected. This allows the user to view and work with different parts of a long document without having to scroll back and forth repeatedly. Also, a different document file can be accessed in any of the windows. For example, a manuscript could be resident in one window with its bibliography in a second window.

  The number of windows allowed varies between programs. So does the size of the windows and their placement (either stacked vertically or side by side). The number of windows that can be functionally used is limited by the size of the display screen—the more windows there are the smaller each one is.

- *Undo*—many programs offer an "undo" command that reverses the effect of the last command executed and restores the document to the condition it was in before that command. This is a very handy option since users invariably make errors or change their minds. Additionally, some commands have a far-reaching impact that would be time consuming to reverse by hand—for example, the deletion of a large block of text.

As noted, the above and other commands are most often selected from menu systems or by using function keys. For example, early IBM-PC keyboards provided ten function keys that could be combined with the Shift, Control, or Alt keys to yield a total of 40 possible commands.

*(iii) Printing Documents*

Once a document has been edited and formatted, it will typically be printed. The type of printer available, in particular its speed and the quality of its print, greatly affects the utility of the word processing software. Nonimpact page printers—especially laser printers—have become the norm.

Different printers have different standards with respect to the type of instructions they must receive from the software in order to function. The portion of the software responsible for issuing such instructions is the device driver. It is important to ensure that the word processing software contains the appropriate device driver for the printer being used. Most major packages include device drivers for several (if not all) of the popular printers.

Printers are dealt with in greater detail in Chapter 7 of this handbook.

## (b) SPECIAL FEATURES

*(i) Spell Checkers and Thesauruses*

Programs with a spell checker can verify spelling in a document, word by word, and advise the user of any errors found. This is a very useful feature that generally takes only minutes, even for lengthy files.

Spell checkers work by referring to a "dictionary" in a disk file. This electronic dictionary holds the correct spelling for a large number of commonly used words—generally 80,000 or more. Any words in a document that are not found in the dictionary are "flagged." These words are either misspelled or are valid words (e.g., proper names, abbreviations, or some other term) not found in the program's dictionary. The user can either correct the spelling of the flagged words or add them to a special supplementary dictionary.

Additional useful features of spell checkers that are sometimes available include help in correcting spelling (the program will search the dictionary for potential correct spellings of a word) and document statistics (such as the total number of words and the number of unique words).

Another feature similar to a spell checker is a thesaurus, which is a list of synonyms for a large number of commonly used words. The thesaurus is typically invoked by a command after the cursor is positioned on the object word in the document. The program returns with a list of synonyms found for that word. Thesaurus files typically cover 100,000 words or more.

*(ii) Grammar Checkers*

As computer memory has become more plentiful and affordable, it has become possible to build in more sophisticated, expertlike systems. One of these is the grammar checker, which, as its name implies, will review text and highlight grammatical errors that require correction. The program does this by analyzing specific words and the relationship between those words within a sentence (i.e., the nouns, verbs, adjectives, adverbs, etc.) and identifying words or relationships between words that don't meet certain criteria for good grammar.

For example, consider the grammatically incorrect sentence "Its my computer." A grammar checker would initially flag this sentence because it contains no verb. Then, depending on the sophistication of the program, it might search a table of common errors and highlight the word "its," suggesting as a replacement the contraction "it's."

As with spell checkers, grammar checkers are particularly worthwhile in organizations that produce documents as their product—e.g., management consulting firms, publishers, etc. Despite the best efforts of writers and editors, human errors are made. Since documents with spelling or grammatical errors reflect badly on the organization, any system that minimizes such errors is particularly welcome.

### (iii) Outline Processors

An outline processor is a program that manipulates ideas or thoughts in much the same way that a word processor works with words. In fact, there are programs on the market that are only outline processors and not word processors.

An outline processor is typically used to plan and organize a large document such as a manuscript or a research paper. The ideas to be developed within the document are input as short phrases, titles, or headings in the planned order, and are referred to as topics. Topics can be moved, deleted, inserted, and copied just as a word processor does with blocks of text.

The topics are assigned levels. Typically, the work is broken down into major topics—sections or chapters—at the top level. The document is then broken down into smaller pieces at the second level, and so on through each level until the user reaches the individual paragraphs to be written. The assigned levels can be easily changed and manipulated.

In programs that integrate an outline processor with a word processor, text is generally input below a given heading and becomes associated with that heading. The user can easily switch between the outline processor view of the document and the actual document since both are part of the same file.

Outline processors may also include additional features, such as automatic numbering (e.g. 1.1.3 or 2.1.3, etc.). But their key benefit is leaving the user free to think about the progression of ideas to be discussed and to try out different sequences easily and quickly until a satisfactory plan is arrived at.

### (iv) Table of Contents and Indexing

Manuscripts, in particular technical books and manuals, often require a table of contents at the front and an index at the back. The process of creating these manually after the document is finished can be very time consuming and tedious.

Some word processors allow the user to mark words in the text that should be included in the table of contents or the index. This is usually done with a special control character or by identifying the entry as a heading. The entries can be marked at any time, either when originally typed or on a subsequent review of the material.

When the program is instructed to create the table of contents or index, it paginates the document and compiles the material. The material can also be recreated or updated later if required.

*(v)  Columnar Printing and Tabulation*

The better programs allow text to be printed in columns on a page, in the same manner as a magazine or newspaper. Usually, the text continues from the bottom of the first column to the top of the next on the same page. The user can specify the number of columns, the amount of blank space or "gutter" to leave between them, and other formatting options such as justification.

*(vi)  Other*

Other typical features of word processing software include:

- Mail merge (personalized form letters and envelope addressing)
- Mathematical functions, usually simple operations such as adding a column of numbers
- Sorting (the ability to sort lists of words or phrases into alphabetical order)
- Help screens and tutorials
- Graphics (the ability to draw boxes around text and/or reserve a space in the document for graphics that are imported from other programs)
- Macros (defined keystrokes that represent a longer command or series of commands) and style sheets (pre-programmed format instructions that can be quickly applied to a block of text)

## (c)  APPLICATIONS

There is a wide range of word processing applications, most of which are quite familiar. In fact, for many users—especially business users—word processing accounts for the highest volume of all computer applications. Some of the typical uses are set out below.

*(i)  Letters and Correspondence*

Ordinary letters and correspondence are probably the most common of all word processing applications, yet curiously they are probably the one application that benefits least from the technology. This is because normal correspondence tends to be short, and a fast and accurate typist can correct a draft and retype it fairly quickly. Put another way, the implications of not having the power of a word processor available are less severe.

*(ii)  Form Letter Mailings (Mail Merge)*

Word processing software can produce form letter mailings and address labels, using the "mail merge" feature available with most of the popular packages. Mail merge is a computer program within the word processor that combines two files, one containing the standard wording of the form letter and the other containing a list of the names and addresses as well as any other data that is to be changed for each document.

The form letter typically contains markers wherever the information from the data file is to be inserted. For example, the address portion of the letter might have four lines that read:

```
<name>
<address>
<city>, <state/prov>
<zip/postal code>
```

The brackets around each item let the program know that it should look in the data file for fields called name, address, and so on, and merge these with the form letter before printing.

Mail merge is a very powerful application, since it saves a significant amount of manual retyping—in some cases hundreds or even thousand of letters. Large mailings can be done without a word processor, for example by photocopying the standard letter and overtyping the addresses and special information on each photocopy. But there are benefits that only a word processor can provide, including:

- A cleaner appearance of the document, giving it the look of an individualized letter rather than a form letter.

- The ability to embed material of varying lengths within the body of a document, rather than simply addresses at a predefined location on the page (this is possible because word processors can reformat each document individually as required).

- The elimination of the need to retype data for subsequent mailings (the data file, typically containing names and addresses, can be used again for subsequent mailings).

*(iii)  Reports and Documents*

Obviously, the key benefit of a word processor is the user's ability to make changes without having to retype an entire document. This benefit is greatest in the case of reports and longer documents.

Legal documents and contracts are an especially important application, since accuracy is crucial. Long book manuscripts are also easier to produce.

## 8.4  DESKTOP PUBLISHING ELEMENTS AND APPLICATIONS

Desktop publishing is the use of a computer system—typically a microcomputer system—to produce printed material that is suitable for distribution or for use as camera-ready artwork in another printing process. The key benefits of desktop publishing are that it

- Eliminates the need for the traditional publishing functions of typesetting and manual paste-up.

- Allows the originator of the material to exercise greater creative control over its final printed appearance.

The desktop publishing process is really no different from the conventional publishing process in that it involves these steps:

- *Create*—write the text and/or draw the art.

- *Edit*—control the quality of the material, amending it as required.

- *Design*—develop a proposed layout or presentation vehicle for the material.
- *Compose*—set the material within the proposed design.
- *Print*—produce the required number of copies of the material, using whatever printing process best meets the needs of the user (normally a trade-off between quality and cost).
- *Distribute*—deliver the material to its intended audience, or make it available to its intended market.

Contrary to popular perception, the desktop publishing revolution has not adversely affected the traditional publishing industry. In fact, it has enhanced that industry by increasing market demand for some existing industry services and by opening up markets for new types of services.

True, there are certain functions—such as the retyping of material into typesetting machines and the manual pasteup of text and graphics—that have been effectively replaced by the new technology. But this is balanced by the increased demand for traditional offset printing (particularly color printing) and by special desktop publishing services such as the disk-to-typesetting machine production of camera-ready art.

The main concern of the big publishing companies has always been the selection, development, and marketing of products. Desktop publishing technology can actually help these companies become more efficient in the product development stage.

A desktop publishing system consists of computer hardware and specialized software, as described in the following two sections.

## (a) HARDWARE

The typical hardware configuration in a desktop publishing system is a microcomputer, display screen, and printer. Optional equipment includes an image scanner and a typesetting machine.

### (i) Microcomputer

The microcomputer is typically the hub of a desktop publishing system; to a large extent it determines what the user's options are for the other components. IBM, IBM-compatible (Windows/Intel), and Apple Macintosh microcomputers are most common in desktop publishing because, among other reasons, there is more software available for these machines.

One attribute of desktop publishing systems is that the microcomputer itself represents a relatively smaller portion of the total cost of the system than is the case for other applications. The other pieces of hardware and software, in total, are usually much more expensive than the main unit.

### (ii) Display Screen

What type of display screen to select is an important consideration for desktop publishing systems. The effectiveness of the system depends largely on the ability of the user to manipulate material on-screen in much the same fashion as more traditional typesetters and graphic artists manipulate material on the pasteboard. Good-quality, high-resolution displays are therefore mandatory.

It is important to note that the quality of the display is not the only factor to be considered. Both the microcomputer and the software must be able to take advantage of the display screen's capabilities.

*(iii) Printer*

Since the ultimate objective of a desktop publishing system is to produce printable material, the printer is arguably the most important hardware component. Nonimpact page printers—in particular, laser printers—are normally the preferred choice because they produce higher-quality output. Dot matrix or ink jet printers may also be used if quality demands are not as stringent, or to produce draft material for later output on a laser printer or typesetting machine.

*(iv) Image Scanner*

An image scanner, sometimes called a "graphics digitizer," is optional for desktop publishing systems. It is used to "read" materials such as photographs or artwork and convert them to digitized information that can be processed by a microcomputer and later printed. The material can be easily enhanced, resized, or otherwise manipulated once it has been digitized.

Optical character recognition (OCR) scanners, which can read text, are also available. Their reliability varies, however, depending on the type of text being read, and they are more expensive than graphics-only scanners. In any case, they do not have the special significance to desktop publishing applications that graphics scanners have.

*(v) Typesetting Machine*

Another possible option for a desktop publishing system, albeit an expensive one, is a typesetting machine. These are very sophisticated devices that can print in a large number of different type styles at higher resolutions than most laser printers.

Laser printers create images on the page by "mapping" a series of highly condensed dots (300 dots per inch or "dpi" for the lower-end models, 600 dpi on most of the newer machines). Typesetting machines can print in the range of 1,000 to 3,000 dpi. Although the untrained human eye cannot distinguish the difference within the 1,000-3,000 range, the difference between 300 dpi and, say, 1,200 dpi is easily discernible.

Typesetting machines generally cost at least $25,000, and optional equipment that enables the machines to perform certain special functions or work with certain software can drive the cost to $100,000. Since this cost is beyond reach for all but the most intensive desktop publishing applications, specialized service companies have emerged that charge fees for transfers from disk to typesetting machine. For example, a newsletter can be produced on an Apple Macintosh using PageMaker software, saved on a $3\frac{1}{2}$-inch diskette, and then taken to a service company where it can be printed out on a typesetting machine.

## (b) Software

Desktop publishing involves more than one type of software. Word processing and graphics software provide some of the basic input material for the system. Page layout, page preview, and page description software then take this basic material and turn it into printed pages.

*(i)  Word Processing*

Initial text input and formatting in a desktop publishing system is normally handled by a word processor. Although most page layout software packages do have text-handling capability, there are generally fewer features available, and the process is more cumbersome than with a word processor.

It is important to ensure that the word processing package selected is compatible with the page layout software. With the major word processing packages, compatibility is virtually assured.

*(ii) Graphics*

Many desktop publishing applications, in order to take maximum advantage of the technology, merge text and graphics on the printed page for a better visual effect. Some word processing and page layout software packages contain simple graphics functions, such as the drawing of boxes and lines and "screening" (the half-toning or shading of certain areas). However, more sophisticated functions normally require a dedicated graphics package.

*(iii)  Page Layout*

Page layout software is typically the central piece of software in a desktop publishing system. As the name suggests, such packages are designed to facilitate the arrangement of text and graphics on the printed page. PageMaker is the most established and still one of the more popular packages on the market.

*(iv)  "WYSIWYG" and Page Preview*

Since one of the characteristics of desktop publishing is that it can manipulate text and graphics on-screen (thus eliminating the need for manual pasteup), it is vital that the image seen on the screen be a realistic representation of what is to be printed. WYSIWYG and page preview are the software features that permit this realistic representation.

WYSIWYG is an acronym for "what you see is what you get." A WYSIWYG system displays on the screen exactly what is to be printed, including the type fonts and graphics.

Certain types of software are not WYSIWYG in their normal mode—that is, while the user is working with the program and manipulating text and graphics on-screen. However, they do have the ability to enter a different mode called page preview mode before the material is printed. This feature enables the user to check the material and determine whether amendments are required before printing. If amendments are required, the user typically must return to normal mode and make the corrections.

Provided the display screen is of sufficient quality, a true WYSIWYG system is more desirable than one that only offers page preview. Many of the major page layout packages are true WYSIWYG.

*(v)  Page Description Languages*

As previously noted, the printing of a page on a laser printer or typesetting machine is accomplished by mapping out a large number of individual dots, which are then condensed together to form a printed image. This image-mapping process can take as long as several minutes (in the case of elaborate graphic images) and is executed by a specialized piece of software known as a page description language. The page description language translates the digitized image received from the microcomputer and maps it onto the page.

A page description language called Postscript (now Postscript Level 2) has emerged as something of a standard. Adobe Systems, which owns Postscript, first licensed it to Apple Computer for its LaserWriter printer. Subsequently, it was licensed to IBM as well. The language has also gained wide acceptance among professional typesetters.

## (c) Applications

The range of desktop publishing applications is, like publishing generally, almost limitless. There are a number of applications, however, on which the technology seems to have had an especially important impact. These are set out below.

### (i) Newsletters

There are two main reasons why newsletters are ideally suited to desktop publishing:

- Unlike books, magazines and similar large publishing ventures, newsletters have always been undertaken by individuals and smaller groups. Desktop publishing offers many of the benefits that individuals and smaller groups want most: for example, reduced typesetting costs and greater creative control over the final printed material.
- Often, newsletters are very time-sensitive; in other words, they must reach their subscribers quickly before they become outdated. Desktop publishing speeds up the process.

Depending on the quality desired, a newsletter can be sent out in black-and-white, or the desktop publishing system can be used to produce camera-ready copy for two-or-more-color offset printing. (Color laser printers or photocopiers are also an option, but compared with offset printing, they are usually only cost-effective for smaller volumes.)

In some ways newsletters have become the quintessential application of desktop publishing. Thousands are now published using the technology, often by individuals working alone but producing material that would appear to require the efforts of many.

### (ii) Advertising and Presentation Materials

Before desktop publishing, good-quality advertising and presentation materials usually demanded the services of specialized graphic artists and/or print shops, slowing down the process and sometimes yielding results that did not meet the needs of the user.

Today, advertising and presentation materials are routinely being produced in-house using desktop publishing systems, even in larger corporate settings. Applications include brochures, letterhead, business cards, resumes, copy for print advertisements, and overheads or slides for seminars.

*(iii)  Longer Manuscripts and Reports*

Reports and manuscripts are not a new application—before desktop publishing, they could be produced much like newsletters were (i.e., using typewriters and word processors). However, both can be greatly enhanced with the technology. The ability of desktop publishing systems to combine text and graphics on the printed page is an especially useful feature. For example, the inclusion of a bar or pie chart in the text of a report can greatly increase reader interest and acceptance.

Desktop publishing is also affecting the way authors produce manuscripts and deliver them to publishers. The submitting of manuscripts on microcomputer diskettes (or even by modem) is commonplace. When a manuscript is submitted in this form, the publisher can often circumvent traditional typesetting. The result is a simpler, faster, and often less expensive publication process.

*(iv)  Other Applications*

Other typical desktop publishing applications include:

- Seminar and course materials
- Term papers
- Magazines
- Blueprints, floor plans, and schematic diagrams
- Price lists
- Restaurant menus

## 8.5  USER NEEDS AND SOFTWARE EVALUATION

### (a)  Matching User Needs and Features

There is a variety of word processing and desktop publishing software available, and the features of each package should be evaluated and matched with the needs of the user. The following subsections discuss some of the important features to investigate. The user should rank these in order of importance before evaluating specific word processing and desktop publishing packages.

*(i)  Do You Need a Desktop Publishing System?*

To some extent, the people who ask this question probably already see the potential benefit of a system in their particular environment. They may already be producing a high volume of material in one or more of the applications set out in the previous section.

A desktop publishing system can yield significant benefits, but it can also cost a great deal to set up—often $10,000 and up. It is therefore especially important that the user's needs be properly assessed and matched with the available systems. Fortunately, the choices are relatively limited compared with those for other information technology products.

These are key questions:

- What are the alternatives to a desktop publishing system?
- What is the cost of those other alternatives?

- What value is placed on the increased creative control and faster turnaround time that a desktop publishing system affords?

- When the cost of a full system cannot be justified, is it feasible to buy a partial system? For example, can a lower-quality printer be used for draft output, with an outside service later used to print the final product?

If the answers to these questions point toward a purchase, then the process of assessing needs and choosing a system begins.

### (ii)  Hardware and Operating System Requirements

The type of hardware, operating system, graphic user interface and/or network that a user is working with will determine the software package the system can run. Many of the more popular packages are offered in a variety of configurations (e.g., Microsoft Word for the Macintosh, MS Windows, LANs) and it's obviously essential that the correct package be chosen. In addition, the user's hardware should have the necessary speed and memory to satisfactorily run the package, as well as any anticipated software upgrades.

Hardware has become more powerful, affordable, and plentiful in recent years, but word processing and desktop publishing software have also grown to take advantage of this additional power and memory. For example, it is not unusual for top-of-the-line programs to require 4 megabytes or more of on-line memory and 8 megabytes or more of storage space for loading on a hard disk. If such programs are to be run under a Graphical User Interface such as Windows 95, a machine based on Intel's Pentium microprocessor (or equivalent) may be the minimum necessary to achieve satisfactory performance.

Another factor is the anticipated size of documents and how the word processing or desktop publishing program handles such documents. Many programs load the entire document file into main memory. Therefore, the size of document that can be processed is limited by the amount of memory remaining after the program and any operating system and interface have been loaded. Additional features such as spell checkers can take up further memory space.

Although software costs in a desktop publishing system can be significant, hardware costs are normally even more so. If the user already has a significant investment in hardware, it may make sense to build the desktop publishing system around that base. Care should be taken in making this assessment, however, and the user should not automatically assume that this is the best route. There are significant differences between desktop publishing systems, and if the applications are important enough to the user, then it may be worth the additional cost to acquire the right system, even if it means starting from scratch.

### (iii)  Printers Supported

As previously noted, word processing and desktop publishing programs need special instructions to control or drive a printer—for example, to process special formatting specifications in a document. These instructions are called device drivers. Most packages include drivers for the more common printers in the marketplace; however, the user should confirm that the package selected has the driver for the printer that will be used.

Some printers can emulate one of the more common printers on the market. For example, Epson has become somewhat of a standard among dot matrix printers. Software that has a device driver for an Epson should work with a printer that can emulate an Epson. However, the user should carefully investigate how well the combination will work if the software does not have a driver specifically for the printer in question.

### *(iv)  Maximum File Size*

As previously noted, many programs load and work with the entire document file in the computer's main memory or RAM. Therefore, the maximum document size that can be processed in one file is limited by the remaining memory after the program itself (which varies in size) is loaded.

Some programs, however, work differently—they store the document on disk and keep in memory only the portion of the document being worked on. Programs like these require frequent disk access, as different portions of longer documents are constantly being swapped in and out of memory.

Because of these and other differences in features—such as automatic table of contents and indexing—software performance varies in the handling of long documents or manuscripts. If processing of very long documents is an anticipated application, users should investigate whether the software is up to the task by asking the manufacturer or salesperson, testing the program for themselves, and so on.

### *(v)  Complexity vs. Ease of Use*

Word processing software varies widely as to ease of use, although most of the more popular packages do rate well in this area. Three of the most important features contributing to ease of use are:

- Well-written and complete documentation
- Availability of tutorials
- Easy command selection via menus and/or logical, simple keystrokes (e.g., Control-D for delete)

With respect to desktop publishing programs, if the user is looking only for the ability to produce basic-looking reports, the occasional overhead, and other mainly-text material, then a simpler and less costly word processing program may suffice. However, if the applications are higher-volume, require especially good-quality output, and/or involve graphics, then a full-featured system (including a powerful microcomputer with a high-resolution display, WYSIWYG software and a quality laser printer) will probably pay off in the long run.

WYSIWYG is one of the most important ease-of-use features. Graphics-based systems that use a mouse to perform the various operations are also preferred by most users. The major packages use this type of system.

Although most of the basic functions of desktop publishing software can be learned fairly quickly, a fair amount of practice is needed to master the systems to the point of obtaining maximum benefit. Success depends more on the creativity of the users than on their ability to follow instructions in a software manual.

*(vi) Software Versions and Software Support*

Inevitably, word processing and desktop publishing software contains errors or bugs that require correction. In addition, software generally improves as technology advances. It is therefore essential that a software package be well supported and updated regularly.

Some experts recommend shying away from the first version of a program or major program upgrade, reasoning that such versions are more likely to contain bugs. They argue that it's better to wait for the first update after such a new release. (Many people argue the same thing for the first model year of a particular car—i.e., that it's better to wait a year, by which time the manufacturer will have corrected any manufacturing flaws.) To counteract this type of resistance on the part of users, some software manufacturers have taken to avoiding the ".0" label for their software. For example, instead of issuing version 5.0, the manufacturer will go straight to version 5.1 to at least give the appearance of more extensive testing.

In addition to the initial price of the package, the user should consider the manufacturer's or vendor's update policies (i.e., how users are notified of updates) and the related cost. The better programs tend to be improved frequently to keep up with the competition.

Support—both vendor and manufacturer—is also a factor. Most major software manufacturers also offer telephone support to registered users. However, a number of the larger manufacturers have begun charging a fee for such services.

*(vii) Compatibility*

A key consideration for many users—especially medium- and large-size organizations—is compatibility with other software owned by the user. For example, if others in the organization are already using a particular package, buying that package will facilitate the exchange of documents within the organization.

Another factor to consider is whether the same manufacturer's software is being used for other applications such as databases or spreadsheets. Sister packages of this kind usually offer greater integration. For example, if graphics are regularly incorporated into reports, such integration may be a key consideration.

Finally, the issue of compatibility extends beyond the organization as well, to the degree that it affects personnel. For example, Microsoft Word and WordPerfect have become somewhat entrenched as standards. As a result, a skilled labor market has developed for these programs, and it is easier to find both permanent and temporary staff who can operate them.

*(viii) Cost*

The price of software has come down substantially in recent years, following the trend in hardware prices. Many word processing programs are also being offered as a package with other programs such as databases, spreadsheets, and graphics software, providing even greater value. (Microsoft Office and Lotus SmartSuite are examples.)

Nevertheless, price comparison is an important step in large organizations that are considering the purchase of site licenses or that operate large networks. In such cases the total purchase cost can run into the tens or even hundreds of thousands of dollars. Training and future upgrade costs also have to be factored in.

### (b)  Where to Buy

Software is frequently sold at a discount from list price. The extent of the discount generally depends on the type of establishment and the after-sales support it offers. The greatest discounts are usually offered by mail order houses that offer no advice. No matter where it's purchased, buyers should ensure that software is sealed in its original packaging. This is important for license/registration purposes and also to ensure it is virus-free.

When you buy a desktop publishing system, you are actually buying a bundle of hardware and software. The one component that is unique to desktop publishing is generally the page layout software. This software is sometimes sold at a discount from list price, although typically not for as large a discount as other types of software.

Some vendors offer demonstration diskettes that run through some of the program's functions on a sample document while the user observes. These can help the user become familiar with the program as well as help him/her evaluate the software.

Although important, the selection of a vendor is less crucial in the case of software than it is for hardware. Nevertheless, after-sale support may be a factor to purchasers who expect to have problems learning and/or operating the package. If support is needed, the higher cost normally charged by a more established vendor with knowledgeable staff may be worthwhile. Many software houses offer telephone support, but that can be frustrating to use because of the lower level of personal attention and the long-distance charges. A local, reputable vendor with whom the user can build a relationship can prove a valuable troubleshooting resource.

### (c)  Other Sources of Information

Some additional sources of information are set out in the following sections.

*(i)  On-Line Tutorials and Help*

Many of the major programs provide a tutorial lesson that leads the beginner through the basics of the word processing or desktop publishing package on the computer's screen, using actual documents.

Most packages also have on-line help. When a defined key is pressed, the software replaces the screen display with information from the manual. Ideally, the help should be "context sensitive," meaning that it is automatically geared to the functions that the user is trying to employ.

*(ii)  Books, Magazines, and Newsletters*

The manuals that accompany the software often are designed more as a reference source for the program's numerous functions than as a teaching tool. As a result, a large number of books have been written to help users actually learn word processing and desktop publishing—especially the major packages—from the ground up. There are also books to help experienced users with advanced functions.

Many of the leading computer magazines carry articles dealing with word processing and desktop publishing packages and/or have columns offering advice and tips. There are even some magazines devoted expressly to desktop publishing, some of which sponsor annual competitions for desktop publishers. As well, some manufacturers publish newsletters on their word processing packages.

*(iii)  Courses and Seminars*

Learning to use a word processing program is usually not very difficult. The primary operation is typing, and a minimum number of commands are needed to execute the basic functions. Nevertheless, operators sometimes require training in order to exploit the powers of the full-featured programs, the advanced functions of which speed up many operations and enhance the appearance of the finished product. As a result, numerous training courses are available for the more popular packages. Ultimately, though, practice is still the best way to learn.

Desktop publishing training courses and seminars are also offered, mainly by computer vendors and consultants. Courses typically last one or two days, with fees ranging from $100 to $500. Given the significant investment required to boot up a desktop publishing system, these courses are well worth considering.

## 8.6  CATALOG OF SELECTED WORD PROCESSING AND DESKTOP PUBLISHING SOFTWARE

The following list (in alphabetical order by package name) represents a cross-section of a few of the popular word processing and desktop publishing packages that are available. The appearance of a specific package on the list should not be construed as an endorsement, nor should its failure to appear be construed as a condemnation. Price estimates are for the fourth quarter of 1996, based on single-copy prices charged by discount retail chains. Full service dealers charge more; multiple-copy site licensees will typically pay less. Prices on the old software version may fall when a new version is released. Lower upgrade prices (usually about 67 percent off the regular price for standalone packages, 33 percent off for suites) are typically offered to existing users and to users of competitive products. Proof that the user is a licensee is required to obtain the upgrade price (for suites, proof of license for a single component is sufficient). Some upgrade packages automatically scan a user's hard disk to ensure they are an existing licensee.

Other publications, in particular computer magazines, regularly publish more complete catalogues and reviews of available software. Several of these publications are listed in the bibliography in Appendix A. Independent software dealers can also provide up-to-date information on specific product options. Finally, the software manufacturers themselves will usually provide complete information on their products. A list of the addresses and phone numbers of several manufacturers appears in the directory of companies contained in Appendix B.

| Word Processing and Desktop Publishing Software | Version Number | Estimated (Best) Price | Manufacturer Name |
|---|---|---|---|
| **1. PageMaker for Macintosh** (page layout software) | 5.0A | $550.00 U.S. $750.00 Cdn. | Adobe Systems Inc. |

*Requirements:* 6Mb RAM, 20Mb hard disk space, System 7.0 or later

| Word Processing and Desktop Publishing Software | Version Number | Estimated (Best) Price | Manufacturer Name |
|---|---|---|---|
| **2. PageMaker for Windows** (page layout software) | 5.0A | $550.00 U.S. $750.00 Cdn. | Adobe Systems Inc. |

*Requirements:* 6Mb RAM, 20Mb hard disk space, Windows 3.1 or later

| Word Processing and Desktop Publishing Software | Version Number | Estimated (Best) Price | Manufacturer Name |
|---|---|---|---|
| **3. Word for DOS** (word processing software) | 6.0 | $280.00 U.S. $390.00 Cdn. | Microsoft Corporation |

*Requirements:* 512K RAM, 5.5Mb hard disk space for full installation, DOS 3.0 or later

| Word Processing and Desktop Publishing Software | Version Number | Estimated (Best) Price | Manufacturer Name |
|---|---|---|---|
| **4. Word for Macintosh** (word processing software) | 6.0 | $280.00 U.S. $390.00 Cdn. | Microsoft Corporation |

*Requirements:* 4Mb RAM minimum (8Mb recommended), 23Mb hard disk space for full installation (9.5Mb minimum), System 7.0 or later

| Word Processing and Desktop Publishing Software | Version Number | Estimated (Best) Price | Manufacturer Name |
|---|---|---|---|
| **5. Word for Windows** (word processing software) | 6.1 | $280.00 U.S. $390.00 Cdn. | Microsoft Corporation |

*Requirements:* 4Mb RAM, 24Mb hard disk space for full installation, Windows 3.1 or later

*Comments:* This package is commonly referred to as WinWord; WinWord is also part of Microsoft Office v4.2 for Windows (along with Excel spreadsheet and PowerPoint presentation packages, and a Mail license), estimated best price $430.00 U.S.; $650 Cdn. Also Microsoft Office Pro (with above plus Access data base package), estimated best price $520.00 U.S., $775.00 Cdn.

| Word Processing and Desktop Publishing Software | Version Number | Estimated (Best) Price | Manufacturer Name |
|---|---|---|---|
| **6. Word for Windows 95** (word processing software) | 7.0 | $340.00 U.S. $475.00 Cdn. | Microsoft Corporation |

*Requirements:* 6Mb RAM, 35Mb hard disk space for full installation, Windows 95

*Comments:* This package is commonly referred to as Word 95. It is also part of Microsoft Office 95 Standard (along with Excel 95 spreadsheet, and PowerPoint 95 presentation package, and Schedule+ 95 time management software), estimated best price $500.00 U.S., $750 Cdn. Also Microsoft Office 95 Professional (with above plus Access 95 data base package), estimated best price $600.00 U.S., $895.00 Cdn.

*(Continued)*

| Word Processing and Desktop Publishing Software | Version Number | Estimated (Best) Price | Manufacturer Name |
|---|---|---|---|
| **7. WordPerfect for DOS**<br>(word processing software) | 6.0A | $240.00 U.S.<br>$350.00 Cdn. | Corel Corporation |

*Requirements:*   520K RAM, 16Mb hard disk space, DOS 3.1 or later

| **8. WordPerfect for Windows**<br>(word processing software) | 6.1 | $240.00 U.S.<br>$350.00 Cdn. | Corel Corporation |
|---|---|---|---|

*Requirements:*   Minimum 4Mb RAM (6Mb highly recommended), 33Mb hard disk space for full installation, Windows 3.1 or later

*Comments:*   Now part of Corel office. This package was part of PerfectOffice v3.0 for Windows (along with Quattro Pro spreadsheet, Presentations presentation, InfoCentral personal information manager, Envoy electronic publisher, and GroupWise e-mail packages), estimated best price $440.00 U.S., $645 Cdn. Also PerfectOffice Pro (with above plus Paradox data base and AppWare visual development packages), estimated best price $550.00 U.S., $775.00 Cdn.

| **9. Word Pro for Windows**<br>(word processing software) | 3.1 | $ 95.00 U.S.<br>$130.00 Cdn. | Lotus Development Corporation |
|---|---|---|---|

*Requirements:*   4Mb RAM, 16Mb hard disk space for full installation (4Mb minimum), Windows 3.1 or later

*Comments:*   Formerly Ami Pro (renamed Word Pro effective with 4.0 release in Summer/95); Word Pro is also part of SmartSuite v3.1 for Windows (along with Lotus 1-2-3 spreadsheet, Freelance graphics, Approach data base, and Organizer personal info mgr), requires 6Mb RAM, 93Mb hard disk space for full installation (33Mb min.), est. best price $460.00 U.S., $630.00 Cdn. Windows 95 version also available.

| **10. XPress for Macintosh**<br>(page layout software) | 3.32 | $595.00 U.S.<br>$795.00 Cdn. | Quark Incorporated |
|---|---|---|---|

*Requirements:* 6Mb RAM, 20Mb hard disk space, System 7.0 or later

*Comments:*       PageMaker's main competition

| **11. XPress for Windows**<br>(page layout software) | 3.32 | $595.00 U.S.<br>$795.00 Cdn. | Quark Incorporated |
|---|---|---|---|

*Requirements:*   6Mb RAM, 20Mb hard disk space, Windows 3.1 or later

# CHAPTER 9

# Spreadsheets and Database Management

<table>
<tr><td>(vi) Software Versions and Software Support</td><td>(ii) Books, Magazines, and Newsletters</td></tr>
<tr><td>(vii) Compatibility</td><td>(iii) User Groups</td></tr>
<tr><td>(viii) Cost</td><td>(iv) Courses and Seminars</td></tr>
<tr><td>(ix) Other Concerns</td><td>(v) Video Training</td></tr>
<tr><td>(b) Where to Buy</td><td>(vi) Consulting Services</td></tr>
<tr><td>(c) Other Sources of Information<br>(i) On-Line Tutorials and Help</td><td>9.6 Catalog of Selected Spreadsheet and Database Management Software</td></tr>
</table>

Chapter 8 dealt with word processing and desktop publishing, which communicate information in the form of written reports and documents. This chapter deals with the manipulation of information, specifically the two most widely used applications that exploit the raw number-crunching and information handling capabilities of computer technology: spreadsheets and database management software.

Although spreadsheets and databases have been packaged and marketed separately for years, the underlying basis for each is quite similar. The familiar row-and-column format of the spreadsheet can be thought of as a specialized way of presenting database information. Each row is the equivalent of a database record, each column a field within that record. Where the task is calculation-oriented and limited in scope (e.g., performing sensitivity or "what if" analysis on a budget forecast), then the traditional spreadsheet format is the most appropriate. Where the task involves manipulating a large volume of similar information (e.g., mailing lists), then more generalized database management tools are needed.

The following material consists of:

- A checklist (Section 9.1), summarizing many of the main points in this chapter.
- A brief treatment of the management, user, and market issues surrounding spreadsheet and database management (Section 9.2).
- Sections on the elements, features, and applications of spreadsheet (Section 9.3) and database management (Section 9.4) software.
- A discussion of the user needs assessment and software selection process (Section 9.5).
- A catalog of selected spreadsheet and database management software, including current version numbers and list prices (Section 9.6).

## 9.1 SPREADSHEET AND DATABASE MANAGEMENT CHECKLIST

The following three-page checklist is designed to assist accountants in decision-making and management relating to spreadsheet and database management software, in their organizations and those of their clients. Generally, all "No" answers require investigation and follow-up, the results of which should be documented. Where there is such additional documentation, the purpose of the "Ref" column is to cross-reference the checklist to the appropriate working paper (or to the notes on the reverse).

The checklist is intended for general use only. If spreadsheet and database management software are of especially vital concern to an organization, the advice of a specialist should be sought.

**Spreadsheet and Database Management Checklist**

|  | Yes | No | N/A | Ref |
|---|---|---|---|---|

**1. Management Issues—Acquisition**

a. Have an appropriate process, timetable, and budget been established for the assessment of user needs, the evaluation of available packages, purchase, training, and implementation?  ☐ ☐ ☐ ___

b. Has the participation of the ultimate users of the spreadsheet or database management software been ensured throughout the process?  ☐ ☐ ☐ ___

c. Have the major user needs been identified (such as the system environment (Mac, OS/2, Windows), size of spreadsheet or database files that must be handled, availability of support, etc.) and has a preliminary identification been made of those packages that may meet these criteria?  ☐ ☐ ☐ ___

d. For each package that might be purchased, have the following issues been addressed?
- Compatibility with hardware and operating systems  ☐ ☐ ☐ ___
- Compatibility with all printers in use  ☐ ☐ ☐ ___
- Compatibility with other software in use  ☐ ☐ ☐ ___
- Compatibility with all networks in use  ☐ ☐ ☐ ___
- Compatibility with possible future upgrades of above  ☐ ☐ ☐ ___
- Adequacy of RAM and hard disk capacity  ☐ ☐ ☐ ___
- Availability of manufacturer and/or vendor support  ☐ ☐ ☐ ___
- Adequacy of documentation and manuals  ☐ ☐ ☐ ___
- Availability of skilled operating personnel  ☐ ☐ ☐ ___
- Availability of training (self-study, seminars, etc.)  ☐ ☐ ☐ ___
- Ability to handle required size of files  ☐ ☐ ☐ ___

e. Has the software been user-tested for appropriateness and ease of use (including all functions and graphics capabilities for spreadsheets, input screens, search and query, and report formats for databases)?  ☐ ☐ ☐ ___

f. Is the software price (taking into account the required number of copies and/or site licenses, training costs, etc.):
- Competitive with other comparable packages?  ☐ ☐ ☐ ___
- Within budget?  ☐ ☐ ☐ ___

|  | Yes | No | N/A | Ref |
|---|---|---|---|---|
| g. Once a package is decided upon, have the related purchase documents (sales agreements, site licenses, etc.) been reviewed, by legal counsel if appropriate? | ☐ | ☐ | ☐ | ___ |

**2. Management Issues—Implementation and Use**

|  | Yes | No | N/A | Ref |
|---|---|---|---|---|
| a. Have all appropriate applications for the software been identified to ensure that maximum use and value are obtained from the software investment? | ☐ | ☐ | ☐ | ___ |
| b. Are appropriate mechanisms in place to ensure that: |  |  |  |  |
| • The organization is aware of future software upgrades? | ☐ | ☐ | ☐ | ___ |
| • All users have the most current software version? | ☐ | ☐ | ☐ | ___ |
| c. Have appropriate policies, procedures, standards, and controls been put in place with respect to: |  |  |  |  |
| • Hiring and training of users? | ☐ | ☐ | ☐ | ___ |
| • File formats and/or templates? | ☐ | ☐ | ☐ | ___ |
| • Full documentation of all files and templates? | ☐ | ☐ | ☐ | ___ |
| • File backups, including off-site backups? | ☐ | ☐ | ☐ | ___ |
| • File security, both electronic and physical? | ☐ | ☐ | ☐ | ___ |
| • File destruction, both electronic and physical? | ☐ | ☐ | ☐ | ___ |

**3. User Issues**

|  | Yes | No | N/A | Ref |
|---|---|---|---|---|
| a. Are users adequately trained in the use of the spreadsheet or database management software, including refresher or update courses when required? | ☐ | ☐ | ☐ | ___ |
| b. Do users observe the following principles of good spreadsheet and database design? |  |  |  |  |
| • Breaking down large designs into smaller modules | ☐ | ☐ | ☐ | ___ |
| • Step-by-step approach (no complex shortcuts) | ☐ | ☐ | ☐ | ___ |
| • Listing of all assumptions used | ☐ | ☐ | ☐ | ___ |
| • Descriptive row, column, field names, and so on | ☐ | ☐ | ☐ | ___ |
| • Adequate column widths, field lengths | ☐ | ☐ | ☐ | ___ |
| • Representing time periods horizontally (as columns) | ☐ | ☐ | ☐ | ___ |
| • Written documentation for the design | ☐ | ☐ | ☐ | ___ |
| c. Do users thoroughly test the design (confirming data, calculations, logic, etc.) to ensure accuracy and completeness before placing reliance on it? | ☐ | ☐ | ☐ | ___ |

|  | Yes | No | N/A | Ref |
|---|---|---|---|---|
| d. Both in theory and in practice, are users aware of the importance and necessity of: | | | | |
| • Frequently saving files? | ☐ | ☐ | ☐ | ___ |
| • Frequently backing up files? | ☐ | ☐ | ☐ | ___ |
| e. Are users aware of and in practice do they follow procedures with respect to: | | | | |
| • File and template formats? | ☐ | ☐ | ☐ | ___ |
| • Diskette labeling and storage? | ☐ | ☐ | ☐ | ___ |
| • Physical security? | ☐ | ☐ | ☐ | ___ |
| • Physical destruction (hard copy, diskettes, etc.)? | ☐ | ☐ | ☐ | ___ |

## 9.2 MANAGEMENT, USER, AND MARKET ISSUES

### (a) MANAGEMENT ISSUES

As with nearly all software, management issues for spreadsheet and database management packages start with the following:

- Making purchase, upgrade, and standardization decisions—these will be based on an analysis of user needs, the available software packages and features, budgets, and so on.
- Ensuring policies and procedures are in place to control and optimize the use of spreadsheet and database management software throughout the organization. This includes:

    Identifying appropriate applications for the software

    Training of staff

    Standardization (e.g., on document formats, diskette labeling and storage procedures, etc.)

    Integration with networks

    Controlling related costs

- Establishing good security, backup and record destruction controls (for both hard copy and electronic media).

Spreadsheet packages are widely used as productivity tools and don't raise unique management control or cost issues. Database packages are another story because most sophisticated designs have implications to the organization far beyond personal productivity. These implications, as well as the significant skills and time required to set up database systems, often warrant custom designing by a programmer or consultant. Alternatively, some specialized database applications, such as accounting, are prepackaged and can be purchased from outside vendors.

Planning and preparation are critical to the success of database applications. Careful thought must be given to the database structure and to the type of data manipulation, information retrieval, and reporting that will be required. Database applications are often not as easily revised as a spreadsheet model, and ad hoc development can lead to disaster. This is especially true for large and complex systems.

As a result of these factors, database packages *per se* tend not to be used as widely as word processing or even spreadsheet packages. Nevertheless, certain applications (e.g., smaller mailing lists that don't have organizationwide significance) can be set up and maintained by individual users without any special assistance or control.

### (b) USER ISSUES

Actually working with spreadsheet and database packages can provide some familiarity; on-line tutorials and courses can also assist. However, becoming proficient with all features (e.g., database screen design) can take many hours of practice. Following are some principles that should be followed:

- For large jobs, break the task down into modules.

- For spreadsheets, summarize the critical results at the top. (This allows the user to see the key results quickly, without having to sift through all of the calculation details.)

- Structure spreadsheets into logical blocks, such as income statement, balance sheet, and statement of cash flow. If possible, keep the size of each block within the limits of the printed page (56 to 60 rows).

- Avoid shortcuts and long, complicated formulas combining several calculation steps; lay out each step of the analysis separately. This will pay off later in maintaining the design.

- Prepare written documentation for designs that are to be used repeatedly in the future, explaining the calculations, describing the layout, and so on.

- Document all assumptions, since these assumptions may be changed later on.

- Include the name of the file on the spreadsheet or database so that it will appear on the printed reports for future reference.

- Use descriptive row and column names for spreadsheets (the same for field names in the case of databases).

- Use columns to represent time periods such as years or months.

- Take the time to confirm properly that the data, calculations, and logic of the design are correct. There is a tendency to presume that computer-generated results are always free from error. This is not necessarily true—for example, if the formulas have been entered incorrectly.

When creating the database structure, field size in particular must be carefully determined. Most database systems use a fixed length of storage for the data fields, set to the value specified in the structure definition. In other words, the program reserves enough storage space to accommodate the maximum specified size of each data element, regardless of how small the actual entries are. Playing it safe by defining unnecessarily large field sizes that will never be approached will waste storage space. In a large database this may impair performance and speed. Nevertheless, you must ensure that the field sizes are big enough to accommodate the largest potential data element.

When using commercial databases that run up fees based on time, follow these steps:

- Prepare search criteria in complete detail before logging on to reduce the volume of extraneous data recovered and to reduce on-line charges.

- Rather than print out or read information while connected, download it to memory or a disk file. This will reduce on-line charges. You can access the stored file later to read, print, or manipulate the data.

- If necessary, upgrade to at least a 14,400 bps or 28,800 bps modem (or even better, an ISDN line), in order to speed up data transfer. (However, be aware that at higher speeds good communication lines are needed to ensure error-free transfer.)

- Some services offer local telephone numbers or toll-free numbers, thereby eliminating long distance charges. If they provide a gateway to a service that otherwise entails a long distance call, the user may be able to reduce costs (depending on the relative on-line and other charges of the respective services).

• Call during nonprime hours, since many services offer reduced rates during these times. Call during hours when the telephone company offers the best discounts. If that time is inconvenient, consider programming the computer to go on-line and execute the required steps during the discount hours. Some telecommunications software packages allow the user to preprogram such procedures.

## (c) MARKET ISSUES

*(i) Historical Background*

The electronic spreadsheet is credited with bringing the personal computer into the serious business market. Before the introduction of VisiCalc for the Apple II in the late seventies, microcomputers had been used primarily by enthusiasts. And whereas most other microcomputer programs began as scaled-down versions of existing software for larger computers, spreadsheets were created on and designed specifically for microcomputers.

VisiCalc (the name stands for "visible calculator") was developed by Software Arts. It was very successful and brought many Apple computers into homes and offices. The paper spreadsheet was used as the on-screen metaphor for VisiCalc. Using this familiar format, almost anything that could be done with pen and paper could be transcribed to the computer, but of course the computer offered the additional benefit of quick corrections and alterations as well as greater numerical accuracy.

The introduction of the IBM PC in 1981 dramatically changed the spreadsheet market. The PC was faster and more powerful than the Apple II but incompatible with the existing Apple software. Software Arts developed VisiCalc for the IBM PC but did not redesign it to take advantage of the PC's new capabilities. One of the first in a new generation of software to do so was Multiplan from Microsoft. The vastly increased memory of the PC meant that the new software was more user friendly and better able to manage larger models.

In 1982 Lotus Development Corporation introduced Lotus 1-2-3; shipments started in 1983. Previously, exploiting the microcomputer's power to produce graphics required spending a lot of time and effort transferring data between spreadsheet and graphics programs. Lotus 1-2-3 added the ability to create graphics directly from the spreadsheet data. It also featured increased size, speed, and ease of use, all because of the increased capacity and power of the IBM PC. It quickly became the top-selling microcomputer program, has been frequently updated over the years, and remains the workhorse package for many PC users.

And VisiCalc? After lengthy legal battles that hurt Software Arts, Lotus Development Corporation bought the company and laid VisiCalc to rest.

Database management systems have been used on large computer systems for many years to handle extensive data collections, such as all of the accounting information for a large corporation. In fact, relational databases were originally developed for large computer systems. The programs were expensive and required large amounts of memory and powerful processors. Moreover, the related processing languages required professional programmers to write applications.

The first database packages for microcomputers in the late 1970s were very primitive and could not be programmed. They were useful for little more than maintaining lists of names and addresses.

The predecessors of today's full-featured programs were introduced in the early 1980s and were based on the larger DBMS software used on mainframes. Their strength lay in their programming features for creating applications; nevertheless, they were developed for 8-bit machines (e.g., dBase II, released in 1981), which limited their power considerably. In 1984 dBase III arrived to take advantage of the increased power of the true 16-bit microcomputers. The current version is dBase V, exploiting today's 32-bit technology.

*(ii)  Market Analysis and Trends*

Lotus 1-2-3 remains a powerful force in the spreadsheet market; however, it no longer dominates as it did throughout most of the 1980s. Microsoft Excel is its major competition.

On the database side, the dominance of dBase during the 1980s has similarly waned, although dBase V is still a popular package. Other players include Paradox (like dBase, a Borland product), Access from Microsoft, Approach from Lotus, and Oracle (the latter mainly in larger, distributed-system environments).

Current microcomputer database programs offer users a level of power that had been available only on mainframes. (In fact, there has been a trend towards the migration of large system databases to the microcomputer environment—e.g., Oracle and Paradox.) The difference is that microcomputer packages are available at a fraction of the cost and are much easier to use. Their capabilities and user-friendliness are developing apace, along with their programming capabilities for customizing applications.

# 9.3  SPREADSHEET ELEMENTS, FEATURES, AND APPLICATIONS

A spreadsheet is essentially a package designed for financial modeling. Financial modeling is the computer analysis of numerical data to assist in making decisions. Normally, financial modeling involves many estimates or assumptions about future events and actions. The main purpose of the model is to predict the different possible outcomes— called cases or scenarios—under these varying estimates or assumptions.

For all but very simple models, the process of projecting numerous scenarios manually is very repetitive and time consuming. Much work and time can be saved by designing a spreadsheet on a computer. Once programmed, the computer is able to produce any number of scenarios very quickly and accurately.

## (a)  GENERAL ELEMENTS AND FEATURES

Spreadsheet software is an electronic form of the paper spreadsheet used in accounting: a large page divided into rows and columns for numerical analysis. The program turns the computer's video monitor into a large spreadsheet that the user writes on with the keyboard, entering and manipulating data.

The intersections of the rows and columns in a spreadsheet form a matrix of locations called cells. The rows are generally numbered from one up and the columns are identified by letters or double letters starting with A. Each cell is referenced by the intersection of its column and row: for example, A1 or F120.

### (i) Creating the Spreadsheet

A spreadsheet model consists of the variables to be examined and a set of formulas defining the relationships between them. The user then builds the model by entering information into the individual cells. This information can be:

- A label: text such as a title or a description.
- A value: a number used in the calculations in the model.
- A formula: a calculation performed by the model using the numbers in one or several cells (e.g., the sum of a number of cells, or one cell multiplied by another; the ability to work with formulas represents the real power of spreadsheets).

### (ii) Working with the Spreadsheet

Spreadsheet software provides a variety of functions called commands that allow the user to manipulate the model. These commands:

- Save the model as a computer file, retrieve models saved in computer files, or combine models.
- Move or copy the contents of cells to other locations.
- Print all or a portion of the model.
- Format the appearance of the model, for example, the number of decimal places displayed, or the width of the columns.
- Transfer data between the spreadsheet and certain other software such as word processing applications.
- Use other special features described in the next section.

The size of the spreadsheet is flexible and expands as the user enters data in new rows or columns. The maximum size is limited by the program but is generally well in excess of the user's needs (usually over 4,000 rows and over 250 columns).

## (b) SPECIAL FEATURES

Virtually all the major packages come with a variety of features that enable users to perform specialized tasks; these include graphics and database functions, linking of spreadsheets, and macros.

### (i) Graphics

Spreadsheets with graphics functions can plot the data within the model on a graph, saving the effort of reentering the numbers into another program. The graph can be displayed on or removed from the screen at the user's request, or printed out on a printer that has graphics capability.

The most common forms of spreadsheet graphics are the line graph, the bar chart, and the pie chart. Programs typically offer many variations of these, including 3-D representations.

### (ii)  Database

This is obviously not a special feature of databases but rather of spreadsheets. In an area of the spreadsheet defined by the user, each row can be treated as a record in the database and each column as a field. Typical functions offered include sorting of records and searching for records matching specified criteria. The functions are limited compared with those of a standalone database program but can be very useful within spreadsheet models.

### (iii)  Linking

Linking means referencing a cell from one spreadsheet to a cell in a different spreadsheet so that the linked cell is updated automatically when the first cell is changed. This feature eliminates the extra time and the potential for error in rekeying data. It is especially important when a user needs to consolidate results of several divisions or entities, each with its own model.

### (iv)  Macros

The better spreadsheet programs support macros, which allow the user to program repetitive tasks to be performed on the spreadsheet. This saves time rekeying the commands each time the repetitive task needs to be carried out.

Sophisticated packages also include programming features within the macro commands, making it possible to design a customized user interface (e.g., a special "menu" that makes it easier for a less knowledgeable user to work with the model).

The utility of macros increases with the size and complexity of the models; another factor is the user's aptitude and dedication in learning how to exploit the potential of the macro feature.

## (c)  ANALYZING DATA AND TRENDS

Spreadsheets allow ledger sheet analysis on most types of numerical data. However, the greatest advantage is gained when the analysis requires regular updating or manipulation. If the work is never to be repeated, then it might be faster to do it by hand rather than to set it up on a model.

Economic and other trends can be analyzed using various spreadsheet functions such as linear regression, exponential smoothing, and moving weighted average. Trends can also be illustrated in a graph, making them even easier to interpret.

## (d)  BUDGETS, PLANS, AND FORECASTS

Budgets, plans, and forecasts are probably the most common of all spreadsheet applications. Models can be written to handle regular budgeting or to forecast the impact of a new project or capital investment on a company.

Projections can be combined with sensitivity analysis, what if analysis, or goal seeking. Each of these is described below.

### (i) Sensitivity Analysis

The purpose of a model containing projections is normally to examine the impact of changing the input assumptions on the critical results. The input assumptions reflect future events that are uncertain and therefore subject to error. An informed investment decision requires knowledge of how the expected return will change if the input assumptions do not match the estimates.

Sensitivity analysis is the process of computing the critical results over a range of values for an input assumption. This can be done easily on a spreadsheet model by repetitively changing an assumption and printing a short summary of the critical results. The computer performs all of the calculations for each scenario.

Certain spreadsheet packages—for example Lotus and Excel—include a function that will create a table listing the critical results obtained over a range of values for an input assumption, thereby performing the sensitivity analysis automatically.

### (ii) "What-If Analysis"

What-if analysis answers the question, "What is the return (or any result) expected if one or more input assumptions are changed to . . . ?" This is similar to sensitivity analysis except that it refers to only one scenario rather than a range of scenarios. For example, a model representing a schedule of mortgage payments might assume an interest rate of 12 percent. A different assumption—say 15 percent—could be input into the model to determine the effect on monthly payments. The model can easily perform any number of what-if analyses in this manner and report the results in a printout.

### (iii) Goal Seeking

Goal seeking answers the question, "What value must be achieved in a selected input assumption (e.g., selling price) to obtain a desired result (e.g., rate of return)?" Spreadsheets might not perform goal seeking automatically but can be manipulated by repeatedly trying input values until the goal is achieved.

## (e) OTHER APPLICATIONS

### (i) Accounting Applications

Spreadsheets are not normally used to handle everyday accounting functions such as general ledger and payroll. Usually these functions are computerized using a dedicated accounting package or a programmable database package.

Nevertheless, specific accounting routines often are modeled, including:

• Consolidation of divisional results or budgets
• Financial statement comparisons to prior periods and budgets
• Tax provision schedules

- Inventory valuation
- Job cost analysis
- Foreign currency translation

*(ii)  Engineering and Scientific Applications*

Complex engineering and scientific analyses can also be modeled using spreadsheets. Examples include the evaluation of experimental results or the computation of load factors in engineering.

Engineering and scientific applications often make use of a variety of mathematical functions provided by spreadsheet software, such as trigonometric, logarithmic, logical, and statistical functions.

## 9.4  DATABASE ELEMENTS, FEATURES, AND APPLICATIONS

A database is a collection of information recorded in an organized structure to facilitate its use. Database management means keeping the database up to date (maintaining) and selectively extracting useful information from it (manipulating). Database programs have long been the centerpiece application in mainframe computer environments, where they are referred to as database management systems or DBMSs. However, databases are now even more popular on microcomputers.

Databases are classified according to the way in which the pieces of information, or data elements, are organized. The two main types are relational and hierarchical:

- *Relational databases*—In relational databases, the data elements are organized in a two-dimensional table with rows and columns. Each row is called a record and contains all of the data elements relating to that record. The data elements are called fields and are put into separate columns. Structurally, the database is analogous to a spreadsheet.

  A relational database application usually consists of a number of separate database files. The program matches records from each of the files based on the information contained in certain fields. The term "relational" derives from the software's ability to relate or link together files in this manner.

- *Hierarchical databases*—In hierarchical databases the data elements are organized in a model that specifies the relationships between them. The model resembles an upside-down tree with the branches representing the relationships connecting the data. The relationships can be one-to-one or one-to-many between an element on one level and the elements below it in the hierarchy. Consider a university where the data elements consist of the professors, the courses, and the students. Each professor is at the top of a tree with branches pointing to the courses taught (on the second level). The courses in turn branch down to the students in each class (on the third level).

Microcomputer database programs usually follow the relational structure, because it tends to be easier to work with and less rigid; however, relational databases make somewhat less efficient use of hardware.

## (a) GENERAL ELEMENTS AND FEATURES

Database programs offer a set of tools with which to organize and manipulate data. The program generally starts up with an open work space and a blank screen. The user executes commands that instruct the database to activate a particular file and/or to perform some action on it. The screen is the program's interface with the user and shows information related to the commands as they are executed.

Typical commands or actions include:

- Adding or deleting records
- Revising the contents of a record
- Adding, changing, or deleting fields
- Selective retrieval (finding records or data elements that match some specified criteria)
- Sorting records into a desired order or changing the order of the records based on predetermined rules
- Linking records in different database files through a common field
- Arithmetic analysis (of numeric fields)
- Generating reports

Many of these operations are dealt with in the following sections.

### (i) Creating the Database Structure

The first step is to define the structure for the database, which means describing the fields that make up each record and their order of appearance. This definition forms one part of the database file; the data are the other part. For each field the user generally specifies the:

- Field name
- Size, or width, of the field
- Type of data the field will store

Data are generally classified into four main types. A given field can store only one type of data. The type of field dictates the form in which data is to be entered and the ways in which the data can be used. The data types are as follows:

- *Text*—text or labels used for any type of description or identification, such as names, addresses, telephone numbers (a separate type of field on some packages), or product model numbers.
- *Numeric*—values or quantities, such as selling price, number of units shipped, or a customer's credit limit.
- *Logical*—a condition dividing the database into two groups, such as male or female.
- *Date*—calendar date consisting of day, month, and year.

Not all database systems recognize logical or date field definitions. Some programs also offer other specialized field types such as dollar, integer, or time, which are variations on the main types listed above.

### (ii)  Defining Key Fields

After the structure is set up and before data are entered, some database programs ask the user to define "key fields." A key field is one that is to be used in later sorting operations.

More than one field can be defined as a key simultaneously, but the keys must be prioritized as primary, secondary, and so on. Sort order is determined on the primary key, but any "ties" (records with identical entries in the primary key) are ordered based on the secondary key.

### (iii)  Data Input and Updating

After the structure and key fields are defined, the user must input the data. The program starts with the first record; once all of the data for that record are entered, the program moves to the next. The software assigns record numbers sequentially, and these are subsequently used to identify the records.

Many programs provide a data input screen that lists all of the field names and highlights a box where the data is to be entered. The cursor cycles through the input areas for each of the fields after confirming that the data input matches the field type. Of course, a field can be left blank if desired.

New records can be added to the database at any time. The additions are appended to the end of the file and again numbered sequentially. The information in the fields of a specific record can be revised or updated using a similar process.

### (iv)  Data Maintenance and Manipulation

Any individual record can be identified and retrieved by referring to its number or searching for one of its elements (e.g., customer name). This allows for easy maintenance of the information in individual records. But the real power of these programs lies in the variety of ways in which larger blocks of data can be selectively manipulated.

The typical selection process involves setting up a condition for a particular field, such as "Sales field > $100,000." In a process known as selective retrieval, the program searches the database and selects only those records for which the condition is satisfied and executes the related command on that subset of the database only.

Some of the primary commands that can be issued to maintain and manipulate databases include the following:

- *Display*—the database can be displayed on the screen, usually in a table format with a new row for each record. Alternatively, the user can view the contents of a single record, usually in the format of the input screen.
- *Delete*—individual records can be deleted from the database. In some databases the remaining records can be renumbered.
- *Replace*—the value of a field can be changed or replaced. For example, in a customer file, a field for discount rates can be selectively revised so that all customers who were receiving a 10 percent discount now receive 12 percent.

- *Sort*—records are first stored in the order in which the data is input. However, the program can rearrange all of the records by ascending or descending order on any key field. Performing such a sort results in the creation of a new file, with the records rearranged into the order selected; the original file remains as it was (however, full-file sorts of this type are more inefficient than indexing, as described later).

- *Analyze*—arithmetic and other functions are available to compute useful statistics on the database, including:

  Count: calculates the total number of records, either in the database or matching the specified conditional expression.

  Sum: adds up the total value of the data elements in a specified numeric field.

  Average: computes the average value of the data elements in a specified numeric field.

### *(v) Report Generation*

The results of data manipulation can be printed out in a report. Normally, the body of a database report is a table consisting of rows and columns; each row represents one record, while the columns represent the fields within each record. The better programs also enable the user to produce custom-designed form reports.

The flexibility of different packages varies with report titles, margins, arithmetic functions, format of output, column widths, and so on. Some programs assist with report design by painting an outline on the screen, allowing the user to see what the report will look like before it is actually printed.

The records to be included in a report can typically be selected using the same criteria and conditional expressions as for any other command. Normally, the report is temporarily created from the information in the database and then printed out; it may not automatically exist as a separate file, unless specifically saved.

## (b) SPECIAL FEATURES

### *(i) Indexing*

As previously described, the records in a database file are stored in the sequence in which the data are input. This is the "physical order" of the information stored on disk. Sorting creates and stores on the disk a second copy of the file with a new physical order reflecting the new sequence. For a large database, this means that a great deal of disk storage space is consumed and that the processing is slowed down as the computer swaps the different sorted versions of the file in and out of memory.

Indexing is an alternative to sorting. The program generates an index to the database—a smaller file consisting only of the record number and the sort key field or fields. The index file is sorted but the original database file containing all of the fields is not. The record number in the index file provides the link to the original database for information on the other fields.

*(ii)  Linking*

In a relational database, different database files can be matched up and manipulated in conjunction with one another. This process, called linking, allows the program to access data elements that belong together but are contained in different files. Repetition of information in each of the files can be eliminated, thereby reducing file size, improving processing speed, and saving data entry time.

Linking involves duplicating one identifying field in both of the related files, such as account number in a customer master file and in a sales order file. Records in the different files with identical entries in that field are linked.

Linking has many accounting applications. Typically, there is information that remains relatively unchanged (e.g., master files containing names and addresses, prices, product descriptions, and employee data) but is needed repeatedly in daily transactions (e.g., sales, purchases, cash receipts, cash payments, and payroll). The master files are set up initially as separate databases, with linking fields to the daily transaction files. Thereafter, the information in the master files does not have to be rekeyed for each of the voluminous daily transactions.

Besides ending the need to enter and store duplicate information, linking is also used to split excessively large databases into smaller, more manageable ones or to accommodate database structures that need more fields or storage size than the maximum allowed by the software.

*(iii)  Processing Modes*

Normally, the user operates a database program by executing commands. A typical session might involve opening a file, inputting new records, indexing the file, performing some computations, linking to other files, and generating a report. This is the primary method of operation for many programs and is called the interactive mode.

Some programs offer a powerful programming alternative to interactive mode called the batch mode. All of the commands required to carry out a processing operation are stored in a command file that is like a computer program.

Software that supports batch mode processing can be considered a type of programming language. The user simply instructs the computer to carry out the command file; all of the commands are then performed in sequence, without intervention by the user.

## (c)  DATABASE APPLICATIONS

Databases are used in a wide variety of environments to manage collections of information. Some typical applications are described briefly in the following sections.

*(i)  Mailing Lists*

Lists of names and addresses (e.g., membership, customer, and subscriber lists) can be manipulated and used to extract target groups for mailing letters or other materials. These files can be supplemented with fields containing personal data such as profession, date of birth, spending patterns, and so on.

Many programs also print mailing labels and address form letters. Some even personalize form letters, although this is crossing over to the realm of word processing software.

### (ii) Accounting

Business bookkeeping and accounting are almost ideal candidates for database applications. Record keeping typically involves a large amount of data that are easily organized by a database package—for example, customer information, inventory, sales orders, and general ledger transactions.

Dedicated accounting systems are essentially specialized and sophisticated versions of database software.

### (iii) On-Line Inquiry

Databases can execute interactive, on-line searches that "interrogate" collections of information and retrieve specific data. Applications include telephone directories, employee data for job assignment or personnel files, customer account histories, and library book collections.

An airline reservation system is an example of a large and sophisticated on-line database application.

### (iv) Custom-Designed Applications

Applications can be custom programmed with database software using batch mode processing—for example, to manage various accounting functions such as inventory control, customer order processing, sales tracking, and commissions.

Commercial add-on products are also available for some of the popular programs—for example to handle complete accounting systems.

## (d) COMMERCIAL DATABASES

Just as libraries have evolved as physical collections of books and information, so commercial databases are evolving as their electronic equivalent.

### (i) General Description

Large collections of information such as newspaper articles, research materials on science and technology, and stock market quotations are available commercially on computer databases for a fee. These on-line information databases allow the subscriber to locate, access, and retrieve information of interest over a telephone line using a microcomputer and a modem. Normally, the user specifies the search criteria, such as a subject of interest; alternatively, the database can be searched for particular words or phrases.

The search criteria include most of the operators used by microcomputer database programs. Additional advanced search techniques are these: synonym or phrasing searching; searching for one word in proximity with another; and wild card searching. (In the latter only some letters or words are specified; those that are unspecified can be anything for the purposes of the software's search.) Some services offer workshops in search techniques; the cost and time invested in these can pay off in reduced on-line charges. Better search techniques save time by weeding out less relevant items to reduce the volume of information retrieved.

Commercial databases are often combined with electronic bulletin boards and/or electronic mail (e-mail) services. Bulletin boards provide a public forum for the exchange of ideas and news. In the case of e-mail, additional fees are often charged for storage of mail on the system.

### (ii)  Fees

Fees are usually based on total time connected plus surcharges for the quantity of information retrieved and/or the number of searches performed. The fees are often discounted during "nonprime hours," which usually means after business hours.

Many services charge a one-time setup fee to subscribers, but may offer some free time on the service to partially offset this cost. Services may also have annual fees and/or minimum charges each time the service is used.

### (iii)  Gateway Services

Gateway services offer users the opportunity to access other commercial databases while signed on and then to return to the main service when finished. If the user wishes to use several services one after the other, this can save the time and effort of logging on and off each one.

The emergence of gateway services is an important trend that increases the attractiveness of commercial databases. These services typically offer the convenience of a single billing, which makes for easier administration for the subscriber.

### (iv)  Types of Information and Services

The variety of information available via commercial databases is almost endless. Any list would include the following:

- News stories (from newspapers around the world)
- Stock and securities quotes
- Corporate financial data
- Indexes and/or abstracts of periodicals and other reference sources
- Government documents such as budgets
- Data on science, technology, trademarks, the law, health and medicine, and the weather
- Bulletin boards and catalogs for home shopping

Some of the well-known general (and gateway) services include America Online ("AOL"), CompuServe, and Prodigy.

## 9.5  USER NEEDS AND SOFTWARE EVALUATION

### (a)  MATCHING USER NEEDS AND FEATURES

There are many spreadsheet and database programs on the market, most of which perform adequately for general applications. Nevertheless, the features of the software being considered should be evaluated and matched with the needs of the user.

The following subsections discuss some of the important features to investigate. The user should rank these in order of importance before evaluating specific spreadsheet or database packages.

*(i)  Hardware and Operating System Requirements*

The compatibility of spreadsheet and database management software with the hardware (e.g., Intel-based, Apple Macintosh) and operating system (e.g., DOS, OS/2, Windows) is obviously critical. The capacity of the system must also be considered carefully.

The spreadsheet and database files in many applications tend to be large. In the case of large databases, the programs are designed to read only a portion of the file into memory (RAM) at any one time. When the program needs to work with a different part of the data file, the computer swaps portions of the file between memory and the disk storage device. Working with large files therefore requires frequent disk access. As a result, the size of RAM and the type of disk storage used greatly affect the performance of database software. In particular, a faster disk storage device improves performance.

It's difficult to generalize on how much capacity is enough, but 8Mb RAM is probably the bare minimum required to run substantial applications using the major spreadsheet or database packages. Available disk space is more of a concern on the database side. With the cost of high-capacity hard disks (1 gigabyte and up) coming down so rapidly, it makes sense to err on the side of excess capacity.

*(ii)  Size of Application*

For spreadsheet software, the power of microcomputers has increased to such an extent that the size of the application is rarely an obstacle. On the other hand, database processing often involves simple manipulations on very large quantities of data. Consequently, the maximum file size can be an important factor. There are a number of other capacity constraints to consider in addition to the total file size, including:

- Number of records per file
- Number of fields per record
- Size of record
- Size of field (which may vary for character and numeric fields)
- Number of key fields

The amount of memory that the program itself takes up and other hardware requirements of the software may impose capacity constraints as well.

*(iii) Complexity of Application*

Two capabilities of spreadsheet packages—linking and macros—can assist with complex applications. These special features were briefly described earlier in this chapter.

For power and flexibility in data manipulation, the ability to access several files simultaneously is very important. Not all databases offer this access. The number of files that can be opened simultaneously may also be limited by the operating system.

Some programs include or offer interfaces to programming languages. This obviously permits the development of more sophisticated applications.

*(iv) Ease of Use*

To some extent, ease of use is a trade-off against the power of the program. The user must determine how much to emphasize one over the other. Features that affect ease of use include:

- On-screen interactive tutorials
- Well-written and complete documentation
- Context-sensitive help screens
- Menu-driven command selection and pull-down menus
- Commands that "read" like English
- Telephone support, especially for complex programs

*(v) Reports Required*

Especially for database packages, the ability to produce reports and flexibility in report design and layout are very important. Database reports are usually tables consisting of selected records as the rows and selected fields as the columns. The report writer should be evaluated for:

- Flexibility in the appearance of printed reports, including number and position of titles, column headings, labels and output values, subtotals, and so on.
- Fonts and print styles available.
- The ability to store report specifications in a file for later use or editing.

Also look for the ability to custom design form reports. And, of course, compatibility with printers (i.e., device drivers) is essential.

*(vi) Software Versions and Software Support*

Inevitably, spreadsheet and database management software contain errors or bugs that require correction. In addition, software generally improves as technology advances. It is therefore essential that a software package be well supported and updated regularly.

Some experts recommend shying away from the first version of a program or major program upgrade, reasoning that such versions are more likely to contain bugs. They argue that it's better to wait for the first update after such a new release. (Many people argue the same thing for the first model year of a particular car—i.e., that it's better to wait a year, by which time the manufacturer will have corrected any manufacturing flaws.) To counteract this type of resistance on the part of users, some software manufacturers have taken to avoiding the ".0" label for their software. For example, instead of issuing version 5.0, the manufacturer will go straight to version 5.1 to at least give the appearance of more extensive testing.

In addition to the initial price of the package, the user should consider the manufacturer's or vendor's update policies (i.e., how users are notified of updates) and the related cost. The better programs tend to be improved frequently to keep up with the competition.

Support—both vendor and manufacturer—is also a factor to consider. Most major software manufacturers also offer telephone support to registered users. However, a number of the larger manufacturers have begun charging a fee for such services.

### (vii)  Compatibility

A key consideration for many users—especially medium- and large-size organizations—is compatibility with other software owned by the user. For example, if others in the organization are already using a particular package, buying that package will facilitate the exchange of files within the organization.

Another factor to consider is whether the same manufacturer's software is being used for other applications such as word processors. Sister packages of this kind usually offer greater integration. For example, if database information is regularly incorporated into reports, easy integration with a word processor may be a key consideration.

### (viii)  Cost

The price of software has come down substantially in recent years, following the trend in hardware prices. Many spreadsheet and database programs are also being offered as a package with other programs such as word processing and graphics or presentation software, providing even greater value. (Microsoft Office and Lotus SmartSuite are examples.)

Nevertheless, price comparison is an important step in large organizations that are considering the purchase of site licenses or that operate large networks. In such cases the total purchase cost can run into the tens or even hundreds of thousands of dollars. Training and future upgrade costs also have to be factored in.

### (ix)  Other Concerns

A number of other features may be important to users—for example, the graphics capability built into the major spreadsheet packages. Other concerns that are especially important for database packages are set out below.

- *Security*—larger database applications are often designed to be used by many individuals. The time spent in the creation of the applications and the data are generally quite valuable. If more than one person will have access to the database, security features to protect the integrity of the files and data therein from accidental or other damage are important. Possible security features include file passwords, write protection, and data encryption (the scrambling of the data).

- *Networking capability*—increasingly, microcomputers are being connected through a local area network (LAN) to share data and hardware resources. Database programs differ in their ability to operate on a LAN, their compatibility with the various types of LANs, their record-update and record-locking abilities (i.e., the program's ability to accept and/or prevent any change to a record), and data security.

- *Data transfer*—it may be useful to transfer data from the database program to some other software. There are many data file transfer formats. Consider which file formats the program is compatible with and can export data in, and which major software packages will accept those formats. Pay particular attention to which software you currently own or anticipate purchasing.

- *Input screens*—consider the default input screen created by the program for data entry or data editing. (The "default" input screen is the one normally displayed by the program when the user enters information into the database.) Consider how much control is allowed over the appearance of the screen, specifically how fields can be presented and their order of presentation. User-defined input screens can speed up the data entry process, contribute to productivity and reduce errors.

## (b) WHERE TO BUY

Software is frequently sold at a discount, the extent of which usually depends on the vendor and the after-sales support it offers. The greatest discounts are usually offered by mail order houses that offer no advice. No matter where it's purchased, buyers should ensure that software is sealed in its original packaging. This is important for license/registration purposes and also to ensure that it is virus-free.

Some vendors offer demonstration diskettes that run through some of the program's functions on a sample file while the user observes. These can help the user become familiar with the program and assist in the software evaluation process.

Although important, the selection of a vendor is less crucial for software than for hardware. Nevertheless, after-sales support may be a factor for purchasers who want support or who expect to have problems learning and/or operating the package. If support is needed, the higher cost normally charged by a more established vendor with knowledgeable staff may be worthwhile. Although software houses offer telephone support, it can be frustrating because of the lower level of personal attention and the long-distance charges. (Also, as noted previously, many manufacturers now charge for telephone service.) A reputable vendor in the same locality with whom the user can build a relationship can prove a valuable troubleshooting resource.

## (c) OTHER SOURCES OF INFORMATION

Training and practice are vital for spreadsheet and especially database programs because they are not as easily learned as word processing packages. Moreover, they do not offer the same sort of entry level from which additional features can be picked up as needed. Some additional sources are set out below.

*(i)  On-Line Tutorials and Help*

Designing spreadsheet and database applications requires a good working knowledge of both spreadsheet and database concepts and the software itself. Learning the software can take some time because it is command-driven. Some programs offer various types of assistance, including the following:

*   *Help screens*—on-line help screens accessed by a defined key can assist the user with problems during a session, especially if the help is context-sensitive.
*   *Menus*—optional menu-driven operation can be slower for experienced users but provides faster access for the beginner. Pull-down menu systems also enhance the learning environment.
*   *On-screen interactive tutorial lessons*—some programs offer these, which lead the user through the basics by simulating the use of the actual software.

*(ii)  Books, Magazines, and Newsletters*

The manuals that accompany the software often are designed more as a reference source for the program's numerous functions than as a teaching tool. As a result, there are many books available to help users learn spreadsheet and database management software (e.g., Lotus 1-2-3, dBase) from the ground up. There are also books to help experienced users with advanced functions and programming.

Many of the leading computer magazines carry articles dealing with spreadsheet and database packages and/or have columns offering advice and tips.

The bibliography in Appendix A includes a list of selected books and magazines.

*(iii)  User Groups*

User networks (e.g., for Lotus 1-2-3 or dBase users) exist throughout North America. User groups often communicate via electronic bulletin boards that are accessible with a modem over telephone lines. Computer magazines and newsletters periodically print lists of such groups in their areas of distribution; your vendor may also be able to assist you in finding one.

Some on-line commercial database and gateway services have subsections for groups of users with special interests. These groups provide a forum for users to pass on information that may be of interest to others.

*(iv)  Courses and Seminars*

Training courses are offered by a variety of firms including computer vendors, public accounting firms, professional bodies (such as societies of accountants), and training institutions. Courses are typically one or two days, and fees usually range from $100 to $500.

A course can provide a good grounding, but afterward the user will need to practice the concepts for some time before putting a spreadsheet or especially a database program to work. Many of the commercially available courses are geared to Lotus (also Microsoft's Excel, which has been helped by the popularity of the Microsoft Office suite) and dBase, since these programs all have a large installed base. However, the user can often benefit by learning concepts applicable to similar programs.

*(v)  Video Training*

Training courses are available on videocassette tapes; they are sometimes advertised in computer magazines. Although the tapes lack the interaction between the instructor and students found in a classroom environment, there are cost advantages for users in remote locations. Also, the tapes can be used by several people.

*(vi)  Consulting Services*

Purchasing custom-designed spreadsheet models or database applications should be considered wherever possible because it saves time and effort by drawing on the expertise of the consultant to design a better application, and it provides greater assurance that the application works correctly. The value derived increases with the complexity of the application and the sophistication of the user.

   Many of the large accounting and management consulting firms provide software-related services. There are also independent consultants who specialize in this field.

## 9.6 CATALOG OF SELECTED SPREADSHEET AND DATABASE MANAGEMENT SOFTWARE

The following list (in alphabetical order by package name) represents a cross-section of a few of the popular spreadsheet and database management packages. The listing of a package should not be construed as an endorsement, nor should its failure to appear be construed as a condemnation. Price estimates are for the fourth quarter of 1996, based on single-copy prices charged by discount retail chains. Full service dealers charge more; multiple-copy site licensees will typically pay less. Prices on the old software version may fall when a new version is released. Lower upgrade prices (usually about 67 percent off the regular price for standalone packages, 33 percent off for suites) are typically offered to current users and to users of competitive products. Proof that the user is a licensee is required to obtain the upgrade price (for suites, proof of license for a single component is sufficient). Some upgrade packages automatically scan a user's hard disk to ensure they are an existing licensee.

   Other publications, in particular computer magazines, regularly publish more complete catalogues and reviews of available software. Several of these publications are listed in the bibliography contained in Appendix A. Independent software dealers can also provide up-to-date information on specific product options. Finally, the software manufacturers themselves will usually provide complete information on their products. A list of the addresses and phone numbers of several manufacturers appears in the directory of companies in Appendix B.

| Spreadsheet and Database Management Software | Version Number | Estimated (Best) Price | Manufacturer Name |
|---|---|---|---|
| **1. Access for Windows** (database software) | 2.0 | $280.00 U.S. $390.00 Cdn. | Microsoft Corporation |

*Requirements:* 8Mb RAM recommended (4Mb minimum), 20Mb hard disk space for full installation, Windows 3.1 or later

*Comments:* This package is also part of Microsoft Office Pro v4.3 for Windows (along with Word word processor, Excel spreadsheet, and PowerPoint presentation packages, and a Mail license), requires 8Mb RAM, 82Mb hard disk space for full installation (29Mb minimum), estimated best price $520.00 U.S., $775.00 Cdn.

| | | | |
|---|---|---|---|
| **2. Access for Windows 95** (database software) | 7.0 | $340.00 U.S. $475.00 Cdn. | Microsoft Corporation |

*Requirements:* 12Mb RAM, 54Mb hard disk space for full installation, Windows 95

*Comments:* This package is commonly referred to as Access 95. It is also part of Microsoft Office 95 Professional (along with Word 95 word processor, Excel 95 spreadsheet, and PowerPoint 95 presentation packages, and Schedule+ 95 time management software), estimated best price $600.00 U.S., $895.00 Cdn.

| | | | |
|---|---|---|---|
| **3. Approach for Windows** (database software) | 3.0 | $ 95.00 U.S. $130.00 Cdn. | Lotus Development Corporation |

*Requirements:* 4Mb RAM, 16Mb hard disk space for full installation (4Mb minimum), Windows 3.1 or later

*Comments:* Approach is also part of SmartSuite v3.1 for Windows (along with Word Pro word processing, Lotus 1-2-3 spreadsheet, Freelance graphics, and Organizer personal info mgr), requires 6Mb RAM, 93Mb hard disk space for full installation (33Mb min.), estimated best price $460.00 U.S., $630.00 Cdn. Windows 95 versions also available.

| | | | |
|---|---|---|---|
| **4. dBase V for Windows** (database software) | 5.0 | $330.00 U.S. $490.00 Cdn. | Borland International |

*Requirements:* 8Mb RAM recommended (6Mb minimum), 14Mb hard disk space, Windows 3.1 or later

| | | | |
|---|---|---|---|
| **5. Excel for Macintosh** (spreadsheet software) | 5.0 | $280.00 U.S. $390.00 Cdn. | Microsoft Corporation |

*Requirements:* 8Mb RAM recommended (4Mb minimum), 22Mb hard disk space recommended (6Mb minimum), System 7.0 or later

| Spreadsheet and Database Management Software | Version Number | Estimated (Best) Price | Manufacturer Name |
|---|---|---|---|
| **6. Excel for Windows** (spreadsheet software) | 5.0 | $280.00 U.S. $390.00 Cdn. | Microsoft Corporation |

*Requirements:* 8Mb RAM recommended (4Mb minimum), 22Mb hard disk space recommended (6Mb minimum), Windows 3.1 or later

*Comments:* This package is also part of Microsoft Office v4.2 for Windows (along with Word word processor and PowerPoint presentation packages, and a Mail license), estimated best price $430.00 U.S.; $650.00 Cdn. Also Microsoft Office Pro v4.3 (with above plus Access database package), requires 8 Mb RAM, 82Mb hard disk space for full installation (29Mb minimum), estimated best price $520.00 U.S., $775.00 Cdn.

| | | | |
|---|---|---|---|
| **7. Excel for Windows 95** (spreadsheet software) | 7.0 | $340.00 U.S. $475.00 Cdn. | Microsoft Corporation |

*Requirements:* 6Mb RAM, 38Mb hard disk space for full installation, Windows 95

*Comments:* This package is commonly referred to as Excel 95; It is also part of Microsoft Office 95 Standard (along with Word 95 word processor, and PowerPoint 95 presentation packages, and Schedule+ 95 time management software), estimated best price $500.00 U.S., $750 Cdn. Also Microsoft Office 95 Professional (with above plus Access 95 database package), estimated best price $600.00 U.S., $895.00 Cdn.

| | | | |
|---|---|---|---|
| **8. Lotus 1-2-3 for Windows** (spreadsheet software) | 5.0 | $300.00 U.S. $410.00 Cdn. | Lotus Development Corporation |

*Requirements:* 4Mb RAM (6Mb recommended), 27Mb hard disk space for full installation, Windows 3.1 or later

*Comments:* Lotus 1-2-3 is also part of SmartSuite v3.1 for Windows (along with Word Pro word processing, Approach database, Freelance graphics, and Organizer personal info mgr), requires 6Mb RAM, 93Mb hard disk space for full installation (33Mb minimum), estimated best price $460.00 U.S., $630.00 Cdn. Windows 95 version also available.

| | | | |
|---|---|---|---|
| **9. Paradox for Windows** (database software) | 5.0 | $240.00 U.S. $350.00 Cdn. | Borland International |

*Requirements*: Minimum 4Mb RAM (6Mb recommended), 33Mb hard disk space for full installation, Windows 3.1 or later

*Comments:* This package was part of PerfectOffice Pro v3.0 for Windows (along with WordPerfect word processor, Quattro Pro spreadsheet, Presentations presentation, InfoCentral personal information manager, Envoy electronic publisher, Groupware e-mail, and AppWare visual development packages), estimated best price $550.00 U.S., $775.00 Cdn.

| Spreadsheet and Database Management Software | Version Number | Estimated (Best) Price | Manufacturer Name |
|---|---|---|---|
| **10. Quattro Pro for Windows** (spreadsheet software) | 6.0 | $240.00 U.S. $350.00 Cdn. | Borland International |

*Requirements:* Minimum 4Mb RAM (8Mb recommended), 28Mb hard disk space for full installation (10Mb minimum), Windows 3.1 or later

*Comments:* This package was part of PerfectOffice v3.0 for Windows (along with WordPerfect word processor, Presentations presentation, InfoCentral personal information manager, Envoy electronic publisher, and GroupWise e-mail packages), estimated best price $440.00 U.S., $645.00 Cdn. Also PerfectOffice Pro (with above plus Paradox database and AppWare visual development packages), estimated best price $550.00 U.S., $775.00 Cdn. Now part of Corel Office.

# CHAPTER 10

# Other Software Categories

| | |
|---|---|
| (v) Software Versions and Software Support | (i) On-Line Tutorials and Help |
| (vi) Compatibility | (ii) Books, Magazines, and Newsletters |
| (vii) Cost | (iii) User Groups |
| (viii) Other Concerns | (iv) Courses and Seminars |
| (b) Where to Buy | (v) Video Training |
| (c) Other Sources of Information | (vi) Consulting Services |

Chapters 8 and 9 dealt with word processing, desktop publishing, spreadsheets, and database management software. This chapter will deal with a few other software categories under the following headings:

- A checklist (Section 10.1), summarizing many of the main points in this chapter.

- A brief treatment of the management and user and issues surrounding some of the software dealt with in this chapter (Section 10.2).

- Sections on three categories of software: Graphics and Presentation Software (Section 10.3), Accounting and Accounting-Related Software (Section 10.4), and Large System Software (Section 10.5).

- A discussion of user needs assessment and software evaluation (Section 10.6).

## 10.1 SOFTWARE CHECKLIST

The following checklist is designed to assist accountants in decision-making and management relating to software, in their organizations and those of their clients. Generally, all "No" answers require investigation and follow-up, the results of which should be documented. Where there is such additional documentation, the purpose of the "Ref" column is to cross-reference the checklist to the appropriate working paper (or to the notes on the reverse).

The checklist is intended for general use only. If software is of especially vital concern to an organization, the advice of a specialist should be sought.

## Software Checklist

|  | Yes | No | N/A | Ref |
|---|---|---|---|---|

**1. Management Issues—Acquisition**

a. Have an appropriate process, timetable, and budget been established for the assessment of user needs, the evaluation of available packages, purchase, training, and implementation? □ □ □ ___

b. Has the participation of the users of the software been ensured throughout the process? □ □ □ ___

c. Have the major user needs been identified—such as the system environment (Mac, OS/2, Windows), size of files that must be handled, availability of support, etc.—and has a preliminary identification been made of those packages that may meet these criteria? □ □ □ ___

d. For each package that might be purchased, have the following issues been addressed?

   • Compatibility with hardware and operating systems □ □ □ ___

   • Compatibility with all printers in use □ □ □ ___

   • Compatibility with other software in use □ □ □ ___

   • Compatibility with all networks in use □ □ □ ___

   • Compatibility with possible future upgrades of above □ □ □ ___

   • Adequacy of RAM and hard disk capacity □ □ □ ___

   • Availability of manufacturer and/or vendor support □ □ □ ___

   • Adequacy of documentation and manuals □ □ □ ___

   • Availability of skilled operating personnel □ □ □ ___

   • Availability of training (self-study, seminars, etc.) □ □ □ ___

   • Ability to handle required size of files □ □ □ ___

e. Has the software been user-tested for appropriateness and ease of use (including all important functions)? □ □ □ ___

f. Is the software price (taking into account the required number of copies and/or site licenses, training costs, etc.):

   • Competitive with other comparable packages? □ □ □ ___

   • Within budget? □ □ □ ___

g. Once a package is decided upon, have the related purchase documents (sales agreements, site licenses, etc.) been reviewed, by legal counsel if appropriate? □ □ □ ___

|  | Yes | No | N/A | Ref |
|---|---|---|---|---|

### 2. Management Issues—Implementation and Use

a. Have all appropriate applications for the software been identified to ensure that maximum use and value are obtained from the software investment?  ☐ ☐ ☐ ___

b. Are appropriate mechanisms in place to ensure that:

   • The organization is aware of future software upgrades?  ☐ ☐ ☐ ___

   • All users have the most current software version?  ☐ ☐ ☐ ___

c. Have appropriate policies, procedures, standards and controls been put in place with respect to:

   • Hiring and training of users?  ☐ ☐ ☐ ___

   • File formats and/or templates?  ☐ ☐ ☐ ___

   • Full documentation of all files and templates?  ☐ ☐ ☐ ___

   • File backups, including off-site backups?  ☐ ☐ ☐ ___

   • File security, both electronic and physical?  ☐ ☐ ☐ ___

   • File destruction, both electronic and physical?  ☐ ☐ ☐ ___

### 3. User Issues

a. Are users adequately trained in the use of the software, including refresher or update courses when required?  ☐ ☐ ☐ ___

b. Do users observe the following principles in utilizing the software?

   • Breaking down large projects into smaller modules  ☐ ☐ ☐ ___

   • Step-by-step approach (no complex shortcuts)  ☐ ☐ ☐ ___

   • Listing of all assumptions used  ☐ ☐ ☐ ___

   • Written documentation for the project  ☐ ☐ ☐ ___

c. Both in theory and in practice, are users aware of the importance and necessity of:

   • Frequently saving files?  ☐ ☐ ☐ ___

   • Frequently backing up files?  ☐ ☐ ☐ ___

d. Are users aware of—and in practice do they follow—procedures with respect to:

   • File and template formats?  ☐ ☐ ☐ ___

   • Diskette labeling and storage?  ☐ ☐ ☐ ___

   • Physical security?  ☐ ☐ ☐ ___

   • Physical destruction (hard copy, diskettes, etc.)?  ☐ ☐ ☐ ___

## 10.2   MANAGEMENT AND USER ISSUES

### (a)  MANAGEMENT ISSUES

As with virtually all software, management issues start with:

- Making purchase, upgrade, and standardization decisions based on an analysis of user needs, the available software packages and features, and budgets.
- Ensuring policies and procedures are in place to control and optimize the use of the software throughout the organization, including:

    Identifying appropriate applications for the software

    Staff training

    Standardization (e.g., on document formats, diskette labeling and storage procedures, etc.)

    Integration with networks

    Controlling related costs
- Establishing good security, backup, and record destruction controls (for both hard copy and electronic media).

### (b)  USER ISSUES

Following are some principles that should be followed:

- For large jobs, break the task down into modules.
- Where applicable, summarize the critical results at the top (this allows the key results to be seen quickly, without having to sift through all of the details).
- Structure projects into logical blocks. If possible, keep the size of each block within the limits of the printed page.
- Avoid shortcuts and long complicated steps; lay out each step of the analysis separately. This will pay off later in maintaining the design or project.
- Prepare written documentation for designs or projects that are to be used repeatedly, explaining the steps and procedures, describing the layout, and so on.
- Document all assumptions, since these assumptions might change.
- Be sure that the name of the file appears on printed output for future reference.

## 10.3   GRAPHICS AND PRESENTATION SOFTWARE

Graphics software is indispensable in preparing visual aids such as slides or overheads and in enhancing the visual appeal of printed reports or any kind of presentation. In fact, graphics software has become somewhat of a subset of *presentation software,* which refers to a number of packages that perform different functions but have the same basic objective: the production of high-quality, attractive output that makes use of both text and graphic elements. Presentation software packages typically bring together such functions as graphics, page layout, and even word processing—for example, the printing of large font sizes for text overheads or slides.

## (a) GENERAL DESCRIPTION

Graphics and presentation software packages assist in creating nontext visual images such as geometric shapes, charts, graphs, diagrams, and drawings. Normally, the graphic is created on the display screen and stored in a disk file. It is then either printed or transferred to another program, where it is merged with other material. The digitized graphic stored in a computer file can also be used to produce overheads and even slides or film with the help of special photographic equipment.

## (b) GRAPHICS AND PRESENTATION ALTERNATIVES

A graphic or presentation aid can be created in a number of ways:

- Automatically, from data supplied by a spreadsheet, database or other software package (for example, many graphics packages can take data and plot it on a line, bar, or pie chart).
- With graphic tools supplied by the graphics or presentation package (for example, most programs have a "palette" of basic geometric shapes [circles, squares, rectangles, etc.] that can be selected and sized to suit the user's needs; geometric shapes or defined areas can also be filled with a variety of different colors or patterns—these are also selected from a menu or palette on the screen, normally with a mouse).
- Freehand, using a graphics tablet that automatically transfers the freehand drawing to the display screen.
- From a library of graphic images and art (these libraries are often included with the graphics or presentation package; in the case of some of the more popular software, libraries are also marketed separately).

## (c) COMMON APPLICATIONS

Some of the more common applications of graphics and presentation packages include:

- Business graphics used to supplement reports (for example, line, bar, and pie charts)
- Presentation materials such as overheads and slides
- The enhancing of advertising and similar promotional material—for example, brochures—with graphic images
- Computer-aided design and computer-aided manufacturing (CAD/CAM), now commonly used in the automobile and other manufacturing industries
- Commercial art

## (d) OTHER CONSIDERATIONS

*(i) Compatibility with Printers and other Devices*

Graphics and presentation software programs need special instructions to control or drive a printer or other output device—for example, to process special formatting specifications in a document. These instructions are called device drivers. Most packages include drivers for the more common printers in the marketplace; however, the user should confirm that the package selected has the driver for the printer that will be used.

Some printers can emulate, or imitate, one of the more common printers on the market. For example, Epson has become somewhat of a standard among dot matrix printers. Software that has a device driver for an Epson should work with a printer that can emulate an Epson. However, the user should carefully investigate how well the combination will work if the software does not have a driver matched to the printer in question.

In the case of graphics and presentation software, similar concerns extend to other output devices such as plotters, or even more advanced and expensive equipment used to produce pictures and slides. Except in high-volume environments, the capital investment required to purchase such equipment may not be justified compared to the cost of using an outside supplier. Even in the latter case, however, users need to ensure that their software and related image files are compatible with the process being used by the outside supplier or service bureau.

*(ii)   Image Size, Resolution, and Speed of Processing*

Image size, resolution, and speed of processing are related variables. The better graphics and presentation software packages digitize images. The greater the resolution, the greater the size of the image—i.e., larger memory and disk storage capacity are required to handle the large number of individual elements making up the image. As resolution and corresponding size of the image increase, speed decreases. As a result, depending on the speed of the hardware and the efficiency of the software, it can take several minutes to process even a single photographic-quality image.

*(iii)   Compatibility*

Finally, the issue of compatibility applies not just within the organization but extends beyond it as well to the degree that it affects personnel. For example, market leaders and/or packages from the major manufacturers—such as Corel Draw, Harvard Graphics, Lotus's Freelance, Adobe Illustrator, and Microsoft's PowerPoint—tend to be better supported and in wider use. As a result, it is easier to find staff who can operate such programs.

## 10.4   ACCOUNTING AND ACCOUNTING-RELATED SOFTWARE

It's been said that an accountant's job is to make order out of the chaos. As you may remember from the Preface, one of the objectives of this handbook is to make order out of information technology chaos. You may also remember that the French word for computer, *ordinateur,* loosely translates as "order keeper." Computers themselves can be thought of as tools that assist us in "making order out of the chaos."

Considering this parallel between the two fields—accounting and computers—it isn't surprising that accounting systems were one of the earliest applications of computers. For many in business, the books and records of a company are like a giant shoe box of forms, check stubs, and adding machine tapes. Computers can help sort it all out.

## (a) MANUAL VS. COMPUTERIZED ACCOUNTING

In a manual system you can keep track of basic information such as asset purchases, the amount of total sales, and the dollar and quantity sales of specific products. While this may be entirely sufficient to produce a set of financial statements at year's end, it often isn't enough information for management to run a business. For example, the sales manager may want to know which salesperson sold the most or sold goods with the greatest dollar gross margin. This kind of management information could be extracted from most manual systems, but only after a great deal of time has been spent sorting through individual transaction records and summarizing them.

Computers are ideal for the slugging through and sorting out process. They excel at reworking data and presenting it in many different ways. The way in which an accounting system can quickly and efficiently prepare management accounting reports to assist key decision makers can be the most important benefit of all, for many businesses.

## (b) HISTORICAL BACKGROUND

Accounting is a long-established application on large computer systems. Such systems are very large and expensive, however, and because of this they are inaccessible to all but the largest businesses.

The first microcomputer-based accounting systems ran on the CP/M (control program for microprocessors) operating system, which became available in the late 1970s. These early programs typically had limited use (and capacity). For example, they would rarely store detailed transaction data past the current month; instead, they would show only a balance forward amount.

The arrival in 1981 of the business-oriented IBM PC switched the focus of accounting software development to the MS-DOS environment. The biggest change, as far as transaction storage capacity is concerned, came the following year with the launch of the IBM PC XT. The XT came complete with a hard disk and a permanent storage medium of 10 megabytes, equivalent to 30 floppy diskettes. This broke the logjam in data storage and allowed program developers to create microaccounting software that could store an entire year's transactions on-line.

The next major development started the following year with the maturation of the first local area networks. These allowed multiple work stations to access a common database. Software developers were able to create multiuser accounting systems for micros, which in turn meant that larger companies with more than one or two people in the accounting function were able to perform all accounting tasks in a coordinated fashion.

## (c) ELEMENTS AND FEATURES

*(i) General Description*

Accounting systems are essentially databases that accumulate records of a business's individual financial transactions, sort and manipulate those records, and produce related reports. The way in which these functions are carried out varies widely from system to system. The particular features of the systems also vary. Even so, the essential process—accumulation, manipulation, and reporting—is always the same.

The major modular functions of most accounting packages are general ledger, accounts receivable, inventory and job costing, accounts payable, and payroll. However, you should note that there is little consistency among vendors of accounting system software as to exactly which functions are contained within a particular module; it is therefore important to get a description of the functions and reports from each vendor in order to be certain of what you are getting.

An accounting system can be either packaged or custom designed, as set out in the following sections.

### (ii)   Custom-Designed Systems

The term "custom-designed system" is a bit misleading, since almost no accounting systems are developed entirely from scratch these days. Usually, the software programmer will use building blocks of previously developed codes that perform basic calculations and sorting. These are then supplemented with a specially written code that prepares special reports or presents information on custom display screens.

Of course, this is still a one-of-a-kind system. The cost will therefore exceed that of a packaged system; and, since it is not available off-the-shelf, it will take time to plan the system and piece it together.

Programmer salaries typically increase because of inflation. Conversely, the price of computer hardware has dropped, on average, by 20 percent a year for the last two decades. The custom-designed software option has therefore become more expensive in recent years.

### (iii)   Packaged Systems

When a standard set of accounting functions is sold to a large number of users at a predetermined fee, the programming costs of developing the software can be amortized over a much larger number of users. One result is that the cost to each individual user will be much lower than that of a custom-designed program.

Packaged systems can be designed for a broad "horizontal" market or for a specifically defined industry, referred to as a "vertical" market.

Most horizontal packages are available in modular form. Each module automates a specific accounting function. The modules of a single vendor's system are designed to integrate or pass information through to other modules very easily. Modules from different vendors will work either not at all or only after some conversion adjustments.

Vertical accounting software, on the other hand, is specifically developed to meet the peculiar reporting requirements of a certain industry. There are vertical systems for many different organizations: law firms, property managers, and construction contractors, for example. Verticals typically cost more than horizontals for the same reason that custom programming costs more than a packaged system—the cost of program development for verticals is spread over fewer users.

Most of the popular, well-publicized programs are horizontal packages. They include top-sellers that are packed with features the software vendor believes will appeal to a wide range of users.

Packaged systems do have their disadvantages. One of the biggest is that a company is often forced to settle for standardized procedures and functions that may not be relevant to its particular organization. The major elements of a packaged accounting system are set out below. Within the same vendor's product line, these elements can usually be purchased as separate modules.

### (iv)  General Ledger

All general ledger systems will accept journal entries and accumulate them to allow print-out of a trial balance. Most will also prepare financial statements, including a balance sheet and income statement.

Financial statements can be formatted in a variety of ways. Entry level systems tend to lock the user into one type of format, which is usually tied into the account number. Better general ledgers provide a "report writer" that lets the user adjust the calculation of report subtotals, placement of headings on the printed page, and the calculation of ratios and percentages.

Some general ledgers also allow you to enter budget figures and prepare reports comparing your actual results with your plan and/or with prior years.

### (v)  Accounts Receivable

All accounts receivable systems allow entry of invoice totals and cash receipts. Users can also prepare an aged trial balance and, in most cases, print out account statements for each customer.

Some systems will only prepare balance forward accounts that show the detail transactions for the current month. Better systems offer the choice of open-item accounts receivable—in other words, they will maintain all transaction details until invoices are paid or otherwise credited.

If you charge interest on delinquent accounts, check to see how interest charges are calculated. There is considerable variation in methods for handling this, with some packages allowing minimum charges, flat finance fees, compounding or simple interest, and so on.

With some accounting systems, the accounts receivable module can be used to prepare and print invoices. Other systems have a separate order entry or billing module that performs this function.

### (vi)  Inventory and Job Costing

All inventory and job costing systems will accumulate costs for goods available for sale. Inventory systems are best for companies that have quantities of identical items in stock; job costing is designed for single-unit, often high-cost items, which are usually available only as a special order.

Costing methods available in inventory systems vary a great deal. Virtually all packages will provide some type of average costing; but if you have other costing requirements such as standard cost, FIFO or LIFO, be sure to confirm that the package will provide it.

The ability to track product sales and stock transfers between multiple warehouses is not always provided in inventory systems. When it is available, some packages will only show product movement during the current month, whereas others will retain this information for three or more years.

If you are considering a job-costing system, determine what your most significant product inputs are (i.e., your major cost components) and evaluate how the accounting system handles these inputs. For example, if labor is a large part of your costs, check to see if the accounting system's payroll module will enable you to transfer labor hours and costs to job cost. If it does, you will only need to enter hours once in order to produce paychecks and cost your jobs.

### (vii) Accounts Payable

Accounts payable modules will accumulate invoices received from vendors and print checks and advices to pay them. You can often determine the sophistication of a vendor's payables module from the accounts receivable module. They are usually similar in capabilities, a mirror image of each other.

Payment selection capabilities can be important. For example, do you want to be able to forecast cash requirements based upon the terms of the payables entered into the system? Some systems will also allow you to hold back a portion of the payable amount; this can be important in construction industries or if you want to be able to allow for billing disputes.

The depth of vendor statistical information can vary greatly from package to package. For example, consider whether you want to keep track of how much you've purchased during the year from a particular supplier.

Finally, some payable modules will let you set up more than one bank account on your books and/or segregate purchases in a foreign currency.

### (viii) Payroll

Payroll systems typically calculate gross pay and statutory deductions. Normally they will also prepare a pay journal and paychecks, with advices detailing the deductions.

Some vendors provide a payroll tax table update service. When income tax rates change, they will either send you a disk with the updated tax tables or a notice advising you of the new values to enter into the program's tax database. It is usually well worthwhile to subscribe to such a tax service.

Pay particular attention to the payroll module if your company's pay structure is unusual. Fractional pay hours, tip sharing, and commissions are not handled by all pay packages. If you have many nonstatutory pay deductions (for a health plan, life insurance, etc.), check to see how many additional deduction categories are available. Many systems allow for only one or two supplementary deductions.

End-of-year governmental pay reporting is not prepared by every payroll package. Not having this feature can lead to a significant amount of year-end paperwork if you have a large number of employees.

### (ix) Other Elements

Some other features offered by certain accounting packages are:

- Fixed assets
- Purchasing

- Time billing and client accounting (important for professionals such as accountants and lawyers)
- Forecasting
- Interface with a spreadsheet such as Lotus 1-2-3, in order to conduct further financial analysis or assist in decision support

(*Important note:* Although it may not be a feature of the software, you should make it a policy to back up your accounting data regularly; in other words, you should treat backups as a key element of your accounting system. To guard against a catastrophe at your main business premises, maintain at least one backup off-site.)

*(x)  Matching User Needs and Features*

There are many high-quality accounting packages on the market, and the process of choosing from the many different systems can quickly become confusing. The best way out of this is to define your own corporate requirements and use them as the standard when you compare all of the systems you are evaluating.

A useful approach to take is to set up a matrix. Down the left-hand side, list the features that are important to you, in order of importance. Across the top of the matrix create a column for each package you intend to evaluate. You can then make notes in each of the cells of the matrix indicating how each package measures up.

The more of your requirements a package comes closest to meeting, the better it will be for you. But you will usually need to make some compromises. If a system can satisfy 90 percent or more of your needs, you must decide how important the remaining functions are. Can you get around them by using another program or by using supplementary, manual procedures?

Prices and features of accounting packages vary widely. For less than $100, you can get a business accounting program that performs basic bookkeeping and provides essential reports; or you can pay more than $5,000 for a high-end modular system that offers complete integration, detailed sales analyses, and sophisticated security features.

The following subsections discuss some of the more important accounting software features.

## Reports

Probably the most important factor to examine when evaluating a system is the quality of the reports it produces. This, after all, is the end product of the accounting system, and you want to see if this product meets your needs.

Check out the flexibility of the reports. For example, can you select ranges of accounts and fiscal periods for reporting purposes? Can you modify the fields (data items) included in a report? Most packages produce 132-column-wide printouts that are good for extensive analytical reports, but some only go to eighty characters across.

## Capacity

Is there a limit to the number of accounts you can set up on the system? Some general ledger packages can accommodate only a few hundred accounts; others can handle over 60,000. Obviously, the first will only handle the books of a small, uncomplicated company.

How many transactions can be stored by the system before a purge (deletion)? Some basic systems automatically delete all transaction details at the close of each month. Better systems will let you retain all the information for a full year or more.

The disk storage capacity of your computer is an important factor here. You must be sure that the disk has room to save the transactions that the program can handle. Programs that can store many entries often come with a file-size estimation guide. The vendor can use this guide together with your estimated transaction volumes to determine the space required for data and program storage.

## Integrity

Accounting systems have improved greatly in this area in the past several years. If you are interested in checking out just how robust a program's data integrity is, try powering down the system—to simulate a power or hardware failure—just as you are entering a transaction. Then turn the machine on again and see what data have been lost or damaged.

Better systems will lose only the entry you were working on, leaving the rest of the information intact and in a usable state. However, other less capable systems will lose data that you may have entered earlier in the session. A few systems will lose most or all of your financial records. Unless this last type of program comes with utilities that can help recover data, stay away from it. The risk of hardware problems corrupting your financial records is too great to put up with a system that has poor error handling.

## Ease of Use

You can't judge ease of use from marketing literature or even from a program's manual. The only way to do that is to attend a hands-on demonstration of a complete working copy of the package. But don't just let the vendor demonstrate the package. Bring a series of sample transactions relevant to your company and enter these yourself, with assistance from the representative if necessary.

Other ease-of-use considerations include whether the program comes with on-line help—in other words, with an on-screen manual that can answer your questions about the program's operations. Also look for an account inquiry feature that allows you to browse through the accounts on the screen until you find the one you want.

Support is one of those things that you don't notice until after you have your system and you need help making it work better. Ask about the type of support, its availability, and its cost before you decide on a purchase. For example, does the vendor provide a telephone hotline you can use to ask questions about the program's operations? (Most major software manufacturers offer telephone support to registered users. However, a number of the larger manufacturers have begun charging a fee for such services.)

As an option a software developer will often provide an extended support contract that usually includes access to the hotline as well as upgrades and enhancements to the accounting system during the period of the agreement. These extended support contracts are usually well worth their cost, which varies but is typically 10 percent to 30 percent per year of the original price of the package.

## Other Factors

An accounting package will either hold your transactions in a batch for later processing or post them directly to the accounts. A batch-based system is more forgiving to learn, since it gives you the opportunity to adjust keying errors before they are irrevocably recorded in your books. A direct update system operates more quickly as it eliminates this interim step. Be sure to set up a suspense account for this latter type of package because most will not allow you to leave the system unless you are in balance. You may not always have the time to investigate your errors first.

If you have three or more employees handling bookkeeping full time, you may need a local area network of linked PCs to handle your volumes. Ascertain whether the system you are considering comes in a network version.

Security of your computerized books is also important, particularly if more than one person is expected to use the accounting system. A good password system will have different codes for each module, allowing you to ensure that only an authorized person can access the sensitive payroll area, for example.

Some systems go even further. They will permit you to limit access to selected menu options within each module. Using this type of menu-level password, you could let a clerk post cash payments to receivables but have the controller process all account write-offs.

## (d) MARKET, MANAGEMENT, AND IMPLEMENTATION ISSUES

The last several years have seen two significant developments in microcomputer-based accounting software: low-cost starter packages and improved user interfaces.

- *Starter packages*—when Dac-Easy Software entered the market with a full-fledged accounting system priced at under $100, the floodgates opened to lower-priced, entry-level accounting programs. Dac and the programs that followed it (e.g., Bedford Integrated Accounting), are priced to fit the pocketbooks of even the smallest business. Product support and tutorials, commonly included or bundled with the purchase of high-end programs, are extra-cost options with many of these new entry-level systems. Some packages also include chapters in their instruction manuals about the fundamentals of accounting for nonaccountants. As a result these programs are often used by neophytes who don't have a firm grasp of either accounting or computer operations.

- *Improved user interfaces*—higher-end packages now have improved capabilities and user friendliness, largely in response to their lower-priced competition. On-line help is quickly becoming standard with these packages, to the point that users often don't need to refer to their manual when using the program. Some programs feature excellent visuals, flexible analysis of accounting data, and a choice of user interfaces.

You should first look at the more generic horizontal packages to see if they will suit your needs. If they don't, search for a specific vertical package for your type of organization. When selecting from any of these programs, the key will be your own requirements. Most packages have hundreds or thousands of users. Only you can decide if you should be next on the list.

It's important to ensure that all of the accounting functions you believe your business may eventually automate are represented in a vendor's module lineup. Only rarely will a module from one accounting family dovetail or integrate with one from a different system. Usually these exceptions are well promoted for the advantages they deliver, but you should not count on them.

One of the key planning steps before you buy a custom system is to define exactly what you expect to get out of it in terms of management reports. Also, you must allow adequate time to test and debug the system. After all, you are not receiving the benefit of changes arising from previous user feedback, as you do with a packaged program. In a sense you're the guinea pig, so it is important to run sufficient tests before implementation if you hope to survive the experiment.

If you retain an outside source to develop your custom system, stage your payment for the programming according to its progress. Pay only for completed work, and allow for a holdback until the entire system is up and running. Agree on standards for system performance (e.g., one-second response time to process a journal entry) and other criteria for acceptance of the system. Once the system passes your acceptance tests, you can safely complete your payments to the vendor or consultant.

Finally, there are three especially important points noted earlier but that are worth repeating here:

- It is generally preferable to ease into computerization of an existing system one or two modules at a time. The first step when planning automation of your accounting system is to determine which functions you'd like to computerize (e.g., the types of transactions) and the reports you need from each. Ideally you should prioritize your list so that you can first convert areas that give you the greatest benefit. If you plan to automate most of your accounting, you may overwhelm your staff if you start the whole system at once. A phased approach in which you initiate one or two modules at a time can help prevent problems. You need to look at the flow of information in the modules and your list of priority functions to decide where to begin. Often general ledger and accounts payable are safe places to start. Save complicated areas like payroll till the end, after the rest of the system is operating smoothly.

- Running your old system in parallel for at least two or three periods is an absolute must. Don't shut down your old system as soon as you start up your new accounting package. Run both in parallel for at least two fiscal periods (usually months) and compare their results. In addition, you should test the new system's ability to handle all of your month-end and year-end procedures. If there are no discrepancies, you can then safely discontinue your old system.

- Accounting systems are among the most difficult of microcomputer packages to install. Even if you initially plan to do it all yourself, you should check to see that you can get extra help if necessary. The dealer who sold you a package is not necessarily the best person to help you assess your accounting requirements and make the right choices in setting it up. Some software developers have set up an installer training and accreditation program to provide third-party assistance. Such professional installers will likely charge more than your dealer; however, they usually have expertise in accounting as well as a good knowledge of the specific computer program.

And again, a regular backup procedure must be implemented for all accounting data; at least one backup copy should be stored off-site at regular and frequent intervals.

## (e) ACCOUNTING-RELATED SOFTWARE

This section deals with the IT-related aspects of some typical accounting-related specialties: audit, tax, financial planning, and practice management. The first three areas deal with specialized packages used by audit, tax, and financial planning professionals, while the last area deals briefly with the IT consulting process.

Users requiring more detailed information should contact professional associations such as the Canadian Institute of Chartered Accountants (CICA), the American Institute of Certified Public Accountants (AICPA), or the Institute of Internal Auditors (IIA). These organizations have publication catalogues and other materials describing a variety of specialized software.

### (i) Audit Systems

Audit systems are those which can assist the independent public auditor in performing the work necessary to express an opinion on a company's set of financial statements. Increasingly, such systems are also being used by internal auditors.

Audit systems generally have two principal functions: preparation of working papers and audit extraction. Of course, there are many other finance-oriented programs that might also be useful during the course of an audit. For example, a statistics package may be used for sampling purposes, and a spreadsheet may be used for general financial analysis. However, these types of packages are not designed principally for auditors.

The two typical functions of an audit system are set out in the following subsections.

### Working Paper Preparation

All packages allow input of preliminary closing amounts from a client's trial balance. You can also organize the chart of accounts into a number of different lead sheets and print them out. Trial balances can be formatted into financial statements. Some systems permit the addition of footnotes.

Journal entries with amounts and brief descriptions can be entered into the system. Sometimes you can segregate entries according to their nature as adjusting entries (affecting profit and loss) or reclassifying entries (balance sheet only).

Some systems let you retrieve financial data from certain other microcomputer-based accounting systems. In practice, this is not much of an advantage for external auditors unless they have many clients using the accounting program that links with the audit system.

### Audit Extraction

These systems are designed to obtain financial information from other accounting systems based in mainframes, minicomputers, and microcomputers. You can usually select data according to the criteria of your own choosing. For example, for an audit of doubtful receivables, you might want to extract the details of all accounts receivable with a balance of $5,000 or more aged 90 days or more. You could then design reports using this data. Some systems might also allow you to create an account confirmation ready to mail out to a client's customers.

Some audit extraction systems are generic, working with any accounting system that can develop plain ASCII flat files. As you might expect, it requires some knowledge of the accounting system to develop these flat files. You may need the services of a special consultant to develop your initial procedures.

Other audit extraction systems can work directly with copies of the original accounting data files. They have enough built-in intelligence about the accounting file structure to extract the data rather painlessly. Although these systems are usually easier to use, they can work only with certain popular accounting packages.

Some of the working paper preparation and audit extraction packages also calculate financial ratios and percentages. For example, these might include the quick ratio and the number of days' sales that are outstanding in accounts receivable. Percentages calculated typically include the change from the prior year's results and the percentage of expenses related to net revenues.

One of the leading audit packages offering audit extraction as well as many other features is Interactive Data Extraction and Analysis (IDEA), developed and marketed by the CICA.

A decision on an audit system should not be taken lightly. Once you have started on a system, you have made an investment in training staff and have committed to a certain method of keying in and summarizing the client's financial data. However, assuming your clients' general ledger formats remain reasonably the same from year to year, the time you spend the second year should be greatly reduced.

Larger auditing firms should determine whether the vendor offers a site license. Such licenses allow all professionals in an office to copy and make use of the program. It usually works out better than the common alternative of buying single copies of the software or the worse alternative of using several, dissimilar audit systems.

Most of the audit systems available on the market are based on packages developed by mid- to large-size public accounting firms.

*(ii)  Tax Systems*

Producing tax returns on a microcomputer can eliminate much of the manual drudgery of tax return preparation, yield professional-looking results with quick turnaround time, provide greater accuracy and efficiency, and enable the processing of quick, on-the-spot adjustments.

The most basic tax program enables you to calculate income tax liability and print the results. Some planning programs stop there; they may not calculate taxes to the exact penny or print returns in a format suitable for filing. Tax preparation programs, on the other hand, print returns that are ready to sign and mail away.

Of course, tax laws, rates, and exemptions typically change from year to year. The program you buy to process this year's returns will not be suitable for next year. Because of this, almost all developers offer an update service to keep you current.

The two basic functions of a tax system—tax planning and tax return preparation—are briefly described in the following subsections.

**Tax Planning**

While you should not expect absolute accuracy from a planning program, many such programs will deliver an estimate of taxes payable that is very close to your actual liability. Most systems also allow you to save more than one tax scenario per individual. This lets you experiment with different tax planning approaches to identify the one that produces the best result.

### Tax Return Preparation

Preparation programs should calculate tax liabilities precisely and prepare most of the common subsidiary schedules that must be filed with a return. Packages vary in their capabilities to produce supplemental schedules and to calculate state or provincial taxes. Be sure that the system you choose can handle your local jurisdiction's requirements.

If the package you are considering uses computer forms to produce the return, be sure to ascertain the forms' costs and availability. If a laser printer is not being used, also consider using three-part forms; they can cost more than twice as much as single-sheets, but they reduce demands on your printer during peak periods.

When choosing a tax-planning program, it is very important to learn whether the current year's tax calculation algorithms will be released in plenty of time. Check to see what the vendor's release date was in previous years.

For tax preparation programs, you should also find out how quickly you can print out the final returns. Many systems now support laser printers that will prepare a complete return on plain paper. This is obviously preferable to changing forms in the printer each time a return is run.

Some vendors offer a service bureau that will print and assemble the completed returns for you. You can send tax data to the service bureau on diskettes or, in some instances, via modem.

Many programs offer a conversion facility to transfer permanent data (name, carry-forward amounts, etc.) from last year's data file to this year's return. This can significantly reduce your keyboarding time in the second year and thereafter. Most users are unlikely to change to another tax package in future years, once they have committed themselves.

Above all, evaluate the software developer before making your commitment. Ask for names of other users in your area and learn whether they have been satisfied with the level of service and support they have received in the past.

### (iii) Financial Planning Systems

Financial planning systems are in many ways analogous to tax systems in terms of their benefits—i.e., they eliminate much of the manual drudgery of preparation, yield professional-looking results with quick turnaround time, provide greater accuracy and efficiency, and enable the processing of quick, on-the-spot adjustments. The ability to perform sensitivity analysis—to examine a variety of what-if scenarios—is a key benefit of financial planning software.

Both personal and business financial planning can be affected by such things as tax and interest rates. As a result, the better packages offer an update service to keep you current.

Specific functions within the business planning category vary from package to package. Typical output include pro forma financial statements, budget, and cash-flow projections. For personal financial planning, separate modules may handle such things as investment portfolios, tax planning, retirement planning, and estate planning.

Two key factors to consider are (i) the comprehensiveness of the program's functions and (ii) whether the program is regularly kept up to date and supported by the manufacturer. Other important factors include ease of use and the quality of the printed output—including such things as printer compatibility.

As with tax software, evaluate the software developer before making your commitment. Ask for names of other users in your area and learn whether they have been satisfied with the level of service and support they have received in the past.

*(iv)  Practice Management Systems; Groupware*

A number of accountants and accounting firms offer IT-related consulting services, sometimes as part of their management consulting practice. Services could include providing advice and guidance on microcomputer installation, through to more specialized areas such as computer security consulting. Some software such as Lotus Notes can assist professional firms in tapping into the knowledge base that is their most important resource.

Expert knowledge and experience are obviously the key prerequisites for an IT consulting practice. Specialized courses are available—for example, the Canadian Institute of Chartered Accountant's Microcomputer Consulting Course—to assist accountants in supplementing or upgrading their professional knowledge in this area. A detailed discussion of IT consulting is outside the scope of this handbook. However, some of the key issues to be considered are set out below:

- *Identification of potential service areas*—this will depend on an assessment of the market (e.g., the needs of existing or prospective clients) and the capabilities of the firm or its ability to acquire such capabilities.

- *Assessing the competition, feasibility studies, and business plans*—all of these are designed to establish that the proposed new service area can be a profitable one for the firm.

- *Development of the proposed service area and related management issues*—these include things such as staffing, establishing policies, procedures, and quality controls for the new service and marketing it to current and potential clients.

- *Delivering the service on a job-by-job basis*—this includes such things as defining job objectives (engagement letters), assigning staff, gathering information, and producing reports.

## 10.5  LARGE SYSTEM SOFTWARE

This handbook is targeted primarily at the nontechnical manager and user of information technology. To some extent, any discussion of mainframes is an anomaly since these systems are very expensive (often over one million dollars for a system) and require a high degree of technical knowledge and sophistication to deal with.

The purpose of including a section such as this in the handbook is not to provide mainframe users with sufficient information to manage and operate their systems. They have already—or should have already—spent thousands or tens of thousands of dollars on training and documentation alone. Rather, the purpose is to provide a general description of these systems—of the environments and applications to which they are especially well suited, of how they compare to microcomputers, and of the industry that manufactures them. In an era during which the networking of microcomputers to larger systems is becoming commonplace, even those who do not own large systems probably require some knowledge of them.

## (a) GENERAL BACKGROUND

Although it doesn't directly relate to software, some general background information is in order.

### (i) Definitions

The word mainframe was derived from the physical structure that held the central processing unit (CPU) of the earliest computers. Semantically, there is no specific technical definition. Mainframe computers are simply the largest and most expensive type of computer, more powerful than either minicomputers or microcomputers. They are particularly adept at performing tasks that require high-speed computing and/or large memory capacity.

Mainframes—which typically cost at least $250,000 and sometimes tens of millions—are most often used by large organizations such as airlines, governments, hospitals, and academic institutions. Three of the major uses of mainframes are:

- Processing of periodic high-volume batch applications, in particular accounting.
- Managing large, centralized databases, including on-line and interactive databases.
- Acting as a host computer in a distributed data processing network.

The last of these applications—distributed data processing—involves the use of relatively smaller computers (typically minicomputers) that are separated physically from the mainframe. In such a configuration the mainframe handles the data processing needs of the firm as a whole, while the various minicomputers located at remote sites handle the more localized data processing needs. The distributed minicomputers can obtain information from the mainframe and transfer the output of their processing to the mainframe as required.

Because of their similarity to mainframes and the increasing capabilities of microcomputers, it is often difficult to distinguish between a small minicomputer and a large microcomputer or a large mini and a small mainframe. Indeed, the minicomputer classification may become all but obsolete with the proliferation of powerful microcomputers based on Intel's 486 and Pentium microprocessors and with the arrival of the P6-based models more recently. Nevertheless, for purposes of this handbook, minicomputers are typically midsize computers costing between $25,000 and $250,000, excluding peripherals.

A distinctive feature of minicomputers is their flexibility. They are generally adaptable to a wide range of applications and can usually be more easily tailored to the users' needs and resources than microcomputers.

### (ii) Linking to Micros

While microcomputers were originally intended to be used by one person at a time (hence the synonym "personal computer"), both mainframes and minicomputers are designed to be accessed by many users simultaneously. Historically, these larger computers have been accessed almost exclusively through terminals. However, microcomputers are becoming an increasingly common substitute for terminals.

Connecting a microcomputer to a larger computer through various communication devices greatly enhances the capabilities of both. A particularly useful combination involves linking a mainframe to a host of microcomputers. Such a micro-to-mainframe link permits:

- Microcomputer users to share information that is of common interest (networking).
- Microcomputers to process information that is stored on the mainframe (downloading).
- Information that is stored on a microcomputer to be used as input to processing on the mainframe (uploading).

In a network a mainframe makes it possible for microcomputers to communicate with one another (when using electronic mail, for example). The message sender need only type a message at his/her micro addressed to the other user's account or ID number, and it will be stored on the mainframe until the other user calls in for messages.

Through downloading, information that is kept on a permanent file or database by the mainframe, such as historical corporate financial data, can be accessed by a microcomputer database package without any need to input the data again. Conversely, through uploading, the results of data manipulation performed by a microcomputer can be relayed to the mainframe to update information that is stored on it.

A micro-to-mainframe link is comparable to a local area network (LAN). However, rather than connecting a smaller computer to a larger one, LANs connect small computers and various peripherals together so that users can, for instance, share files and printers.

*(iii)  Historical Background*

The history of computers is often described in terms of generations. The first generation was heralded by the introduction in the early fifties of a mainframe known as UNIVAC 1, the first general-purpose electronic digital computer. Computers of this generation were very large and emitted intense heat as a result of their use of vacuum tubes.

The second generation of computers began in the late fifties when the vacuum tube was replaced by the transistor. This substantially reduced the size and increased the power of computers, and as a result their popularity spread rapidly.

The third generation of computers commenced with the introduction of the IBM System/360 series in 1964. This series made use of integrated circuits, whereby all the elements of an electronic circuit were contained on a small chip. Once again, the size and speed of computers were greatly affected. The third generation also marked the emergence of software as a means of utilizing the capabilities of computers more efficiently.

The fourth generation of computers—which is the current generation— began in 1971 with the introduction of the microprocessor. Since then, the mainframe has had to share the spotlight with the microcomputer.

## (b) ELEMENTS OF LARGE SYSTEMS

*(i) Nonsoftware Elements*

Before proceeding to a discussion of software, the hardware elements are briefly reviewed for the sake of completeness.

### Central Processing Unit

The CPU of a mainframe computer is more powerful than that of any other type of computer. Actually, the tremendous processing speed of mainframes is due to the fact that they typically contain several processors as opposed to just one.

The word length of a mainframe processor generally ranges from a powerful 32 bits to 64 bits. This distinguishes it from micro and mini processors, which until the early 1990s were generally limited to 16-bit word lengths.

The powerful CPU of a mainframe permits it to:

- Run extremely large programs that smaller computers cannot.
- Handle many users simultaneously (this is an especially important capability in certain environments, such as airline reservation systems and automated banking machines).

Although the speeds of mainframe systems are difficult to compare, two common measures are MIPS (millions of instructions per second) and FLOPS (floating point operations per second). The former attempts to quantify how fast the computer can carry out instructions. The latter gives an indication of the speed at which the computer can perform a mathematical calculation. There are a number of problems with such measures, however, including the fact that they refer specifically to the CPU and thus do not take the speed of the overall system (input and output devices, etc.) into account.

Though the practice is being discredited in some circles, the MIPS figure is often related to the price of a mainframe in order to derive a "cost/MIPS" ratio.

### Terminals

Video display terminals, commonly known as cathode ray tubes (CRTs), are the devices that typically allow users to interface with mainframes. They are often stationed at remote sites and can be classified into three categories:

- *"Dumb" terminals*—terminals that are only capable of transmitting each character that is keyed in by a user and displaying information from the mainframe.
- *"Smart" terminals*—terminals that provide additional features such as formatting and editing of inputted data (such terminals are characterized by a "cursor" that can move in all directions to indicate the location of the next character to be input).
- *"Intelligent" terminals*—terminals that are user-programmable such that they can process data on a limited basis without the assistance of the mainframe and can store data temporarily until they are transmitted to the mainframe.

Since the cost of adding additional features to terminals is low, virtually all terminals used within a mainframe environment are either of the "smart" or the "intelligent" variety. In fact, there is very little difference between using "intelligent" terminals—which are composed of keyboards, screens, storage, and processors—and using a series of more general-purpose microcomputers in a micro-to-mainframe link. As a result, most terminals destined for the mainframe market are now "smart" terminals.

Some have speculated that the falling prices of microcomputers, coupled with the increased acceptance of the benefits of using microcomputers to interface with mainframes, will eventually lead to the demise of the terminal market. However, it is unlikely that this will occur because:

- Operating a microcomputer generally requires a higher level of expertise than operating a terminal.
- Terminals will remain significantly less expensive than microcomputers.

IBM's 3270 terminal family and Digital Equipment Corporation's VT100 are two of the most popular terminal models used in mainframe environments.

**Secondary Storage Devices**

The types of secondary storage devices used with mainframe computers are similar in principle to those used with microcomputers. Magnetic disks, drums, and tape are commonly used. However, since the scale of processing is much greater with a mainframe—sometimes billions of bytes of storage are necessary—these secondary storage devices are much larger and more complex.

For instance, while many microcomputers use a hard disk to fulfill their secondary storage needs, mainframes typically use hard disk drives that store data on removable disk packs. A disk pack contains a number of hard disk platters—usually 11—each of which generally stores 10 to 20 megabytes of data. Mainframes are designed to use many such disk packs, which is why their on-line storage capacity, when combined with off-line storage, is so vast.

Reel-to-reel magnetic tape is also popular among mainframe users, primarily for its low cost. For example, a 2,400-foot tape can hold more than 40 million bytes of information at a cost of less than $30.

Since magnetic tape is substantially less expensive than magnetic disks, normally only the most current data is kept on disk while the remainder is maintained on tape. Tape is also the preferred storage medium for those applications that require sequential as opposed to direct processing, such as payroll. In addition, magnetic tape is often used to copy information maintained on-line on magnetic disk, as a means of backup.

Secondary storage devices for mainframes, depending on their speed and capacity, can cost between a few thousand and several hundred thousand dollars. The cost, however, is falling significantly, while the amount of available storage in these devices is increasing as the technology advances.

**Printers**

The types of printers used within a mainframe environment are technically no different from those used with microcomputers or minicomputers. However, the printing capabilities of a mainframe configuration are typically more flexible because mainframes typically have several different types of printers connected to them (dot matrix, letter quality, etc.). This enables users to choose the print quality they need, and to accommodate the printing needs of various users simultaneously.

For all computers the printers and other peripheral devices are much slower than the processors. If not compensated for, this can drastically reduce the effectiveness of the system. Fortunately, two options exist to overcome the problem.

First, there is the "spool queuing" system, whereby a spooler program allows the processor(s) to alternate between processing data and controlling the order in which various user documents are "lined up" for printing. The spool queue uses secondary storage or a block of primary storage to store documents until they are printed.

Second, a specialized, temporary storage area called a buffer can be used to store documents before they are printed. The buffer releases the documents at the speed at which the printing device is capable of printing. This option is especially useful if the processing demands on the mainframe require most of the available storage space.

As you might expect, mainframes can produce printed matter much faster and more copiously than any other type of computer system; some of mainframe printers (typically laser page printers) can operate at about 20,000 lines per minute. Although printers with this capability can cost over $100,000, such a cost can be justified by large corporations, which may print hundreds of thousands of pages per month.

### (ii)  Security Considerations

While mainframes, and in particular micro-to-mainframe links, can provide considerable benefit, there is potential for abuse from both inside and outside the organization. The mere fact that more users have access to data stored on the mainframe increases the possibility that mainframe security measures might be thwarted.

For example, authorized users within the organization might inadvertently erase vital corporate data, intentionally embezzle corporate funds by making unauthorized transactions, or access sensitive documents and sell them to competitors. Likewise, computer hackers from outside the organization could conceivably gain access to a mainframe and wreak havoc.

The most effective means of dealing with security problems of the type outlined above is through prevention. The most common form of prevention is access control, which is usually accomplished with the use of passwords. A number of other security measures are also advisable and are dealt with in greater detail in Chapter 13 of this handbook.

### (iii)  Large System Software

Mainframe computer software is somewhat different from software for micros, in part because it often has to be developed internally and/or custom-tailored to meet the organization's needs. Another major difference is the fact that mainframe software must be capable of being addressed by a large number of users simultaneously.

There is a wide range of mainframe software available for virtually any application, including such conventional ones as word processing and graphics. Sometimes these are purchased off the shelf, and at other times they are custom-developed. In all cases, however, mainframe software is considerably more expensive than the micro variety. The systems that are especially relevant to mainframes are set out in this section. But first two important concepts need to be described.

*(iv)   Virtual Storage*

Virtual storage is the ability of large computer systems to assign more memory space to a program than is actually available. That may sound like a contradiction, and in a sense it is; but it's a contradiction that lies at the heart of the mainframe's power.

Mainframes divide their main memory into pages, and the number of pages available is finite. If it weren't for virtual storage, all of the available pages might be taken up by some very large and complex applications. Under such conditions the system would effectively grind to a halt, at least from the point of view of other users who wanted to run other applications at the same time.

Virtual storage allows the mainframe to circumvent this problem by swapping in and out of memory only those pages of the program that need to be used at any one time. The rest of the program is written to secondary storage (i.e., to disk). The operating system of the computer keeps track of where the various pages of the program are, but the program itself operates as if it had been assigned all the necessary space in main memory.

As an aside, Microsoft introduced Windows 3.0 in 1990. This represented an MS-DOS operating system enhancement for microcomputers that at the time used Intel's 386 and 486 microprocessors. Among other improvements, Windows 3.0 included a virtual memory routine similar in principal to that used by mainframes. This further illustrated the trend that the distinction between micros, minis, and mainframes was blurring.

*(v)   The Virtual Machine*

In a similar vein, mainframes can actually allocate their main memory to more than one operating system. At any point in time, operating system 1 might be in control and running a database system; an instant later, operating system 2 might be in control and running a word processing package for a different user.

This means that it is possible to have several operating systems running at the same time, each constituting a virtual machine in its own right. This is especially important when converting programs from one operating system to another because it means the program can be converted and debugged in smaller chunks, even while running in its entirety.

*(vi)   Operating Systems*

As you can tell from the preceding discussion, the operating system is the most vital piece of mainframe software. In addition to handling virtual storage and sharing control with other virtual machines, it must also manage many hardware sites and terminals and ensure that users establish proper identification for security purposes.

Mainframes manage multiple users through a time-sharing system whereby each terminal is allocated a small portion of CPU time. During that time information or instructions keyed in at a terminal are processed before the operating system directs the CPU to proceed to the next terminal, and so on. Fortunately, the CPU of a mainframe can typically return to each terminal several times per second; users are normally unaware that they are sharing the CPU with others.

Because the operating systems of mainframes are such large and complex programs, they often require a staff of full-time systems programmers to maintain them. Moreover, unlike microcomputer operating systems, which can run on a variety of different machines, mainframe operating systems normally only work with a specific type of mainframe.

Popular operating systems for IBM mainframes include the VM series (e.g., VM/SP, VM/XA and VM/CMS), MVS series (e.g., MVS/SP, MVS/XA), and DOS/VSE.

### (vii) Accounting Systems

The major elements of an accounting system include general ledger, accounts receivable, accounts payable, inventory and job costing, and payroll. If the volume of such transactions is large, it may be more effective to have a mainframe process them as opposed to a micro, for the following reasons:

- Processing time, which is critical in many of the subsystems identified above, is much faster with a mainframe.

- Provided that the management information systems (MIS) department is efficiently run, accounting applications of such a scale can be performed at a lower cost on a mainframe.

- The integrity of sensitive data (such as payroll) can be more easily protected on a mainframe, which is less accessible to unauthorized personnel.

Mainframe manufacturers sell their own accounting software, and there are also independent software companies producing these systems, including Computer Associates. A number of companies also produce vertical packages, which are designed for specific industries (e.g., banks).

An accounting system can in fact be viewed as a specialized form of database management, as discussed in the next section.

### (viii) Database Management Systems

A database is essentially an accumulation of information organized into records and files to facilitate information retrieval and processing. A database is typically stored on a secondary storage device and is accessed using an applications program known as a database management system (DBMS).

Since mainframes typically manage huge collections of data, traditional file processing—whereby data are organized, stored, and processed in independent files—can be cumbersome and costly. In particular:

- With an independent data file structure, the same data may be stored in several files. As a result, when the data has to be updated, each file must be updated separately.

- If a user requires information from several different files, the computer must retrieve the necessary data from each file.

- If the format of data must be changed, changes must be made to all of the programs that use the affected files.

Fortunately, there is another way to arrange information. A database consists not of independent files but of records and files of logically related data that are used as a common source for all of the various application programs.

Database management systems are software packages that facilitate the creation, maintenance, and use of databases. The DBMS:

- Relieves programmers from having to develop detailed data-handling procedures using a programming language (e.g., BASIC, COBOL) each time a program is written.
- Enables users to access information in the data by using a simple "query language" such as PROLOG or INTELLECT.
- Enhances the integrity and security of the data in the database by placing responsibility for it in the hands of a specialist known as a database administrator.

Typically, an organization will purchase or lease commercially available DBMS software packages for its mainframe to avoid the time and cost involved in developing such systems internally. DBMS software for mainframes can cost over $100,000.

In addition to the mainframe manufacturers themselves, a number of independent vendors produce DBMS packages. Among the industry leaders is Oracle.

### (ix) Custom Software

Although there are many application software packages available for use with mainframes, many organizations choose to develop their own custom software. Generally speaking, custom software is developed for a unique application for which no "canned" package exists or for which modifications to any existing package would be so extensive that they would be equivalent to starting from scratch. Considering that many mainframe users are highly specialized organizations (airlines, governments, hospitals, etc.), it isn't surprising that many users have custom applications.

For those organizations that require custom software, a staff of computer specialists including systems analysts and programmers is retained to both create and maintain it. Typically, the process followed is to:

- Specify what the program is to solve or achieve.
- Gather and analyze data about current processing operations to determine whether they can be of assistance in development of the new application.
- Separate the program specifications into the specific input/output, calculation, logic, storage, and retrieval operations required to develop the new program.
- Convert the operations identified above into a custom program, which is written in a computer language that is compatible with the organization's hardware.
- Test, implement, and maintain the custom program.

While computer specialists are involved in the development of custom software throughout the process, it is also critical that the end users be involved to the maximum extent possible.

As should be obvious, the development of custom software is a complex process that requires considerable company resources. It is therefore highly desirable to adapt an existing program to the specific needs of the organization, if at all possible. This alternative offers the advantages of reduced risk of error, faster implementation, and lower cost.

## (c) THE LARGE SYSTEM INDUSTRY

Mainframes are manufactured by several large firms including IBM (the clear market leader), Unisys, NEC, Fujitsu, and Hitachi. These companies typically produce "families" of mainframes that allow users to upgrade to larger models with little or no change to the programs being used. Some general and historical background is set out in the following paragraphs.

Up until about 1975, over 80 percent of computer industry sales could be attributed to mainframes. By the end of the 1980s, however, mainframes represented only about 25 percent of the total. Nevertheless, yearly mainframe sales (in dollars) continued to grow—from just over $10 billion in 1975 to about $30 billion by the end of the 1980s. The drop in the share of total industry sales therefore reflects an increase in the rate at which microcomputer sales are growing relative to mainframe sales rather than the demise of the mainframe market. The increasing popularity of distributed data processing networks and client/server configurations has also contributed to mainframes' loss of market share to smaller computers.

Prices for small- to medium-size mainframes range from $250,000 to $1 million; the largest models can cost from $1 million to $5 million and up. These prices are for the mainframes themselves; the total system cost can run even higher. Because of the high cost, mainframes are typically leased rather than purchased; the maintenance contract alone can be a significant element of the total cost.

Another development in the industry was the plug-compatible mainframe (PCM), which can be used to replace or augment an existing system and which can also use the software and peripherals of the existing system. In practice, the term PCM most often refers to the replacement of an IBM system or peripheral equipment, since IBM has historically dominated the market and the IBM System/370 became somewhat of an industry standard.

IBM's line of mainframes was split into four groups (Groups 10, 20, 30, and 40). At the low end were IBM's smaller 9370 models. In the mid-range were the 4361 and 4381. At the top were mainframes such as the 3090. All of these are considered part of the aforementioned 370 line, the number referring to the architecture of the CPU in these machines.

Finally, a trend in the industry was started with the tiered software pricing structure that IBM implemented and other independent houses followed. Essentially, this pricing structure means that the cost of software is tied to the model of mainframe on which it is run. IBM bases its software prices on the group category into which the mainframe falls (i.e., the aforementioned Groups 10, 20, 30, or 40).

The dividing line between mainframes and minicomputers is not distinct. The essential difference is that minis are somewhat less powerful and less expensive. The basic elements of a minicomputer system differ little from those of a mainframe; the differences are subtle. Generally, minicomputer hardware tends to be somewhat more modular, such that a variety of hardware options can be incorporated or interchanged to tailor a system to a user's requirements. Additional terminals, large-capacity disk drives, multiple printers, and the like can be added to the system relatively easily.

Minicomputer manufacturers place a high priority on the compatibility of their products with the larger systems that they produce, existing software, and competitors' systems. The intention is to enable users to upgrade their systems easily as their business and computing needs grow. This has resulted in the trend toward the totally compatible computer "families" that many large manufacturers now offer.

Minicomputers also feature extensive communication capabilities that facilitate the sharing of company databases and other resources, such as peripheral equipment. This is often accomplished through a LAN. For instance, LANs allow users who are in relatively close proximity to transmit information without having to physically share a floppy disk or convert it into a file so that it can be sent by way of a modem.

Finally, the communications capabilities of minicomputers also make it possible to establish the micro-to-mainframe link more cost-effectively. Simply linking many microcomputers directly to a mainframe can make communication costs prohibitive. If a minicomputer is used to control the data flow between micros and mainframes, a significant portion of the cost can be averted. In addition, the security of the mainframe is enhanced in such a configuration.

A full range of software is available for minicomputers, including major programming languages (FORTRAN, COBOL, BASIC, RPG, etc.), operating systems, and application software packages. The range of application software is diverse enough that it is seldom necessary for minicomputer users to develop their own.

In order to maintain the flexibility of minicomputers, the software that is supplied with the hardware usually consists only of what is necessary to support the basic hardware functions. The UNIX operating system is most prevalent among minicomputer users.

The wide variety of minicomputers is reflected in the wide range of prices in the marketplace. Most minicomputers cost between $25,000 and $250,000, excluding peripherals. However, "superminis," computers that perform like mainframes but are cheaper, can cost many hundreds of thousands of dollars. As with microcomputers, the cost of peripherals can equal or exceed the cost of the processor.

The minicomputer market is being squeezed by supermicros at the low end and by superminis and small mainframes at the upper end. The top manufacturers are IBM (e.g., the very popular AS 400, which superseded the System/36 and 38), DEC (which historically carved out a good share of the market with its VAX computers) and Hewlett-Packard. Minis can be purchased directly from regional offices of these manufacturers or in some cases through independent distributors.

Mainframe sales are expected to continue to grow in dollar terms. Their unparalleled ability to process high-volume applications, manage large centralized databases, and serve as the hub in distributed data processing networks ensures that mainframes will maintain a significant presence in the computer marketplace.

The same cannot be said for minicomputers. The increasing capabilities and reduced cost of higher-end micros will probably lead to the extinction of the traditional minicomputer market.

Another likely trend is the incorporation of artificial intelligence capabilities into mainframes. Specifically, expert systems—software packages that duplicate a human expert's decision-making process—are increasingly being offered by vendors as an enhancement to standard applications rather than as standalone items.

If you're in the market for a mainframe or minicomputer, it's advisable to retain the services of an independent consultant. Obviously, you're dealing with a purchase decision of great magnitude, and the consultant can help you wade through the myriad of choices as well as the conditions that should exist in the maintenance contract that will accompany your purchase. This contract greatly affects the overall effectiveness and ultimate cost of your system.

For additional information on mainframes, computer periodicals such as *Computerworld* are a good source.

## 10.6  USER NEEDS AND SOFTWARE EVALUATION

### (a)  MATCHING USER NEEDS AND FEATURES

The features of the software being considered should be evaluated and matched with the needs of the user. The following subsections discuss some of the factors to be considered.

*(i)  Hardware and Operating System Requirements*

The compatibility of the software with the hardware (e.g., Intel-based, Apple Macintosh) and operating system (e.g., DOS, OS/2, Windows) is obviously critical. The capacity of the system must also be considered carefully. The files in many applications tend to be large. It's difficult to generalize on how much capacity is enough, but 8Mb RAM is probably the bare minimum required to run substantial applications (16Mb is becoming increasingly common).

*(ii)  Size and Complexity of Application*

Some applications (e.g., accounting packages) involve the manipulation of very large quantities of data. Consequently, the maximum file size can be an important factor. There are a number of other capacity constraints to consider in addition to the total file size, including number of records and size of records. The amount of memory that the program itself takes up, and other hardware requirements of the software, may impose capacity constraints as well.

*(iii)  Ease of Use*

Ease of use is a trade-off against the power of the program. The user must determine how much to emphasize one over the other. Here are some features to look for:

- On-screen interactive tutorials
- Well-written and complete documentation
- Context-sensitive help screens
- Menu-driven command selection and pull-down menus
- Easily readable commands
- Telephone support, especially for complex programs

*(iv)  Reports Required*

Especially for accounting packages, the ability to produce reports and flexibility in report design and layout are very important. The report writer should be evaluated for:

- Flexibility in the appearance of printed reports, including number and position of titles, column headings, labels and output values, subtotals, and so on

- Available fonts and print styles
- The ability to store report specifications in a file for later use or editing.

Also look for the ability to custom design form reports. And, of course, compatibility with printers (i.e., device drivers) is essential.

### (v)  Software Versions and Software Support

Inevitably, software contains errors or bugs that require correction. In addition, software generally improves as technology advances. It is therefore essential that a software package be well supported and updated regularly.

Some experts recommend shying away from the first version of a program or major program upgrade, reasoning that such versions are more likely to contain bugs. They argue that it's better to wait for the first update after such a new release. (Many people argue the same thing for the first model year of a particular car—i.e., that it's better to wait a year, by which time the manufacturer will have corrected any manufacturing flaws.) To counteract this type of resistance on the part of users, some software manufacturers have taken to avoiding the ".0" label for their software. For example, instead of issuing version 5.0, the manufacturer will go straight to version 5.1 to at least give the appearance of more extensive testing.

In addition to the initial price of the package, the user should consider the manufacturer's or vendor's update policies (i.e., how users are notified of updates) and the related cost. The better programs tend to be improved frequently to keep up with the competition.

Support—both vendor and manufacturer—is also a factor to consider. Most major software manufacturers also offer telephone support to registered users. However, a number of the larger manufacturers have begun charging a fee for such services.

### (vi)  Compatibility

A key consideration for many users—especially medium- and large-size organizations—is compatibility with other software owned by the user. For example, if others in the organization are already using a particular package, buying that package will facilitate the exchange of files within the organization.

Another factor to consider is whether the same manufacturer's software is being used for other applications such as word processors. Sister packages of this kind offer greater integration. For example, if spreadsheet or database information is regularly incorporated into reports or presentations, easy integration with a graphics or presentation package may be important.

### (vii)  Cost

The price of software has declined substantially in recent years, following the trend in hardware prices. Many software programs are also being offered as a package with other programs such as word processing and database management software, providing even greater value. (Microsoft Office and Lotus SmartSuite are examples.)

Nevertheless, price comparison is an important step in large organizations that are considering the purchase of site licenses or that operate large networks. In such cases, the total purchase cost can run into the tens or even hundreds of thousands of dollars. Training and future upgrade costs also have to be factored in.

*(viii)  Other Concerns*

A number of other features may be important to users:

- *Security*—software is often designed to be used by many individuals. The data and the time spent in the creation of the applications are generally quite valuable. If more than one person will have access to the files, security features to protect the integrity of the files and data therein from accidental or other damage are important. Possible security features include file passwords, write protection, and data encryption (the scrambling of the data).

- *Networking capability*—Increasingly, microcomputers are being connected through a local area network (LAN) to share data and hardware resources. Software programs differ in their ability to operate on a LAN, their compatibility with the various types of LANs, their record-update and record-locking abilities (i.e., the program's ability to accept and/or prevent any change to a record), and data security.

- *Data transfer*—It may be useful to transfer data from a graphics program to some other software such as a word processor. There are many data file transfer formats. Consider which file formats the program is compatible with and can export data in, and which major software packages will accept those formats. Pay particular attention to which software you own or might purchase.

## (b)  WHERE TO BUY

Software is frequently sold at a discount that usually depends on the type of establishment and the after-sales support it offers. The greatest discounts are usually offered by mail order houses that offer no advice. No matter where it's purchased, buyers should ensure that software is sealed in its original packaging. This is important for license/registration purposes and also to ensure that it is virus-free.

Some vendors offer demonstration diskettes that run through some of the program's functions on a sample file while the user observes. These can help the user become familiar with the program and assist in software evaluation.

Although important, the selection of a vendor is less crucial for software than it is for hardware. Nevertheless, after-sales support may be a factor for purchasers who want support or who expect to have problems learning and/or operating the package. If support is needed, the higher cost normally charged by a more established vendor with knowledgeable staff may be worthwhile. Many software houses offer telephone support, but that can be frustrating to use because of the lower level of personal attention and the long-distance charges. (Also, as noted previously, many manufacturers now charge for telephone service.) A reputable vendor in the same locality with whom the user can build an ongoing relationship can prove a valuable troubleshooting resource.

## (c)  OTHER SOURCES OF INFORMATION

Training and practice are often vital in mastering the use of software. Some additional sources of information are set out below.

*(i)  On-Line Tutorials and Help*

Some programs offer various types of assistance including:

- *Help screens*—on-line help screens accessed by a defined key can assist the user with problems during a session, especially if the help is context-sensitive.
- *Menus*—optional menu-driven operation can be slower for experienced users but provides faster access for the beginner. Pull-down menu systems also enhance the learning environment.
- *On-screen interactive tutorial lessons*—some programs offer these, which lead the user through the basics by simulating the use of the actual software.

*(ii)  Books, Magazines, and Newsletters*

The manuals that accompany the software often are designed more as a reference source for the program's numerous functions than as a teaching tool. As a result, a large number of books have been written to help users learn various software packages from the ground up. There are also books to help experienced users with advanced functions and programming.

Many of the leading computer magazines carry articles dealing with different categories of software and/or have columns offering advice and tips.

The bibliography in Appendix A includes a list of selected books and magazines.

*(iii)  User Groups*

There are user networks for various software products throughout North America. User groups often communicate via electronic bulletin boards that are accessible with a modem over telephone lines. Computer magazines and newsletters periodically print lists of such groups in their areas of distribution; your vendor may also be able to assist you in finding one.

Some on-line commercial database and gateway services have subsections for groups of users with special interests. These groups provide a forum for users to pass on information that may be of interest to others.

*(iv)  Courses and Seminars*

Training courses are offered by a variety of firms, including computer vendors, public accounting firms, professional bodies (such as societies of accountants), and training institutions. Courses are typically one or two days, and fees usually range from $100 to $500.

A course can provide a good grounding, but afterwards the user will need to practice the concepts for some time before putting the software to work. Most of the commercially available courses are geared to the major packages, since these programs have a large installed base. However, the user can often benefit by learning concepts applicable to similar programs.

### (v)  Video Training

Training courses are available on videocassette tapes; they are sometimes advertised in computer magazines. Although the tapes lack the interaction between the instructor and fellow students found in a classroom, there are cost advantages for users in remote locations. Also, the tapes can be used by several people.

### (vi)  Consulting Services

Many of the large accounting and management consulting firms provide software-related services. There are also independent consultants who specialize in this field.

# CHAPTER 11

# Telecommunications

Telecommunication means communication over a distance, especially the technology that supports electronic communication between intelligent devices across significant distances: telephones, computers, and many other devices.

## 11.1  TELECOMMUNICATIONS VS. CONNECTIVITY

Telecommunication relates to technology itself. It's a subset of connectivity, which is a broader concept that includes telecommunications and all of its applications. The chapter that follows in this part deals with the main application of telecommunication technology: networking.

Except for hard-core "techies," the practical application of technology is more important and interesting than the technology itself. Likewise, this chapter—focusing as it does on telecommunication classifications and explanations—may be less important and interesting for the target audience of this handbook than the others. Nevertheless, a broad overview of the technology is appropriate for the sake of completeness and to provide some context for the more practical chapters.

## 11.2  HISTORICAL BACKGROUND

The first practical development in telecommunication was the invention, by Morse in 1835, of a telegraph operating on the principle of the magnetic deflection of a needle. In the most widely used version of his invention, a small needle was positioned between two small cylinders so that when it was deflected by the current in a wire running past it, the needle would strike one or the other cylinder. The distinctive sounds produced allowed the operators to hear which way the needle turned and to transcribe the series of sounds into letters. The famous Morse code was invented for this purpose. When the needle moved one way it was a dash; the other way was a dot. These and similar sounding mechanisms were the basis of all electric communications until the end of the nineteenth century.

Many of the terms invented in the early days of telegraphy are still current today. For instance, the states of any two-state digital or analog communications link are called "mark" and "space." These are derived from an early recording telegraph that used a pen to mark a moving strip of paper. But whereas the terms in the 1840s referred to the pen either marking or spacing over a strip of paper, current terminology uses "mark" to designate the idle condition on a line and "space" for when the line is active.

In 1855 Hughes produced the first practical telegraph for printing the messages in letters of the alphabet. This invention was expanded by Baudot in 1874 to allow several machines to share the same set of wires and to use Baudot's five-level code. The first transatlantic cable was laid from France to the United States in 1866.

(The telegraphs developed by Morse and Hughes evolved into the Telex and TWX networks that eventually spanned the globe. These networks still used the five-level code invented by Baudot, but intelligent devices were also connected to the networks to handle message sending, receiving, and printing.)

In 1875 Alexander Graham Bell, a native of Scotland who lived in Canada and worked in the United States, invented a mechanism that would carry the sound of a voice over wires. Previous inventions had had partial success. Bell's equipment varied an electric current in proportion to the acoustic pressure of the speaker. In this way, his telephone was able to reproduce all the sonic qualities of the source; other telephone inventions neglected pitch or loudness, or both. By the close of the nineteenth century, the famous "daffodil" telephone was being produced by the American Bell Telephone Company.

By the early 1900s the American Telephone and Telegraph (AT&T) company had gained control of the significant patents involving telephone equipment. Through its subsidiaries it dominated the manufacture, supply, and service of the American telephone network. (Until 1975 most large telephone companies, including Bell Canada, were wholly or partially owned subsidiaries of AT&T. The most sweeping change in American telecommunications occurred on January 1, 1984, when, after years of dispute, the American courts ordered AT&T to divest itself of all operating companies and to restrict its local services.)

Modems were first used to send digital signals over telephone lines in the early 1960s. By the end of the decade, multiplexers and concentrators became more important in the design of cost-effective networks in burgeoning computer facilities. Modem speeds were forced up by customer pressure, and common carriers responded with special equipment and circuits to carry signals at speeds up to several hundred bits per second. This was still not sufficient, and digital transmission networks independent of the telephone networks were introduced in the early 1970s.

Today, the proliferation of terminals and other equipment in corporate branch and regional offices has increased the complexity of private networks. There has also been a need to connect computers between companies and between countries. A major advance in this direction was the introduction in 1976 of an international standard (X.25) for packet switching networks.

By the mid-1980s almost every industrialized country had at least one network based on the X.25 standard and connected with the international network. Ten years had seen the world of data communications change from one dominated by point-to-point leased lines to one based on interconnected private and public data networks. Carrying it all one step further, the 1990s have seen the appearance of commercial Internet service providers, which for a fee allow anyone access to this international network of networks (well, at least to those networks that choose to hook up with the Internet).

## 11.3 TYPES OF TELECOMMUNICATION

Telecommunication technology is often categorized in two separate ways, voice vs. data, and analog vs. digital. These categories are described in the following sections.

### (a) VOICE VS. DATA

As you can gather from the history given in the last section, telecommunications has followed two separate paths in its development—voice and data. This is because terminal devices—the equipment to which the communications links are connected—have historically been of two very different varieties. The telephone systems were optimized to handle analog signals and switch among multitudes of telephone sets, and the receivers were people. The data communications devices were designed to recreate messages out of the ones and zeros they received.

This historical separation has persisted until very recently. Not only was voice communications equipment very different from that for data communications, but the two were designed, manufactured, and sold by different companies and purchased by different departments in most organizations. Many companies still have one group responsible for telephone communications, usually under the vice president of administration, and another group, usually part of the computer department, responsible for data communications.

In a typical example of technology driving the businesses that use it, the integration of voice and data services is now setting in motion a radical change in the way these technologies are used and managed. The dividing line between voice and data is becoming less distinct; it makes the most sense today to treat them as different aspects of the same technology.

## (b) ANALOG VS. DIGITAL

Whereas the difference between voice and data is one of convention, the difference between analog and digital is one of technology. Either technique can be used to communicate voice, data, or any other type of message.

The central challenge in telecommunications is, simply, distance. When it is necessary to move data from computer memory to the processor, the distances are very small, and multiple conductors can easily be built to transfer the data 8, 16, 32, or more bits of information at a time. This is called parallel communications. However, when moving data from one building to another, or worse yet, across the country, it is not feasible to run multiple conductors, and another method is required.

An additional constraint on digital communications is the electrical limitations of the wires and other equipment used to carry the signal. If you have a regular "dumb" terminal connected to a computer in the same room, it can send and receive digital signals on a conventional cable of up to about 50 feet without special equipment. But the longer the cable, the greater the natural resistance of the conductors, which causes the signal to lose its strength. Furthermore, if digital signals were sent through the conventional telephone network, they would encounter circuitry especially designed to block digital signaling.

To solve the distance problem, the conventional telephone network uses analog transmission technology. Sound (e.g., a human voice) is transformed into an alternating current that can pass through the pair of wires leading from the phone, through all the switching gear provided by the telephone companies, and into the telephone at the other end, where it is re-formed into acoustic vibrations.

The challenge for data transmission was to find a way to carry digital pulses within an analog signal in order to make use of the telephone network. A way was found, and it proved to be the basis of all telecommunications until the late 1970s. Since then, fiber optics and other advances in electronics have made it possible to provide a network separate from the conventional telephone network to carry digital signals.

## 11.4  VOICE FACILITIES

Conventional voice telecommunication is achieved through a combination of telephone equipment and the central office facilities of the telephone company as described in Sections a and b. Sections c, d, and e deal briefly with more specialized voice topics: long distance, cellular, and PBX.

## (a) TELEPHONES

Telephone equipment is most conveniently divided into two major categories: customer premises and central office. Customer premises equipment is installed at the user organization's location—in equipment rooms and cupboards, under desks, on top of desks, and so on. This includes the station equipment (i.e., the telephone sets themselves) and the common equipment (i.e., everything else that provides lights, intercoms, and other peripherals). Common equipment has two important categories: key equipment and PBX.

To generalize, small offices (i.e., 40 phones or less) use key equipment whereas larger offices use PBXs. Key equipment makes it possible for each telephone to pick up an outside line directly. If you want to choose among five lines at your telephone, you will need five buttons, one for each line. If you want to talk to someone in your office, you can either dial one of the lines that appear on his/her telephone (inconvenient), or use an intercom to dial the correct code (possibly intrusive if the person is already on another call).

As far as the central office is concerned, a key system looks the same technically as a telephone set installed in your home. When the central office has to signal an incoming call, it rings one of the key system lines and expects one of the key system sets to pick it up. In the event of a system problem, you could replace any key system with a simple telephone set and be able to receive and place telephone calls.

The PBX, which stands for private branch exchange, puts into the customer premises the kind of switching power found in the central office. Each telephone is given an extension number of two to five digits. This can be used to dial directly to any telephone on that PBX. To make a call outside of the PBX, you dial 9 to signal the beginning of an outside number, and then the rest of the digits. The PBX finds a spare trunk and places the call for you. PBXs are described in more detail later in this chapter.

The range of station equipment available is enormous; the basic dial (or touch-tone) and talk telephone, also known as the "plain old telephone" (POT), has been replaced in both the office and the home by a plethora of feature-rich alternatives. Telephone sets are now available with built-in speakerphones, clocks, calculators, number storage and speed-dial, desk pads, computer terminals, and even video cameras. With the upgrading of telephone networks, other features previously available through PBXs have also become more commonplace, such as conferencing, camp-on, incoming call identification, and call cost monitoring.

Figure 11.1 is a diagram of the classical telephone system components described above.

### (b) THE CENTRAL OFFICE

The central office (CO)—actually many offices—provides all the call routing necessary to connect the caller to the number called. The North American telephone network has a common numbering and traffic routing plan that facilitates simple access to any telephone number.

The North American telephone switched network is divided into 12 regions (two in Canada, ten in the U.S.A.), each controlled by a regional center. Each region is divided into sections and each section into primary areas. These are served by sectional and primary centers, respectively. This hierarchical arrangement of centers—see Figure 11.2—provides an efficient means of connecting the over 200 million telephones in the U.S.A. and Canada.

All telephones are connected to an end office that contains unique originating equipment (OE) for each number. Local numbers consist of a three-digit exchange or CO code and a four-digit station number. When a station dials a number, the OE recognizes the number as belonging to either the same end office or another end office. In the first case, the switching equipment in the CO is able to connect the caller to the called party directly.

In the second case, the end office routes the call to a toll center, which determines how the call is to be routed to its destination. This involves switching the call over trunk

**Figure 11.1** Telephone System Components

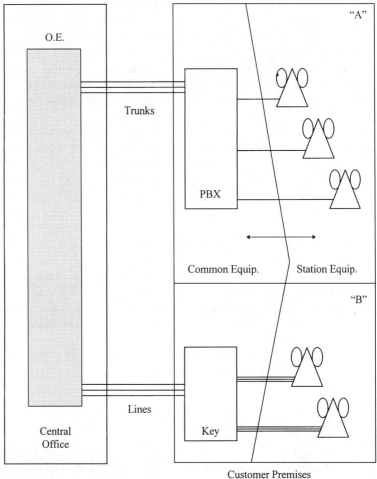

lines between various offices until the appropriate end office is located. Where possible, trunks directly connecting class 2 and 3 offices are used (high-use trunk groups). If they are busy or if the offices are not connected to one another, the final trunk groups are used to route the call up to the regional center, across to the regional center of the called party, and down through the centers to the end office.

## (c) LONG-DISTANCE TELEPHONY

Central office exchanges are grouped into rate centers for the purposes of determining long-distance costs. Generally, calls among points in a rate center are billed at normal rates, and calls outside a rate center are billed at time- and distance-sensitive rates. This procedure varies with the complications arising out of the reconfiguration of the American telephone system into local access transport areas (LATAs) and by the advent of measured service in some telephone companies throughout North America.

**Figure 11.2** Hierarchical Central Offices

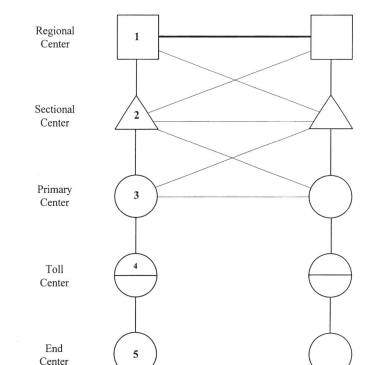

Regional Center — 1

Sectional Center — 2

Primary Center — 3

Toll Center — 4

End Center — 5

————————— **Final Trunk Group**

– – – – – – – – High-Use Trunk Group

Measured service is one of a number of new charging options available to telephone subscribers. With the increasing competition for personal and corporate communications budgets, the telephone companies are allowing subscribers to customize their billing to compensate for high- or low-use patterns.

Both LATAs and the growing complexity of the American long-distance system are outside the scope of this handbook. The main point is that intelligent planning and design of telephone facilities can yield significant savings in both the American and Canadian long-distance markets if these complexities are sufficiently understood.

## (d) CELLULAR TELEPHONES

Basically, a cellular telephone is a portable unit that supports telephone calls to any telephone number in the world. It can be installed in a car or carried around in a briefcase.

The technology behind cellular telephones existed over 20 years ago, but it was only in the latter half of the 1980s that it was widely implemented. The delays were primarily regulatory, as the authorities had to decide who would be allowed to provide the service in various areas. Since cellular telephony involves radio frequencies, portable electronics, interconnection to the telephone network, and billing for local and long-distance calls, the administrative hurdles took some time.

What makes cellular telephones different from older technologies is the arrangement of the antennas. Radio telephones worked through radio signals exchanged with a large antenna in the city of operation. Once the vehicle was outside the range of this single antenna, the signal quality would deteriorate to the point of disconnecting the call. Cellular overcomes this limitation by placing numerous antennas throughout the geographic area served by the service vendor. Computers monitor the position of every unit that has a call in progress, and when one moves closer to another antenna they switch the call to it. This occurs so quickly that the people on the line (usually) do not notice that it is happening.

Large expanses of metropolitan areas in North America are now served by cellular telephone networks. Cellular is the largest growth area in telecommunication technology, and significant advances—including conversion to digital technology—are being made.

### (e) PBXs

Private branch exchanges (PBXs) were created to move some of the switching performed in the exchange into the customer premises. Lines to PBXs are given the same name as the lines between central offices—trunks. The activities that take place over trunks are significantly different from those that occur over lines to key telephone systems.

A PBX has several main components. Line cards (or line terminating equipment) are connected to the telephone sets. Trunk cards connect to the CO trunks. Both line and trunk cards are responsible for handling the signaling used for each type of equipment.

The line and trunk cards are connected to a control mechanism that is either electromechanical (as relays are) or computer-based. This control mechanism arbitrates all the resources in the PBX and connects the lines and trunks through the switching matrix as required. The switching matrix actually makes the connections between a telephone extension and a trunk, in the case of an outside call, or among telephone extensions for inside calls.

A diagram of a PBX system appears in Figure 11.3.

## 11.5 DATA FACILITIES

### (a) DATA COMMUNICATIONS FUNDAMENTALS

*(i) Information Encoding*

Regardless of the transmission technology used, a communications channel is equivalent to a stream of bits. A bit of information goes in one end and it comes out the other, followed by the next bit that was put in, and so on. In order for an exchange of information to occur, each end has to agree on what the bit stream means—in other words, on how to interpret the bits as codes or characters.

If you are sending a paragraph of text from one computer to another, the bit stream must be correctly interpreted as a series of characters. This is the purpose of the international standards ASCII (American Standard Code for Information Interchange) and EBCDIC (Extended Binary-Coded Decimal Interchange Code). These two coding ar-

**Figure 11.3** Private Branch Exchange (PBX) System

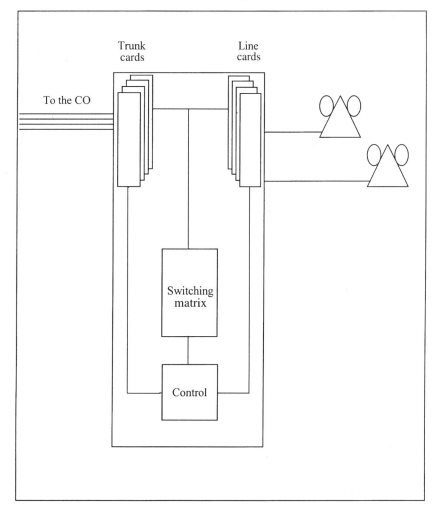

rangements associate characters with sequences of bits. If both ends of a communications link agree to use one or the other, the information will be passed correctly.

For example, to send the character *N* using ASCII, a computer would send the bit stream 01001110. These bits can only be interpreted as an *N* by a computer using ASCII. If it were using EBCDIC, this pattern of bits would represent a +. As originally designed, eight bits gave the ASCII code 128 different characters plus a parity bit that could be used for error detection. The EBCDIC code does not have a parity bit and therefore can represent 256 different characters.

*(ii) Asynchronous vs. Synchronous*

It is also necessary for the two ends of the communications link to know where the characters start and stop. If the receiving end adds another zero to the beginning of 01001110, the ASCII *N* turns into a single quote, and there is a zero added to the next character, making it incorrect as well.

Synchronization involves keeping the beginnings and ends of characters in agreement between two ends of a communications link. There are two means of maintaining synchronization—synchronous and asynchronous clocking. These two important data communications technologies are fundamentally different.

With asynchronous timing, the sending end prefixes each character with one or two start bits and affixes each character with a stop bit. When each character is received, the equipment (a modem, described in the next section) starts its clock and has time to set the correct speed before the actual data bits start coming in (this happens in a few milliseconds). When the stop bit is clocked in, the equipment knows to stop the clock and wait for the next start bit. This is sufficient for slow communications, such as a person typing at a terminal, but it wastes too much time on the line when the sender has a lot of information that it can send in one burst. Asynchronous communication has historically been used with microcomputers and dumb terminals.

With synchronous timing, the receiving end of the line starts a clock when it receives two or more special characters, called SYN characters. The clock stays running until the entire block of characters is received. This is the typical manner of communicating for cluster controllers and on packet switching networks, to cite two very different examples.

### (iii) Modems

The devices that translate the digital information from the terminal or the computer into signals that can travel on communication lines are called modems. They take their name from their function—they MOdulate and DEModulate the acoustic signal across a telephone line.

Different modems are designed to work with different kinds of communication links. The most widely used modems are for the switched voice network—the same network that you use for all normal telephone calls. This network is optimized to carry the sound of a voice over great distances, hence the name "voice grade line." These kinds of modems modulate an acoustic signal in patterns recognizable as ones and zeros.

The speed of voice grade modems is limited by the sound quality of the line. The modulations of the carrier signal must be clearly distinguished by the other end despite the noises introduced on the switched telephone network. The line over which two modems are communicating might travel for hundreds of miles through switching centers, past noisy electrical equipment, and alongside other signals that interfere with the information being exchanged.

Until the 1970s voice grade modems for use with the switched network could not operate faster than 300 bits per second (bps), but developments in encoding technologies pushed this much higher: the 1980s saw microcomputers using 2,400 bps modems; 14,400 bps modems are now common, and 28,800 bps units are increasingly common.

A note about data transmission speeds is appropriate here. The old term for speed was baud (named after Emile Baudot, the inventor who first encoded characters using patterns of bits with fixed lengths, in 1874). Precisely speaking, bauds measure the number of signal elements per second. What is more important to modern applications is the number of bits per second.

Because many modern modems use signal elements encoded with two, eight, or more bits, the term baud has become ambiguous and incorrect. For instance, if you were considering a modem rated at 4,800 baud, you would have to know how it encoded data to know whether it operated at 2,400 bps, 4,800 bps, 9,600 bps or some other speed.

Speeds faster than those possible over switched voice-grade lines can be achieved by leasing a line from the telephone company. Such a line does not get routed through any central office switching equipment and is quieter as a result. Additionally, it is common to add conditioning filters to the line to enhance the frequency characteristics and suit the modems being used. Speeds as high as 1.5 million bits per second are common on specially conditioned lines.

### (iv) Digital Circuits

To further address the problems of speed and reliability, various common carriers (telephone companies and others) have developed all-digital networks in the last 20 years. These make it possible to avoid modems entirely, as the signal does not need to be transformed into analog form. In the modems' place, data sets are installed to mediate between the computing devices—usually medium to large computers—and the network.

These types of networks offer the equivalent of private line facilities, often at speeds of 1.544M bps.

## (b) TRANSMISSION TECHNOLOGIES

### (i) Copper Wire

The oldest, most fundamental, and most pervasive transmission medium is the network of copper wires that was constructed for the public telephone network. Virtually every home and office building is connected by at least one pair of copper wires to the nearest telephone central office.

These wires have the advantage of being the most widely understood and used medium. Almost any communications equipment will work with copper. It is the lowest common denominator of transmission media.

Nevertheless, copper has significant problems with interference, bandwidth, and security—interference because wires running for great lengths along the underground cables are susceptible to picking up the signals on adjacent wires. You may be able to carry on a conversation despite the noise from other voices in the background, but computers do not have a human's sense of discrimination.

Bandwidth is a problem because the voice network to which most of these copper wires are connected is optimized to support the 3,000 Hz signal used for voice. Early experiments in acoustics established that a recognizable and intelligible human voice can be carried using frequencies from about 300 Hz (or cycles per second) to 3,100 Hz. If you attempt to send frequencies outside the voice band range, they will be filtered out at the central office by equipment specifically designed to do so.

Finally, copper has the security problems associated with its omnipresence: wiretaps to a given line can be attached at the terminal, elsewhere on the floor at the customer premises, in the basement of the customer's building, in manholes along the street, on poles along the highway, in the central office itself, or in other locations too numerous to mention. At every one of those points there is the opportunity for physical interference with the line ranging from monitoring to disconnection.

*(ii) Fiber Optics*

Current commercial fiber optic technologies can send data at one billion bps over a single strand of glass fiber. That fiber is completely insensitive to interference, safe against undetectable tapping or monitoring, and robust enough to be installed underground and across oceans. Because of all this, there has been a major shift towards fiber optics for data communication.

Most visibly, the long-distance carriers are replacing many of their high-traffic intercity trunks with fiber. These cables, typically with 12 to 144 individual fibers, can support over 80,000 voice circuits (or their data equivalent), with great savings over copper cables. The signal quality on fiber optics is also noticeably better.

Fiber is also being installed for private networks to interconnect buildings or computer installations that need to exchange large volumes of data. Fiber optic cables are significantly smaller than copper cables with a similar capacity, which makes fiber an attractive solution within buildings that have very crowded ceilings and conduits.

*(iii) Satellite Communications*

Satellites were first viewed as a medium for worldwide television broadcasts and long-distance telephone calls. Fortunately for the satellite industry, other applications arose to take advantage of the satellite's unique features: coverage of long distances, broadcast capabilities, high-volume capacity, and independence from land-based communication systems. This last point is significant because adding a base station for a satellite signal simply involves mounting a dish and plugging in the interface equipment; the telephone company doesn't get involved, land lines aren't needed, and other interface complexities are avoided.

Satellite facilities are strongest for applications that involve one to many signal paths, for example, in configurations between a headquarters and field offices.

*(iv) Microwave*

There are two kinds of microwave facilities: long-haul and short-haul. Long-haul microwave has been an important part of long-distance voice and video communications in North America for decades. The large towers with various types of megaphonelike units mounted on them are part of a coast-to-coast relay for microwave voice and video signals. These microwave antennas operate in the 2 to 6 GHz range (GHz stands for Giga-Hertz or billions of cycles per second).

Organizations wanting to use microwave as part of a private network will likely select short-haul technology. The antennas are smaller and consequently cheaper, and the data rates are faster (between 18 and 23 GHz). They are used primarily for interbuilding links, where they can provide reliable alternatives to underground cabling.

## (c) THE NEED FOR PROTOCOLS

*(i) Overview*

We have seen that both ends of a communication link must agree how to encode the data being exchanged. In real life, communication links have to deal with a variety of other conditions that complicate the sending and receiving of data and necessitate more complex protocols. These include:

- Detecting errors and retransmitting when necessary
- Equipment failures
- Processing delays
- Sharing facilities with other devices

The rules for handling these situations are called protocols. This is an extremely technical area, and it's a challenge even to present a conceptual framework for it. Nevertheless, we'll try.

One of the most important concepts in the design of a protocol is that of levels. A protocol specifies what to do at one or more levels of an information exchange so that other levels not defined in that protocol may exist independently. It's like a person typesetting a book: the typesetter is concerned only with the level defined by the characters on the page, not with what they mean. The author is responsible for the meaning, but not the typography. As long as they each perform correctly at their different levels, their work will be done correctly and efficiently.

Similarly, data communication is divided into several distinct levels. Be warned, however. A particular protocol classified today as relating to a particular level might expand to include several levels tomorrow, either by merging with or adopting other protocols or because the protocol developer expands its scope. As we indicated, it's all rather complicated.

### (ii)  Interface Level

The bottom or most basic level is the interface level, which is used to define the physical (i.e., electrical and mechanical) aspects of a communications connection. For instance, RS-232 defines the electrical voltages and meanings for the 20 different conductors used in connecting data terminal equipment (DTEs, like CRT terminals or microcomputers) to data communications equipment, (DCEs, like modems). The distinction between DTE and DCE is important when you actually get down to plugging cables into these two types of equipment, as a different portion of the interface standard applies to each.

Newer interface protocols, like X.21, replaced the approach used by RS-232 with the sending of codes between the DTE and DCE. As more intelligence has become available in communicating devices, this has become the more accepted approach.

### (iii)  Data Link Level

The data link level governs the logical (as opposed to the physical, electrical, and mechanical) link between the DTE and the DCE. This includes such things as initialization and termination of the link, synchronization, error detection, and recovery over the link. It provides an error-free channel for the exchange of information initiated by the higher levels.

Examples of data link protocols include binary synchronous communication (BSC), synchronous data link control (SDLC) from IBM, and high-level data link control (HDLC) from the International Standards Organization.

*(iv) Network Level*

The network level establishes a logical path between systems and provides flow control to accommodate different data acceptance rates. It also provides addressing in situations where one device has the capability to connect to more than one other device. Examples of network protocols are X.25 level 3 for packet switching, the system network architecture (SNA) path control from IBM, and transmission control protocol or Internet protocol (TCP/IP), which, as the name implies, is the protocol used throughout the Internet.

With this third layer it may appear that we have solved our entire data communications problem; but this is not the case. There are still many other things that need doing somewhere in the connection, including:

- Flow control from end to end
- Assembling and disassembling the data into blocks or packets
- Dealing with the need to use a communication facility (as opposed to a local computer resource)
- Code and character set conversions

Before the mid-1970s each communications software program dealt with these and other issues in an entirely arbitrary manner. As the need to communicate became more widespread, it became obvious that a general solution would be preferable.

*(v) SNA*

The need for a general solution was not lost on industry. IBM announced its system network architecture (SNA) in 1974. It is a set of definitions of protocols and formats for communicating among the various components of IBM's product line. It is not a product per se, but since 1975 IBM has released products that conform to or build on SNA for most communications needs.

Although we referred to SNA in the last section, we also indicated previously that protocols may cut across or encompass several levels. The SNA set of protocols is such an animal. The set consists of six layers, ranging from the top layer that handles the network-addressable units (an NAU—any network entity that can be addressed by the network), to the bottom, or physical, layer. The SNA path control protocol we referred to in the last section falls between the two (the third level up from the bottom).

Although originally perceived as a marketing strategy by IBM to lock out competition and sidestep international standards activities, to some extent SNA became another IBM-generated *de facto* standard. It is widely used, and many vendors of IBM-compatible products also provide support for it.

*(vi) OSI Reference Model*

Even with IBM's strength in the market for large computer systems, it was not expected that all other vendors would conform to SNA. Instead, it was necessary to develop a standard that all vendors, large and small, could embrace and rely on—one that would not be tied to a single vendor and yet would be specific enough that products and services could be built around it. The International Standards Organization (ISO) began work in 1975 on such a standard. In 1983 their Draft Proposal 7498 (TC 97/SC 16N 890 in the exact numbering scheme of the ISO's technical committees) was adopted as an international standard.

The ISO calls this standard a Reference Model for Open Systems Interconnection (OSI). The primary objective of the model is "to provide a common basis for the coordination of standards development for the purpose of open systems interconnection, while allowing existing standards to be placed into perspective within the overall Reference Model." The term "open system" refers to the standard's objective, which is to be independent of vendors, products, and systems.

The OSI Reference Model, as depicted in Figure 11.4, consists of seven layers. From lowest to highest level these are:

**Figure 11.4**   OSI Reference Model

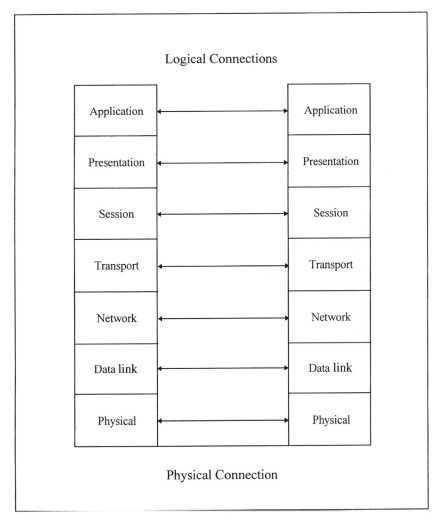

- Physical
- Data Link
- Network
- Transport
- Session
- Presentation
- Application

The first three are roughly equivalent to those dealt with earlier in this chapter. The other levels define the higher functions needed in order for user application programs to successfully communicate with each other and with other users.

*(vii) X.400*

One of the first major post-OSI communications standards was X.400 for electronic mail. Electronic mail can run on private, in-house systems, or public service bureaus. Within one system it is relatively simple to identify whom any given message should be sent to and how it should get there. What was missing until X.400 was a standard that would allow different messaging systems to exchange messages.

## 11.6  INTEGRATED FACILITIES

Integrated facilities (facilities that handle both voice and data) are becoming increasingly common and will eventually become standard. This section covers these integrated technologies: PBX, teleconferencing, and ISDN.

### (a)  PBXs

PBX is an advanced technology that implements integrated voice and data communication. Early advanced PBXs used computers to perform control and switching functions but did not provide data services as such. Subsequent PBXs carried voice and data signals through the same cables and provided similar features for each, such as last-number redial and traffic monitoring.

Now that the hurdle of treating voice and data separately has been cleared, significant new capabilities are possible. Telephones on desks can now be replaced with intelligent workstations that are analogous to personal computers but take full advantage of their telephone antecedents. Electronic mail messages can be read over the phone to the user from voice-synthesis units, and conference calls can share data as well as voice signals.

### (b)  TELECONFERENCING

Teleconferencing, a combination of voice and data technologies, allows people to meet across long distances. It can take the form of a simple audio hookup with speakers and microphones, or a full-scale, multimedia conference center of the kind provided by some telephone companies and hotel chains.

Telecommunications technologies allow two rooms to be connected with a multiplexed signal that carries the two-way audio channel, numerous video signals from cameras in each location, auxiliary graphics information from drawing boards or projectors, and computer data for display or analysis. For very long distances a technique called freeze-frame video is available that reduces the amount of video information communicated by taking a visual frame off a camera every few seconds or minutes instead of the fractions of a second used in conventional, full-motion television.

### (c)  ISDN

ISDN—an acronym for integrated services digital network—deals with the exchange of data signals among intelligent devices, including telephones, fax machines, televisions, and computers. The services supported by ISDN include voice telephony, data communications, broadcast video and audio, messaging and information services, and telemetry. ISDN is designed for both home and business installation. True ISDN systems are eventually expected to replace the current telephone switching and digital data communications networks worldwide.

A terminal or workstation on ISDN is able to handle complete voice and data switching, display caller number identification, monitor and log call-in-progress information, process alarm and environmental controls for security and energy management, and perform all of the other functions now provided by a telephone on a PBX (e.g., camp-on). This is all achieved through a common interface similar in appearance to the telephone jack now used in most homes, except that the interface is faster and more reliable, especially for data communications.

ISDN addresses the need to manage and exchange an enormous diversity of information as effectively and efficiently as possible and is expected to break down many barriers to widespread information exchange.

## 11.7  SOME FINAL THOUGHTS

Telecommunication is becoming increasingly important to businesses of all sizes and to the economy in general. There are several reasons for this, including

- Pressure to reduce overhead costs in a competitive environment.
- Greater need for information access, driven by both competitive and regulatory pressures.
- Corporate diversification and decentralization, and the related need to control and coordinate operations.
- Increasing numbers of acquisitions and mergers.
- Executives' maturing attitudes towards computers and information.

Telecommunication has developed past the point where it merely facilitates information distribution; it can now drive the direction of new products and markets and stimulate the reorganization of work at both a personal and a corporate level. Banks that provide automatic teller machines and multibranch banking capabilities, newspapers that offer on-line access to their copy databases, auditors who perform remote tests or collect information on site to be analyzed at another location—all of these are examples of businesses discovering new products and services that arise out of telecommunication technology.

Telecommunication is also playing an integrative role. Voice and data technologies are merging to create a unified network for voice, data, graphics, and image exchange. This explains the integration of computers and communications technologies in the design and manufacture of information technology products.

Every enterprise must learn to recognize this new role of telecommunications at the strategic planning level in order to best take advantage of the possibilities. Telecommunication technology no longer merely serves the information needs of an organization—it can actually propel the business.

In this environment the most important aspect of planning any installation is to future-proof it. Anticipate excessively high data traffic requirements and surprisingly quick changes in technology. Do not make any major long-term commitments to even partially mature technologies if there is no upgrade path available at a minimum cost.

Finally, adopt a technique of experimentation or piloting. Have some in-house exposure to advanced technologies that you are possibly going to use in the future. As your understanding of each new technology develops and it proves to be potentially suitable, create a pilot for its use in part of your organization. If your assumptions about its suitability are wrong, you can get out with minimum cost and maximum information. If your assumptions prove right, you will have learned how the technology responds in your environment and will be better prepared to expand its use.

# CHAPTER 12

# Networking

This chapter deals with networking, one of the primary applications of telecommunication technology. Networking is the use of telecommunications to connect computers and related devices to facilitate the transfer of information and the sharing of peripherals.

Looking at it another way, networking is what happens when you use telecommunications in a nontrivial way. Thus, a small computer connected to a single terminal in another building would be excluded from the definition, because such a setup is too simple to be called a network. Today, networks involving dozens of mainframe computers and thousands of terminals are common.

Management issues for networks start with:

- Making purchase, upgrade, and standardization decisions (this will be based on an analysis of user needs, the available network configurations and features, budgets, etc.).

- Ensuring that policies and procedures are in place to control and optimize the use of networks throughout the organization, including:

255

Identifying appropriate applications for the network

Training of staff

Standardization (e.g., on software, etc.)

Controlling related costs

- Establishing good security, backup, and record destruction controls (for both hard copy and electronic media).

Planning and preparation are critical to the success of network building and implementation. Careful thought must be given to the network structure. This is especially true for large and complex networks. Personnel with network management expertise are critical to success.

The following material consists of:

- A checklist (Section 12.1), summarizing many of the main points in this chapter.
- Sections on the Types and Elements of Networks (Section 12.2); Local Area Networks and Client/Server Technology (Section 12.3); and Distributed Networks, Electronic Data Interchange, and the Internet (Section 12.4).
- A discussion of the user needs assessment and network selection process (Section 12.5).

## 12.1 NETWORKING CHECKLIST

The following checklist is designed to assist accountants in decision-making and management relating to networking, in their organizations and those of their clients. Generally, all "No" answers require investigation and follow-up, the results of which should be documented. Where there is such additional documentation, the purpose of the "Ref" column is to cross-reference the checklist to the appropriate working paper (or to the notes on the reverse).

The checklist is intended for general use only. If networking is of especially vital concern to an organization, the advice of a specialist should be sought.

**Networking Checklist**

|  | Yes | No | N/A | Ref |
|---|---|---|---|---|

**1. Management Issues—Acquisition**

a. Have an appropriate process, timetable, and budget been established for the assessment of user needs, the evaluation of available networks, purchase, training, and implementation?     ☐ ☐ ☐ ___

b. Has the participation of the users of the network been ensured throughout the process?     ☐ ☐ ☐ ___

c. Have the major user needs been identified (such as the existing hardware, software and operating system environments, size of the network that must be managed, e-Mail, availability of support, etc.), and has a preliminary identification been made of those networks that may meet these criteria?     ☐ ☐ ☐ ___

d. For each network that might be set up, have the following issues been addressed?

   • Compatibility with hardware and operating systems     ☐ ☐ ☐ ___

   • Compatibility with existing printers in use     ☐ ☐ ☐ ___

   • Compatibility with software in use     ☐ ☐ ☐ ___

   • Compatibility with possible future upgrades of above     ☐ ☐ ☐ ___

   • Adequacy of network capacity (e.g., number of users)     ☐ ☐ ☐ ___

   • Availability of manufacturer and/or vendor support     ☐ ☐ ☐ ___

   • Adequacy of documentation and manuals     ☐ ☐ ☐ ___

   • Availability of skilled technical and management personnel     ☐ ☐ ☐ ___

   • Availability of training (self-study, seminars, etc.)     ☐ ☐ ☐ ___

e. Has the network been user-tested?     ☐ ☐ ☐ ___

f. Are network security features adequate?     ☐ ☐ ☐ ___

g. Is the network price (taking into account the required number of copies and/or site licenses, training costs, etc.):

   • Competitive with other comparable networks?     ☐ ☐ ☐ ___

   • Within budget?     ☐ ☐ ☐ ___

h. Once a network is decided upon, have the related purchase documents (sales agreements, site licenses, etc.) been reviewed, by legal counsel if appropriate?     ☐ ☐ ☐ ___

|                                                                                                                                              | *Yes* | *No* | *N/A* | *Ref* |
|----------------------------------------------------------------------------------------------------------------------------------------------|-------|------|-------|-------|
| **2. Management Issues—Implementation and Use**                                                                                              |       |      |       |       |
| a. Have all appropriate applications for the network been identified to ensure that maximum use and value are obtained from the investment?   | ☐     | ☐    | ☐     | ___   |
| b. Are appropriate mechanisms in place to ensure that the organization is aware of future network upgrades?                                  | ☐     | ☐    | ☐     | ___   |
| c. Are appropriate policies, procedures, standards and controls in place with respect to:                                                    |       |      |       |       |
| • Network documentation?                                                                                                                     | ☐     | ☐    | ☐     | ___   |
| • Network security (passwords, etc.)?                                                                                                         | ☐     | ☐    | ☐     | ___   |
| • Filing and storage, both electronic and physical?                                                                                          | ☐     | ☐    | ☐     | ___   |
| • Data backups, including off-site backups?                                                                                                   | ☐     | ☐    | ☐     | ___   |
| **3. User Issues**                                                                                                                           |       |      |       |       |
| a. Are users adequately trained in the use of the network, including refresher or update courses when required?                              | ☐     | ☐    | ☐     | ___   |
| b. Both in theory and in practice, are users aware of the importance and necessity of:                                                       |       |      |       |       |
| • Network security, including physical security?                                                                                             | ☐     | ☐    | ☐     | ___   |
| • Frequently saving and backing up files?                                                                                                    | ☐     | ☐    | ☐     | ___   |
| • Physical destruction (hard copy, diskettes, etc.)?                                                                                          | ☐     | ☐    | ☐     | ___   |

## 12.2  NETWORK TYPES AND ELEMENTS

### (a)  TYPES OF NETWORKS

*(i)  Local vs. Distributed*

Networks can be of many sizes and many types. One of the most important variances has to do with the geographical extent of a network. The farther apart the elements of a network are spaced, the more constraints there are on how you can interconnect them. If you want to network a collection of microcomputers in one office, there are a number of possible ways to do so, including fat and thin twisted pair cables, coaxial cables, fiber optic cables, infrared sensors, and so on. If you want to connect insurance agents' terminals across the country to several mainframe computers at headquarters, most of these alternatives are not possible.

Local area networks (LANs) usually involve distances of less than a mile (typically inside one building, for example) and, consequently, data speeds in excess of one million bits per second. Distributed or wide-area networks, on the other hand, can span the globe and typically operate at speeds of 9,600 to 56,000 bps.

Obviously, the technologies used to implement each type of network are radically different. However, it should be noted that as high-speed technologies such as fiber optics break down distance barriers, LAN techniques have become possible for wide-area networks as well.

*(ii)  Public vs. Private*

If you own all the facilities that comprise your network, it is a private network. This is only feasible if the data rates or security issues are such that they can justify exclusive use of communication resources.

Most users draw on a mix of private and public facilities, choosing from among many voice and data carriers for a broad range of services.

### (b)  ELEMENTS OF A NETWORK

This section outlines the characteristics of the main technical elements of a network.

*(i)  Terminals*

Terminals, or workstations, are the devices the user employs to access remote computer facilities. Many devices can play the role of terminal in a network, including microcomputers, larger computers, advanced telephones, and even television sets.

Computers expect every terminal to follow a definite protocol. It can be a very simple one, such as the TTY or "dumb terminal," in which the terminal is treated like a simple line-by-line printer. This type of protocol is the lowest common denominator of terminal protocols and can be relied on to work with most computer systems. Other common terminal protocols include IBM's 3270 and DEC's VT100. Most terminals copy, or emulate, one or more of these protocols: the user is responsible for instructing the terminal as to which protocol to use to correctly communicate with the remote device.

The above protocols cover most interactive uses: i.e., those in which the user is making inquiries of another system and looking at information on the screen. When users want to retrieve larger amounts of information from a computer (download) or send larger amounts of information to the computer (upload), more extensive protocols are required that can handle error detection and correction, file names, and other exigencies of transferring files. Examples of standards used in microcomputer networks are Xmodem and Kermit.

### (ii) Modems

As discussed in the last chapter, modems are needed to transform a computing device's digital information into a form that can be sent serially across large distances. Each modem is usually dedicated to one device and one communications link, which is sufficient when the amount of use does not justify a larger expense.

### (iii) Multiplexers

When there are several communicating devices in one location that all need to connect to a device in another location, a multiplexer can be used in place of several sets of modems and lines. Multiplexers take advantage of low line utilization by encoding several data streams into one higher-speed stream. That stream is then sent out through a single high-speed modem to the other end, where a similarly configured multiplexer takes the signals apart and connects them to the intended devices.

It is important to recognize that a multiplexer is invisible, or transparent, to the communicating devices (terminals, computers, etc.). These devices do not recognize that their signals are being handled by a multiplexer, and so one can be installed without disrupting any other communications activities. The advantage of a multiplexer is not its efficiency but rather its cost.

Technical advances are now making complex multiplexer networks possible. In these, switching, network management, and other advanced features are added to the basic multiplexing function at little extra cost.

### (iv) Communications Processors

Communications processors are a class of devices that apply a high level of intelligence to the communications function. In an effort to reduce the load on the main computer for protocol handling, error recovery, network management, and other functions, special-purpose computers called front-end processors (FEPs) are installed between the computer and the communication lines.

In some cases, FEPs support several computers; and users switch from one to the other, depending on what applications they need to use. The most common FEPs in IBM computer sites have been the 3705s or the later 3725s.

### (v) Network Control and Management

With all these devices interconnected across different types of facilities, a significant effort is necessary to keep it all running, especially with the increasing decentralization and diversification that many corporations are implementing. Most networks need some form of a network control center from which the network can be controlled and managed.

Network management involves gathering various kinds of information, including:

- Line availability and quality
- Line utilization
- Cost allocation

Network control also involves maintaining network operations through close monitoring, remote testing, and responding to emergencies as they arise (e.g., by using alternative facilities, equipment, or other contingency plans).

All of this information must be analyzed, correlated, and discussed in the context of the business objectives that relate to information communications.

# 12.3  LOCAL AREA NETWORKS (LANS) AND CLIENT/SERVER TECHNOLOGY

The first typical network environment involves the linking of computers or workstations locally within an organization, hence the term *Local Area Network* or LAN. During the earliest days of LANs (essentially, from the mid to late 1980s), connectivity was largely limited to the sharing of peripheral devices by standalone computers. Microcomputers were simply not powerful enough to control networks in the way that mainframes could control a network of terminals.

By the 1990s, however, the power of micros had increased so much that so-called Client/Server Technology (and the related terms Client/Server Architecture and Client/Server Computing) had become a high-growth field. Client/server architecture is basically an expansion of the LAN concept, whereby a powerful microcomputer holds the primary processing and file server capability at the center of a network. Many large organizations are backing down from their mainframes onto this type of configuration.

## (a)  TYPES OF LANs AND CLIENT/SERVER ARCHITECTURE

The two most distinctive physical characteristics of LANs and Client/Server Technology are the transmission technology used to pass the signal among devices and the physical arrangement of the connecting medium, called the topology.

*(i) Transmission Alternatives*

The transmission medium and signaling technique determine the cost and performance characteristics of a network. The two most common media are twisted-pair copper wire (identical to or derived from telephone cabling) and coaxial cables. Each has advantages and disadvantages over the other. A third media—fiber optics—is also increasingly being used in LANs and Client/Server Technology.

Twisted-pair wiring is the least expensive to install and maintain; in many cases, sufficient wiring has already been installed with the telephone equipment. However, unshielded twisted-pair cable is very susceptible to interference from any electromagnetic source (e.g., a ringing telephone or electric motor). It also has an upper data rate of about one million bits per second, the lowest of the three media.

Coaxial cable carries either a baseband or broadband signal. Each has very different characteristics that need to be distinguished. Baseband coax uses an all-digital signaling method to broadcast a single channel to every receiving station. Computer circuitry is needed to recognize which messages belong to the receiving station and to correctly seize control of the channel and broadcast its own outward messages. Data rates are typically around ten million bps. Because of the digital nature of the signal, special cable is required, but installation is simple, and tapping into the cable can be done at any time without disrupting an active network. Ethernet is the best known example of a baseband LAN.

Broadband coax uses the same analog technology as cable TV—each signal is multiplexed onto a particular frequency, and the receiving station is tuned into the channel that it uses to send and receive messages. Signals other than a LANs data can be easily carried by a broadband coax network—for example, voice, video, or telemetry data. Although the hardware technology is widespread, broadband installations are more expensive than baseband because radio frequency converters are needed for every station; also, tapping into the line involves cutting the cable and disrupting the network.

Finally, fiber optics are finding greater use in local area networks because of their speed, reliability, and security; however, installation seems delayed by the difficulties involved in actually tapping into and connecting fiber links.

### (ii) Topology Alternatives

The topology of a network is the overall shape of the medium that connects the various devices. Most LANs use one of three topologies: bus, ring, or star. Client/Server Architecture typically follows the star topology.

A bus LAN, exemplified by the Ethernet network, consists of a single length of cable (typically coax) to which the workstations connect through taps fastened onto the cable. To attach an additional device, one need only attach another tap onto the cable and plug the new system into the tap's interface. Bus topologies are broadcast media: any signal on the bus is "listened to" by all devices on the LAN but only acted on by the one device that recognizes that message as belonging to it.

A ring LAN arranges the stations in a circle and connects each to its immediate neighbor over a length of cable. Because of the access method used on most rings, each device usually has an "in" and an "out" socket for connecting to the systems on either side of it in the ring. Each station on the ring processes the signal before sending it to the next station.

A star LAN or Client/Server Architecture connects each device to a central network manager that is responsible for dispatching data messages to each system through its unique point-to-point connection.

Each topology has different strengths and weaknesses with respect to traffic throughput, reliability, and resilience to component failures. Bus networks are excellent for environments with low to medium traffic but can only be connected to a limited number of devices. When the capacity of the LAN is reached, all stations are adversely affected. Nevertheless, a failure in one device may not stop the whole network, the master cable is usually easy to install, and adding new devices is a straight-forward process.

Ring networks guarantee the minimum delay for handling data regardless of the traffic presented by any one device. They can usually handle very fast speeds and are often used for minicomputer interprocessor communications. However, a break anywhere in the ring cable will typically stop the entire network; also, problems can be difficult to diagnose and correct.

A star network relies entirely for throughput and reliability on the central network manager. There is a fixed limit to the number of devices and the volume of information that it can handle without upgrading or replacing the central controller. On the other hand, the failure of any other device or connection does not have any effect on the rest of the network, and controlling and managing the network is made simple by the centralized design.

## (b)  PBX LANs

The above section described dedicated LANs that rely on specialized LAN hardware and the workstations themselves to run the network. An alternative is offered by several major PBX vendors (for example, AT&T) in which the PBX itself can run the LAN functions. This has several advantages over a separate LAN:

- The cost of switching data signals and managing the network is shared with voice users.
- The functionality and capacity of the PBX can be much higher than on a special-purpose LAN.
- Some or all of the wiring may already be in place from the telephone installation.
- Workstations on a PBX-based LAN can take advantage of the telephony features supplied by the LAN, such as access to the world outside the office.

## (c)  IBM AND COMPATIBLES; APPLETALK

Most local area networks have been designed for use with IBM and compatible micro-computers. LANs offer the only truly effective solution for sharing printers, modems, and data files among the growing number of PCs. By adding software, special add-on cards, and some cable to a micro, you can connect with a common pool of data resources.

Leading vendors in this area include Novell and Microsoft as well as the PBX LAN vendors.

In a somewhat different approach from that of the IBM add-on LANs, Apple supplies all the computers in its Macintosh line with a built-in LAN called AppleTalk. Connecting computers, printers, and other devices together is as easy as plugging the shielded twisted pair cable into an adapter with an open socket.

Although Apple's software has built-in capability for printer sharing and other basic functions, it is left to other vendors to supply hardware and more elaborate network management software to support partitioned disks, links to Ethernet networks, file transfer, and pooled remote-system access.

## 12.4 DISTRIBUTED NETWORKS, ELECTRONIC DATA INTERCHANGE (EDI), AND THE INTERNET

While distributed networks can and do exist within large, geographically dispersed organizations, the more typical or "generic" scenario for this type of network involves communication between organizations. For example, such networks can be thought of as linking financial organizations with their clients, commercial databases with their customers, participating organizations in an EDI environment, or cybersurfers with the World Wide Web.

### (a) DIAL-UP VS. DEDICATED NETWORKS

In the choice between dial-up and dedicated networks, the factors to consider are convenience and practicality. For example, networks in which the remote ends are regional office computers having high data-exchange requirements with the head office data center will in most cases be connected with dedicated facilities leased from one or more of the common carriers.

Networks that include traveling sales staff, time-sharing users in many locations, or remote warehouses with low data-exchange requirements can be served most effectively by dial-up facilities. A typical configuration could look like this:

- There might be 25 remote oil-drilling sites, each with a microcomputer and a modem attached to a telephone.
- Since the head office expects that a maximum of five sites will be calling in at any one time, the central site has five modems on dedicated telephone lines connected to their computer.
- To use the central computer, a site dials the number of the central site and connects to one of the modems—long distance charges are incurred for the length of the call only.

When the overall data volume is low, dial-up is generally more cost-effective than dedicated lines. Additionally, many sites install dial-up facilities in parallel to dedicated lines for use when the main line is damaged in any way.

### (b) MICRO-MAINFRAME NETWORKS

Mainframes are continuing to improve their processing and storage capabilities, while microcomputers continue to improve and proliferate. The first is a centralizing trend, the second encourages decentralization. Several attempts have been made to develop products that would integrate these two divergent trends, thus extracting users from a major dilemma.

Unfortunately, no generally acceptable solution has been found other than to equip micros with the necessary hardware and software to emulate a mainframe terminal. This solves the problem of how to allow the micro user access to mainframe information, but it opens the mainframe environment to an enormous security exposure. Control over who accesses the mainframe directly or through dial-in lines is now in the hands of the micro user instead of the mainframe EDP department (see also Chapter 13 of this handbook, "Computer Security and System Recovery").

### (c)  PACKET NETWORKS

Packet networks offer a very flexible alternative to dial-up or leased lines. In most countries in the world, one or more common carriers have constructed a network of switching nodes and high-speed lines across the country. Each of these networks can be connected to by means of the international packet switching standard, X.25; they can also communicate with one another using other common international standards.

The user connects to the network with a terminal or a computer and pays a small fixed charge for that connection. All other charges are use-dependent, so light users are lightly charged even though they can establish a link to almost anywhere on the globe. Many computer networks of conglomerate companies are based on the global packet switching networks because of the availability of X.25 interfaces from all major computer vendors, the universality of the networks, and the reasonable cost.

### (d)  ON-LINE COMMERCIAL DATABASES

A significant service available to business and personal users alike is the commercial database. These databases are available for every conceivable research request and are a direct result of telecommunications technologies that have made it easy and cheap to retrieve information from faraway places.

Commercial databases are of two types: one provides a small set of specialized databases focused on a limited range of topics—medicine, the stock market, or computer engineering, for example. They cater to professional users in private or public libraries or to specialized corporate environments.

The other kind of information provider acts as a broker, liaison, or "gateway" for the first kind of information provider. Examples of this kind of service are America Online, CompuServe and Prodigy.

### (e)  ELECTRONIC DATA INTERCHANGE

Local Area Networks and Client-Server Technology are essentially applications of connectivity *within* organizations (although the organization may be geographically dispersed). EDI is a still-emerging application of information technology that is most significant because it involves connectivity *among* organizations.

EDI is an acronym for Electronic Data Interchange. EDI is the transfer of information among computers in independent organizations, using an agreed-upon structure or standard.

In practice EDI involves the transfer of transaction-based information and documents—for example purchase orders, receiving reports, invoices, and bank account debits or credits—between companies that have adopted standards to facilitate such transfers.

Electronic Commerce is another term sometimes used to describe the EDI concept.

The basic elements of EDI are:

• Hardware, specifically computer and telecommunications equipment.

• Software, in particular (a) accounting and/or database software that store the documents and/or information to be electronically exchanged; and (b) communications software to transmit and receive the information.

- Specific, widely agreed-upon standards governing data and data transmission.
- Formal, written agreements between the parties participating in the EDI system.

For any organization the costs of setting up, entering into, and implementing an EDI environment must be weighed against the potential benefits—reduced information processing costs (including staffing), more timely information, reduced receivables, lower cost of capital, and so on—once the system has been set up.

Organizations interested in studying the EDI option should obtain information from the EDI association in their jurisdiction, if one exists. Alternatively, there may be EDI standards that have been developed by and for particular industry groups. Examples in the United States include the Transportation Data Coordinating Committee (TDCC) for the transportation industry, Uniform Communication Standards (UCS) for the grocery industry, Warehouse Industry Network Standard (WINS) for the warehouse industry, and American National Standard Industry (ANSI) X12 standards for general business.

## (f) THE INTERNET

*Internet* is the buzzword that's been commonly used to describe the international network of computer networks. In a sense the Internet can be thought of as a global client/server configuration. Every person who accesses the Internet through his or her personal computer or workstation is a client. Typically, clients use the software on their machines to access the network, make queries, download and store data, and so on. The server computers on the Internet are all those that contain resources that clients wish to access. These resources could include databases, sounds and images, software, games, newsgroups, on-line conferences, and home shopping. Client computers—which can be located anywhere in the world—may provide resources directly to clients or act as "gateways" to other networks that provide the resources (hence the phrase "network of networks").

The concept of client/server computing as it applies to commercial databases is long established. In the mid-1980s it was possible to use a modem to dial up a remote database, use search criteria to gather information, and download it to your PC. There were also gateway services available which provided one-stop access to multiple commercial databases as well as electronic mail systems for those who subscribed to the gateway service. Why then all the fuss about the Internet? Some still argue that there is no good answer to this question and that the Internet is mainly hype, the hula-hoop of the 1990s. However, in fairness, there are at least two factors that distinguish the current Internet:

- A *common protocol*—the Internet has developed around a common protocol known as TCP/IP, an acronym for Transmission Control Protocol/Internet Protocol. This protocol was originally developed by the U.S. Department of Defense to link computers at various military installations, private-sector contractors, and academic institutions. Adoption of the protocol for wider use has meant that the system managers of server computers—and the developers of resources contained thereon—do not have to worry about how to develop links with different types of computers. In other words, all the computers in the network speak the same language.

- *Explosion in use*—throughout most of the 1980s, an ordinary user could typically only obtain a TCP/IP connection through an academic institution that had access to it. The very late 1980s and early 1990s saw the arrival of commercial Internet service providers that sold access to anyone with a computer, modem, and communications software. From that point on, the Internet began to feed on itself. As more users—in particular home computer users, the highest growth area of the computer industry in the 1990s—accessed the Internet, more resource providers entered the fray to sell their wares. Companies felt it necessary to set up Internet (especially World Wide Web) addresses, lest they miss out. Finally, media hype about the Internet and its growth has fueled even more growth.

One of the key elements of the Internet is the identification of specific computer sites. For computers and computer users to communicate, they must obviously know where to find one another—they need the computer equivalent of an address or telephone number. Accordingly, every server (host computer) on the Internet has a numeric IP address, consisting of four sets of numbers separated by periods. Over time, the use of domain names has proliferated as a substitute for these numbers, since numbers are difficult to remember. However, the numbers themselves still lie underneath.

Registered numeric IP addresses and domain names are obtained from different organizations depending on the country where the server is located. For example, in Canada addresses are obtained from the CA*net IP Registry. In practice most users will arrange domain name registration through their commercial Internet service provider. However, most users do not need their own domain name, and they simply lease the commercial service provider's domain name. The proliferation of users in this manner—some having their own domain names, others leasing it from a service provider—and the desirability of identifying the type of user has led to a specific format for Internet addresses—*yourname@domain.category*. The elements of this address are as follows:

- The middle or *@domain* portion is the key element since it represents the numeric IP address of the host computer. The @ symbol, along with the period that follows the domain name, are necessary because they delineate the domain name from any other elements which precede and follow it.

- The *yourname* portion is a descriptive used to identify the specific user. The commercial Internet service provider would use it to identify the users who have leased its domain name, for purposes of billing as well as distributing electronic mail. Alternatively, the *yourname* portion could identify a specific employee within an organization that has its own domain name. In either case, someone will be assigned the task of administering names on the host computer (adding, deleting, ensuring that names are unique, etc.), much as a network administrator would on a local area network. In the case of sole users who have their own domain name, the *yourname* portion is simply an additional descriptive that they choose.

- The *category* portion is another descriptive which can be either (i) a two-character country code as defined by the International Standards Organization (for example *.ca* for Canada); or (ii) a three-character code describing the activity of the host computer (for example, *.com* for a commercial enterprise, *.edu* for an educational institution, *.gov* for government, *.org* for an organization, and so on). Infrequently, it is possible for this *category* portion to be split into two (for example, in Canada some addresses have a provincial code followed by *.ca*).

As an example of how the system might work, if John Robert Smith worked for Acme Inc. somewhere in British Columbia, his address might be *jrs@acme.bc.ca*.

## 12.5  USER NEEDS AND NETWORK EVALUATION

### (a)  MATCHING USER NEEDS AND FEATURES

The features of the network being considered should be evaluated and matched with the needs of the user. Some factors to be considered are:

- *Hardware and operating system requirements*—the compatibility of the network with the hardware (e.g., Intel-based, Apple Macintosh) and operating system (e.g., DOS, OS/2, Windows) is obviously critical.
- *Size and complexity of network*—the network must meet current as well as anticipated needs; otherwise, the investment could prove a short-term waste.
- *Manufacturer and vendor support*—inevitably, networks contain errors or bugs that require correction. In addition, networks generally improve as technology advances. It is therefore essential that a network package be well supported and updated regularly.
- *Price*—in addition to the initial cost of the network, the user should consider the manufacturer's or vendor's update policies (i.e., how users are notified of updates) and the related cost. The better networks tend to be improved frequently to keep up with the competition.
- *Compatibility*—a key consideration for many users (especially medium- and large-size organizations) is compatibility with other networks owned by the user. For example, if others in the organization are already using a particular network, building on that network may be the best alternative.
- *Security*—networks are by definition designed to be used by many individuals. Protecting the integrity of files and data from accidental or other damage is therefore critical. A password system is essential.

### (b)  OTHER SOURCES OF INFORMATION

In addition to network documentation, sources of information include:

- Books, magazines, and newsletters
- Courses and seminars
- Consulting services

Training courses are offered by a variety of firms, including network vendors, public accounting firms, professional bodies (such as societies of accountants), and training institutions. Courses are typically one or two days, and fees usually range from $100 to $500.

Many of the large accounting and management consulting firms provide network-related services. There are also independent consultants who specialize in this field.

# CHAPTER 13

# Computer Security and System Recovery

Whether the concern is accidental damage or deliberate acts such as fraud and commercial crime, prevention is the best medicine. Establishing and maintaining adequate computer security is a vital part of any prevention strategy.

This chapter features the following:

- The next section (13.1) contains a checklist that summarizes the key points in this chapter.
- Section 13.2 introduces the key management issues surrounding computer security.
- The following sections deal with the specifics of physical security (13.3), logical security (13.4), and system recovery (13.5).
- The last section (13.6) presents some final thoughts on computer security.

While the focus is on prevention, the chapter deals with computer security issues in a comprehensive way.

## 13.1 COMPUTER SECURITY CHECKLIST

The following three-page checklist is designed to assist accountants in dealing with computer security in their organizations and those of their clients. Generally, all "No" answers require investigation and follow-up, the results of which should be documented. Where there is such additional documentation, the purpose of the "Ref" column is to cross-reference the checklist to the appropriate working paper (or to the notes on the reverse).

The checklist is intended for general use only. Use of the checklist does not guarantee the adequacy of computer security, and it is not intended as a substitute for audit or similar procedures. If computer security is an especially vital concern or if computer fraud is suspected, the advice of a specialist should be sought.

## Computer Security Checklist

|  | Yes | No | N/A | Ref |
|---|---|---|---|---|
| **1. Physical Security** | | | | |
| a. Are adequate fire detection and suppression systems in place (e.g., computer room construction to a minimum one hour fire resistance rating, smoke detectors, fire alarms, sprinklers)? | ☐ | ☐ | ☐ | ___ |
| b. Are adequate systems in place to protect against water damage (e.g., underfloor water detectors, floor drains, waterproof equipment covers)? | ☐ | ☐ | ☐ | ___ |
| c. Where power supplies are unreliable or the nature of processing is critical, are suitable precautions in place (e.g., batteries or backup generators, surge protectors)? | ☐ | ☐ | ☐ | ___ |
| d. Are appropriate environmental controls in place with respect to temperature, humidity, and dust? | ☐ | ☐ | ☐ | ___ |
| e. Is access to especially sensitive computer installations restricted (e.g., through key locks, combination or cypher locks, or card access systems)? | ☐ | ☐ | ☐ | ___ |
| f. Is overall computer security on the premises adequate? | ☐ | ☐ | ☐ | ___ |
| **2. Communications Security** | | | | |
| a. Is a user ID and password system in place? | ☐ | ☐ | ☐ | ___ |
| b. Is the ID and password system properly administered (e.g., is the distribution of new IDs controlled, and are terminated users promptly deleted from the system)? | ☐ | ☐ | ☐ | ___ |
| c. Are users aware of the responsibility associated with their password (e.g., are they instructed to maintain password secrecy and not to choose simplistic or easily guessed passwords)? | ☐ | ☐ | ☐ | ___ |
| d. Are passwords changed regularly (e.g., every 30 days)? | ☐ | ☐ | ☐ | ___ |
| e. Does the system monitor and control use (e.g., by restricting users to specific terminals or specific times, automatically logging-out inactive users, limiting the number of log-on attempts, and recording all usage for later follow-up and investigation if required)? | ☐ | ☐ | ☐ | ___ |
| f. For especially sensitive systems, is security to control remote access in place (e.g., callback devices)? | ☐ | ☐ | ☐ | ___ |

|  | Yes | No | N/A | Ref |
|---|---|---|---|---|

### 3. Data Security

a. Is access to on-line data limited to authorized persons only through built-in software restrictions or screening? ☐ ☐ ☐ ___

b. For extremely sensitive data, has data encryption been considered as a security measure? ☐ ☐ ☐ ___

c. Are data files stored on magnetic media (including all backups) kept in a physically secure location to which only authorized persons are allowed access? ☐ ☐ ☐ ___

d. Are all printed reports subject to appropriate control, and appropriate destruction (e.g., shredding) when no longer required? ☐ ☐ ☐ ___

### 4. Software Integrity

a. Is access to production versions of all software tightly controlled by a production librarian or another authorized person? ☐ ☐ ☐ ___

b. Is access to all software programming code controlled so that tested and approved software cannot be subsequently altered by programmers or others? ☐ ☐ ☐ ___

c. Are appropriate policies in place to guard against computer viruses (e.g., prohibiting the installation of any copied or borrowed software and screening all software with virus detection programs)? ☐ ☐ ☐ ___

### 5. Operations Security

a. Do detailed operator instructions (e.g., manuals) exist? ☐ ☐ ☐ ___

b. Are computer operations personnel prohibited from altering program code and the Job Control Language (which should match the program and data files to be run)? ☐ ☐ ☐ ___

c. Are all software and data storage media clearly and correctly labeled, including dates, to avoid errors? ☐ ☐ ☐ ___

d. Are data files reconciled from run to run? ☐ ☐ ☐ ___

e. Are all data storage media erased (wiped clean) before being disposed of? ☐ ☐ ☐ ___

f. Is computer activity logged and any unusual operator activity investigated? ☐ ☐ ☐ ___

|  | *Yes* | *No* | *N/A* | *Ref* |
|---|---|---|---|---|

**6. System Recovery**

a. Are copies of all data files and software made on a regular basis (e.g., weekly, with daily backups of transaction files)?  ☐ ☐ ☐ ___

b. Is at least one backup copy of all data files and software stored off-site?  ☐ ☐ ☐ ___

c. Has training been provided, and are there written instructions for disaster recovery procedures?  ☐ ☐ ☐ ___

d. In the case of catastrophic failure, are there alternate processing arrangements?  ☐ ☐ ☐ ___

e. Is there insurance adequate to cover computer equipment, software, recovery expenses, and business interruption?  ☐ ☐ ☐ ___

## 13.2 MANAGEMENT ISSUES

In today's business environment the computer is no longer regarded as simply a "number cruncher" used to process accounting transactions such as receivables and payables. It has become an integral part of business and of numerous business processes. For example, the computer is increasingly being used to:

- Store sensitive and confidential information on products, employees, or customers in a central location, to which access should be controlled and expanded for corporate benefit.
- Provide timely information to assist in decision making—for example, revised projections of performance against marketing plans and budgets.
- Improve the personal productivity of employees—for example, analysis of data, preparation of correspondence and reports, and electronic mail.
- Gain a competitive advantage by reducing order turnaround time and improving customer service.

As more and more organizations implement applications of this nature, their reliance on computer processing increases, which in turn increases the need for an effective computer security program, because criminals also use computers—both their own and those of others—in committing fraud and commercial crime.

In addition, information itself is being increasingly recognized as an asset of value. Individuals, companies, and even governments covet the information held by others as a source of financial gain, power, or other advantage. Now that computers are the main depositories of information, this change in perception has also highlighted the requirements for effective security over automated systems. Security is no longer viewed as an option; it is a necessary element of business survival and therefore a critical management responsibility.

### (a) THE CONCERNS

Managers in business and government have recognized the growing importance of computer processing to their organizations and, over the last few years, have expressed their concerns in a wide variety of publications. These concerns generally fall into one of the following three categories.

*(i) Theft of Confidential Information*

Recognizing that more and more information is being stored in computer systems, management is seeking assurance that this information is well protected and that only appropriately authorized persons have access to it.

For example, theft of proposed pay scales prior to labor negotiations could be detrimental to the process and result in increased production costs. Theft of marketing or pricing plans might result in a loss of competitive advantage. Similarly, theft of personal or financial customer information could result not only in embarrassment, but also a direct loss of business and possible litigation.

*(ii) Information Integrity*

Because of the large volume of information processed by computers, it is usually not feasible to confirm the validity or accuracy of processing results. Management therefore seeks assurance on the integrity of computer-generated information—that the information is protected against computer viruses, hackers, unauthorized tampering by employees, or other forms of sabotage.

For example, tampering that results in inaccurate reporting of sales figures could in turn cause inappropriate production, excessive inventory levels, and lost sales. Unauthorized altering of the accounts payable records could result in altered mailing labels or shipping amounts and direct financial loss.

*(iii) System Availability*

Recognizing the organization's dependence on the data processing service, management is seeking assurance that not only has everything been done to reduce the likelihood of disruption, but also that there are plans in place for the resumption of data processing in the unlikely event of a major catastrophe. The total or partial loss of data processing services would make it difficult, perhaps impossible, for most organizations to perform routine business operations.

## (b)  SECURING COMPUTER SYSTEMS

An effective computer security program can help alleviate such concerns. The design of an effective computer security program must take into account the nature of the risk and the nature and cost of the controls required to reduce exposure. This in turn requires that the following areas be addressed.

*(i) Accidental vs. Deliberate Events*

The events that create confidentiality, integrity, or availability problems may be accidental or deliberate or may result from actions internal or external to the organization.

Clearly, the most likely variant is an internal accident such as an employee deleting an essential data file. It has been claimed that 25–35 percent of an organization's information systems budget is wasted through errors, accidents, or omissions.

Deliberate sabotage—theft of information, malicious damage, viruses, and so on— is much less likely than inadvertent damage. However, for purposes of this handbook, this distinction has little relevance. Accidents can be arranged by would-be perpetrators of fraud, and a well-designed computer security program will consider all possible events, both accidental and deliberate. The focus should be on minimizing the possibility of the most likely crises, while also considering less likely problems that could result in greater financial loss. To achieve the most cost-effective level of security in any organization, a combination of controls is required.

*(ii) Prevention, Detection, and Recovery Controls*

Obviously, the best and most appealing way to minimize the impact of an unwanted event that will affect information confidentiality, integrity, or availability is to prevent the event from occurring. In the case of deliberate acts, preventive controls will reduce opportunity and thereby remove temptation.

Preventive controls, however, cannot fully guarantee that a problem will not occur. As a result, it is common to find complementary detective controls that will highlight any actual or attempted security violation. As an example, software features may exist that prevent unauthorized users from gaining access to data. In such a situation it is also usual for a report to be produced that documents all attempts by users to gain access to information to which they had no right—the detective control.

In addition to preventive and detective controls, it is necessary to provide for recovery from events that might occur. Using the example of the deletion of a data file, the existence of a backup copy will constitute such a recovery control.

A well-designed security program will include elements of all three types of control: preventive, detective, and recovery. The mix of controls used will depend on the nature of the information stored on the computer, the reliance placed on the computer, and management's willingness to accept the associated risks.

## 13.3  PHYSICAL SECURITY

### (a)  INTRODUCTION

Physical security is the generic term used to describe the protection of the computing facility. The controls exercised under the heading of "physical security" are typically preventive and detective in nature.

Physical security primarily addresses availability and attempts to minimize the potential for system loss as a result of equipment damage. To achieve this objective, consideration must be given to each of the areas dealt with below.

### (b)  COMPUTER ROOM CONSTRUCTION

The most concise definition of recommended computer room construction is found in the National Fire Prevention Association (NFPA) standards. In summary, to provide an appropriate level of protection, computer room perimeter walls should be constructed to a minimum of a one-hour fire resistance rating. These walls should extend from concrete ceiling to concrete floor (slab to slab).

The purpose of such construction is to minimize the possibility of fires originating in general office areas and migrating to the computer room before they can be extinguished. The use of glass partitions to segregate the computer room from the general office environment will not usually provide sufficient protection against such a migration fire.

### (c)  FIRE DETECTION AND SUPPRESSION

Fire detection and suppression systems are essential in the computer room if the investment in computer equipment, and the information stored thereon, is to be protected. They are designed to detect and suppress fire before it advances to a serious state. Automated detection and suppression systems are recommended since they reduce the dependence on manual fire-fighting techniques that may prove unsatisfactory.

The most common fire suppression systems are water sprinklers and Halon 1301 gas. Water sprinkler systems may be "wet" or "dry." Wet systems contain water in the pipes at all times, while a dry pipe system does not contain water until an alarm goes off, at which point a valve is automatically opened to charge the system.

Fire detection systems can also provide a direct linkage to other significant support functions, such as opening fire exits, shutting off equipment and fans, and immediate notification of an alarm company or the fire department via a communications link.

## (d)  WATER PROTECTION

Water and electrical systems do not mix, but both are generally found in computer rooms to operate the equipment and to cool the equipment or environment. It is, therefore, important to ensure that precautions are taken to detect and remove water leakage before it contacts the electrical supply. Water protection usually involves the provision of:

- Under-floor water detectors, normally in the vicinity of the air conditioning units (water detection systems are usually monitored in the same manner as fire alarms).

- Floor drains to remove any water buildup (unless specified during construction, floor drains are not usually provided in modern office towers).

- Waterproof equipment covers (where sprinkler systems or other above-floor water sources are present, there should be equipment covers or rolls of plastic that can be pulled over the equipment in the event of a problem).

## (e)  ELECTRICAL POWER RELIABILITY

A disruption to the electrical power supply will, unless suitable precautions are taken, result in the loss of computer service. The provision of backup power sources can be expensive, and its cost may not be justified if the computer center is in an area where the electric power supply is reliable. If the electric power supply is unreliable, or the nature of processing critical, consideration should be given to the provision of:

- Uninterruptible power supply (UPS), which provides battery backup in the event of power failures or brownouts (the regular power supply is monitored at all times, and battery power is automatically provided when required).

- Backup generators, since UPS can only provide battery backup power for a limited time (in computer centers that provide critical processing services or in areas where electric power is unreliable, UPS systems are often supported by diesel generators that can produce electric power for an indefinite period).

Finally, regardless of the local power supply outage record, it is likely that power conditioners will be used in larger computer installations. Power conditioners monitor the electric power supply and remove voltage sags and surges.

## (f) ENVIRONMENTAL CONTROL

Environmental control is an issue that has primarily been a concern for the larger mainframe computer environments. But even smaller machines that manufacturers claim can operate in a general office environment cannot totally ignore the environmental issues set out below.

- *Temperature control*—computers cannot operate in extreme temperatures. It is true that the range of operating temperatures has been increasing. However, even where the specifications indicate that the machine will operate in a fairly wide temperature range (e.g., 15–32 degrees Celsius or 59–90 degrees Fahrenheit), it is not advisable to operate near either the lower or upper limits, and air conditioning is usually installed to reduce the likelihood of system outage or damage as a result of overheating.

- *Humidity control*—the computer manufacturers normally indicate a range of humidity that is acceptable for their machines—for example, a 20–80 percent humidity tolerance. Humidity control is normally provided by the air conditioning unit.

- *Environment contamination*—dust can cause major problems in a computer environment. If dust gets into a disk pack, it may cause a head crash and render the information on that disk inaccessible. In addition, accumulations of paper dust from printers represent a potential fire hazard. To minimize the potential for dust contamination, it is advisable that the areas where dust normally accumulates be regularly vacuumed.

## (g) PHYSICAL ACCESS CONTROLS

The importance of physical access controls over all assets and related records is obvious. Such controls help to reduce the risk of fraud and commercial crime for the following reasons:

- Physical access controls are often the most visible to potential perpetrators. As such, strong controls in this area send a powerful deterrent message—i.e., that the other controls in the system are also strong. Conversely, loose physical controls invite challenge.

- Many frauds require the perpetrator to come into physical contact with either (a) the asset being misappropriated, or (b) the related asset records in order to cover up the fraud. Reducing physical access reduces opportunity.

- Even if fraud and commercial crime is not prevented through access controls, these controls can often help an investigation (e.g., the determination of what actually happened and the narrowing of suspects).

Physical security over computer installations and equipment is especially important. It should be noted that white-collar criminals and irate employees can resort to so-called "blue-collar" crimes like arson and destruction of property. When they do, even blue-collar crimes may be classified as commercial or economic in nature.

The only employees who should have access to computer equipment are those responsible for its operation. Any third-party engineers performing maintenance should be accompanied by operations staff at all times. To provide more liberal access increases the potential for vandalism, mischief, and accidental error, any of which can result in processing disruptions.

Limiting access to the computer room involves securing the doors and keeping them closed at all times. A variety of devices are available for this, including:

- *Key locks*—these are the cheapest to install but are usually the least secure since duplicate keys can be made and distributed without control.
- *Cypher locks*—push-button combination devices are generally more secure if the combination is changed on a regular basis.
- *Card access devices*—these are probably the most secure mechanisms because cards cannot be readily duplicated and card distribution can be controlled.

### (h) PHYSICAL SECURITY FOR MICROCOMPUTERS

Much of the preceding discussion relates to computer systems of any size. Some especially important measures for physically securing microcomputers include the following:

- Restrict physical access—lock doors during off hours or when an office is vacant.
- Use the locks and other security features provided on many microcomputers, which prevent their use by unauthorized persons.
- Ensure that the receptionist and others watch for unauthorized personnel in the area around the microcomputers.

## 13.4 LOGICAL SECURITY

### (a) INTRODUCTION

Logical security is the term used to describe the protection of information stored on a computer system. The controls involved are usually a blend of preventive and detective controls. Logical security addresses confidentiality and integrity concerns and helps to reduce the potential for inappropriate information disclosure, modification, or deletion.

Achieving an appropriate level of logical security requires consideration as to how the user gains access to information. Diagrams and flow charts can assist in this regard. For example, Figure 13.1 depicts computer access in an IBM mainframe environment; in addition to the security controls for the data, it is necessary to consider the controls over the software that provides access to the data and to the system. The following issues need to be addressed.

### (b) COMMUNICATIONS SECURITY

Communications security focuses on controlling the various methods of access to the computer system. Of course, the primary purpose of communications security is to ensure that

**Figure 13.1**    Logical Security

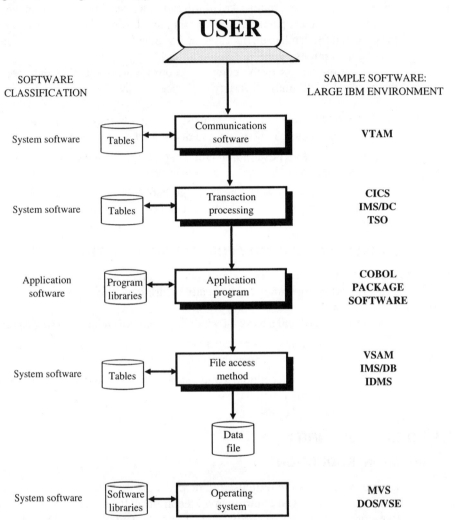

valid transmissions between computer systems are complete and accurate; however, such security also presents an obstacle to criminal activity.

*(i) Passwords and Administration*

The provision of a valid user identification (ID) and password is the first line of access control on most computer systems. The validation of the ID and password by a computer program represents the preventive part of the control, and the rejection and recording of an invalid ID or password represents the detection control. The detective aspect of password control requires the investigation of all reported access failures.

For passwords to be an effective control, procedures must also be in place to ensure that:

- Passwords are not simplistic in nature (e.g., initials, wife/husband's name or other similar personal passwords, since simplistic passwords can be readily guessed and the system compromised).
- Passwords are changed regularly, say every 30–90 days, depending on the nature of the information accessed.
- New user IDs and passwords are distributed to users in a controlled manner.
- Users who have left the organization have their IDs and passwords revoked on a timely basis.

*(ii) Network Security Features*

The programmed network security features that are available vary from system to system. Some of the common features include:

- Providing a maximum number of log-on attempts—if the user has not successfully logged on in the specified number of attempts, the session is terminated and the incident recorded on a log for investigation. On some systems the user's account is locked to prohibit further attempts until action is taken by the operators or security officer function. This feature is intended to prevent unauthorized users from repeatedly attempting to gain access.
- Automatic log-out of inactive terminals—if an employee leaves a terminal logged on, anyone who gains access to that terminal has the access rights of the previous user. Password security is effectively breached. In recognition of this, many systems now provide for users to be logged out automatically if the terminal has been inactive for a defined period of time.
- Restrictions of users to specific terminals and/or specific times of the day.
- Echo checking of transmitted information to ensure that the information is complete and accurate—this is achieved by a retransmission of the message to the source terminal for validation.

*(iii) Dial-up Security*

Hackers have received considerable publicity in recent years, having successfully gained access to numerous computer systems. In response to the problems created by hackers, several companies have developed and marketed security devices to control dial-up access. The purpose of these devices is to limit dial-up access to authorized employees.

One common device available to help control dial-up access is the callback device. When an employee dials in, the call is intercepted by the device, a special code is entered by the employee, and the device then calls back to the phone number associated with the code entered. The communication link is then established, and the user ID and password entered in the normal way.

## (c) DATA SECURITY

Inappropriate access to information can result in its disclosure, modification, or deletion. Appropriate data security demands an evaluation of the sensitivity of the data to ensure a level of protection commensurate with the value of the information. Data security addresses the issue of protecting information stored on computer files, magnetic media, and hard copy reports.

### (i) "On-line" Data Files

On-line data files are the files stored on disk that can be directly accessed by the users of a computer system. Two effective techniques are available to secure on-line data files:

- *Software restrictions*—a program, or series of programs, is used to reference established security tables to determine whether the requesting user is allowed the requested access (e.g., read or write in the requested data file). If the request is valid, the user will be permitted access; if not, access is denied and the access violation reported on a log file for subsequent investigation. This process is illustrated by the flowchart in Figure 13.2.

**Figure 13.2**    Security Software

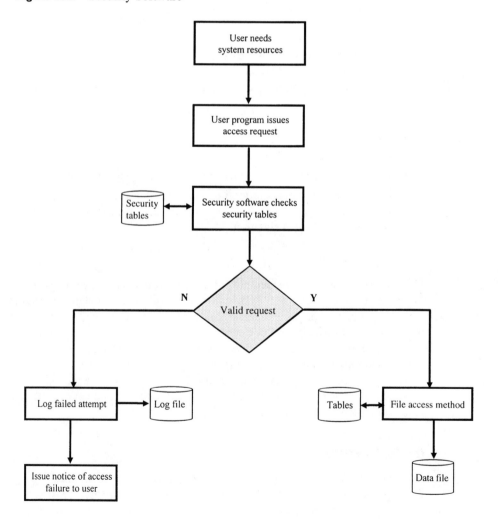

On some computer systems the software restriction facility is an integral part of the operating system, while others require a separate security software product that interfaces with the operating system.

- *Data encryption*—data encryption can be used to scramble information using a predefined algorithm or key so that it is not meaningful to anyone who gains access to the disk file. A data encryption standard (DES) has been approved for use by the U.S. National Bureau of Standards.

The use of data encryption remains relatively limited outside of the defense sector. Data encryption and decryption add an additional system overhead that most users find unwarranted.

### (ii)  "Off-line" Data Files

Off-line data files represent the information stored in libraries on magnetic tape, exchangeable disks, and diskettes. The information stored on these media is as readily susceptible to inappropriate disclosure, amendment, and deletion as on-line data files unless it is properly controlled. The preventive controls usually applied include:

- Keeping the media library in a physically secure room where the door is locked at all times when authorized staff are not present.
- Media library procedures that require that the files are issued only from the library for approved purposes (e.g., production use and transport to off-site storage).

The detective controls normally consist of an investigation of all media issued but not returned in a reasonable time and the performance of a periodic inventory check. However, many smaller organizations consider the use of comprehensive library procedures impractical because of limited staff availability. In these situations and in microcomputer environments, computer information (e.g., on hard disks and diskettes) should be backed up regularly and stored in a secure location.

### (iii)  Reports and Documents

It is not difficult to become preoccupied with protecting information on computer systems and to neglect information on input forms and on printed computer reports.

Generally, reliance is placed on internal controls exercised by user departments to ensure that data approved for input are not modified before they are entered into the computer. However, less concern is typically given to securing input documents before and after input. Yet these input documents contain all of the confidential information ultimately stored on disk.

Attention must be given to printed output, which should include the following:

- *Printing control*—any partially printed reports resulting from printer problems should be destroyed.
- *Distribution control*—verify that printed computer reports are distributed only to authorized recipients, particularly reports containing sensitive or confidential information.

- *Secure storage*—computer reports should be appropriately secured in the user department outside of regular office hours.

- *Controlled destruction*—all reports should be appropriately destroyed when no longer required (this applies to all offices, not just computer areas). Even when information is out-of-date, inappropriate disclosure may still prove embarrassing.

## (d) SOFTWARE INTEGRITY

The integrity of information depends on the integrity of the programs that produce and use it, the communications software, the transaction processors, the file access software, the security software, and the operating system (known collectively as the system software, which controls the operation of—and may be used by—application programs).

Software integrity refers to the protection of software during storage on magnetic media, and also during transfer (for example, the migration of programs to production).

### (i) "On-line" Software Libraries

Computer programs are stored on disk files in libraries or software directories. The most effective means of restricting access to those libraries is through security software restrictions, as described earlier for on-line data files (Section 13.4(c)(i)), although library control of software might also help.

Programmers require access to copies of the programs to do their job. They do not, however, require access to the production version. Providing programmers with direct access to the production version compromises software control and increases the possibility that unauthorized changes may be made. In general, only a production librarian should have access to the production programs and only that person should copy new versions of programs into production.

### (ii) "Off-line" Software

Off-line software refers to the backup copies of program libraries or directories stored on magnetic tape, exchangeable disks, and diskettes. The controls required to secure these versions of the software are identical to those discussed for off-line data files earlier in this chapter.

### (iii) Migration of Programs to Production

If a programmer can gain access to a program and make changes while tests are being performed by the user, and before the program is put into production, the version used in production may not be that which was tested and approved. Changes might be introduced that could affect information integrity and risk financial loss. This problem can be addressed in a variety of ways, including:

- Restricting access to the test version of the program to the users who are running the test and the librarian function responsible for the transfer to production.
- Monitoring the time when the last change was made, if that information is retained by the system or library control software (the date of the last change

should not be later than the date when the tests were run and the software approved for use).

### (e) COMPUTER OPERATIONS SECURITY

The proper operation of computer programs and, therefore, the integrity of information can also be affected by improper operator intervention. In particular, computer operators can create problems by:

- Running the incorrect version of a program against the correct data files (this might introduce errors through the use of an untested program code or the possibility of fraud through the use of unauthorized code).
- Running the correct version of the program against incorrect versions of data files (the results produced by this action would be incorrect and could have serious implications).

To effectively control operator activity, a number of measures can be taken, including:

- Restricting the operator's ability to change the job control language, which directs the processing of a program, identifying the program to be run and the data files to be used.
- The use of internal tape and/or disk label checking, to ensure the correct file is being used.
- The provision of detailed operations instructions to reduce the possibility of accidental error.
- Monitoring operator intervention by reviewing the computer activity/console logs and investigating unusual activity.
- Reconciling data file totals from run-to-run to ensure that the correct version of the file was used.

### (f) LOGICAL SECURITY FOR MICROCOMPUTERS

Here are some of the important points to note about logical security for microcomputers:

- Be wary of leaving sensitive information on hard disks. Consider using removable cartridge devices such as the Bernoulli Box or Zip Drive.
- Use cryptic passwords, and don't leave passwords lying around next to the microcomputers.
- Regularly back up hard disks to microcomputer diskettes or tape.
- When erasing a hard disk, remember that the normal erase procedures of some operating systems leave the file on the disk (i.e., it may only remove the file from the directory). To prevent any possible recovery of sensitive files, use the disk-wiping functions provided by special utilities programs (e.g., Norton Utilities).

## 13.5 SYSTEM RECOVERY

### (a) INTRODUCTION

The preventive and detective controls provided by physical and logical security will, if properly applied, minimize the possibility of problems. However, problems—either accidental or deliberate—do occur. System recovery procedures are intended to promote an orderly and controlled return to normal operations after a problem.

Recovery controls address the availability concern, i.e., the need to ensure that the system can be restored after a failure or a disaster. They are necessary in order to address problems expected to be short-term in nature, as well as to address more catastrophic long-term events.

### (b) RECOVERY FROM OPERATIONAL FAILURES

Operational failures are those problems that occur during the performance of day-to-day processing. Examples include:

- The use of incorrect files
- The deletion of disk files
- The destruction of disk files
- Job processing failures
- Computer equipment failure

Overcoming problems of this nature requires an appropriate combination of backup and written recovery procedures.

*(i) Data File and Software Backup*

To protect against accidental or deliberate destruction (for example, by hackers), it is essential that copies of all data files and software libraries/directories be made regularly. How often is regular? This will vary from installation to installation. In determining an appropriate backup cycle, consider the following factors:

- How often the file, library, or directory is updated (for example, if system software libraries are rarely changed, it may be more appropriate to make backup copies only after a change has been made).
- How many transactions are processed each time the file is updated (this determines the amount of effort required to reprocess all transactions entered since the last backup).
- The amount of processing time available for backup.

In the past a backup cycle tended to be determined application by application. Today it is more usual to find organizations taking a weekly copy of all files and libraries and supplementing this with daily incremental backup. Incremental backup takes copies of only those files and libraries that have been updated during the day.

To assist in recovery from day-to-day operational failures, a backup copy of the data files and software should be kept on-site. A copy should also be sent off-site for use in the event of more catastrophic problems where all on-site material is either unavailable or destroyed. (This area is dealt with in Section 13.5(c).)

*(ii) Recovery Procedures*

In addition to the backup copies of the files and libraries, detailed written instructions are required for the operators to ensure that recovery can be efficiently and effectively achieved. These procedures, which usually form part of the computer operations manual, should address such matters as the following:

- Application failure recovery, procedures normally documented for each application and for each job step within the application—these describe how the operators can restore processing at an earlier point and reprocess transactions. In some cases this may not be possible, and direction should be provided on obtaining programming or technical support.

- The use of utilities to recover from backup copies—the involvement of operators in recovery varies from organization to organization. In some installations the operators copy the files and libraries to a predefined recovery area on disk, and it is a user or support group's responsibility to copy them from the recovery area to the production area. Other organizations will recover directly to the production areas.

- Obtaining vendor support for equipment failures or head crashes—all equipment failures should be documented together with details of the request for vendor assistance and the vendor's response.

## (c) DISASTER RECOVERY PLANS

Disaster recovery plans are intended to aid recovery from a more catastrophic event. They are not intended to deal with day-to-day operational failures. The term "disaster" is used in the broadest sense—it need not be an act of God. As previously noted, white-collar criminals can also arrange "disasters" to cover up their crimes.

*(i) Definition*

A disaster-recovery plan is a documented description of the action to be taken, the resources to be used, and the procedures to be followed before, during, and after the data processing capability is disrupted.

Given the reliance now being placed on computers in the business environment, many executives would probably find a lengthy loss of the computer center inconceivable. However, the same executive's organization has likely taken no action on developing a contingency plan. A survey done several years ago suggested that less than 50 percent of the *Fortune* 1,000 companies had disaster recovery plans and of those that did, only half were workable.

*(ii) Elements of Effective Disaster Recovery Plans*

Before a disaster occurs, be sure that off-site backup is capable of supporting recovery operations. Off-site backup copies of data files and software should be kept far enough from the principal site so that access to it will not be denied in the event of a disaster affecting the local geographic area. (The 1979 train derailment in Mississauga, Ontario, provides a good example. In this case the authorities closed access to a sizable city area for five days because of a dangerous chemical spill. Any organization whose data center and off-site storage were in that geographical area would have had difficulty invoking its recovery plan.)

In addition, keep off-site supplies of other materials required for processing. Examples include blank check forms, special invoice forms, forms for laser printers, operations documentation, and a copy of the recovery plan.

Perhaps the most important actions to be taken before a disaster occurs are the documentation of detailed recovery procedures and regular testing. Disaster recovery operations require that information be channeled to management in order to assist in decision making during the chaos of a disaster. If the reporting channels and decision points are not clearly identified in advance, inappropriate action may be taken.

Similarly, detailed procedures should be prepared for system recovery since operations staff may not perform standard procedures as expected when under the stress created by a disaster. Regular testing ensures that the plan is workable and helps to keep the plan up to date.

During the disaster the staff with recovery responsibility should follow documented procedures to:

- Notify all necessary parties that a problem has occurred.
- Assess the extent of the damage and the expected period of system outage for communication to the recovery team.
- Report to a predetermined emergency control center.

After the disaster recovery plan has been invoked, the recovery staff should follow the documented procedures for:

- Recovering the critical systems at the identified alternate processing location.
- Operating at the alternate site.
- Refurbishing or replacing the damaged site.
- Returning to normal operations once the damaged site has been refurbished.

It should be noted that only critical systems are normally recovered at the alternate processing site. These are the application systems that must be run to ensure continued business operations. If sufficient resources exist at the alternate site to run other systems, they should not be recovered until the critical systems are running.

A schematic of an approach to developing a disaster recovery plan that will address all of these elements is set out in Figure 13.3.

## (d) INSURANCE

For most businesses that rely heavily on computer processing, an effective disaster recovery plan is likely the only effective means of ensuring continued business survival following a major computer system disruption. However, it is possible to mitigate some of

**Figure 13.3** The Disaster Recovery Planning Process

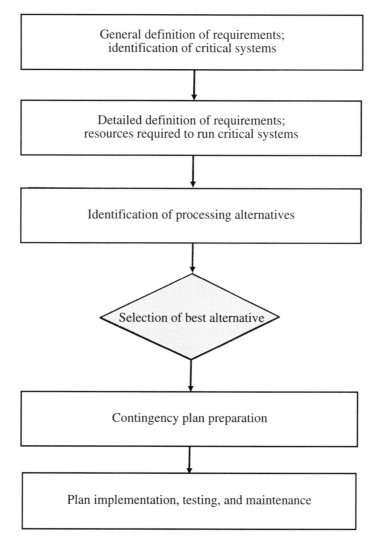

the financial loss through insurance coverage. Some examples of the types of insurance coverage available are set out below:

- *Data processing equipment coverage*—to assist in defraying the cost of replacing computer hardware and air conditioning equipment. Some policies also cover the cost of removing the debris from covered equipment.
- *Data, computer programs, and media coverage*—these policies cover only data and programs in computer format, not hard copy. Insurance can be taken out to cover the estimated potential loss if data and programs are destroyed.

- *Extra expense coverage*—this covers the extra expenses involved in continuing data processing operations if the equipment, air conditioning, or building housing the equipment is damaged.
- *Business interruption*—covers the business losses incurred following a disaster in the computer department, subject to limits on the amount to be paid per day, and a total amount payable.

### (e) SYSTEM RECOVERY FOR MICROCOMPUTERS

Equipment failure for microcomputers is generally not as great a concern as it is for larger systems. Normally another machine is available or can be obtained with relative ease. The biggest concern is the potential loss of data stored on hard disk or diskettes.

A regular policy of backing up hard disks is advisable. Norton Utilities and similar programs should also be considered, because under certain conditions they enable the recovery of files that have been accidentally erased.

## 13.6 SUMMARY

### (a) MANAGEMENT'S RESPONSIBILITY

Management is responsible for providing protection for the organization's assets, including protection against dishonest employees and outside criminal acts. The information asset, administered in most organizations by the information systems or computer department, is as vital and vulnerable as any other asset. While many organizations have invested heavily in developing computerized systems to support their business operations, they have not yet put the appropriate effort into establishing a security program to protect that investment. Computer security is often neglected because of the pressures to deal with day-to-day operating needs first; yet security can be fundamental to business survival.

The implementation of effective security can be achieved through the identification of the:

- Information in your organization that requires protection.
- Current level of protection provided for that information.
- Risks and exposures to which that information is currently vulnerable.

Using this approach, it is possible to achieve a level of security appropriate to the organization's requirements. This program should incorporate the development of policy, standards, guidelines, and procedures; the assignment of security responsibility; and the monitoring of progress.

### (b) POLICY, STANDARDS, GUIDELINES, AND PROCEDURES

It is generally unwise to assume that employees will act in a security-conscious manner if the organization's expectations have never been communicated to them. This can be achieved through the development and implementation of corporate policy statements on computer security. Emphasis should be placed on security and fraud awareness.

To be effective, the policies must be short and succinct. If they are too detailed and lengthy, it is unlikely that they will have the desired effect (especially with junior-level employees). Brevity is best achieved by cross-referencing more detailed standards rather than by attempting to include this material in the policy statement itself.

The policy, standards, guidelines, and procedures provide a framework for effective security in any organization.

## (c) THE SECURITY FUNCTION

Having recognized the importance of computer security to the organization, management must assign responsibility for this function. The person identified to take on the security function will usually be responsible for:

- Assisting in the development of policies, standards, guidelines, and procedures.
- Developing a formal security program to improve the level of security in accordance with management's expectations.
- Raising security and fraud awareness.
- Reporting on progress to senior management.
- Liaising with specialists in case of a crisis (e.g., police, forensic accountants, specialists in computer viruses, etc.).

Depending on the size of the organization, this may be a full-time or part-time responsibility. Even in the latter case, it will probably be a full-time job to set up the program.

## (d) POLICING

Once the security program is under way and the policy, standards, guidelines, and procedures are in place, it is necessary to ensure continuing compliance with expectations. This is a policing function.

Most organizations have an internal audit department that performs the policing function for controls that operate in other areas of the business. As such, internal audit may be ideal for testing compliance with corporate security expectations. Alternatively, external auditors or consultants can fill this role.

# CHAPTER 14

# Information Technology and the Law

In both Canada and the United States information technology law falls under several different jurisdictions. In both countries the federal government has exclusive constitutional jurisdiction in the area of patents and copyright. International, and interstate/interprovincial trade and commerce fall under federal jurisdiction as well. The federal governments have exercised their jurisdiction in the form of a variety of legislation, some of which is discussed below.

The provinces and states have jurisdiction in general civil matters, including commerce within their borders. In addition to commercial codes and statutes, there are consumer protection laws affecting the information technology field.

Information technology law falls into two principal areas: laws relating to the protection of intellectual property rights and laws relating to the purchase, sale, and use of information systems.

## 14.1 INTELLECTUAL PROPERTY LAW

Most of the special legislation in information technology deals with intellectual property. The reason for this has to do with the very essence of information technology—its ability to deal with information in purely electronic form. The laws that preceded the information technology explosion were developed at a time when most things of importance existed in a physical state.

For example, the original law of copyright stated that an author's thoughts had to be fixed in readable form before they could enjoy the law's protection. With modern technology, however, information can be created, stored, retrieved, and used without having to be fixed in a permanent medium. The concept that a completely intangible thing should be protected by the law has raised many knotty problems.

## 14.2 GENERAL BUSINESS LAW

The purchase, sale, and use of computer systems is much more familiar territory for the law. The common law of contract, sale of goods, and torts offers many effective tools for ensuring stable commerce. Consumer protection laws can readily be applied as well. From a purely business point of view, there are few very difficult problems raised by information technology.

## 14.3 PROTECTION OF INTELLECTUAL PROPERTY

The predominant feature that sets a computer apart from other mechanical devices is its programmability. A computer is at once omnipotent and impotent. Equipped with a stored program of instruction, the computer can do a vastly wide variety of tasks. Without a program of instruction, however, the computer is simply a rather inefficient room heater.

A computer program is the creation of the human mind, the child of many hours of arduous work. The resulting program has value purely as the practical expression of human intellectual effort. The computer hardware's value is a function of its physical ingredients and the manufacturing of the ingredients. In the physical sense, computer software has virtually no value whatsoever, except that it can command an inanimate object to follow the directions of a human mind.

### (a) GENERAL PRINCIPLES

In both Canada and the United States the federal government has jurisdiction over most intellectual property, including copyright, patents, and trademarks. Commercial interests lie behind all of the legislation in these areas. The main argument that businesses make is that their investment in developing new products should be protected. The physical products themselves can be protected against everyday theft; the ideas that led to the creation of those products are much more difficult to protect. The first ball-point pen took a long time to invent, but the design is very easy to copy. A novel may take years to write but can be reprinted very cheaply.

At the same time, free enterprise and competition must be encouraged. A patent—and, to a lesser extent, a copyright—creates a monopoly for the creator. Societies and economists generally view monopolies as bad but are willing to give a limited monopoly to enable the creator to reap rewards for the investment underlying the invention.

The common law offers some protection to intellectual property through the concept of trade secrets. A trade secret is a process, formula, or compilation of information that is known only to its owner and its owner's employees and gives its owner an advantage over competitors. An often cited example is the secret recipe for Coca-Cola.

Because trade secrets do not need to be expressed in tangible form, they may offer a wider scope of protection than copyright or patents. The essence of a trade secret is its confidentiality—once the secret has been released to outsiders, it ceases to enjoy trade secret protection. For that reason computer vendors may seek express acknowledgment of the confidential nature of their software before licensing it to users. They may also insist upon nondisclosure agreements before discussing the details of their computer systems with prospective purchasers or licensees.

Trade secret law is under the constitutional jurisdiction of the provinces and states. No Canadian province has enacted trade secrecy laws, but many American states have done so.

## (b) STATUTES

The main statutes dealing with protection of intellectual property are the Patent Act, the Copyright Act, and various Criminal Code provisions. In addition, the United States has a Semiconductor Chip Protection Act aimed at protecting its semiconductor industry from unfair foreign competition.

### (i) Patent Act

Patents are limited monopolies granted to inventors to allow them to exploit their creations. (The reason legislators created patents was to encourage inventiveness.) The patent applies to the idea underlying the invention, not just to the physical product itself. This is even more protection than copyright affords.

Patents are useful for protecting some parts of computer hardware but may not be available to protect software. Patent protection may, however, be available for computer programs when they form part of an overall industrial process. The applicability of patents to software is a changing area of law; particular problems in this area should be referred to a lawyer.

As a practical matter patents are expensive and take a long time to obtain. For this reason alone, most software creators turn to other methods to protect their creations.

### (ii) Copyright Act

Copyright is a statutory right that protects the expression of a creator's ideas. It gives a limited monopoly to the creator and allows the creator to restrain others from duplicating the protected work.

Copyright does not, however, protect the ideas themselves. A classic example of the difference is a cookbook. Mrs. Beeton's recipe for making rabbit pie may be protected by copyright, but the making of the rabbit pie itself certainly would not be. Moreover, anyone else would be free to come up with his or her own recipe for rabbit pie, and it would not be an infringement of Mrs. Beeton's copyright, even if the pie looked and tasted exactly the same as Mrs. Beeton's.

This limitation of copyright is what enables competitors to produce computers that are functionally identical to those made by major manufacturers such as Apple and IBM. The essential software embedded in read-only memory chips within the computer performs specific functions required by the computer. A competitor is free to figure out what those functions are and to write another program that produces the same result.

To establish limits on the scope of copyright, the legislatures and courts have established several requirements. Historically, one requirement was that the protected work be expressed in a tangible, readable form. This requirement related to the distinction between the idea itself and the expression of the idea—a useful distinction in traditional print technologies, but one that raised many problems in the computer area. A computer program in its machine form is hardly readable by a human; in fact, it need not be fixed in any tangible form at all to be useful to a computer.

Amendments to the Copyright Act of the United States in 1984, and more recently in 1988 and 1993 in Canada, have solved these problems. It is now clear that copyright extends to computer programs, whatever their medium or format.

Nevertheless, the degree of protection offered in Canada is different from that in the United States. In Canada copyright gives the creator the right to take court action to prevent unauthorized use, to recover infringing copies, and to claim compensation for any provable losses that the infringement caused. Remedies under the American legislation go beyond that, including statutory damages and attorney's fees and costs. The copyright acts of both countries also establish criminal offenses for infringement in certain circumstances.

Copyright comes into existence automatically upon creation. The author owns the copyright unless, under a contract of employment, the copyright is given to the employer. Although the basic rights come into existence on creation of the work, there are some formal requirements associated with some aspects of copyright enforcement. In order to take advantage of the protection of international copyright conventions, and in order to pursue other statutory remedies, the copyright owner must mark a work with a copyright symbol and a copyright notice.

In Canada, there is no formal requirement for registering a copyright. In the United States, works need not be registered, but registration affords additional statutory protection.

From a business perspective, copyright protection has the great advantage of simplicity and speed. There are few formal requirements, and protection is immediate. The disadvantage is that the copyright holder must take (and pay for) court action to enforce a copyright infringement. As a practical matter, this may often be more trouble than it's worth. A notable exception, however, lies with large corporate defendants. Successful action has been taken against large corporations that allowed their employees to engage in software piracy. In such cases the damages may be large enough to make a lawsuit worthwhile.

The costs and practical difficulties associated with copyright enforcement actions are mitigated to a degree by the availability of criminal sanctions for copyright infringement.

*(iii) Criminal Laws*

The copyright acts of both Canada and the United States establish criminal penalties for commercial infringement of copyright. The courts have made it clear that these criminal sanctions are available in cases of theft of computer software or data.

*(iv) Semiconductor Chip Protection Act*

The United States has a unique law designed to protect the semiconductor industry from unfair foreign competition. Semiconductor chips are very expensive to design but relatively easy to duplicate. Chips are made using a process involving a drawing of the circuit, which is photographed and used to guide sophisticated machinery in producing individual chips. Copyright protection is available for the drawing itself but not for objects made from the drawing. The reasoning is similar to that used in the rabbit pie example given earlier.

The Semiconductor Chip Protection Act protects semiconductor chip masks and the chips made from them. It does not, however, prevent reverse engineering (i.e., taking apart a chip for study to determine how to make a similar or better one). Remedies under the act include injunctions, damages for actual monetary losses (including any profits earned by the infringer), impoundment of infringing goods, and exclusion of infringing products from importation into the United States.

## 14.4 BUSINESS LAW ASPECTS OF IT

Computers are economic goods and are therefore subject to commercial dealings. We therefore look to the normal laws of commerce for solutions to many of the problems that arise from the sale and use of computers.

### (a) CONTRACT LAW

At the center of commercial law is the law of contract. Before examining the terms commonly found in computer contracts, it is important to consider the concept of a contract of adhesion. This term refers to contracts whose terms are dictated by one party to the transaction and that must be accepted, without negotiation or modification, by the other party. Examples include contracts for air travel, credit cards, and banking arrangements.

An adhesion contract contains standard terms offered by the vendor that are not open to negotiation. In fact, most contracts of this type contain a specific provision excluding any possibility of modifying any of the terms. Such contracts are usually found in cases when the bargaining power of one party to the transaction is very much greater than that of the other. If you want to fly on that airline, you must agree to its standard terms. It's a take-it-or-leave-it proposition.

In common law jurisdictions, the courts have long recognized the principle of freedom of contract. The principle is that parties to an agreement are free to make whatever bargain they wish. The court's role is first to determine whether a contract exists; second, to determine what the terms of the contract are; and third, to enforce those terms. The courts have taken the view that it is not up to them to decide what the parties should have agreed to. They are only to decide what they in fact have agreed to, good or bad.

The principle of freedom of contract works very well in many circumstances. It works rather poorly in others. When a dispute arises out of a transaction covered by a contract of adhesion, the courts recognize the fact that one of the parties had no opportunity to negotiate favorable terms. In particular, the courts are aware that the party dictating the terms often attempts to exclude its liability for any and all imaginable shortcomings and deficiencies.

The courts will, if at all possible, give a very restricted interpretation to exclusion clauses in a contract of adhesion. If the court can find a way to declare the exclusion clause to be ambiguous or too far-reaching, then the clause will be struck out. This is particularly likely if the effect of the exclusions would be to completely remove all obligations from one party. The courts rather sensibly conclude that the parties could not have intended to make a deal in which one party had to pay money and the other had to do absolutely nothing.

Contracts of adhesion occur frequently in information technology. Major vendors, for example, all have standard form agreements covering hardware purchase terms, software licenses, and maintenance. They usually take the position with a customer that these terms are nonnegotiable.

It should be noted, however, that if a transaction is large and/or if the customer is an established business, then it is less likely that the courts will treat a contract as one of adhesion. Businesses are presumed to be aware of the terms of the contracts they sign, and in fact computer vendors often are willing to negotiate the terms of their contracts. If an acquisition involves a substantial commitment, the purchaser should therefore obtain independent legal advice before signing even a standard contract.

### (i)  Hardware Purchase Contracts

A purchase contract is created whenever anyone buys anything. In very simple transactions the contract may be purely oral. In other cases the contract may be in writing.

There is no formal requirement that a computer transaction be in writing; an oral contract is equally binding on the parties. The main difficulty with an oral contract, of course, is that of establishing just what was agreed to. This is especially difficult given the fact that the need to do so almost always arises in conjunction with some disagreement between the contracting parties.

Hardware purchase contracts vary in formality and complexity. At the low end the contract may simply consist of standard terms on a vendor's order form. Alternatively, the contract terms may be found in a vendor's written quotation that has been accepted by the purchaser. Purchase contracts for more costly computer systems may involve elaborate contracts that are many pages in length.

Typical terms in a hardware purchase contract include:

- Systems specifications (including performance standards)
- Cost and timing of payment
- Target delivery dates
- User training
- Maintenance
- Remedies

The systems specifications are often set out in the purchaser's formal request for proposal (RFP), which may be included in the final contract. Purchasers should strive to include the vendor's presale representations found in the RFP and their reply to it, even if the vendor resists. It may help if the purchaser warns the vendor in advance that the RFP and the reply will be included verbatim in the contract. This might at least alert the vendor's sales staff that their legal department should be involved at an early stage.

Delivery is often a difficult area. Some of the equipment may still be under development at the time of purchase, and the vendor's promised delivery dates may prove impossible to meet. The purchaser must ensure that delivery dates are specific and that there is a plan for dealing with delays should they occur. One alternative is for the vendor to make alternate compatible equipment available to the customer. Another is to provide for a monetary penalty for late delivery. There should also be a provision for cancellation of the entire contract if all of the equipment has not been delivered by a final deadline date.

Maintenance contracts usually refer to a maximum time for responding to service calls. This may be four hours, same day, or within twenty-four hours. Unfortunately, most contracts do not say what will happen should the vendor fail to meet promised response times. Without a specific remedy in the contract, the purchaser is forced to either accept the deficient service or litigate.

Acquisition of small systems often does not involve a formal hardware purchase agreement. The purchaser simply pays cash and accepts immediate delivery. Microcomputers are being sold as a commodity, like other consumer goods. The sale terms may be found on the reverse of an order form, in the case of a purchase from a computer dealer, or be absent entirely. In the latter case the purchase would be governed by the normal laws of sale of goods applicable in the jurisdiction.

### (ii)  Major Software License Agreements

A computer cannot operate without software. Software never wears out (although it may grow obsolete), and in some ways is more akin to a service than a consumable product. In large systems, software requires continuous maintenance. The need for ongoing software modifications arises from the need to correct programming errors, enhance performance, and adapt the software to changes in the hardware configuration. A major piece of software becomes less and less useful unless it is maintained.

Major systems software is usually supplied by the hardware manufacturer, who has an interest in maintaining control over it. For these and other reasons, vendors usually do not sell software outright; instead, the vendor and customer enter into a licensing agreement under which the customer has the right to use the software for a specified period subject to certain conditions. Ownership of the software remains with the vendor.

Major system software licensing agreements offer significant protection to the vendor, who is usually able to dictate the terms of the software license and create just about any rights it wishes. Under the principle of freedom of contract, courts generally respect the right of the parties to make any bargain they desire. An effective software license therefore means that the vendor need not rely on statutory or common law for protection of its intellectual property rights.

A major expenditure for a computer system generally calls for careful thought and planning on the part of the purchaser. For example, a purchaser can be expected to seek legal advice before concluding purchase and licensing agreements. In most cases the final contracts are signed following deliberate thought and consideration of their terms.

### (iii)  Minor Software License Agreements

Smaller purchases are typically made without a great deal of consideration and negotiation. Personal computer software is often purchased from a retail outlet or department store or even by mail order. There is almost certainly no negotiation of purchase or licensing terms. The transaction is much more akin to an outright purchase of a good than it is to a contract for services or a license to use.

Imagine, then, how surprised most retail purchasers would be if they were told that after paying $195 to the clerk and walking out with their software in a bag, they did not in fact own the software at all, that the software was still the exclusive property of the manufacturer, and that they had somehow entered into an agreement giving them only limited rights. Imagine your surprise if, after buying a book in a bookstore, you learned that you didn't own it—that all you had was the right to read it, and that, moreover, after reading it you were prohibited from letting anyone else read it. To be sure, you would not be permitted to photocopy the book and give copies away to your friends or to extract portions of the book and sell them as if they were your own creations. But those restrictions arise out of the law of copyright and have nothing to do with the direct purchase transaction.

This, however, is precisely what the software manufacturers strive to achieve. Microcomputer software is almost invariably sold with what appears to be a licensing agreement attached to it. If you read the agreement, it declares that the relationship between the customer and the manufacturer is to be governed by the terms of the agreement, which, of course, restricts the rights of the customer.

The difficulty with the manufacturer's approach is that there has in fact been no opportunity for the customer to consider the terms of the purported agreement before paying for the software. The seller already has the money, and although it may be possible for the customer to bring the software back to the store, it is certainly impossible for the customer to negotiate the terms of the license. The traditional legal analysis of this sort of dealing is that a buyer is not bound by contractual terms that were not brought to the buyer's attention before the transaction was completed. Once a purchase has been made, it is too late for one party to impose new terms. If this analysis is correct, then the transaction is not a license arrangement at all; it is an outright purchase governed by the law of sale of goods.

To overcome this rather serious difficulty, the software manufacturers have tried to devise ways to induce the customer explicitly to agree to a licensing agreement after the software has been purchased. The most common approach is known as the "shrink wrap" license agreement. When the customer opens the box, he or she discovers that the diskette containing the software is enclosed in plastic shrink wrapping. Plainly visible through the shrink wrap is a notice that says something like the following:

IMPORTANT—READ CAREFULLY BEFORE OPENING

SOFTWARE LICENSE

*By opening this package, you are agreeing to the terms of this license agreement. If you do not agree to these terms, then you may return the software for a full refund.*

The idea here is to establish some conscious act of acceptance of the license agreement. There is still, however, a major legal difficulty: if the purchaser has already purchased the right to open the package, then how can he or she be called upon to give up more concessions before exercising that right?

Despite the rather questionable enforceability of shrink wrap licenses, they remain in wide use. It may be that improved statutory copyright protection will make it unnecessary for a vendor to try to enforce a shrink wrap license.

### (b) THIRD-PARTY LIABILITY

When a purchaser has difficulties with a computer system, the most direct target for redress is the vendor. The contract between the customer and the vendor determines the relationship between them. The contract may be formal or informal, but it always exists. Unfortunately for the purchaser, the terms of the purchase or license agreement may not be very favorable. It will typically limit the vendor's liability for damages, especially damages related to the consequences of using the computer.

Consequential losses arise when the computer's deficiencies affect the company's business affairs in ways that go beyond the direct use of the computer. For example, a computer that constantly breaks down may cause a company to lose customers who are dissatisfied with poor service. A disruption in cash flow caused by the computer may lead to cancellation of credit lines as well as other losses. Most computer contracts exclude liability for consequential losses such as these. An aggrieved company may therefore seek other defendants against whom to make a claim.

Some possible candidates include the computer hardware manufacturer, the software designers, consultants, or others. The laws governing the liability of third parties are complex and call for specific legal advice.

## 14.5  COMMON QUESTIONS

### (a) CAN I COPY SOFTWARE?

In the United States, the Copyright Act specifically protects computer software. The act prohibits the owner from copying the software, just as it prohibits audiophiles from making and distributing taped copies of compact disc recordings. In the case of computer software, however, there is an important exception: the act allows the owner to make a copy of the software for archival purposes. Accordingly, in the United States, you have a statutory right to make a backup copy of the software. However, you may not use the copy for any other purpose. You're not permitted to sell, give, or lend it to anyone else, nor can you use the copy within your own organization for day-to-day use.

The more recently revised (1993) Copyright Act in Canada also covers computer software. Even prior to the statute revisions, court decisions in Canada had made it clear that computer software is a literary work that is protected in the same way as books. However, under the law of copyright, there is a principle known as fair use. The principle permits a student, for example, to make a photocopy of portions of library books for personal study. The student may not sell the copies, however, nor copy the entire book for a personal library. Similarly, a business may not make photocopies of a commercial newsletter and distribute the copies to members of its staff. These examples go beyond what is considered to be fair use.

The fair use principle permits a software purchaser to make an archival backup copy of the software. The copy would have to be purely for archival purposes, however; its use would not be permitted unless the original were damaged.

### (b) ARE COMPUTER CLONES LEGAL?

Unless a mechanical or electronic device is patented, it is perfectly legal for another manufacturer to produce a machine that performs exactly the same functions. Copyright law does not cover machinery, but it does cover a key portion of a computer, as described below.

Software is stored on magnetic disks, but the computer cannot load programs from the disk unless it knows how to operate the disk drives. It gets this knowledge from a small program called a bootstrap loader. The bootstrap loader is contained in an area of permanent memory called ROM. Copyright protection extends to the bootstrap loader program (and any other program segments contained in ROM). You cannot legally copy it and include it in a clone computer.

For example, the original IBM Personal Computer had major portions of its operating system program in ROM. The basic input/output system (BIOS) routines were embedded in ROM. For a clone to be fully compatible with the IBM PC, it had to contain a BIOS in ROM that behaved exactly like the IBM BIOS. Some early clone manufacturers fell to the temptation and simply duplicated the IBM BIOS exactly. That was illegal, and IBM took prompt action to protect its intellectual property rights.

To overcome the problem the clone makers had to design their own bootstrap and BIOS ROMs. They did so by reverse engineering. In most circumstances it is perfectly legal to examine a copyrighted program, analyze it to figure out how it does what it does, and then write a program that carries out the same functions. Independent companies did this successfully with the IBM BIOS and mass-produced their own ROMs for use in clone computers. Clones that used these legitimate BIOS ROMs were, and continue to be, perfectly legal.

### (c) CAN I GET MY MONEY BACK AFTER PURCHASE?

The purchase of a computer product is governed by the general law of sale of goods. If there is a specific purchase contract binding on both parties, then that contract will determine your rights to return the goods. If there is no specific purchase contract, the purchase terms will be determined by statute and common law.

In most jurisdictions consumers have the right to return goods if they are defective or not fit for the purpose for which they were sold. However, consumers have no legal right to a refund if they simply change their mind about the purchase.

A liberal return policy is one reason for purchasing computer products from a reputable dealer. As a simple matter of good business, many dealers will accept goods for return within a reasonable period, possibly with a restocking fee. Check this out with the dealer before you buy, and make sure that your return privileges are recorded in writing.

### (d)  CAN I SUE MANUFACTURERS, VENDORS, AND CONSULTANTS?

You can sue whomever you wish. The outcome of the lawsuit, however, will depend on the legal rights and relationships between you and the defendant. Some of those rights are described above, but there are many others. If your real losses are substantial enough to lead you to consider litigation, you should get professional legal advice.

Manufacturers have a duty to those who ultimately use their products to exercise reasonable care in the design and manufacture of their goods. The fact that a product has a defect, however, does not necessarily mean that the manufacturer will be liable. Much depends on the nature of the defect and the severity of the losses that might result from a defect.

Your rights against the vendor are governed by various consumer protection statutes and by the general law of sale of goods described earlier. You may also be able to claim negligence against a vendor, although this is usually more difficult to establish.

Consultants give advice, and they owe a duty to their clients to give reasonably competent advice. They are in the same position as lawyers, accountants, and other professional givers of advice. Professional negligence claims arise when the professional fails to exercise the degree of skill and care that a reasonably competent professional would exercise in the circumstances. The duty of care extends not only to the immediate client but also potentially to anyone whom the adviser should reasonably expect to be affected by the advice given. This is a complex and difficult area that clearly calls for specific legal advice.

## 14.6  THE EFFECT OF IT ON THE LEGAL PROFESSION

Information technology has two main effects on the legal profession: its effect on the practice of law, and its effect on the law itself. Each of these issues is dealt with in the following sections.

### (a)  EFFECT ON THE PRACTICE OF LAW

*(i)  Practice Management*

Running a law practice raises many issues in common with other businesses. Although other factors must be considered as well, lawyers usually base their fees on the amount of time spent on the case. Keeping track of that time and assigning it to specific client files is a significant clerical chore. Also, disbursements must be allocated and recovered.

Computers are well suited to tasks such as these and have become widely used in the legal profession. As a byproduct of their bookkeeping functions, computers can also analyze lawyers' activities. Typical examples are reports of unbilled time by lawyer and by client, unbilled disbursements, and total billings by type of legal work.

Some aspects of legal practice raise unique accounting and information systems problems. Perhaps the most important is the problem of accounting for client trust (escrow) funds. The rules of professional conduct in most jurisdictions call for strict control over trust accounting. The easiest and most common way to be disbarred is to misappropriate client trust funds. Law firms are therefore particularly sensitive to the need for adequate controls in this area. Law office management software must embody these controls.

Generic financial management tools, such as electronic spreadsheets and financial graphics software, are also useful aids to law practice management. Other useful tools include databases of client names, addresses, and other data, mailing list systems, diary systems, and electronic mail.

### (ii)  Writing

Most of what lawyers produce eventually finds its way onto paper. Law firms might be viewed as document factories, and it should therefore be no surprise that they have been major consumers of word processing technology for years. Word processing systems offer significant economies, especially for large documents that are assembled from pre-existing text libraries and modified to suit particular transactions.

Document-outlining software is also a superb tool for organizing a complex agreement, brief, or appeal factum. Writing style analyzers point out legal jargon, ambiguous language, and complex sentence structures. Other writing aids include on-line thesauruses, document comparison programs to highlight revisions, and systems for managing projects involving multiple authors and editors.

### (iii)  Case Law and Other Research

Lawyers often need to research points of law that arise in a case. The traditional tools of legal research are the published volumes of law reports and statutes. Other printed material includes journals, digests, and textbooks. The lawyer's role is first to analyze the matter at hand in order to identify the relevant legal issues, and second to find out what the current law is with respect to those issues. The first part of this task is something for which present technology offers little help. Legal analysis is still a very human skill, poorly imitated by computers (although some progress is being made). The second part of the task, however, is one that computers can help with a great deal.

There is an immense and rapidly growing body of statutory and case law, and much of it is already available on computer systems that can be searched from anywhere in the country (assuming you have a computer, modem, and communications package). The most popular systems in Canada have included QuicLaw from QL Systems and Can/Law from Canada Law Book. American systems have included WestLaw from West Publishing Company and Lexis from Mead Data.

Lawyers also use general business and technical databases such as Dow-Jones News Retrieval. These databases are rich sources of information and are very useful for product liability cases, environmental disputes, mass tort litigation, and many other types of cases. Unfortunately, the tools are not used as often as one might expect, except in large firms, because lawyers do not have the time to learn the intricacies of a variety of databases for what they perceive to be a "one-of" problem. The information industry needs to do a better job of providing intelligent front ends for these databases so that they are more accessible to the infrequent user.

### (iv)  Litigation Support

Complex litigation involves vast amounts of evidence in two main forms—oral and documentary. Oral evidence is given during the discovery process before trial and during the trial itself. Documentary evidence takes many forms, and in this age of the photocopier and facsimile machine, it is available in great abundance. Some lawsuits involve hundreds of thousands of documents. While such monster cases are rare, cases with several thousand documents are not at all uncommon.

The lawyer's task is to analyze the mass of evidence—both oral and documentary—and to organize it according to the issues in the case. The computer can help a great deal.

To help analyze oral evidence, the computer must first have it in machine-readable form. The court reporter uses word processing or specialized court reporting computer systems to produce a transcript of the oral evidence on diskette. The diskette can then be processed by any number of retrieval systems. These typically permit key-word searching using methods similar to those used in large research databases. The lawyer uses the system to locate pertinent portions of testimony quickly.

Document retrieval systems serve a similar purpose but are rather more complex. Oral evidence is created during the course of the lawsuit, and lawyers can control the processes used to collect it. Documentary evidence, on the other hand, is created before the lawsuit begins. Lawyers cannot control its format, and much of it has historically been difficult to convert to machine-readable form. The situation is changing, however, with the advent of more powerful hardware and document storage software that incorporates optical character recognition capabilities. Document storage and retrieval software also accepts document summaries or abstracts. A team of trained coders reads each document and produces a summary of it for input into the computer document retrieval system. From there it is extracted and analyzed using ordinary retrieval techniques.

The advent of powerful, inexpensive microcomputers has meant that most law firms can now afford to use litigation support systems even for cases of modest size. The main obstacle to wider use of these and other computer applications is simply that many lawyers remain unfamiliar with the tools. The situation is, however, improving rapidly. On the one hand new law school graduates, familiar with computer methods, are entering the established firms. On the other hand, corporate clients expect their lawyers to use the most modern and cost-effective tools available. Simple competition may ultimately be what stimulates the legal profession to make better use of information technology.

## (b)  EFFECT ON LAW ITSELF

*(i)  New Laws*

Information technology has advanced much more rapidly than the law's ability to react. In general, laws arise retrospectively, not prospectively. Civil cases, for example, can only come forward when something has already gone wrong. Before a legal issue arising from a new area of technology can be established, one or more cases must proceed through the litigation process. This may involve various levels of appeal over several years. In the meantime, computer technology advances relentlessly.

Legislation often lags far behind technology as well. Legislators are not particularly well known for anticipating problems and taking steps to create new laws to deal with them. This is especially troubling in the area of information technology, where changes occur very rapidly. An additional complication is that information technology is itself a new field. The lawmakers often have a weak understanding of the technological issues and therefore find it especially difficult to deal with them.

There has been some progress, however. In the United States the Semiconductor Chip Protection Act marked an important legislative response to a unique problem in the semiconductor industry. Copyright Act amendments have been or soon will be passed in many western countries. New laws are being considered in the area of international data flow, where information as a valuable resource has been crossing borders with little or no effective regulation. Electronic fund-transfer systems, including automated teller machines, have raised new legal problems. Legislation in these and other areas is under consideration in Canada and the United States.

### (ii) New Branches of Law Practice

Any area of human endeavor that operates in an environment where the rules are unclear is fertile territory for lawyers. It is not the lawyers who are to blame; the actors in the technology arena do not know the rules because the rules remain unclear. They therefore get into arguments over them.

As more disputes arise over information technology, lawyers unavoidably get more legal work in that field. This has led to the creation of whole new areas of practice, including computer contracting, software distribution, computer crime, computer contract litigation, computer software copyright, and trade secret protection. Most large law firms have computer law departments. Computer law specialty firms are also beginning to appear.

### (iii) Information Technology in the Courtroom

In cases tried by a judge alone, the judge faces the same problems as the lawyers presenting the case. If the case involves many documents, the judge must be able to locate key passages from thousands of pages of material. If the case involves many weeks of testimony, the judge must review it all before making a final assessment on difficult factual issues. If the case involves an unusual legal point, then the judge must be able to review the relevant legal authorities. When a trial decision goes to appeal, whether from a judge alone or from a judge and jury, the appeal court must review the evidence of the case, including the transcript of oral testimony and the documentary evidence presented during the trial. Computer systems are available to assist in each of these areas. They are the same tools that lawyers use.

Trial and appellate judges also must draft often lengthy decisions explaining the facts as they find them, the law as it applies to those facts, and the outcome. Word processing programs, writing style analyzers, outlining programs, and other software tools are therefore beginning to be used by judges as well.

### (iv) A Final Thought

The information technology explosion touches nearly all aspects of life in the modern world. The changes it brings will inescapably lead to friction between groups with opposing interests. Law, as the primary means of resolving disputes, will have to adapt to these continuing changes with new laws and new ways of applying old laws. Its main challenge will be to keep up.

# CHAPTER 15

# Artificial Intelligence and Expert Systems

The terms "artificial intelligence" and "expert systems" have been frequently used—indeed overused—in the literature in recent years. Throughout most of the 1980s and even into the 1990s, both have had relatively limited practical application compared with other areas of information technology, and neither is very well understood. Yet they remain hot topics, possibly because they carry a vaguely futuristic connotation that many find appealing.

    A very detailed or technical treatment of artificial intelligence and expert systems is beyond the scope of this handbook. The following material is designed to provide an overview and general understanding of the concepts involved.

Artificial intelligence (AI) is a scientific discipline concerned with developing computer systems that can perform functions normally requiring human intelligence. As with expert systems—which are in fact the pragmatist's subset of artificial intelligence—the term has been used liberally, and its meaning has therefore become somewhat imprecise.

Whereas typical computer systems are designed for intensive numeric calculation, AI is concerned more with nonnumeric symbols and language and with processes akin to human reasoning and problem solving.

An expert system is a computer system designed to act as a substitute for a human expert.

The problem with the above and any other definition of an expert system is that the term has been used so liberally—as has artificial intelligence—that the concept itself has become muddled. For example, to the degree that an architect is an expert at drawing up blueprints, some might try to argue that a simple graphics package is an expert system. But it isn't. The important distinction is that the graphics package by itself would not enable a nonarchitect to draw up a meaningful set of blueprints. It does not capture the expertise of the architect; it is only a tool that enhances the productivity of a human expert.

Another term, "knowledge-based system" or simply "knowledge system," is often used interchangeably with the term "expert system."

## 15.1 A BRIEF HISTORY

Artificial intelligence derives from the studies of logic and cognitive psychology, both of which predate the computer. In fact, the first computer, developed by the University of Pennsylvania in the mid-1940s and called ENIAC, was essentially a calculator that used switching circuits to apply the rules of logic to mathematical problems.

AI began to emerge as a separate discipline in the late 1950s, and intensive research and development continued throughout the 1960s. However, this research tended to focus on general problem-solving rather than on practical applications. Actual results were restricted to such things as chess-playing computer programs, which had little significance outside the academic (or chess!) community.

Beginning in the 1970s, there was a shift in focus to specialized applications that later evolved into a subdiscipline of AI called expert systems. However, the advances still tended to be restricted to academia, especially the large U.S. institutions such as MIT, Carnegie-Mellon, and Stanford.

The 1980s saw for the first time the emergence of practical expert systems for business, both the commercially available variety (including expert system "shells," described later in this chapter) and those custom-designed by larger business organizations. In addition, a large number of corporations and entrepreneurs have entered the field in anticipation of greater commercial acceptance of AI and expert systems.

## 15.2 ARTIFICIAL INTELLIGENCE

### (a) OBJECTIVES OF ARTIFICIAL INTELLIGENCE

The objectives of artificial intelligence (AI) are analogous to but somewhat broader than the objectives of expert systems. Specifically, AI seeks to:

- Better understand the rules of logic and cognitive psychology that are the basis of the processes of human reasoning and problem solving.
- Utilize this better understanding to identify opportunities where computer technology can be used to simulate or substitute for human intelligence.
- Develop systems that perform at a level normally associated with human intelligence.

## (b) MAJOR ARTIFICIAL INTELLIGENCE APPLICATIONS

Some of the major areas of research in the area of artificial intelligence are set out in the following sections.

### (i) Natural Language Systems

This branch of AI involves the development of computers that can read and/or speak in ordinary, everyday language. It is the most difficult area of AI and the furthest from achieving meaningful results.

Voice recognition and speech synthesis programs do exist, but these do not represent true natural language systems. To meet this definition the system must actually have an understanding—or at least be able to emulate human understanding—of the language.

### (ii) Robotics

Robotics is the branch of AI concerned with the development of computers that have the sensory capability (primarily visual) to interact with the surrounding environment. These sensory capabilities are much better understood and are therefore easier to simulate than language skills.

Robotics has many applications, from manufacturing (e.g., auto assembly) to environmental safety (e.g., handling of hazardous waste or operating in hazardous areas) to space exploration (e.g., the Viking mission to Mars).

### (iii) Expert Systems

Expert systems are a special branch of AI concerned with the development of limited-application computer programs that can substitute for a human expert. They are dealt with later in this chapter.

## (c) TOOLS, CONCEPTS, AND ISSUES IN AI

Some of the major tools, concepts, and issues in the area of artificial intelligence are set out below.

### (i) LISP and PROLOG Languages

Conventional computer languages such as COBOL and FORTRAN can be used to create simple artificial intelligence programs. However, they are not the preferred languages because they tend to be numeric rather than text-oriented.

LISP (an acronym derived from LISt Processor), a programming language developed at MIT in the 1950s, has been the preferred AI tool because it is designed to handle strings of words and execute program instructions based on the content of those strings.

PROLOG (an acronym based on PROgramming language for LOGic) is a special programming language designed to help build expert systems. It was initially developed in the early 1970s at the University of Marseilles, and has been selected by Japan for its fifth-generation computer project.

Although PROLOG is less complex than many conventional programming languages, its first appearance represented a major leap forward in the way computer programming was looked at. Unlike other languages, PROLOG does not require the programmer to specify the precise sequence of tasks that the computer must carry out. It is only necessary to define the task itself. When called upon by a user, PROLOG automatically searches for and carries out the necessary steps to perform that task. This is a rather inefficient way of using computer power, but even so, the rapid growth in the availability of such power has made PROLOG-type languages the way of the future.

### (ii) Fifth-Generation Computers

Current computer technology, especially software technology, is inadequate for many artificial intelligence and expert system applications. Such applications typically require an enormous amount of nonnumeric processing for which existing machines and languages were simply not designed.

The next generation of computers, the fifth generation, is expected to better address this problem by making possible the:

- Processing of huge amounts of knowledge, not just numbers.
- Parallel processing of several programs simultaneously.
- Modification of a program's knowledge base by the program itself, thus allowing the system to "learn."

The most famous effort in the area of fifth-generation computers is the one announced by Japan in 1981. Over $500 million is to be spent on the project, with the goal of implementing commercial applications by the end of the 1990s.

Other efforts similar to Japan's are being undertaken by IBM, MCC (Microelectronics Computer Technology Corporation, a joint venture of IBM's major competitors), ESPRIT (European Strategic Program for Research and Development in Information Technology, a European Economic Community initiative), and a number of agencies of the U.S. government, including the Department of Defense.

### (iii) Is AI Relevant to Business?

The answer is yes, but in most cases it only has long-term relevance. There are tools on the market now—specifically, expert systems and expert system-building tools for large computer systems (and, to an increasing extent, for microcomputers as well). But for the most part these are rather simple systems that cannot fundamentally change the way business operates. The cost of very sophisticated applications remains prohibitive for the vast majority of businesses.

The one clear exception to the above is the information technology industry itself, where AI most certainly does have relevance. In fact, it is expected to be one of the major growth areas for the remainder of the century.

*(iv)  Current and Future Research*

The most relevant work currently being done is on the expert systems subbranch of AI, as described in the next section. However, even in this area the major advances will likely have to wait for the advent of fifth-generation computers. Some advances have been made in the area of robotics, and in fact many practical applications already exist in this area. Natural language systems are probably the furthest from yielding results.

In the long term the challenge is to build systems that combine natural language capability and huge knowledge bases with the ability and flexibility to learn. This objective probably will not be achieved until well into the next century.

## 15.3  EXPERT SYSTEMS

### (a)  OBJECTIVES OF EXPERT SYSTEMS

As previously noted, the objective of an expert system is essentially to act as a substitute for a human expert. It follows that the ideal expert system, like a human expert, should be able to:

- Identify the problem, when necessary interacting with the people affected.
- Analyze the problem, getting help from other sources if needed.
- Solve the problem.
- Explain how it derived the solution.
- Help implement the solution.
- Learn from the experience.

Clearly, no expert system can meet all of the above objectives, and therefore, the ideal system does not yet exist. However, the technology is moving in that direction, and even today, these systems can be helpful for certain types of applications.

### (b)  ELEMENTS OF AN EXPERT SYSTEM

As depicted in Figure 15.1, expert systems can be divided into four main elements: the user, the user interface, the knowledge base, and the processing system. How well these four elements interact determines how effective the system is in achieving its objectives.

*(i)  The User*

Expert systems don't have problems—people do. Many expert systems, indeed many computer systems generally, fail because they don't pay enough attention to the fact that the user is an integral part of the system. The user's needs must be paramount. Typically these needs are straightforward:

**Figure 15.1**    Elements of an Expert System

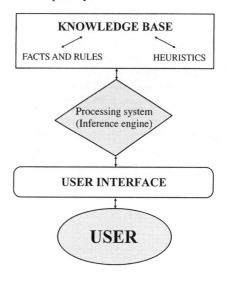

- To be able to understand how to use the system.
- To have the system solve their problem or assist them in solving it.

It may also be necessary to understand how the problem was solved—that is, to learn from the system—and to be able to influence or "teach" the system. The basic user needs are reasonably well met by many expert systems; these secondary needs are sometimes overlooked.

*(ii)  The User Interface*

The user interface is the portion of the expert system responsible for interacting with the user. The most common hardware for this is a keyboard and display screen, or a mouse and display screen in the case of graphical user interfaces.

The software driving the interface is the most important consideration because it determines the way in which questions or prompts are put to the user. There is no substitute for well-designed, menu-driven input screens and logical question-answer sequences.

The ultimate user interface would be one based on a combination of normal speech, pointing devices, and keyboard entry, permitting flexible and natural use of expert systems in everyday tasks. Although voice recognition and speech synthesis do exist and are a continuing subject of research, in practice they are not often used in expert systems.

*(iii)  The Knowledge Base*

The knowledge base is the centerpiece element of an expert system, and essentially consists of two parts:

- *Facts*—these are basic, generally-agreed-upon information or problem-solving rules relating to the field of expertise.

- *Heuristics*—these are rules of thumb designed to embody the judgment of an expert in the field.

Facts and problem-solving rules can generally be gathered and built into an expert system without actually having to consult an expert, although it is preferable to do so. Heuristics, however, can only be developed in consultation with an expert in the field.

### (iv)  The Processing System

At its core an expert system is a computer program. The user interface and the knowledge base are the parts of the program the user sees (or at least their existence is evident). The processing system is the black box part of the program that the user does not see—the part that drives the program through information gathering, analysis, and solution.

The processing system is also referred to as the inference engine: "engine" because it drives the program and "inference" because its purpose is to analyze the user's inputs and the knowledge base and then draw relevant conclusions or inferences about how to proceed. Specifically, the inference engine determines whether the expert system:

- Asks for additional information from the user.

- Makes assumptions concerning information.

- Works with the facts, rules, and heuristics in its knowledge base.

- Draws conclusions and makes recommendations.

The processing system may also determine the degree to which a recommendation is qualified or, in the case of multiple solutions, the ranking of those solutions.

More sophisticated processing systems also have the ability to adjust their own knowledge base, to learn from the results of earlier analysis. Such systems are in fact entering the realm of more generalized artificial intelligence applications.

There is no general-purpose processing system that represents a standard for all expert systems. However, this is a subject of continuing research, and there are a number of expert system shells available, as noted below.

## (c)  KNOWLEDGE ENGINEERING AND ENGINEERS

Creating an expert system is a task that in itself requires an expert, sometimes referred to as a knowledge engineer. The knowledge engineer works with the human expert in the field, and with computer scientists, to define the task and see it through. Knowledge engineering involves:

- Defining the knowledge base

- Developing the processing system or inference engine

- Implementing the expert system

These tasks are highly specialized, and the skills of knowledge engineers are therefore very much in demand.

## (d) EXPERT SYSTEM SHELLS

In the context of expert systems, a shell refers to the building tools used by a knowledge engineer to design expert systems. A shell provides:

- Much of the basic computer code that would otherwise have to be created
- The methodology for developing the processing system and knowledge base of the specialized expert system application

The first shells for the IBM PC appeared on the market in the mid-1980s (e.g., ES/P Advisor, INSIGHT Knowledge System). Shells have been evolving rapidly through the mid-1990s, and will to a large extent determine the course of expert system development into the next century.

## (e) MAJOR TYPES OF EXPERT SYSTEMS

The emergence of expert systems that have practical application is a relatively new development, and specific packages are not discussed in detail here. However, there are certain fields that more easily lend themselves to the development of expert systems. Some of the most effective expert systems can be expected to emerge from these areas, as discussed below.

### (i) Medical Diagnostic Systems

Medical diagnostic systems are among the most common forms of expert systems. In fact MYCIN, a system developed at Stanford in the mid-1970s to diagnose infectious diseases (especially meningitis and bacterial infections), was the very first large-scale expert system. Later, INTERNIST/CADUCEUS—one of the most sophisticated expert systems, the knowledge base of which deals with the entire field of internal medicine—was developed at the University of Pittsburgh.

Universities remain at the forefront of research in this area. Medical schools and hospitals are envisaged as the primary users, followed by general practitioners.

### (ii) Tax Systems

Taxation is an almost ideal candidate for expert system development, since in theory tax experts ought to be able to describe in rather clear-cut terms how their decisions are made. It is a field that, more than almost any other, depends on rule-based logic.

It is important to make a distinction between a tax system that is a true expert system and one that is merely a sophisticated tax calculator designed only to assist a tax expert. A real expert system in this area must be able to interact with a nonexpert and deal with tax planning areas that require solutions and recommendations that go beyond "This is your tax payable."

The large public accounting firms, which have a vested interest in these types of expert systems and the resources to develop them, are most likely to emerge as leaders in this type of system.

### (iii) Audit Systems

Auditing, to a greater degree than tax, involves judgments by the expert that are not so easily codified into an expert system's knowledge base. Nevertheless, auditing is an area for which expert systems can be envisaged to:

- Evaluate internal controls—including computer controls—in an accounting system
- Assess an allowance for bad debts
- Perform statistical sampling for audit testing and/or design statistical systems

As with taxation, large public accounting firms are developing expert systems in this area. Again, it is important to distinguish between a true expert system and a limited tool that only assists an expert.

### (iv) Other Systems

A number of other types of expert systems have been developed or are logical candidates for development, including:

- Scientific systems such as PROSPECTOR (Stanford), which assists geologists in finding ore deposits; DENDRAL (Stanford), which assists in determining the chemical structures of compounds; and MACSYMA (MIT), which is used to solve complex mathematical problems.
- Business systems designed to handle especially complex areas such as order processing (e.g., XCON, developed by Digital Equipment Corporation to assemble VAX computer system orders) or maintenance (e.g., DELTA/CATS-1, developed by General Electric to help with maintenance of GE diesel locomotives).

## (f) DEVELOPING AN EXPERT SYSTEM

It is quite common for the user to develop expert systems from scratch. In fact, it is more common than in other types of computer programs. This is primarily because expert systems, and the needs of their users, are often highly specialized and therefore require custom development.

Developing an expert system involves the following steps:

- Identifying the application
- Ensuring resources are in place to develop the system, especially human resources (i.e., a knowledge engineer with the necessary expertise)
- Building the system
- Implementing the system

*(i) Identifying the Application*

The suitability of an application as a candidate for an expert system depends on several factors, including:

- How well-bounded the knowledge base of the particular field is (fields with relatively unbounded knowledge bases are poor candidates for expert system development).
- How well the application can be codified into a set of facts, rules, and heuristics to develop the knowledge base.
- The complexity of the application (generally, the more complex the task, in terms of the permutations and combinations analyzed before arriving at a solution, the better suited it is to expert system development).
- Especially for commercial ventures, the cost of an expert system (since the cost is generally high, the benefits must also be, which usually means that the application must be integral to the user's business operations).

*(ii) Resources Required*

The financial and human resources required to build an expert system are considerable. Although very simple systems can be built in a matter of months, complex ones can take several years and cost hundreds of thousands of dollars. Generally only the largest organizations and academic institutions can justify the cost of developing such systems.

Of course, two other necessary and important resources are computer capacity and expertise. Both are often in short supply.

*(iii) Building and Implementing the System*

In building a system, a knowledge engineer will:

- Assess the application and learn as much as possible about it.
- Specify a set of goals or objectives against which the system can be judged.
- Decide on the type of computer and computer language to be used to build the system.
- Develop the system and implement it (this is usually a circular process as the system goes through the prototype, testing, and implementation phases).

Throughout this process the knowledge engineer will also need to consult with a human expert.

*(iv) Pitfalls to Avoid*

Common problems in expert systems include:

- Selecting an application or task that is poorly suited to expert system development (for example, choosing a field with an unbounded knowledge base).
- Underestimating or not having the resources necessary to develop the system.

- Building a system that is not user friendly.
- Building a system that is not flexible enough to meet changing needs.
- Building inadequate and/or inaccurate knowledge bases (in practice, this is the biggest and most difficult task: capturing the knowledge necessary to make the system work).
- Encountering human resistance, in some cases from the human experts themselves, to the idea of a particular kind of expertise being automated.

Finally, unrealistic expectations for expert systems can also be a problem. Although well-designed systems can assist in their particular domain, expert systems are still far from perfect.

## 15.4 SUMMARY

Artificial intelligence and expert systems are growth areas in the information technology industry. They are also important to larger businesses that have the resources to develop big systems; often in so doing they maintain their competitive advantage. However, for smaller businesses, AI and expert systems are still just over the horizon.

If you are contemplating acquiring or developing applications in this area, you should:

- Follow the general steps and avoid the common pitfalls set out previously in this chapter.
- Recognize that you will almost certainly need to seek outside assistance (partnerships between the private sector, government, and academia are common).
- Be prepared for a relatively long process of design and testing before the application can be implemented.

There are many books and magazines dealing with artificial intelligence and expert systems. In addition, you may want to approach a company involved in the field or a university department doing this type of research. There may also be research programs funded by your government agencies responsible for high technology.

Finally, don't go into the process with unreasonable expectations. For many, the terms "artificial intelligence" and "expert systems" stir up expectations that the current technology is unable to meet. Any extraordinary claims, by software manufacturers or others, should be viewed with caution.

# APPENDIX A

# ASCII Table

| | | | | | |
|---|---|---|---|---|---|
| 0 | NUL | 32 | SP | 64 | @ |
| 1 | CTRL A | 33 | ! | 65 | A |
| 2 | CTRL B | 34 | " | 66 | B |
| 3 | CTRL C | 35 | # | 67 | C |
| 4 | CTRL D | 36 | $ | 68 | D |
| 5 | CTRL E | 37 | % | 69 | E |
| 6 | CTRL F | 38 | & | 70 | F |
| 7 | CTRL G | 39 | , | 71 | G |
| 8 | CTRL H | 40 | ( | 72 | H |
| 9 | CTRL I | 41 | ) | 73 | I |
| 10 | CTRL J | 42 | * | 74 | J |
| 11 | CTRL K | 43 | + | 75 | K |
| 12 | CTRL L | 44 | ' | 76 | L |
| 13 | CTRL M | 45 | - | 77 | M |
| 14 | CTRL N | 46 | . | 78 | N |
| 15 | CTRL O | 47 | / | 79 | O |
| 16 | CTRL P | 48 | 0 | 80 | P |
| 17 | CTRL Q | 49 | 1 | 81 | Q |
| 18 | CTRL R | 50 | 2 | 82 | R |
| 19 | CTRL S | 51 | 3 | 83 | S |
| 20 | CTRL T | 52 | 4 | 84 | T |
| 21 | CTRL U | 53 | 5 | 85 | U |
| 22 | CTRL V | 54 | 6 | 86 | V |
| 23 | CTRL W | 55 | 7 | 87 | W |
| 24 | CTRL X | 56 | 8 | 88 | X |
| 25 | CTRL Y | 57 | 9 | 89 | Y |
| 26 | CTRL Z | 58 | : | 90 | Z |
| 27 | ESC | 59 | ; | 91 | [ |
| 28 | FS | 60 | < | 92 | \ |
| 29 | GS | 61 | = | 93 | ] |
| 30 | RS | 62 | > | 94 | ^ |
| 31 | US | 63 | ? | 95 | - |

| | | | | | |
|---|---|---|---|---|---|
| 96 | ? | 107 | k | 118 | v |
| 97 | a | 108 | l | 119 | w |
| 98 | b | 109 | m | 120 | x |
| 99 | c | 110 | n | 121 | y |
| 100 | d | 111 | o | 122 | z |
| 101 | e | 112 | p | 123 | { |
| 102 | f | 113 | q | 124 | | |
| 103 | g | 114 | r | 125 | } |
| 104 | h | 115 | s | 126 | ~ |
| 105 | i | 116 | t | 127 | DEL |
| 106 | j | 117 | u | | |

# APPENDIX B

# Directory of Companies

**Acer America Corporation**
2641 Orchard Parkway
San Jose, California 95134
(408) 432-6200; Fax (408) 922-2953

*Main Products:* Microcomputers

*Other Numbers:* (800) 574-2237 [574-ACER] (customer information, U.S. and Canada)

*Web Site:* http://www.acer.com

**Acer Canada Ltd.**
5155 Spectrum Way, Unit 9
Mississauga, Ontario
Canada L4W 5A1
(905) 602-8200; Fax (905) 602-7799

**Adobe Systems Inc.**
1585 Charleston Road, P.O. Box 7900
Mountainview, California 94039
(415) 961-4400; Fax (415) 961-3769

**Adobe Systems Canada Inc.**
145 King Street West, Suite 1000
Toronto, Ontario
Canada M5H 3X6
(416) 360-2317; Fax (416) 360-2917

*Main Products:* Postscript (page description language); Illustrator (drawing); Photoshop (image editing); PageMaker (page layout software); fonts

*Other Numbers:* (800) 833-6687 (product and update information, U.S. and Canada); (800) 872-3623 (technical support, U.S. and Canada); (408) 986-6587 (faxback service)

*Other Addresses:* P.O. Box 6458, Salinas, California, USA 93912 (customer orders); ftp@adobe.com (Internet downloads)

*Web Site:* http://www.adobe.com

**Aldus Corporation**

*Comments:* Developed PageMaker; acquired by Adobe Systems in September 1994

**Amdahl Corporation**
1250 East Arques Avenue, Box 3470
Sunnyvale, California 94088-3470
(408) 746-6000; Fax (408) 773-0833

**Amdahl Canada Limited**
12 Concorde Place, Suite 300
North York, Ontario
Canada M3C 3R8
(416) 510-3111; Fax (416) 510-3353

*Main Products:* Mainframe computers

*Other Addresses:* 2330 Millrace Court, Mississauga, Ontario Canada L5N 1W2 (Canadian distribution center), (905) 821-9034; Fax (905) 821-9312

*Web Site:* http://www.amdahl.com

**Amdek Corporation**

*Comments:* Monitor manufacturer bought by Wyse Technology several years ago

**America Online, Inc.**
8619 Westwood Center Drive
Vienna, Virginia 22182
(703) 448-8700; Fax (703) 883-1509

*Main Services:* Commercial on-line service

*Other Numbers:* (800) 827-6364 (customer information and support, U.S., and Canada); (800) 827-3338 (technical service, U.S., and Canada)

**American Telephone & Telegraph**

See AT&T.

**Ansa Software**

*Comments:* Developed Paradox; acquired by Borland several years ago

**Apple Computer, Inc.**
1 Infinite Loop
Cupertino, California 95014
(408) 996-1010; Fax (408) 996-0275

**Apple Canada Inc.**
7495 Birchmount Road
Markham, Ontario
Canada L3R 5G2
(905) 477-5800; Fax (905) 477-6305

*Main Products:* Macintosh computer line; Macintosh Operating System; laser printers (Personal LaserWriter and LaserWriter Select series); wide variety of other microcomputer hardware and software

*Other Numbers:* (800) 776-2333 (product information, U.S.); (800) 538-9696 (dealer and service provider information, U.S.); (800) 767-2775 (technical support, U.S.); (800) 665-2775 (dealer and product information, Canada); (800) 293-3394 (technical support, Canada)

*Web Site:* http://www.APPLE.com

---

## Ashton-Tate

*Comments:* Developed dBase; acquired by Borland in July 1991

---

## AST Research Inc.
16215 Alton Parkway
Irvine, California 92718
(714) 727-4141; Fax (714) 727-9355

## AST Canada Inc.
255 Matheson Boulevard West
Mississauga, Ontario
Canada L5R 3G3
(905) 507-3278; Fax (905) 507-8278

*Main Products:* Microcomputers

*Other Numbers:* (800) 876-4278 (customer information, U.S. and Canada)

*Comments:* Started out as manufacturer of expansion cards and boards

*Web Site:* http://www.ast.com

---

## AT&T (American Telephone & Telegraph)
295 North Maple Avenue
Basking Ridge, New Jersey 07920
(908) 221-2000

## AT&T Canada Inc.
320 Front Street West
Toronto, Ontario
Canada M5V 3C4
(416) 595-5696; Fax (416) 204-2912

*Main Products:* Wide range of telecommunication equipment and computer hardware

*Other Numbers:* (513) 445-5000 (AT&T Global Information Solutions, including former NCR); (416) 599-4627 (AT&T Global Information Solutions Canada Ltd.); (905) 826-9000 (customer support center, Canada)

*Other Addresses:* AT&T Communications Canada Inc., 4950 Yonge Street, North York, Ontario, Canada, M2N 6K1

---

## Atari Corp.
455 South Matilda Avenue
Sunnyvale, California 94086
(408) 328-0900; Fax (408) 328-0909

*Main Products:* Game systems (Jaguar, Lynx); microcomputers (Falcon) and peripherals

*Web Site:* http://www.atari.com

## AutoDesk Inc.
111 McInnis Parkway
San Rafael, California 94903
(415) 507-5000; Fax (415) 507-5100

## AutoDesk Canada Inc.
90 Allstate Parkway, Suite 201
Unionville, Ontario
Canada L3R 6H3
(905) 946-0928; Fax (905) 946-0926

*Main Products:* AutoCAD (CAD/CAM software)

*Other Numbers:* (800) 445-5415 (AutoCAD information line, U.S. and Canada)

*Web Site:* http://www.autodesk.com

## Avery Dennison Corporation
20955 Pathfinder Road
Diamond Bar, California 91765
(909) 869-7711; Fax (909) 598-2905

## Avery Dennison Canada Inc.
200 Baseline Road East
Bowmanville, Ontario
Canada L1C 1A2
(905) 623-6311; Fax (905) 623-9751

*Main Products:* Label products for use with microcomputers and printers

*Other Numbers:* (800) 462-8379 (consumer service, U.S. and Canada)

## Bedford Software Corp.

*Comments:* Developed Bedford Accounting software; acquired by Computer Associates several years ago

## Borland International
100 Borland Way
Scotts Valley, California 95066
(408) 431-1000

## Borland Canada Software Inc.
200 Conrad Crescent
Markham, Ontario
Canada L3R 8T9
(905) 477-4344; Fax (905) 477-6657

*Main Products:* dBase; Paradox (database); Quattro (spreadsheet); development tools (C++, Turbo Pascal)

*Other Numbers:* (800) 461-3327 (customer service and upgrades, U.S. and Canada)

*Web Site:* http://www.borland.com

## Brother International Corporation
200 Cottontail Lane
Somerset, New Jersey 08875-6714
(908) 356-8880; Fax (908) 356-4085

## Brother International Corporation Ltd.
1 Hotel de Ville
Dollard des Ormeaux, Quebec
Canada H9B 3H6
(514) 685-0600; Fax (514) 685-0700

*Main Products:* Laser and other printers

*Other Numbers:* (800) 284-4357 (customer information and support, U.S.); (800) 361-6465 (customer information, Canada); (800) 853-6660 (technical support, Canada)

*Web Site:* http://www.brother.co.jp

---

**Canon USA**
One Canon Plaza
Lake Success, New York 11042
(516) 328-5000

**Canon Canada Inc.**
6390 Dixie Road
Mississauga, Ontario
Canada L5T 1P7
(905) 795-1111; Fax (905) 795-2020

*Main Products:* Photocopiers; fax machines; laser printers; print engines; toner

*Other Numbers:* (800) 848-4123 (customer information, U.S.); (800) 387-1241 (customer information, Canada)

*Web Site:* http://www.usa.canon.com

---

**Commodore Business Machines**

*Comments:* Commodore 64 and the Amiga were the company's most notable products; the company has ceased operations, but its rights were reportedly bought by a German company that may start up an Amiga 4000 line

---

**Compaq Computer Corp.**
20555 State Highway 249
Houston, Texas 77070
(713) 370-0670

**Compaq Canada Inc.**
45 Vogell Road
Richmond Hill, Ontario
Canada L4B 3P6
(905) 707-1715; Fax (416) 229-8898

*Main Products:* Microcomputers and related hardware

*Other Numbers:* (800) 231-0900 (customer information, U.S.); (800) 652-6672 (technical support, U.S. and Canada); (800) 263-5868 (customer support, Canada)

*Web Site:* http://www.compaq.com

---

**CompuServe**
5000 Arlington Ctr Blvd, PO Box 20212
Columbus, Ohio 43220
(614) 457-8600; Fax (614) 457-0378

*Main Services:* Commercial on-line service

*Other Numbers:* (800) 848-8199 (signup and service, U.S. and Canada)

*Comments:* Owned by H&R Block

**Computer Associates International**
2880 Scott Boulevard
Santa Clara, California 95050
(408) 562-8800; Fax (408) 562-8282

**Computer Associates International**
5935 Airport Road
Mississauga, Ontario
Canada L4V 1W5
(905) 676-6700; Fax (905) 676-6734

*Main Products:* Accounting and other software for microcomputers and larger distributed systems

*Other Address:* Corporate Headquarters, 1 Computer Associates Plaza, Islandia, New York, USA 11788-7000; Tel. (516) 342-5224; Fax (516) 342-5734;

*Other Numbers:* (800) 225-5224 (customer information, U.S. and Canada)

*Web Site:* http://www.cai.com

---

**Corel Corporation**
P.O. Box 3595
Salinas, California 93912
(800) 772-6735

**Corel Corporation**
1600 Carling Avenue
Ottawa, Ontario
Canada K1Z 8R7
(613) 728-3733; Fax (613) 761-9176

*Main Products:* Drawing and graphics software (CorelDRAW), Corel Office

*Other Numbers:* (800) 772-6735 [77COREL] (customer information, U.S.); (800) 818-1848 (technical service, U.S. and Canada); (800) 394-3729 (customer information, Canada)

*Web Site:* http://www.corelnet.com

---

**Cricket Software**

*Comments:* Developer of draw programs (e.g., CricketDraw); acquired by Computer Associates several years ago

---

**Dac Easy Inc.**
17950 Preston Road, Suite 800
Dallas, Texas 75252
(214) 248-0305

**Dac Easy Canada Inc.**
3075 14th Avenue, Suite 201
Markham, Ontario
Canada L3R 0G9
(905) 940-3314; Fax (905) 940-0308

*Main Products:* Accounting software (DacEasy)

---

**Data General Corporation**
4400 Computer Drive
Westboro, Massachusetts 01580
(508) 366-8911; Fax (508) 366-1319

**Data General (Canada) Inc.**
350-7070 Mississauga Rd.
Mississauga, Ontario
Canada L5N 7J8
(905) 567-8340; Fax (905) 819-5413

*Main Products:* Microcomputer hardware

*Web Site:* http://www.dg.com

**Dell Computer Corporation**
2214 West Braker Lane, Station "D"
Austin, Texas 78758-4053
(512) 338-4400; Fax (512) 728-3653

**Dell Computer Corporation**
255 Consumers Road, Suite 240
North York, Ontario
Canada M2J 1R4
(416) 758-2100; Fax (800) 387-5753

*Main Products:* Microcomputers

*Other Numbers:* (800) 879-3355 (customer information and support, U.S. and Canada)

---

**Delrina Technology Inc.**
(see Symantec)

**Symantec Delrina Group**
895 Don Mills Road, 500-2 Park Centre
Toronto, Ontario
Canada M3C 1W3
(416) 441-3676; Fax (416) 441-0333

*Main Products:* WinFax; screen savers; other utility software

*Comments:* Acquired by Symantec in July 1995

*Web Site:* http://www.delrina.com

---

**DEST Corporation**

*Comments:* Produced scanners in the 1980s and early 1990s, later under the name New DEST; no further information available

---

**Digital Equipment Corporation (DEC)**
111 Powdermill Rd.
Maynard, Massachusetts 01754
(508) 493-5111; Fax (508) 493-8780

**Digital Equipment of Canada Ltd.**
4110 Yonge Street
Willowdale, Ontario
Canada M2P 2C7
(416) 730-7000; Fax (416) 730-7070

*Main Products:* Wide range of hardware and software, including large distributed systems

*Other Numbers:* (800) 344-4825 ("DEC direct" customer information, U.S. and Canada); (800) 354-9000 (technical support, U.S. and Canada)

*Other Addresses:* 146 Main Street, Maynard, Massachusetts, USA 01754-2571

*Web Site:* http://www.digital.com

---

**Digital Research, Inc.**

*Comments:* Developed CP/M (an early disk operating system) and DR-DOS (which was unsuccessful in competing with Microsoft's MS-DOS during the 1980s); the company was acquired by Novell in 1991

**Dow Jones & Company Incorporated**
P.O. Box 300
Princeton, New Jersey 08543-0300
(609) 520-4000; Fax (609) 520-4000

**Dow Jones Canada Inc.**
60 Yonge Street, 9th Floor
Toronto, Ontario
Canada M5E 1H5
(416) 365-7171; Fax (416) 777-5590

*Main Services:* News retrieval service

*Other Address:* Harborside Financial Center, 600 Plaza 2, Jersey City, New Jersey, USA 07311-3992; Tel. (201) 938-4000; Fax (201) 938-5011

*Other Numbers, Sites:* (609) 452-1511 (customer service, Dow Jones News Retrieval); http://bis.dowjones.com

**Eastman Kodak**

See Kodak.

**Electrohome USA Inc.**
181 Cooper Avenue, Suite 100
Tonawanda, New York 14150
(716) 874-3630; Fax (716) 874-4309

**Electrohome Ltd.**
809 Wellington Street North
Kitchener, Ontario
Canada N2G 4J6
(519) 744-7111; Fax (519) 749-3131

*Main Products:* Monitors; projectors

*Other Numbers:* (909) 466-3816 (California sales office for western U.S.)

*Web Site:* http://www.electro.com

**Enable Software**
Northway Ten Executive Park, 313 Ushers Road
Ballston Lake, New York 12019
(518) 877-8600; Fax (518) 877-5225

*Main Products:* Enable software (integrated spreadsheet, database, word processor)

**Epson America Inc. (Seiko Epson)**
20770 Madrona Avenue
Torrance, California 90503
(310) 782-0770; Fax (310) 782-5220

**Epson Canada Limited**
550 McNicoll Avenue
Willowdale, Ontario
Canada M2H 2E1
(416) 498-9955; Fax (416) 498-4574

*Main Products:* Printers; microcomputers

*Other Numbers:* (800) 873-7766 [(800) USEPSON] (customer information, U.S.); (800) 463-7766 [(800) GOEPSON] (customer information, Canada)

*Web Site:* http://www.epson.com

## Exabyte Corporation
1685 38th Street
Boulder, Colorado 80301
(303) 442-4333; Fax (303) 417-7170

## Exabyte Canada
3800 Steeles Avenue West, Suite 121
Woodbridge, Ontario
Canada L4L 4G9
(416) 744-6006; Fax (416) 740-8119

*Main Products:* Tape backup systems

*Other Numbers:* (800) 392-2983 (customer information, U.S. and Canada)

*Comments:* Acquired Tallgrass Technologies in 1994/95

*Web Site:* http://www.exabyte.com

## Fujitsu Computer Products of America
2904 Orchard Parkway
San Jose, California 95134-2009
(408) 432-6333; Fax (408) 894-1709

## Fujitsu Canada Inc.
2800 Matheson Boulevard East
Mississauga, Ontario
Canada L4W 4X5
(905) 602-5454; Fax (905) 602-5457

*Main Products:* Wide range of hardware from mainframes to printers

*Other Numbers:* (800) 626-4686 (customer information, U.S.); (800) 263-8716 (customer information, Canada); (905) 475-1221 (Fujitsu Business Systems Canada)

## Gandalf Systems
501 Delran Parkway
Delran, New Jersey 08075
(609) 461-8100; Fax (609) 461-4074

## Gandalf Canada Ltd.
130 Colonnade Road South
Nepean, Ontario
Canada K2E 7M4
(613) 274-6500; Fax (613) 274-6501

*Main Products:* Communication hardware (e.g., multiplexers, modems)

*Other Numbers:* (800) 426-3253 (800 GANDALF)

*Other Addresses:* 235 Yorkland Boulevard, Suite 200, Willowdale, Ontario, Canada M2J 4Y8, (416) 491-6070; Fax (416) 491-0454

*Web Site:* http://www.globalx.net

## Gateway 2000
610 Gateway Drive
North Sioux City, South Dakota 57049
(605) 232-2000; Fax (605) 232-2023

*Main Products:* Microcomputers

*Other Numbers:* (800) 523-2000 (customer information, U.S. and Canada)

*Web Site:* http://www.gw2k.com

## Global Village Communication
1144 East Arques Avenue
Sunnyvale, California 94086
(408) 523-1000; Fax (408) 523-2407

*Main Products:* Communication hardware (modems)

*Other Numbers:* (800) 736-4821 (customer information and sales, U.S. and Canada); (404) 984-9958 (PC support); (408) 523-1050 (Macintosh support); (800) 340-8007 (faxback Macintosh support)

*Web Site:* http://www.globalvillage.com

## GRiD Systems Corporation

*Comments:* Was a laptop computer maker in the late 1980s, possibly through the early 1990s; no further information available

## Hayes Microcomputer Products, Inc.
5835 Peachtree Corners East
Norcross, Georgia 30092
(770) 840-9200; Fax (770) 441-1213

*Main Products:* Communication hardware (modems, several makes and models)

*Other Numbers:* (770) 441-1617 (customer service); (770) 449-0087 (fax customer service); (800) 429-3739 (fax on demand technical service, U.S. and Canada)

*Web Site:* http://www.hayes.com

*Comments:* Practical Peripherals operates as a separate division

## Hercules Computer Technology
3839 Spinnaker Court
Fremont, California 94538
(510) 623-6030; Fax (510) 623-1112

*Main Products:* Graphics boards

*Web Site:* http://www.hercules.com

## Hewlett-Packard Co.
P.O. Box 10301
Palo Alto, California 94304
(415) 857-1501; Fax (415) 857-5578

## Hewlett-Packard (Canada) Ltd.
5150 Spectrum Way
Mississauga, Ontario
Canada L4W 5G1
(905) 206-4725; Fax (905) 206-4739

*Main Products:* Laser printers; wide range of hardware and software

*Other Numbers:* (800) 752-0900 (customer information, U.S. and Canada); (208) 323-2551 (technical support); (905) 206-4383 (customer information center, Canada)

*Other Addresses:* 19310 Pruneridge Avenue, Cupertino, California, USA 95014;

*Web Site:* http://www.hp.com

---

### Hitachi America Limited
50 Prospect Avenue
Terrytown, New York 10591
(914) 332-5800; Fax (914) 332-5834

### Hitachi (HSC) Canada Inc.
6740 Campobello Road
Mississauga, Ontario
Canada L5N 2L8
(905) 821-4545; Fax (905) 821-1101

*Main Products:* Wide range of hardware from mainframes to monitors

*Other Numbers:* (800) 448-2244 [HITACHI] (customer information, U.S. and Canada) (800) 906-4482 (customer support, Canada)

*Other Addresses:* Hitachi Home Electronics, 1290 Wall Street West, Lyndhurst, New Jersey, USA 07071; (201) 935-8980; Fax (201) 935-4869; Hitachi Data Systems Inc. (Canada), 2550 Victoria Park, Suite 601, Willowdale, Ontario, Canada M2J 5A9, (416) 494-4114; Fax (416) 494-1934

---

### Intel Corporation
2200 Mission College Boulevard
Santa Clara, California 95052
(408) 765-8080; Fax (408) 765-1992

### Intel Semi Conductor of Canada Ltd.
190 Attwell Drive, Suite 500
Rexdale, Ontario
Canada M9W 6H8
(800) 628-8686 (to obtain direct #, no switchboard)

*Main Products:* Integrated circuits (e.g., Pentium chip) and boards

*Other Numbers:* (800) 628-8686 (customer information, chips and boards, U.S. and Canada); (800) 538-3373 (network and other products, U.S. and Canada)

*Web Site:* http://www.intel.com

---

### International Business Machines Corporation (IBM)
Old Orchard Road
Armonk, New York 10504
(914) 765-1900

### IBM Canada Ltd.
3600 Steeles Avenue East
Markham, Ontario
Canada L3R 9Z7
(905) 316-9000; Fax (905) 316-2535

*Main Products:* Wide range of hardware and software (mainframes to microcomputers)

*Other Numbers:* (800) 426-3333 (customer information, U.S.); (800) 426-2968 (IBM PC Direct sales line, U.S.); (800) 465-6600 (customer information, Canada); (800) 465-7999 (IBM PC Direct sales line, Canada)

*Web Site:* http://www.ibm.com (Web Site: http://www.can.ibm.com)

**International Data Corporation**
5 Speen Street
Framingham, Massachusetts 01701
(508) 872-8200; Fax (508) 935-4015

**IDC (Canada) Ltd.**
36 Toronto Street, Suite 950
Toronto, Ontario
Canada M5C 2C5
(416) 369-0033; Fax (416) 369-0419

*Main Products:* Industry statistics and market research reports

*Web Site:* http://www.idcresearch.com

---

**Internex Online**
(N/A; see UUNET)

**Internex Online Inc.**
10 Bay Street, Suite 1001
Toronto, Ontario
Canada M5J 2N8
(416) 363-8676; Fax (416) 363-8713

*Main Services:* Internet service provider

---

**Iomega Corporation**
1821 West Iomega Way
Roy, Utah 84067
(801) 778-1000; Fax (801) 778-3190

**Iomega Corporation**
130 Spadina Avenue
Toronto, Ontario
Canada M5V 2L4
(416) 504-6032

*Main Products:* Removable hard disk cartridges (Bernoulli Box, Zip Drive, Ditto Drive)

*Other Numbers:* (800) 777-6654 (customer information, U.S. and Canada)

*Web Site:* http://www.iomega.com

---

**Kodak Corporation (Eastman Kodak)**
343 State Street
Rochester, New York 14650
(716) 724-4000

**Kodak Canada Inc.**
3500 Eglinton Avenue West
Toronto, Ontario
Canada M6M 1V3
(416) 766-8233; Fax (416) 766-5814

*Main Products:* Color laser and thermal dye printers; color photocopiers

*Other Numbers:* (800) 242-2424 (customer information, U.S. and Canada); (800) 465-6325 (digital and applied imaging products, Canada)

*Other Addresses:* 901 Elm Grove Road, Rochester, New York, USA 14653

*Web Site:* http://www.kodak.com

## LaserMaster Corporation
7156 Shady Oak Road
Eden Prairie, Minnesota 55344
(612) 944-6069; Fax (612) 944-6932

*Main Products:* Laser printers

*Other Numbers:* (612) 944-9330 (sales department); (612) 944-0522 (fax, sales department)

*Web Site:* http://www.lasermaster.com

## Leading Edge Products
14 Brent Drive
Hudson, Massachusetts 01749
(508) 562-3322; Fax (508) 568-3618

*Main Products:* Microcomputers

*Other Numbers:* (800) 245-9870 (customer information, U.S. and Canada); (800) 387-6211 (SHL Technical Services, Canadian support line)

## Lexmark International
740 New Circle Road
Lexington, Kentucky 40511
(606) 232-2000; Fax (800) 522-3422

## Lexmark Canada Inc.
160 Royal Crest Court
Markham, Ontario
Canada L3R 0A2
(905) 477-2311; Fax (905) 477-0864

*Main Products:* Laser printers

*Other Numbers:* (800) 438-2468 (customer information, U.S. and Canada); (800) 358-5835 (customer information line, Canada)

*Web Site:* http://www.lexmark.com

*Comments:* Purchased IBM's microcomputer printer division in 1991; IBM is a minority shareholder.

## Logitech, Inc.
6505 Kaiser Drive
Freemont, California 94555
(510) 795-8500; Fax (510) 792-8901

## Logitech Canada, Inc.
5025 Orbitor Drive, Building 6, Suite 200
Mississauga, Ontario
Canada L4W 4Y5
(905) 629-2006; Fax (905) 629-2868

*Main Products:* Scanners; microcomputer input devices; ergonomic devices

*Other Numbers:* (800) 231-7717 (customer information, U.S. and Canada); (510) 795-8100 (technical support)

*Web Site:* http://www.logitech.com

---

**Lotus Development Corp.**
55 Cambridge Parkway
Cambridge, Massachusetts 02142
(617) 577-8500

**Lotus Development Canada Limited**
10 Bay Street, Suite 1700
Toronto, Ontario
Canada M5R 2J8
(416) 364-8000; Fax (416) 364-1547

*Main Products:* Wide variety of software (Lotus 1-2-3, Freelance, Ami Pro)

*Other Numbers:* (800) 872-3387 [TRADEUP] (customer service, U.S.); (800) 465-6887 [GOLOTUS] (customer service, Canada)

*Web Site:* http://www.lotus.com

*Comments:* Acquired by IBM in June 1995

---

**Manhattan Graphics**

*Comments:* Produced a popular page layout package called ReadySetGo, subsequently marketed by a company called Letraset; no further information available

---

**Mannesmann Tally Corp.**
P.O. Box 97018
Kent, Washington 98064-9718
(206) 251-5500; Fax (206) 251-5520

**Mannesmann Tally Corp.**
125 Traders Blvd., Unit 9
Mississauga, Ontario
Canada L4Z 2E5
(905) 890-4646; Fax (905) 890-4567

*Main Products:* Printers

---

**Maxtor Corporation**
2190 Miller Drive
Longmont, Colorado 80501
(303) 651-6000; Fax (303) 678-2165

*Main Products:* Hard disk drives

*Comments:* Acquired Miniscribe in early 1990s

---

**Media Cybernetics Inc.**
8484 Georgia Avenue, Suite 200
Silver Spring, Maryland 20910
(301) 495-3305; Fax (301) 495-5964

*Main Products:* Software (Image Pro, Windows-based graphics package)

*Other Numbers:* (301) 495-4808 (international sales and support line)

*Comments:* Also produced a popular graphics package called Dr. Halo (now discontinued)

## MicroPro International Corp.

*Comments:* Developed WordStar; subsequently renamed WordStar International

## Microrim Inc.
15395 SE 30th Place
Bellevue, Washington 98007
(206) 649-9500; Fax (206) 746-9350

*Main Products:* Database software (R:Base)

*Other Numbers:* (800) 628-6990 (sales, U.S. and Canada)

## Microsoft Corp.
1 Microsoft Way
Redmond, Washington 98052-6399
(206) 882-8080; Fax (206) 883-8101

## Microsoft Canada Inc.
320 Matheson Boulevard West
Mississauga, Ontario
Canada L5R 3R1
(905) 568-0434; Fax (905) 568-1527

*Main Products:* Wide variety of software (MS-DOS, Windows, Word, Excel)

*Other Numbers:* (800) 426-9400 (customer information, U.S.); (206) 936-8661 (automated information, U.S.); (800) 563-9048 (product and upgrade information, Canada); (905) 568-3503 (technical support, Canada)

*Web Site:* http://www.microsoft.com

## MicroTek Data Corporation
3715 Doolittle Drive
Redondo Beach, California 90278
(310) 297-5000; Fax (310) 297-5050

*Main Products:* Scanners

*Other Numbers:* (800) 654-4160 (customer information, U.S. and Canada); (310) 297-5101 (automated faxback system)

## Miniscribe Corporation

*Comments:* Disk drive manufacturer; acquired by Maxtor in early 1990s

**Mitsubishi Electronics America, Inc.**
Information Systems Division
5665 Plaza Drive
Cypress, California 90603-0007
(714) 220-2500; Fax (714) 236-6172

**Mitsubishi Canada Limited**
Commerce Court West, Suite 5101
Toronto, Ontario
Canada M5L 1A5
(416) 362-6731; Fax (416) 365-1384

*Main Products:* Monitors

*Other Numbers:* (800) 843-2515 (customer information, U.S. and Canada)

*Other Addresses:* 6200 Dixie Road, Mississauga, Ontario, Canada, (905) 670-8711 (semiconductor division)

---

**Motorola Inc.**
1303 East Algonquin Road
Schaumburg, Illinois 60196
(708) 576-5000

**Motorola Canada Limited**
Info Systems and Computer Division
400 Matheson Boulevard West
Mississauga, Ontario
Canada L5R 3M1
(905) 507-7200; Fax (905) 507-7230

*Main Products:* Semiconductors (chips); cellular phones; wide range of hardware

*Other Numbers:* (800) 451-2369 (customer information, U.S.); (800) 668-8973 (customer information, Canada)

*Other Addresses:* 5000 Bradford Drive, Huntsville, Alabama, USA 35805; (205) 430-8000, Fax (205) 430-8926 (modem division); 400 Victoria Park Ave., Toronto, Ontario, (416) 497-8181 (semiconductor products, Canada); 5875 Whittle Road, Mississauga, Ontario, (905) 890-2355 (cellular phone products, Canada)

---

**National Semiconductor Corporation**
P.O. Box 58090
Santa Clara, California 95052-8090
(408) 721-5000; Fax (408) 739-9803

**National Semiconductor Canada Ltd.**
5925 Airport Road, Suite 615
Mississauga, Ontario
Canada L4V 1W1
(905) 678-2920; Fax (905) 678-2535

*Main Products:* Semiconductors (chips)

*Other Numbers:* (800) 272-9959 (customer response center, U.S. and Canada)

---

**NCR Corporation**

*Comments:* Acquired by AT&T (see AT&T Global Information Solutions)

---

**NEC Technologies Inc.**
1414 Massachusetts Avenue
Boxborough, Massachusetts 01719
(508) 264-8000; Fax (508) 264-8245

**NEC Canada Inc.**
6225 Kenway Drive
Mississauga, Ontario
Canada L5T 2L3
(905) 795-3500; Fax (905) 795-3540

*Main Products:* Microcomputers; monitors

*Other Numbers:* (800) 632-4636 (customer information, U.S. and Canada); (905) 795-3545 (customer service, Canada)

---

## New DEST Corporation

*Comments:* Produced scanners in the 1980s and early 1990s, originally under the name DEST; no further information available

---

## Nikon Electronic Imaging
1300 Walt Whitman Road
Melville, New York 11747
(516) 547-4355; Fax (516) 547-0305

## Nikon Canada Inc.
1366 Aerowood Drive
Mississauga, Ontario
L4W 1C1
(905) 625-9910; Fax (905) 625-0103

*Main Products:* Electronic imaging products (e.g., scanners, digital printers)

*Other Numbers:* (800) 526-4566 [52NIKON] (customer information, U.S. and Canada)

---

## Northern Telecom (Nortel)
200 Athens Way
Nashville, Tennessee 37228
(615) 734-4000

## Northern Telecom (Nortel)
2920 Matheson Boulevard East
Mississauga, Ontario
Canada L4W 4M7
(905) 238-7000; Fax (905) 238-7350

*Main Products:* Telephones; telecommunication equipment

*Other Numbers:* (800) 466-7835 [4NORTEL] (customer information, U.S. and Canada)

---

## Norton Computing

*Comments:* Full name is Peter Norton Computing; developed Norton Utilities; acquired by Symantec Corporation several years ago

---

## Novell Inc.
1555 North Technology Way
Orem, Utah 84057
(801) 429-7000

## Novell Canada
3100 Steeles Avenue East, Suite 500
Markham, Ontario
Canada L3R 8T3
(905) 940-2670; Fax (905) 940-2688

*Main Products:* Networking products; WordPerfect

*Other Numbers:* (800) 453-1267 (customer information, U.S. and Canada); (800) 638-9273 (customer support, U.S. and Canada)

*Comments:* Acquired WordPerfect in 1994 (later sold to Corel)

**Okidata**
532 Fellowship Road
Mount Laurel, New Jersey 08054
(609) 235-2600; Fax (609) 424-7219

**Okidata**
2735 Matheson Boulevard East
Mississauga, Ontario
Canada L4W 4M8
(905) 602-6400; Fax (905) 602-4755

*Main Products:* Printers

*Other Numbers:* (800) 654-3282 [OKIDATA] (customer information, U.S. and Canada); (609) 273-0300 (technical support)

**Olivetti Office USA**
Office Products Division
765 U.S. Highway 202
Bridgewater, New Jersey 08807
(908) 526-8200; Fax (908) 526-8405

**Olivetti Canada**
2235 Sheppard Avenue East, Suite 1200
North York, Ontario
Canada M2J 5B5
(416) 492-8250; Fax (416) 758-6514

*Main Products:* Wide range of hardware and software

*Other Numbers:* (800) 387-9660 (customer information, U.S. and Canada); (800) 457-1451 (computer products information, U.S. and Canada); (800) 222-2310 (printer and fax products information, U.S. and Canada)

**Oracle Corporation**
500 Oracle Parkway
Redwood Shores, California 94065
(415) 506-7000; Fax (415) 506-7200

**Oracle Corporation Canada Inc.**
110 Matheson Boulevard West
Mississauga, Ontario
Canada L5R 3P4
(905) 890-8100; Fax (905) 890-1207

*Main Products:* Database software (Oracle)

*Other Numbers:* (800) 672-2531 [ORACLE1] (sales and marketing, U.S. and Canada); (800) 363-3059 (customer information, Canada)

**Packard Bell Electronics Inc.**
31717 La Tienda Drive
Westlake Village, California 91362
(818) 865-1555; Fax (818) 865-0379

*Main Products:* Microcomputers (Legend series)

*Other Numbers:* (800) 733-4411 (customer information, U.S. and Canada); (801) 579-0161 (technical support)

**Panasonic Industrial Company**
One Panasonic Way
Secaucus, New Jersey 07094
(201) 348-7000

**Matsushita Electric of Canada Ltd.**
5770 Ambler Drive
Mississauga, Ontario
Canada L4W 2T3
(905) 624-5010; Fax (905) 624-9714

*Main Products:* Wide range of hardware

*Other Numbers:* (800) 222-0584 (technical support, U.S.)

**Patriot Computers**
25 Minthorn Court
Thornhill, Ontario
Canada L3T 7N5
(416) 969-8123; Fax (416) 969-8121

*Main Products:* Microcomputers

**PC World Communications, Inc.**
501 Second Street, #600
San Francisco, California 94107
(415) 243-0500

*Main Products:* Publications (PC World)

**Peter Norton Computing Inc.**

*Comments:* Developed Norton Utilities; acquired by Symantec several years ago

**Polaroid Corporation**
549 Technology Square
Cambridge, Massachusetts 02062
(617) 386-2000; Fax (617) 446-4600

**Polaroid Canada Inc.**
350 Carlingview Drive
Etobicoke, Ontario
Canada M9W 5G6
(416) 675-3680; Fax (416) 675-3228

*Main Products:* Computer imaging systems; diskettes

*Other Numbers:* (800) 225-1618 (customer support, U.S. and Canada)

## Practical Peripherals, Inc.

5854 Peachtree Corner S.E.
Norcross, Georgia 30092
(404) 840-9966; Fax (404) 734-4601

*Main Products:* Modems

*Other Numbers:* (800) 225-4774 (customer information, U.S. and Canada); (404) 840-9996 (technical support)

*Comments:* Acquired by Hayes in late 1980s; now operates as a division of Hayes

## Princeton Graphics Systems

*Comments:* Monitor manufacturer, ceased operations in March 1992; repairs by Ultimate Display, (404) 664-1010

## Prodigy Services Company

445 Hamilton Avenue
White Plains, New York 10601
(914) 448-8000; Fax (914) 448-8083

*Main Services:* Commercial on-line service

*Other Numbers:* (800) 776-3449 [PRODIGY] (customer service, U.S. and Canada)

## QMS Inc.

One Magnum Pass
Mobile, Alabama 36618
(334) 633-4300; Fax (334) 633-4866

## QMS Canada Inc.

2600 Skymark Avenue, Building 5
Mississauga, Ontario
Canada L4W 5B2
(905) 206-0848; Fax (416) 206-0903

*Main Products:* Laser printers

*Other Numbers:* (800) 523-2696 (customer information, U.S. and Canada); (334) 633-4500 (technical support)

## Quadram Corporation

*Comments:* Printer manufacturer; operated for a time as Q Corp.; no longer operating; repairs by Authorized Computer Repair (ACR), (404) 923-6666

## Quark Incorporated
1800 Grant Street
Denver, Colorado 80203
(303) 894-8888; Fax (303) 894-3399

*Main Products:* QuarkXpress (page layout software)

*Other Numbers:* (800) 788-7835 (customer service, U.S. and Canada)

## Qume Corporation

*Comments:* Printer manufacturer during the 1980s and early 1990s; no further information available

## Rodime Inc.

*Comments:* Hard disk drive manufacturer during the 1980s and early 1990s; no further information available

## Roland Digital Group
15271 Barranca Parkway
Irvine, California 92718
(714) 727-2100; Fax (714) 727-2112

*Main Products:* Plotters; engraving machines

*Other Numbers:* (800) 542-2307 (customer information, U.S. and Canada)

## Samsung Information Systems America Inc.
105 Challenger Road
Ridgefield Park, New Jersey 07660
(201) 229-4000; Fax (201) 229-4110

## Samsung Electronics Canada Inc.
7037 Financial Drive
Mississauga, Ontario
Canada L5N 6R3
(905) 542-3535; Fax (905) 542-3835

*Main Products:* Fax machines; printers; monitors; wide range of hardware

*Other Numbers:* (800) 726-7864 [SAMSUNG] (customer information, U.S.); (800) 767-4675 (dealer locations, U.S. and Canada); (800) 268-4947 (customer information, Canada)

**Seagate Technology**
920 Disc Drive, P.O. Box 66360
Scotts Valley, California 95067-0360
(408) 438-6550

*Main Products:* Hard disk drives

*Other Numbers:* (408) 438-1111 (sales); (408) 438-8222 (technical support)

**Seiko Epson**

See Epson

**Sharp Electronics Corporation**
Sharp Plaza
Mahwah, New Jersey 07430
(201) 529-8200

**Sharp Electronics of Canada Ltd.**
335 Britannia Road East
Mississauga, Ontario
Canada L4Z 1W9
(905) 890-2100; Fax (905) 890-0375

*Main Products:* Copiers; fax machines; notebook computers; wide range of hardware

*Other Numbers:* (800) 237-4277 [23SHARP] (customer information, U.S. and Canada)

**Silicon Graphics**
2011 North Shoreline Boulevard
Mountainview, California 94043-1389
(415) 960-1980; Fax (415) 961-0595

**Silicon Graphics Canada**
2550 Matheson Boulevard East
Mississauga, Ontario
Canada L4W 4Z1
(905) 625-4747; Fax (905) 625-4476

*Main Products:* Workstations

*Other Numbers:* (800) 800-7441 (automated sales and information line, U.S. and Canada)

**Software Arts**

*Comments:* Developed VisiCalc, the first successful spreadsheet; Lotus purchased the company in the early 1980s and discontinued VisiCalc

**Software Publishing Corporation**
3165 Kifer Road
Santa Clara, California 95051
(408) 986-8000; Fax (408) 450-7921

**Software Publishing Canada**
Valleywood Corp. Ctr, 60 Columbia Way,
Suite 300
Unionville, Ontario
Canada L3R 0C9
(905) 940-2600; Fax (905) 940-2979

*Main Products:* Software (Harvard Graphics)

*Other Numbers:* (800) 234-2500 (customer information, U.S. and Canada)

---

### Sony Corporation of America
3300 Zanker Road
San Jose, California 95134
(408) 432-0190; Fax (408) 943-0740

### Sony of Canada
405 Gordon Baker Road
Willowdale, Ontario
Canada M2H 2S6
(416) 499-1414; Fax (416) 497-1774

*Main Products:* Monitors; diskettes; wide range of hardware

*Other Numbers:* (800) 352-7669 [352-SONY] (customer information, U.S. and Canada); (416) 499-7669 (consumer product information, Canada); (416) 499-7759 (customer relations, Canada)

---

### Sun Microsystems Incorporated
2550 Garcia Avenue
Mountainview, California 94043
(415) 960-1300

### Sun Microsystems of Canada Inc.
100 Renfrew Drive
Markham, Ontario
Canada L3R 9R6
(905) 477-6745; Fax (905) 477-9423

*Main Products:* Workstations

*Other Numbers:* (800) 821-4643 (customer information, U.S. and Canada)

---

### Sybase Incorporated
6475 Christie Avenue
Emeryville, California 94608
(510) 922-3500; Fax (510) 658-9441

### Sybase Canada Ltd.
1 Robert Speck Parkway
Mississauga, Ontario
Canada L4Z 3M3
(905) 273-8500; Fax (905) 273-8550

*Main Products:* Database software

*Other Numbers:* (800) 933-0044 (customer information and support, U.S. and Canada)

---

### Symantec Corporation
10201 Torre Avenue
Cupertino, California 95014-2132
(408) 253-9600; Fax (408) 366-5949

### Symantec Canada
250 The Esplanade, Suite 200
Toronto, Ontario
Canada M5A 1J2
(416) 366-0423; Fax (416) 366-4453

*Main Products:* Software (e.g., Norton Utilities)

*Comments:* Acquired Delrina in July 1995

## Tallgrass Technologies Corporation

*Comments:* Manufacturer of tape backup systems; acquired by Exabyte Corporation in 1994/95

## Tandon Corporation

*Comments:* Manufacturer of hard disk drives; in Chapter 11 bankruptcy since March 1993 (TSL Holdings)

## Tandy Corp., Radio Shack Division
1900 One Tandy Center
Fort Worth, Texas 76102
(817) 390-3700

## Radio Shack
279 Bayview Drive, Box 34000
Barrie, Ontario
Canada L4M 4W5
(705) 728-6242; Fax (705) 728-2012

*Main Products:* Wide range of hardware and other computer products

*Other Numbers:* (800) 843-7422 (customer information, U.S.)

*Comments:* Canadian Radio Shack is not a subsidiary of Tandy U.S. (was divested in the 1980s)

## Texas Instruments Incorporated
P.O. Box 6102 , MS 3255
Temple, Texas 76503
(817) 774-6001

## Texas Instruments Canada Ltd.
280 Centre Street East
Richmond Hill, Ontario
Canada L4C 1B1
(905) 884-9181; Fax (905) 884-7739

*Main Products:* Microcomputer hardware; calculators; business equipment

*Other Numbers:* (800) 527-3500 (customer information, U.S. and Canada); (800) 336-5236 (response center, all products, U.S. and Canada); (800) 848-3927 [84TEXAS] (notebooks, printers, calculators, and educational toys, U.S. and Canada)

## 3Com Corporation
5400 Bayfront Road
Santa Clara, California 95052
(408) 764-5000; (408) 764-5001

## 3Com Canada Inc.
2225 Sheppard Avenue East, Atria 3, Suite 1204
North York, Ontario
Canada M2J 5C4
(416) 498-3266; Fax (416) 498-1262

*Main Products:* Local area networks

*Other Numbers:* (800) 638-3266 [638-3COM] (customer information, U.S. and Canada)

**Toshiba America Information Systems Inc.**
9740 Irvine Boulevard
Irvine, California 92718
(714) 583-3000; Fax (714) 583-3140

**Toshiba of Canada Limited**
191 McNabb Street
Toronto, Ontario
Canada L3R 8H2
(905) 470-3500; Fax (905) 470-3490

*Main Products:* Laptops; monitors; wide range of hardware

*Other Numbers:* (800) 334-3445 (customer information, U.S.); (800) 663-0378 (computer products technical support, Canada); (905) 470-3456 (office products group, Canada); (905) 470-3478 (information systems group, Canada)

---

**Unisys**
P.O. Box 500
Blue Bell, Pennsylvania 19424
(215) 986-4011

**Unisys Canada Inc.**
2001 Sheppard Avenue East
North York, Ontario
Canada M2J 4Z7
(416) 495-0515; Fax (416) 499-3833

*Main Products:* Wide range of computers from mainframes to micros; information management consulting

*Other Addresses:* Information Systems Customer Support Center, 61 Middlefield Road Scarborough, Ontario, Canada, (416) 609-7700

*Comments:* Formed in late 1980s through merger of Burroughs and Sperry Univac

---

**US Robotics, Inc.**
8100 North McCormick Boulevard
Skokie, Illinois 60076
(708) 982-5010; Fax (708) 982-5800

**c/o Megahertz Corp (division of US Robotics)**
4220 North Service Road
Burlington, Ontario
Canada L5L 6C7
(905) 336-8168 ext. 25; Fax (905) 336-7380

*Main Products:* Modems

*Other Numbers:* (800) 762-6163 (fax on demand, U.S. and Canada); (708) 933-5552 (fax line for customer support); (708) 982-5092 (computer bulletin board service); (708) 982-5151 (support hotline)

*Other Addresses:* support@usr.com (Internet support) GO USROBOTICS (CompuServe)

## UUNET Technologies
3060 Williams Drive
Fairfax, Virginia 22091
(703) 206-5600; Fax (703) 206-5601

## UUNET Canada Inc.
20 Bay Street, Suite 1910
Toronto, Ontario
Canada M5J 2N8
(416) 368-6621; Fax (416) 368-1350

*Main Services:* Internet service provider

*Other Numbers:* (800) 488-6384 [4UUNET4] (customer information, U.S. and Canada)

*Comments:* Local access numbers in major cities

## ViewSonic Corporation
20480 Business Parkway
Walnut, California 91789
(909) 468-5800; Fax (909) 468-5838

*Main Products:* Monitors

*Other Numbers:* (800) 888-8583 (customer information, U.S. and Canada)

## Western Digital Corporation
8105 Irvine Center Drive
Irvine, California 92718
(714) 932-4900; Fax (714) 932-4012

## Western Digital Canada Corporation
50 Burnhamthorpe Road West, Suite 710
Mississauga, Ontario
Canada L5B 3C2
(905) 566-4702; Fax (905) 566-4711

*Main Products:* Hard disk drives (IDE high capacity drives)

*Other Numbers:* (800) 832-4778 (customer information and support, U.S. and Canada)

## WordPerfect Corporation

*Comments:* Acquired by Novell in 1994; Corel in 1996

**Wyse Technology**
3471 North First Street
San Jose, California 95134
(408) 473-1200; Fax (800) 742-6335

**Wyse Technology (Canada) Ltd.**
44 East Beaver Creek, Unit 16
Richmond Hill, Ontario
Canada L4B 1G8
(905) 886-9973; Fax (905) 886-0415

*Main Products:* Monitors

*Other Numbers:* (800) 800-9973 (Wyse/Amdek customer information, U.S. and Canada); (800) 792-6335 (Amdek monitor division, U.S. and Canada)

*Other Addresses:* Amdek division, 9020-II Capital of Texas Highway North, Suite 400, Austin, Texas, 78759

*Comments:* Acquired Amdek several years ago

---

**Xerox Corporation**
901 Page Avenue, Box 5030
Fremont, California 94537
(510) 635-2020

**Xerox Canada Inc.**
5650 Yonge Street
North York, Ontario
Canada M2M 4G7
(416) 229-3769

*Main Products:* Photocopiers; printers (including color printers); wide range of hardware

*Other Numbers:* (800) 275-9376 [ASK-XEROX] (customer information, U.S. and Canada); (203) 968-3000 (Headquarters, U.S.)

---

**Zeos International (Now Micron Electronics)**
2295 Walnut Street
Roseville, Minnesota 55113
(612) 486-1900; Fax (612) 486-1967

*Main Products:* Laptop and microcomputers

*Other Numbers:* (800) 423-5891 (customer information, U.S. and Canada)

*Comments:* Merged with Micron Electronics in April 1995.

# GLOSSARY

**Alphanumeric**—A character that is a letter, number or symbol; also, a string of characters containing any combination thereof.

**Analog**—Refers to the representation of data on a continuous physical scale—for example, temperature and pressure are typically measured on an analog scale; electronically, analog scales use variable voltage to measure quantities—the other form of representation is digital.

**Applications software**—Software dedicated to a specific purpose, such as word processing or desktop publishing; the other forms of software are operating systems and programming languages.

**Artificial intelligence (AI)**—A scientific discipline concerned with developing computer systems that can perform functions normally requiring human intelligence.

**ASCII**—American Standard Code for Information Interchange; this is a standard that defines alphanumeric codes used by computers and other devices.

**Assembly language**—A programming language written to facilitate access to a computer's machine language; although easier to use than machine language, it is nevertheless cumbersome.

**BASIC**—Beginner's All-purpose Symbolic Instruction Code; BASIC is the most popular microcomputer programming language.

**Baud rate**—The rate at which signal elements are transmitted over a serial path; the name is derived from J.M.E. Baudot (1845–1903), a French telegraphy pioneer (note: Baud is often erroneously used as a synonym for "bps," which means bits per second, not signal elements per second).

**BIOS**—Basic input/output system, the hardware or software that enables a computer to communicate with other external devices.

**Bit**—An abbreviation of "binary digit," the basic unit of information recognized by a computer; a bit has one of two values, either 0 or 1, and is therefore often compared to an on-off switch.

**Booting**—The process of turning on a computer, causing it to seek instructions from a ROM chip or from the operating system; the computer is said to "pull itself up by its own bootstraps."

**Buffer**—A storage area for data used to compensate for differences in the speed of two devices.

**Byte**—A series of eight bits of information processed as a unit by the computer; a byte typically represents one character.

**Central processing unit**—*See* CPU.

**Chip**—An integrated circuit, usually made of silicon, typically used as the CPU or as main memory in a microcomputer.

**Client/server architecture or client/server technology**—An expansion of the LAN concept, whereby a powerful microcomputer holds the primary processing and file server capability at the center of a network; many large organizations are backing down from their mainframes and using this type of configuration.

**COBOL**—COmmon Business Oriented Language, a high-level programming language particularly well suited to business applications.

**Command**—An instruction given to a computer program.

**Compatible**—An attribute of hardware or software that refers to its ability to work with or act in an identical manner to another piece of hardware or software; often used in conjunction with an industry standard—for example, "IBM compatible" or "Lotus compatible."

**Compiler**—Software that translates a high-level programming language into machine language.

**Computer**—A machine that processes information.

**Control characters**—Special codes that represent instructions given to a computer or peripheral device.

**CPU (central processing unit)**—The computer's command center, it performs arithmetic and logic functions, and controls input and output.

**Cursor**—An indicator on a display screen that shows where the next character will appear.

**Database**—A collection of information recorded in an organized structure to facilitate its use.

**Debugging**—The process of finding and correcting errors in a computer program.

**Desktop accessory**—A piece of software designed to assist in some common office function or to replace some common device; the typical example is an on-screen calculator.

**Desktop publishing**—The use of a small computer system, typically a microcomputer system, to produce printed material that is suitable for distribution or for use as camera-ready artwork in another printing process.

**Digital**—Refers to the representation of data using binary numbers, which consist of a series of ones and zeroes that can be compared with an on-off switch.

**Disk**—The most common medium for storing information electronically.

**Driver**—A program necessary to operate a particular piece of hardware such as a printer.

**80286**—An Intel 16-bit microprocessor used in the IBM-PC AT and similar machines.

**80386**—An Intel 32-bit microprocessor used in some IBM Personal System/2 Models, Compaq Deskpro 386, and similar machines.

**80486**—An Intel 32-bit microprocessor used in the more advanced microcomputers such as the IBM Model 95 XP 486.

**80586**—The generic name—also referred to as simply "586"—for the Pentium microprocessor manufactured by Intel (in an attempt to thwart clone-makers, Intel has adopted the registered trademark Pentium for this microprocessor); Intel's name for the next generation chip is the P6.

**EDI (Electronic Data Interchange)**—The transfer of information between computers in independent organizations, using an agreed-upon structure or standard.

**Expert system**—A computer system designed to act as a substitute for a human expert in his or her particular field of knowledge.

**Financial modeling**—The computer analysis of numerical data to assist in making decisions.

**FORTRAN**—FORmula TRANslation was the first high-level programming language and is particularly well suited to scientific and engineering applications.

**Graphics**—Nontext information.

**Hard copy**—Computer output printed on paper.

**Hardware**—The physical parts of a computer system, as contrasted with software.

**Hertz (Hz)**—A measurement of frequency equaling one cycle per second: one KHz represents 1,000 Hz; one MHz represents 1,000,000 Hz.

**Icon**—A pictorial representation or symbol, used by some types of software as a substitute for a typed command.

**Image scanner**—A device used to read printed matter, text, photographs, or artwork electronically and convert it to digital form.

**Information center**—The department within an organization responsible for managing the information resource and responding to the information needs of users.

**Information technology**—The name given to the tools and methods used to collect, retain, manipulate, or distribute information; it is most often associated with computers and related technologies.

**Kilobyte (K)**—1,024 bytes.

**LAN (local area network)**—A group of computers (typically microcomputers) and related devices connected together to facilitate the transfer of information and the sharing of peripherals.

**Machine language**—Instructions to a computer in the form of binary code (a series of ones and zeroes).

**Macro**—A combination or series of keystrokes that represents a lengthier command or series of commands.

**Mainframe computer**—The largest and most expensive type of computer, more powerful than either minicomputers or microcomputers.

**Megabyte (Mb)**—1,048,576 bytes.

**Menu**—A list of choices offered to a user by a computer program.

**MHz**—*See* Hertz.

**Microcomputer**—A relatively small and inexpensive computer capable of satisfying most of the computing needs of a single user or, in some cases, a small group of users.

**Minicomputer**—Typically a midsize computer costing between $25,000 and $250,000, excluding peripherals.

**Modem**—MOdulator-DEModulator, a device that makes it possible to transmit or receive digital information over a telephone line.

**Mouse**—A pointing device connected to a computer, typically used in lieu of the keyboard to move the cursor and execute commands.

**MVS**—Multiple virtual storage, one of the more popular operating systems for IBM mainframe computers.

**Networking**—The use of telecommunications to connect computers and related devices, for the purpose of facilitating the transfer of information and the sharing of peripherals.

**Office automation**—The technique of making any office apparatus, process, or system operate automatically or in such a way as to reduce the expenditure of human time and effort; it is most often associated with the use of computers in the office environment.

**Operating system**—A specialized type of software that controls a computer and its peripheral devices.

**Optical character recognition (OCR)**—Refers to the ability of a scanner to read text.

**Parallel interface**—A method of connecting a computer and peripheral, whereby information is transmitted simultaneously over separate channels; contrast with serial interface.

**Peripheral**—Any hardware device, other than the CPU, that is used with a computer.

**QWERTY**—The typical typewriter keyboard design, named after the first six keys in the home row.

**RAM**—Random access memory, the primary storage area accessible to a CPU.

**RGB**—Red-green-blue, the three primary colors. Typically used in reference to an RGB monitor, which has a separate transmitter for each of the primary colors and can therefore produce crisper images than composite color monitors.

**ROM**—Read only memory, a storage area accessible to the CPU but the contents of which cannot be changed.

**Serial interface**—A method of connecting a computer to a peripheral whereby information is transmitted in series over a single channel; RS-232, the most common form of serial interface, contrast with parallel interface.

**Software**—Programs that provide direction to computer hardware.

**Telecommunication**—The technology that supports communication between intelligent devices across significant distances.

**Topology**—The physical structure of a network; bus, ring, and star are the most common topologies.

**UNIX**—A powerful operating system commonly used with minicomputers and some powerful microcomputers; a key feature of UNIX is its multiuser capability.

**Window**—A portion of a display screen that contains information independent from the rest of the screen; windows are typically used to work with two different parts of a file, or two different files, at the same time.

**Word processing**—The creation, manipulation, and printing of written material using a computer system.

**WYSIWYG**—"What-you-see-is-what-you-get"; refers to the ability of software to display on the screen exactly what is to be printed.

**Xenix**—A UNIX-like operating system typically used with the IBM and compatible microcomputers.

# REFERENCES

## GENERAL BOOKS

Augarten, Stan. *Bit by Bit: An Illustrated History of Computers*. New York: Ticknor & Fields, 1984.

Fertig, Robert. *The Software Revolution*. New York: North-Holland, 1985.

Freiberger, Paul and Michael Swaine. *Fire in the Valley: The Making of the Personal Computer*. Berkeley: Osborne/McGraw Hill, 1984.

Juliussen, Egil and Karen Juliussen. *The Computer Industry Almanac*. New York: Simon & Schuster (Brady), (published annually).

Manes, Stephen and Paul Andrews. *Gates: How Microsoft's Mogul Reinvented an Industry—and Made Himself the Richest Man in America*. New York: Doubleday, 1993.

Porter, Kent. *The New American Computer Dictionary*. New York: New American Library (Plume), 1983.

Vorwald, Alan and Frank Clark. *Computers: From Sand Table to Electronic Brain*. New York: Whittlesey House, 1964.

Wulforst, Harry. *Breakthrough to the Computer Age*. New York: Charles Scribner's Sons, 1982.

## LARGE COMPUTER SYSTEMS

*Auerbach Series*. Boston: Auerbach Publishers, Inc., (updated periodically).

*Datapro Series*. Delran: McGraw-Hill Publishing Company, (updated periodically).

## MICROCOMPUTER HARDWARE AND SOFTWARE

*Byte,* P.O. Box 558, Hightstown, NJ, USA 08520-0558 ($29.95 U.S. per year—14 issues)

Grout, Bill et al. *Desktop Publishing from A to Z*. Osborne/McGraw-Hill.

Lawrenson, H. Denman, et al. *The Canadian Business Guide to Microcomputers*. Prentice-Hall Canada Inc., (published annually).

*PC Magazine,* Ziff-Davis, P.O. Box 54093 Boulder, Colorado USA 80322 [subscriptions: (303) 665-8930 (Outside U.S.) ($49.97 U.S. per year—22 issues; Canada $85.97)].

*PC World,* PC World Communications, P.O. Box 55029, Boulder, Colorado, USA 80322-5029 [subscriptions: (303) 604-1465 ($29.97 U.S. per year—12 issues; Canada $47.97)].

*Que Series,* e.g.: Campbell, Mary V. *Using Excel;* LeBlond, Geoffrey T. and Douglas Ford Cobb. *Using 1-2-3.* Indianapolis: Que Corporation (revised with each new software version).

## ADVANCED TOPICS

*Data Communications,* a magazine published monthly by McGraw-Hill Inc.

*Open System,* ed. Harold C. Folts. New York: McGraw-Hill. The encyclopedic reference to all worldwide data communications standards by CCITT, ISO, ECMA, ANSI, EIA, and so on (6 volumes, 1990).

*Auerbach Data Security Management.* Boston: Auerbach Publishers, Inc., (updated bimonthly).

Anthony Ralston, *Encyclopedia of Computer Science and Engineering,* 3rd ed., New York: Van Nostrand Reinhold Company, 1993.

Nimmer, Raymond T. *The Law of Computer Technology.* Boston: Warren, Gorham & Lamont, 1985.

# Index

DATE DUE

F9
OCT 0 3 1997

OCT 2 3 1997

11/14/97

Demco, Inc 38-293